EVERYTHING I KNOW ABOUT LIFE I LEARNED FROM JAMES BOND

Everything I Know About Life I Learned From James Bond

John L. Flynn
and
Bob Blackwood

INTEGRATED MEDIA
NEW YORK

All rights reserved, including without limitation the right to reproduce this book or any portion thereof in any form or by any means, whether electronic or mechanical, now known or hereinafter invented, without the express written permission of the publisher.

Copyright © 2015, 2022 by John L. Flynn

ISBN: 978-1-5040-8421-5

This edition published in 2023 by Open Road Integrated Media, Inc.
180 Maiden Lane
New York, NY 10038
www.openroadmedia.com

We would like to dedicate this book to those in the James Bond family who have passed away in the last few years.

Pedro Armendariz, Jr.	Christopher Lee
George Baker	Desmond Llewelyn
John Barry	Michael Lonsdale
Paul Bhattacharjee	Patrick MacNee
Honor Blackman	Zena Marshall
Khan Boils	Joaquin Martinez
Charlotte Brosnan	Lois Maxwell
Peter Burton	Michael D. Moore
Adolfo Celi	Roger Moore
Sean Connery	Barry Nelson
Linda Christian	Donald Pleasence
Gert Frobe	Michael Reid
Richard Graydon	Nadja Regin
Marvin Hamlisch	Diana Rigg
David Hedison	Tanya Roberts
Julius Harris	Harold Sakata
Geoffrey Holder	Telly Savalas
Clifton James	Vincent Schiavelli
Louis Jourdan	Angela Scoular
Curt Jurgens	Mark Sutton
Richard Kiel	Herve Villechaize
Yaphet Kotto	Josephn Wiseman
Bernard Lee	

They were all shining stars in the world of 007, and now they have all gone onto a better place . . . for The World Is not Enough.

INTRODUCTION

At a recent science fiction convention, while we were discussing the impact of the James Bond films on popular culture at a well-attended panel, I blurted out, "Everything I know about life I learned from James Bond," and my long-time friend and writing partner Dr. Bob Blackwood echoed my sentiments, saying "That's absolutely true!" Everything that we know about women, cars, food and drink, fashion, guns and gadgets, travel, and life in general we learned while watching James Bond movies. In fact, I wondered where we would be without James Bond.

For the adolescent male growing up in the 1950s and 1960s, 007 was everything that we were not. He was sexually irresistible to women. He was well dressed and well groomed, socially astute, clever and witty, athletic, debonair, dangerous, and heroic. He drove the coolest cars, possessed the greatest gadgets, traveled to the most exotic places, made love to the most beautiful women, and had the most fun of any cinematic figure we knew. Over the years, he has certainly had his rivals, from Derek Flint and Matt Helm to Indiana Jones and Austin Powers, but he was, by and far, the greatest and the best. James Bond represented everything that the two of us wanted to be. And now, as we look

INTRODUCTION

back over the years as middle-aged adults, we both realize how Bond helped re-define our understanding of what it meant to be manly, particularly at a time in our culture when the roles of men and women were becoming so fractured and confused.

For fifty years, since the release of ***Dr. No*** in 1962, movie-goers have been fascinated and thrilled by the James Bond films. In fact, a recent statistic states that one fourth of the world's population has seen a James Bond movie or read a James Bond novel. That's over a billion and a half people! The stories with their magical power to trans port us to thrilling locations, to introduce us to larger than life characters, and to place us right in the middle of exciting adventures have always captivated audiences in a way that overwrought big-budget epics, intimate real-life tearjerkers, stultifying high-minded literary adaptations, elephantine bio-pics or other Hollywood prestige films could not. The James Bond films are simply a great deal of fun, and inspire us to memorize whole passages of dialogue, spend millions of dollars each year on toys and books and posters, dress in a tuxedo as our favorite hero, and attend yearly conventions to argue and discuss the finer points of film production. They bring out the inner geek in us all, and certainly have made us the men that we are today.

Like Robert Fulghum's bestseller, this book provides witty and insightful aphorisms about everyday things, ranging from girls to food and drink, cars to clothing and style, and life lessons to fun facts about culture and civilization, as reflected through the prism of James Bond, the world's most stylish and cultured secret agent. Author Ian Fleming once wrote that "Bond lives in the details," and the specifics of his character's discriminating tastes, defining principles, and worldly interests form much of the magic of the James Bond films. The world according to 007 includes fast cars and even faster women,

INTRODUCTION

deadly villains, high-stakes gambling, hard drinking and smoking, thrilling locations, fabulous food, expensive clothing, cool gadgets, pithy one-liners, and the best of culture. This book is nothing more or less than a celebration of the inner geek that still feels like he is thirteen again when his pulse quickens at the famous staccato beat of the James Bond theme music and he hears those famous words "My name is Bond. James Bond." While few (if any) of us film geeks live the fast-paced lifestyle of 007, we are still fascinated by his shaken (not stirred) martinis, the specially-equipped Aston Martins, battered pigskin attaché cases, the Saville Row suits, and deadly Rolex watches. The "details" of Bond's world have revealed helpful insights about life and everyday things. In fact, everything we know about life we learned from James Bond . . . We learned that women with cold lips or red hair were not to be trusted. We learned . . . that vodka martinis were best shaken and not stirred . . . that Royal Beluga caviar from north of the Caspian Sea was best served on soft toast with sour cream . . . that Delta 9 nerve gas was fatal . . . that diamonds were the hardest substance known to man . . . that the Orient Express travels from Istanbul, Turkey, to Calais, France. We learned that it was dangerous to fire weapons in the passenger compartment of an airplane at thirty-five thousand feet . . . that we should always cut the red wire (instead of the green wire) to disable an atomic bomb, and that we should never EVER bet against another player holding nine in *chemin de fer*. We learned that certain orchids from South America caused sterility . . . that there were strict rules of golf that determined the outcome of the game . . . that it was impossible to reason with Baron Samedi and his Voodoo curse . . . and that we had to keep fit and trim, or we'd wind up at Shrublands. And finally, we learned there are things that only James Bond could do.

Each of those "details" has helped, in some way, to define the

INTRODUCTION

people we are today, and while thankfully, we no longer pretend we're James Bond while driving our family wagon on the interstate or recite the line, "Bond . . . James Bond," each time we wear a tuxedo to formal affairs, we still love James Bond books and movies. This book reflects our lifelong love affair with 007, and not something that showcases our scholarship or academic standing. For Bob, a fellow journalist like Ian Fleming living in Chicago, his first exposure to James Bond was the novels in the late fifties. He can still remember those Signet paperback editions, in particular the cover illustration of the fat ugly face of Mr. Big from **Live and Let Die**. For me, it was the movies in the early Sixties. I can still remember seeing **Goldfinger** at age ten at the Coral Theater in the suburbs of Chicago, and then a week later attending the double feature re-release of **Dr. No** and **From Russia with Love**. James Bond has been our constant companion, especially when our buddies ditched us to hang out with girls. We learned a lot about girls and cars (naturally), gambling, food and drink, travel, clothing and style, culture, and the world from 007. We are admittedly film geeks, and we have tried to keep this fun and entertaining by celebrating the inner geek in us all. We trust what distinguishes this volume from others is its focus, which includes those "details" that we have learned, and its good-humored approach to the films. But please don't think for one moment that, because we are both Ph.D's and academics, this is some kind of dry, high-browed dissertation. Other scholars and esearchers have already written that kind of book, and for better or worse their efforts are available at your local bookstore or library. Instead of being forgotten on a stuffy old bookshelf with all of the other film books, we'd like to see ours sitting next to the television, or placed on top of the DVD player, or folded in someone's pocket as they head off on a first date. We'd like to imagine ours to be the perennial

INTRODUCTION

favorite on every geek's gift list. With this book, we are celebrating 007's amazing adventures, his beautiful women, his incredible enemies, his thrilling locations, his fabulous gadgets, and all things James Bond.

The aim of this book is to pay tribute to the twenty-four films in the canon made by EON Productions and the handful of independents (including **Casino Royale**, 1967, and **Never Say Never Again**, 1983) made by other studios that we grew up watching as kids and that we still enjoy watching today. We have tried to capture that gee-whiz feeling with each of our chapters devoted to the "details" of Bond's world. So, in contrast to other works that have concentrated almost exclusively on a didactic or pedantic approach to the Bond films, we have attempted to circumvent this limited notion of the series and their impact on popular culture by covering aspects that have always given us the greatest amount of pleasure and glee. If you've ever cheered when a Bond trailer played on screen, or if you ever fantasized that your car was a gadget-laden Aston Martin, or if you have ever pretended you were Bond while ordering a martini, shaken, not stirred . . . then this book is for you.

As a mark of this new and somewhat tongue-in-cheek perspective, for this volume we have adopted a fairly freewheeling approach to the James Bond films that has never been done before. Rather than bore you with lots of statistics about each film or a blow-by-blow plot summary or endless commentary about how the films were made, we have chosen to focus on those specific elements that make the Bond movies fun. We've talked about this with other film geeks, and we all agree that we watch the films for the babes or the cars or the gadgets or the clothes or the cool, imaginative ways that 007 handles each new situation. We have included lots of interesting fun-filled facts, trivia questions, and other revealing factoids. But if you're

INTRODUCTION

looking for a blow-by blow plot summary of each movie or an in-depth analysis about the making of the films, may we recommend John Brosnan's ***James Bond in the Cinema*** (A.S. Barnes, 1977; 1981) or ***The Incredible World of James Bond*** (Citadel, 1995) by Lee Pfeiffer and Philip Lisa. Our book is more like a practical guide to surviving in the real world with the knowledge that we've gleaned from the James Bond films. Once you have read through our work, we are hoping that you will come back many times to consult it before you go out on a date, head to the shopping mall, or embark on your own secret missions.

007 fans, this book is for your eyes only!

—John L. Flynn, Ph.D.
September 6, 2015

EVERYTHING I KNOW ABOUT LIFE I LEARNED FROM JAMES BOND

CHAPTER ONE

A PORTRAIT OF JAMES BOND 007

He always runs while others walk,
He acts while other men just talk,
He looks at this world and wants it all,
So he strikes like Thunderball.

—Tom Jones, ***Thunderball*** (1965)

Author Ian Fleming once wrote that "Bond lives in the details," and the specifics of his character's discriminating tastes, defining principles, and worldly interests form much of the mystique of the man we celebrate with this book. Commander James Bond is a cool, handsome, and deadly agent who works for Great Britain's Secret Intelligence Service MI6; his code number, 007, indicates that he has a discretionary "licence to kill" in the line of duty. Fleming named 007 after the famous American ornithologist James Bond who had written ***Birds of the West Indies***. A keen bird watcher while living in Jamaica, Fleming kept a copy of Bond's bird book on his desk, and chose the name for his hero because it was "brief, unromantic, Anglo-Sax on, and yet a very masculine name"—exactly what he needed. Fleming based elements of Bond upon himself for he had served briefly in the British Secret Service during the war, and he also drew upon aspects of some of the world's greatest spies to complete his character. Like those real-world counterparts, James Bond travels the world and relies on his wits, exceptional knowledge, fighting skills, and assortment of high-tech gadgets to battle super-villains bent on world domination. Some of Bond's idiosyncratic traits, which have now become famous, were also those Fleming himself embraced. The British author was known for his glamorous lifestyle and his sexual prowess with the ladies. He also preferred his martinis made with vodka and "shaken, not stirred." He drank champagne and bourbon whiskey heavily, and smoked up to seventy cigarettes in one day. He relied on a Walther PPK as his favorite handgun, and had a habit of introducing himself last name first, followed by his complete full name. And thus, "Bond ... James Bond" was born.

James Bond is the son of a Scottish father, Andrew Bond, and a Swiss mother, Monique Delacroix, both of whom perished in a mountain climbing accident when he was just eleven years-old. Their family motto is Orbis *non sufficit*, or "The World Is not Enough" (translated from the Latin), and they had a family estate named *Skyfall* in the northern part of Scotland. The future secret agent was born near Essen, Germany, on November 11, 1920 (according to **John Pearson's Unauthorized Biography of 007**) or 1924 (according to an obituary in Ian Fleming's **You Only Live Twice**). After his parents' deaths, he and his younger brother Henry were raised by their aunt. Bond bought his first car in 1933, a 4.5 litre Bentley Convertible Coupé with an Amherst Villers supercharger (which he drove in several early

EVERYTHING I KNOW ABOUT LIFE
I LEARNED FROM JAMES BOND

novels and in *From Russia with Love*, 1963). This date, which would have made Bond either thirteen-years-old or nine-years-old when he purchased his first automobile, seems to contradict both of his birthdates. Chronologically, these were the first of many instances where biographical contradictions occur in the life of James Bond. The only explanation for why Ian Fleming appears to be rather careless in connecting the dots of 007's early years is that he never really intended to write as many James Bond adventures as he did. In fact, in the concluding chapter of *From Russia with Love*, Fleming leaves 007 for dead in much the same way that Sir Arthur Conan Doyle tired of Sherlock Holmes and killed him off at the hands of his nemesis, Moriarity. But of course James Bond didn't die from the poison in Rosa Klebb's shoe, and lived to die another day. Many Fleming and Bond biographers do agree that Bond lost his virginity on his first trip to Paris at the age of sixteen to Marthe de Brandt, the notorious madam and brothel owner who worked as a spy for the other side. In his teens, he played two rounds of golf a day at the Royal St. Marks outside London. Bond was taught how to ski by Hannes Oberhauser (Christoph Waltz's name in *Spectre* [2015] is Oberhauser) at the Hannes Schneider School at St. Anton in Alberg, Austria, and won the Golden K when he was just a teenager. He briefly attended Eton College, but was expelled after his sexual indiscretion with a maid was discovered. He then attended the prestigious Fettes College in Edinburgh, Scotland, and the University of Geneva; he also took a First in Oriental Languages at Cambridge University. Apparently, he also speaks French, German, and Russian, which he studied at Oxford while impersonating a Russian scientist. While attending numerous academies, he fought as a light weight boxer and founded a judo class. And just prior to World War II, he worked with René Mathis of the Deuxième Bureau and the British Secret Service observing a team of Romanian cheaters at Monte Carlo, whom he later cleaned out of a large sum of money through gam bling.

Thunderball (1965) Italian Poster © United Artists [IT] / Eon Productions

In 1941, James Bond lied about his age in order to join the Royal Navy's Volunteer Reserve as a lieutenant; the fact that he was only seventeen-years-old in 1941 seems to suggest that he was born in 1924 rather than 1920. He met his best friend, Bill Tanner, when they were both midshipmen during the war. He served in the Royal Navy, notably on HMS Ark Royal, and earned the rank of Commander before he was recruited by MI6 at the end of the war. In fact, Tanner first recommended James Bond to Admiral Sir Miles Messervy, or M, as his replacement when he was injured during a sabotage mission in 1944 and subsequently became M's Chief of Staff. At first, Bond reported to a Mr. Clements, but later earned the Admiral's trust and admiration, and reported directly to him for all future assignments. He soon met the Admiral's secretary, Miss Moneypenny, and was equipped by the armorer Q.

A four-part miniseries, airing on British television titled **Fleming: The Man Who Would Be Bond**, (2014), explores the life of Ian Fleming (as played by Dominic Cooper, the man

EVERYTHING I KNOW ABOUT LIFE
I LEARNED FROM JAMES BOND

who should be the next James Bond), at the outset of WWII when he is nothing but a mischievous playboy living off his mother's (Lesley Manville as "Em" Fleming) fortune and living in the shadow of his much more famous brother, novelist Peter Fleming (Rupert Evans). Ultimately, he is recruited into Naval Intelligence, and works on a number of secret plans to take down the Nazis, with Samuel West as Rear Admiral John Godfrey and Anna Chancellor as Second Officer Monday (not Moneypenny). Written by John Brownlow and Don Macpherson and directed by Matt Whitecross, the miniseries is fun and imaginative, and shows how Fleming created 007. Two other television productions attempted to dramatize the wartime exploits and romantic adventures that influenced Fleming's life, including **GoldenEye: The Secret Life of Ian Fleming—the Real James Bond** (1989), with Charles Dance as Fleming and **Spymaker: The Secret Life of Ian Fleming** (1990), with Sean Connery's son Jason in the role of Fleming, but the plot or each TV-movie was greatly removed from Fleming's real-life story. Only the 2014 miniseries came close. He earned his 00-number during the war for killing a Japanese cipher expert in New York and a Norwegian double-agent in Stockholm. He was also briefly stationed in Hong Kong at the end of the war, where he discovered a fondness for silk pajamas tops. Bond was then sent to Jamaica for an extended assignment to prevent Communists stationed in Cuba from infiltrating the Jamaican unions. In 1953 or 1954 (depending on the source), he earned a Companion to the Order of St. Michael and St. George citation for his work, but he later re fused knighthood on the grounds that he was basically a Scotch peasant. 007 was smuggled into Hungary during its anti-Soviet uprising in 1956, and trained rebels to fight against the Communists. In 1957, James Bond helped foil an attempt by Greek commandoes to rescue Arch bishop Makarios III from his exile in the Seychelles. His first literary assignment (in *Casino Royale*, 1953) came when he was recruited by the Head of Station S of the British Secret Service to dispose of a high-profile Russian agent, Le Chiffre, through a high-stakes game of baccarat at a French casino.

Not long after this assignment in France, James Bond was reluctantly re-equipped by Q-Branch with a 7.62mm Walther PPK pistol which replaced his small caliber Beretta automatic pistol that he had used for the last ten or fifteen years. Both the literary and the cinematic James Bond had just returned from six months in the hospital, recovering from wounds suffered in his last job when the Beretta jammed. Several decades later, Bond adopts the Walther P-99 as his weapon of choice.

Though he tends to eat rather plainly when in England, when traveling abroad, he indulges in the finest food and drink available. He is famous for ordering his vodka martinis "shaken, not stirred" and for indulging his taste for Beluga caviar. Throughout the novels, 007 orders his martinis with a slice of lemon peel, perhaps in honor of his lover Vesper Lynd (from *Casino Royale*). He also drinks gin and bourbon and all manner of alcoholic beverage to excess; in the films, he drinks champagne thirty-two times, and consumes twenty vodka martinis. He prefers Turkish cigarettes and practically lives on grilled sole, eggs coquotte, and cold roast beef. Back at his home in Chelsea, of course, Bond is cared for by his elderly, Scottish housekeeper, May, who makes him an English breakfast every morning.

Ian Fleming described James Bond's physical resemblance to singer Hoagy Carmichael, and thus far, only actor Timothy Dalton (who twice played the character in the late 1980s) resembles Fleming's description. He was tall (over six feet) with a three-inch, vertical scar on his left cheek (absent from the

EVERYTHING I KNOW ABOUT LIFE
I LEARNED FROM JAMES BOND

cinematic versions); he had blue-gray eyes, a cruel mouth, and short, dark hair with a comma that fell on his forehead. He has had many girlfriends, but has only been married once. His wife, Tracy di Vicenzo, was killed by Ernst Stavro Blofeld in the novel and cinematic versions of ***On Her Majesty's Secret Service*** shortly after their wedding ceremony in Portugal. Essentially, like his boss M, he is married to his job.

Although licensed to kill, James Bond dislikes killing; in the novels, he resorts to flippant jokes or off-handed remarks after he has killed, and many misinterpret this verbal release as cold-bloodedness. He is haunted by the memories of the people that he has murdered in the line of duty, and sometimes regrets those that he has killed. John Pearson's unauthorized biography suggests that Bond first killed as a teenager, but there doesn't seem to be much corroborating evidence of this. In the novel ***Goldfinger***, Bond is haunted by the memory of a small time, Mexican gunman he had killed with his bare hands days earlier. In ***GoldenEye*** (1995), Alex Trevelyan-009 taunts him with memories of all the women Bond has failed to save. In ***The World Is not Enough*** (1999), James Bond is forced to kill an unarmed Elektra King in order to stop a nuclear catastrophe, and later regrets his ctions.

In the novel ***You Only Live Twice***, James Bond is struck by a bullet while fleeing Blofeld's hideaway in a helium balloon, and crashes into the sea. Kissy Suzuki finds him suffering from amnesia, and conspires with the Japanese islanders to hide Bond from his superiors. 007 is presumed dead, and his obituary appears in *The Times*. Some months later, he finds the word "Vladivostok" on a piece of paper, which triggers memories of his life as a secret agent, but not as an SIS agent. Bond sets off for Russia, and is captured and brainwashed by the KGB. He leaves behind Kissy, who is carrying his son. When 007 re-appears at SIS headquarters in Fleming's last novel *The Man with the Golden Gun*, he tries to assassinate M, but his attempt is thankfully foiled. Bond is restored to normality by electroshock therapy, and dispatched on his next mission to kill Francisco Scaramanga, the world's great assassin. After defeating him in a thrilling shoot-out, 007 returns, but he is never quite the same. According to John Pearson, Bond retires shortly thereafter.

However, as we all know, James Bond 007 continues to be very active as a secret agent in the subsequent novels by John Gardner, Raymond Benson and other authors, and in the highly successful film series that has captured the imagination of moviegoers worldwide. Every film, except *Dr. No* (1962), concludes with the line: "James Bond will return . . ." or "James Bond will be back," and we can rest assured that he will return to thrill us with all new adventures.

CHAPTER TWO

ESPIONAGE AND SPYING 101

Meeting you, with a view to a kill,
Face to face, in secret places.
Feel the chill.
Nightfall covers me,
But you know, the plans I'm making
Still over see,
Could it be the whole earth opening wide?

—Duran Duran, **A View to a Kill** (1985)

The James Bond of the Fleming novels was envisioned as a "blunt instrument" for Great Britain, a weapon used to crush his nation's enemies, "Mr. Kiss Kiss Bang Bang." 007 was plainly, and simply, a hired gun, and he had no illusions about this fact. But on his way to the big screen, Bond changed. He was no longer simply a hired gun, but a sophisticated gentleman agent who dressed well and enjoyed all of the finer things in life. He wore a Rolex Oyster Perpetual Watch, drove an Aston

Martin DB-5, and drank Dom Perignon Champagne. Critics have always maintained that a real secret agent would not call so much attention to himself with the expensive jewelry, clothes, and cars; the real secret agent is one who completely submerges his or her identity in a cover that is often very dull and boring. But 007 makes the gritty world of espionage and spying seem almost glamorous. In movie after movie, Bond moved further and further away from the reality of espionage to the fantasy world of spy versus spy. Yet ironically, Agent 007 was created by a former member of Britain's Secret Intelligence Service, and based on the world's greatest spies. Those who know only the literary James Bond would never recognize his cinematic counterpart. By the last reel of **Moonraker** (1979), for example, James Bond had overcome so many obstacles and had traveled quite literally to outer space in his battle to save the world from Sir Hugo Drax that there was very little our well-dressed secret agent could not accomplish. He seemed like a larger-than-life superhero! Let's face it, when Bond merely glances at the complex schematic of the deadly rare orchid in **Moonraker**, and declares, "That's the chemical formula of a plant," 007 had moved beyond the boundaries of this world into the next! Ian Fleming never envisioned his hero as a Sherlock Holmes—or a Buck Rogers, for that matter—and the producers found it necessary to bring James Bond back to earth. So, in **For Your Eyes Only** (1981) and the subsequent films, the producers tried to re-imagine 007 as a real-world spy with adventures firmly entrenched in the real world, a move which has been received by the moviegoing public. The Daniel Craig films, including **Casino Royale** (2006) and **Quantum of Solace** (2008), have an even grittier feel to them, placing James Bond in the early stages of his career as a secret agent.

Though neither of us has ever been enlisted as spies for MI6,

EVERYTHING I KNOW ABOUT LIFE
I LEARNED FROM JAMES BOND

the Central Intelligence Agency, or a foreign power to spy for them, both of us feel like we know a great deal about espionage from watching the Bond films. Leave it to 007 to teach us about the real—and the fictional world—of spying . . .

MI6.

During his initial briefing with 007, M (Bernard Lee) tells James Bond that he has recently taken charge of MI6, which was overdubbed so that he says MI7 instead, possibly for fear of offending the real-life organization. In later Bond films and novels, however, 007 clearly works for MI6 or the Ministry of Intelligence, Bureau Six of the Secret Intelligence Service. MI6 originated in 1909 as the Foreign Section of the Secret Ser vice, and was charged with gathering foreign intelligence using highly covert methods. RNR Commander, later Captain, Sir Mansfield Cumming, the first M or head of the bureau actually signed himself with the letter "C"and each of his successors have done so ever since.

By 1922 Cumming's section had become so successful at gathering intelligence that a separate Service with the title SIS or Secret Intelligence Service was created. (A different agency, known as MI5, was assigned the role of internal security, much like the FBI in the United States.) The principal role of SIS is the production of secret intelligence in support of Her Majesty's Government's security, defense, foreign and economic policies within the framework of requirements laid down by law. Just as the CIA or Central Intelligence Agency is known as "The Company," SIS is known internally as "The Firm" and to other agencies as "The Friends," SIS was first based in Whitehall Court, then moved to Kensington, St. James Park, and Lambeth, before finally settling into brand new building at

85 Albert Embankment, Vauxhall Cross in London (known to those who work there as "Legoland"). In the early novels, Bond reports to work at an innocuous building overlooking Regent's Park, and the Sean Connery films place his headquarters, under the code name Universal Exports, there in Re gent's Park. The Roger Moore films move the headquarters to the Ministry of Defense building opposite the House Guards, not far from 10 Downing Street, in Whitehall. In the later Pierce Brosnan films, MI6's real location at Vauxhall Cross is used. In *Skyfall*, due to the cyber-terrorist attack of Silva, which temporarily destroyed M's office, MI6 is forced to move to Winston Churchill's World War II underground bunker. The members of MI6 mistakenly believed Silva would not yet have found an access route to this new location.

M.

James Bond's boss in the early novels was Admiral Sir Miles Messervy or simply M, and in the later books Barbara Mawdsley. Historically, RNR Commander, later Captain, Sir Mansfield Cumming was the first M or head of the bureau, and usually signed important document with the letter "C" and each of his successors have done so ever since. In real life, Mr. David Spedding is the individual who commands the SIS today. In the Bond films, the character of M is played by several actors and one actress. Bernard Lee originated the role of M in ***Dr. No*** (1962), and played the head of MI6 in ten other films, ***From Russian With Love*** (1963) to ***Moonraker*** (1979). Lee was a very popular character actor in Great Britain and had appeared opposite future Bond villain Orson Welles in ***The Third Man*** (1949). He also played a thinly disguised M, with the name Commander Cunningham, in

EVERYTHING I KNOW ABOUT LIFE
I LEARNED FROM JAMES BOND

Operation Kid Brother (1967), the James Bond spoof with Sean Connery's brother Neil. Robert Brown, who had been Admiral Hargreaves in ***The Spy Who Loved Me*** (1977), took over the role of M in ***Octopussy*** (1983), when Lee got sick and died. He played M in the subsequent ***A View to a Kill*** (1985), and two of the Timothy Dalton Bonds, ***The Living Daylights*** (1987) and ***License to Kill*** (1989). Judi Dench became the first female M in ***GoldenEye*** (1995), and played the character through Skyfall (2012). Arguably, she could be characterized as the most cold-blooded M, as she showed in her decision to "take the shot" which put Bond in danger in ***Skyfall***. Dench had a good run and was replaced by Ralph Fiennes as Gareth Mallory. Several other actors have also played M, including John Houston in ***Casino Royale*** (1967) and Edward Fox in ***Never Say Never Again*** (1983).

00-Licence to Kill.

For the first time, and certainly not the last, James Bond is reminded by his boss M in ***Dr. No*** (1962) that he has a special 00-licence to kill. According to the novel ***Casino Royale***, agents are awarded 00-numbers when they have had to kill someone in cold blood in the line of duty. James Bond gained his number 007 for killing a Japanese cipher expert in New York and a Norwegian double-agent in Stock holm, both during World War II. In the novels and then later in the films, other 00-agents are mentioned, including the most famous (or is that notorious?) 006 Alec Trevalyan from ***GoldenEye*** (1995). Despite the fact that Bond's agency is based on the real-life MI6, no agents in the Secret Intelligence Service are as signed a 00-number or given a "licence to kill."

Q-Branch.

Q-Branch, which is short for Quartermaster Branch, is the department of MI6 or the Secret Intelligence Service responsible for arming James Bond for each of his dangerous assignments. Major Boothroyd (played by Peter Burton in the first film, and thereafter by Desmond Llewelyn) is referred to simply as the "armorer" in ***Dr. No***. The character of Boothroyd, who would go on to become known as Q, also appears in Ian Fleming's original novel. He is named for Geoffrey Boothroyd, who wrote to Fleming complaining about Bond's use of a Beretta in the early Bond books and recommending Bond use a Walther PPK instead. This detail was included in the novel, and then later incorporated in the film, establishing Q-Branch as part of the SIS. During World War II, Fleming worked as a secret agent for MI6 and became friendly with Charles Fraser-Smith who designed spy gadgets called "Q-devices" for field operatives, and the character of Q is also loosely based upon him. Throughout the course of the James Bond films, Q's handy little devices would save the life of 007 many, many times. In both ***Skyfall*** and ***Spectre***, the character of Q re-appears as a twenty-something computer geek (played by Ben Whislaw). While he is sharp and formidable, he seems much too young and wet-behind-the-ears to be head of Q-branch.

The Central Intelligence Agency.

Felix Leiter (played by a variety of actors) and Jack Wade (Joe Don Baker) keep popping up in James Bond films because, as members of the CIA, they are equivalents to James Bond's membership in MI6. The CIA was founded in 1947, an outgrowth of "Wild Bill" Donovan's World War II Office of

Strategic Services that gathered intelligence abroad. Its job was to centralize all intelligence from the Army, Navy, Air Force, and the FBI. Over the years, we have seen arguments that, instead of being the central agency, it has become a rival agency to the other intelligence services of the USA. This matter of continued rivalry may be resolved by the restructuring under President George W. Bush's Homeland Security Agency. During World War II, MI6 trained OSS personnel, and MI6 continues to be an ally to the CIA. The difference between them is that MI6 is even more secretive about its activities than the CIA. MI6 has the power to censor stories in the British press by issuing "D" notices under the authority of the Official Secrets Act.

SMERSH.

Most of Ian Fleming's early novels featured villains from SMERSH, a secret branch of the MGB (prior to it becoming the KGB). A contraction of Smiert Spionam (which meant "Death to Spies"), SMERSH was a very real organization that operated both with in the Soviet Union and overseas with about forty thousand operatives prior to 1955. When 007 is assigned to deal with Le Chiffre in the first James Bond novel *Casino Royale* (1953), he learns of SMERSH from a dossier sent to M. Apparently, SMERSH assassinated Trotsky in 1940 as part of its mission to eliminate all forms of treachery, both within the USSR and aboard. SMERSH was organized into five departments (or Otydels): Department 1 was responsible for intelligence and counterintelligence among all Soviet organizations; Department 2 dealt with Operations and Executions, as headed by Colonel Rosa Klebb; Department 3 was Administration and Finance; Department 4 focused on Investigations, and finally Department 5 had the ominous title Prosecutions.

In the novel version of *From Russia with Love*, SMERSH's headquarters are located in Leningrad, and Colonel General Grubozaboyschikov, known as "G." In later novels, Dr. No, Mr. Big, and Auric Goldfinger, all worked for SMERSH. SMERSH itself was disbanded by Khrushchev in 1958, and replaced by the Special Executive Department of the MVD.

Smiert Spionom.

In the Fleming novel *From Russia with Love*, readers learn that the organization SMERSH is taken from the two Russian words "smiert spionom" which means "death to spies." Nearly thirty years later, the phrase resurfaces in *The Living Daylights* (1987) when General Koskov informs British Intelligence that the new KGB head General Leonid Pushkin is pursu ing a policy known as "Smiert Spionom," which is the assassination of all Western spies. Later, with orders to kill him, James Bond tracks Pushkin down, and demands some answers. According to the new KGB head, Smiert Spionom was a "barrier operation in Stalin's time" that was deactivated some twenty years earlier. We don't doubt Pushkin's sincerity with 007, particularly not with a gun to his head, but we need to clear up some of the disinformation that he told Bond. If we date the events in *The Living Daylights* to 1987, then we have to point out that the real Soviet military counterespionage organization known as SMERSH was actually disbanded (not deactivated) forty-one years earlier in 1946. Many of its objectives were taken over by the Third Chief Directorate of the MGB (later known as the KGB), including assassination, but the organization itself (not an operation, as Pushkin contends) ceased to be an actual government department. Of course, the word SMERSH is not mentioned in the film, but most of us Bond fans know that "smiert spionom" refers to SMERSH.

EVERYTHING I KNOW ABOUT LIFE
I LEARNED FROM JAMES BOND

SPECTRE.

SPECTRE is an acronym for the **Sp**ecial **E**xecutive for **C**ounterintelligence, **T**errorism, **R**evenge, and **E**xtortion. Dr. No refers to them as "the four great cornerstones of power headed by the greatest brains in the world," and we learn in the later films that Ernst Stavro Blofeld is the head of SPECTRE. In reality, no such agency exists. As the Cold War was winding down and the evil empire of the Soviet Union was getting soft and flabby, Ian Fleming needed a new counterpart to SMERSH, which was a real organization in Russia, to become Bond's nemesis. Flemng created SPECTRE, and made it an international agency, not connected to any single government.

In the novel *Thunderball*, SPECTRE is based at No. 136 Boulevard Hoaussman in Paris, behind the cover of an organization called FIRCO, which supports people who served in the French resistance during World War II. In the film version, SPECTRE meets at a Parisian building with the cover organization being the "Centre International D'Assistance Aux Personnes Deplacées" (International Center for Assistance to Displaced Persons). Behind the secret entrance, Blofeld (with his white Persian cat in his lap) presides as the Supreme Commander, with Largo and twenty other members as the inner circle. His SPECTRE organization consists of former members from other criminal or enforcement organizations— Sicilians from the Mafia, Corsicans from the Union Corse, Russians from SMERSH, surviving members of the Gestapo, etc.—who can only be ruled by fear. Dr. No had been an associate of SPECTRE as he prepared to extort money from the Americans. When Rosa Klebb, formerly of SMERSH, set out to obtain the Russian Lektor cipher machine, she was working directly for SPECTRE under the guidance of Kronsteen. While

Largo and Volpe don't survive their attempts on Bond, we will see Blofeld again in *You Only Live Twice*, though as an independent operator. The SPECTRE logo is an octopus, as seen on Blofeld's ring and the various symbols of his operatives. With Blofeld's seeming demise in *For Your Eyes Only* (1981), his organization re-surfaces in *Never Say, Never Again* (1983) and again in 2015's *Spectre*. (Note: a new revitalized SPECTRE, under the control of Blofeld's daughter, was to have been at the heart of the doomsday scenario in an early draft of the script for *The Spy Who Loved Me* (1977), but a dispute over rights to use the criminal organization SPECTRE with Kevin McClory torpedoed that earlier enterprise.)

Mossad.

Mossad, the Central Institute for Intelligence and Special Missions, is the equivalent of Britain's Secret Intelligence Service, or MI6. Israeli newspapers and broadcasting services are prohibited from writing about Mossad, and an impenetrable cloak of secrecy surrounds its covert operations. According to reports, Mossad's largest operational branch is the Collections Department, which is responsible for intelligence-gathering operations abroad. The Collections Department is split into separate "desks" or branches that cover different regions of the world. Branch A is designated for Spain, Egypt, Cyprus and Algeria. Branch C covers London, Paris and Marseilles. All clandestine operations are handled by the highly-secretive Metsada, which runs small units of combatants all around the world. Ironically, future 007 Daniel Craig played a Mossad agent in Steven Spielberg's *Munich* (2005), the year before he earned his license to kill.

EVERYTHING I KNOW ABOUT LIFE
I LEARNED FROM JAMES BOND

The Deuxième Bureau or Direction Générale de la Sécurité Extérieure.

The French Government maintains its own secret service known as the Deuxième Bureau or Direction Générale de la Sécurité Extérieure. Formed during World War II by General de Gaulle, the Free French activities struck at the German occupiers behind enemy lines. The secret services continued to assist de Gaulle in many ways during the post-war struggle against Communism in France. During this era, the French were also struggling to retain some semblance of control over their overseas colonies. This included a serious commitment of troops in Vietnam, Algeria, French Polynesia, and the Middle East. Today, the Direction Générale de la Sécurité Extérieure works closely with MI6 and the CIA. In the novels, Bond works closely with René Mathis of the Deuxième Bureau.

Japanese SIS.

In the novel and film version of You Only Live Twice, James Bond journeys to Japan, and joins forces with Tiger Tanaka, the head of Japanese SIS, and his agents to defeat a common enemy. In reality, Japan's Secret Intelligence Service is one of the most secret and closed organizations in the world; no foreigners can gain access to its top secret inner circle of leaders. So, even if 007 was Britain's top agent, he would never have gotten close to the head of the organization, and would have had to content himself to deal with underlings like Aki. A secret police force has existed in Japan going back to its medieval days when samurai were chosen by the ruling shogun to maintain order and the security of the state. During World War II, the secret police controlled internal dissent as well as provided Japan with much needed intelligence about the Allied forces; the forerunner to Japan's SIS controlled every aspect of life, including the postal service and communications industry. Before the Allied forces under General MacArthur crushed its headquarters, it included an extremely loyal ten-thousand-man army alongside eighty-six thousand regulars, and owned its own prisons, munitions plants, and construction firms. After the war, the Japanese secret police was disbanded, and the Japanese Secret Intelligence Service was formed as a legitimate organization to deal with intelligence, counterintelligence, infiltration, eavesdropping, and disinformation campaigns to harass and destroy groups not friendly to the new regime. In subsequent years, Japanese SIS allied itself with Britain's MI6 and America's CIA in an effort first to fight Communists and then, later, terrorist organizations.

Ninjas.

Tiger Tanaka (Tetsuro Tamba), the head of Japanese SIS, enlists an army of Ninjas to assault Blofeld's volcano hideaway. He tells James Bond that his ninjas are trained in "the art of concealment and surprise," and they are also armed with the latest in advanced weaponry. From the Japanese word "ninja," which means "stealer in," these warriors are most often associated and sadly stereotyped with spying, infiltration, and assassination. They date back to a class of fourteenth century assassins who were trained in martial arts, carried a short sword, and were hired for espionage and murder by wealthy patrons. In their day, ninjas were legends, supposedly capable of disappearing into thin air or turning into animals.

EVERYTHING I KNOW ABOUT LIFE
I LEARNED FROM JAMES BOND

For Eyes Only.

According to the United States Department of Defense, certain classifications are used to identify the level of restriction for important documents. In fact, the Defense Message System (DMS) has formalized hierarchical categories for the dissemination of all information. Each item meant for a U.S., Allied, or NATO member must be marked on the first page with "This Message Contains (—a specific security label is used—) Information." A "security label" is defined by NSTISSI No. 4009 as "information representing the sensitivity of a subject or object by its hierarchical classification." The hierarchical classification is UNCLASSIFIED, RESTRICTED, CONFIDENTIAL, SECRET, TOP SECRET, and FOR EYES ONLY. Thus, unclassified documents are meant for everyone, restricted documents are meant for those who have restricted access to information, and so on. For Eyes Only is the label used for the highest level of security access.

Checkpoint Charlie.

"You Are Leaving the American Sector" were the ominous words on a sign that stood at the border between East and West Berlin for nearly thirty years. During the Cold War, Checkpoint Charlie was one of three gates of the Berlin Wall that separated East from West. With the construction of the wall in August of 1961, the U.S. Army, which was charged with protecting Berlin from the Soviets, erected three gates or checkpoints that would allow foreign tourists, diplomats and other individuals to cross between the two sectors of the city. Named following the conventions of the NATO phonetic alphabet, the three checkpoints were Alpha, Bravo, and Charlie. Checkpoint Alpha was erected at Helmstedt at the autobahn crossing; Checkpoint Bravo was built at the western edge of Berlin where motor traffic crossed at Dreilenden, and Checkpoint Charlie was erected at Friedrichstrasse, at the very heart of the city. In time, Checkpoint Charlie became synonymous with the words separation and freedom. On November 9, 1989, all travel restrictions for East Germans were lifted, and tens of thousands of people flooded through the gate into the western part of the city. Not long after, the Berlin Wall fell, and all three checkpoints were closed for good. The guardhouses were removed on June 22, 1990, and are now located in the Allied Mu seum in Zehlendorf. A copy of the booth and sign that once marked the border was re-erected a year later. For the first time in the James Bond series, 007 crosses Checkpoint Charlie to East Berlin with forged papers and identity cards as Charles Morton. Checkpoint Charlie was also featured in one of the segments of the James Bond spoof *Casino Royale* (1967), and in *Octopussy* (1983), where Bond is driven across the border at "Checkpoint Charlie," after receiving a new ID and travel documents from M.

Enemies and Friends.

James Bond learns the meaning of the old Arab proverb "the enemy of my enemy is my friend" when he allies himself with Kamran Shah and the Mujahedeen against their common enemy, the Soviets. While the old Middle Eastern axiom may date back to antiquity, the meaning is very clear, and is a life lesson well learned, particularly with those who are threatened or at war. The term "enemy" de notes an opposing group or individual that threatens one's own identity or group; therefore, other groups that oppose your enemy would be considered a friend and valuable ally.

EVERYTHING I KNOW ABOUT LIFE I LEARNED FROM JAMES BOND

Enemy Action.

In the novel, Goldfinger tells Bond that "once is happenstance; twice is coincidence, and the third time is enemy action." As a life lesson, particularly when dealing with new people that you don't know, this is very good advice. Happenstance is a chance meeting, and our lives are comprised of many circumstances that create these chance encounters with others. Coincidence is the occurrence of events that happen at the same time seemingly by accident but have some connection. Enemy action is the deliberate manipulation of events so that people are thrown together at a specific time and place.

Microdots.

James Bond discovers a microdot embedded on the photograph he steals from Osato's safe, and relies on Tanaka's men to decipher it in *You Only Live Twice* (1967). Relics of the Cold War, microdots are text or photographic images that are reduced down to the size and shape of a period to prevent their viewing by unintended recipients, and then sent in an innocent-looking document containing periods. Professor Zapp in Germany is regarded as the inventor of microdots; a spy kit for microdot production was called a Zapp outfit. His technique was first used by the Germans in World War II, and then later employed by many countries to pass messages through insecure postal channels. Later microdot techniques used film with special dyes to avoid detection by counter-espionage agents.

Retinal Scan Identification.

When Jack Petachi put his eye in the retinal scan device and was identified as the President of the USA, we felt a bit uneasy. Could a corneal implant work? The answer is... maybe, but not likely. Is retinal scanning a good method of identification? Frankly, it is a bit intrusive. People worry that during the close-up infrared scan of the blood vessel patterns at the back of the human eye their eyes will be damaged. Also, it takes up to ten seconds to make a comparison between a person's retina and that person's filed copy. Yet, because of its low false reject rates, a nearly zero percent false accept rate and small data template linked with quick identity confirmation, retinal scanning systems have been used by the CIA, FBI, NASA and USA defense contractor General Dynamics. The less intrusive method of eye identification is the passive iris system which enables the unique pattern and colors of the flecks on your iris to be read by a camera from a distance of from one to three feet. Iris-scanning technology has been used at London's Heathrow Airport for frequent flyers who wish to avoid queuing up at the passport control station. They just have to walk through past the camera to be recognized. In any case, should you see an attractive passport officer during your regularly scheduled international flight, you could, if you choose, explain your wink as the result of the iris scan. It's a way to start a conversation. What you do from that point is up to you.

Rogue Agents.

At one point in ***Licence to Kill***, James Bond is referred to as a "rogue agent." The first time most Americans heard that term was during the investigation of President John F. Kennedy's assassination when "rogue agents" of the CIA were alleged to be involved in the assassination, though this allega-tion was never substantiated. As we look at James Bond after the incident when M asked for his weapon (which was never given to him) in ***Licence to Kill***,

EVERYTHING I KNOW ABOUT LIFE
I LEARNED FROM JAMES BOND

we find some difficulties. First, M seemed to be acting under some duress. He was buttressed by two American agents and a third American agent was determined, when the meeting went sour, to take out Bond with a sniper rifle. Later, in M's London office, Moneypenny and M have a brief discussion. M knows that Bond is going after Sanchez to kill him in Isthmus and says that he must be stopped. He leaves Moneypenny's desk. Moneypenny quickly telephones Q. The next time we see Q, he is visiting Bond in his hotel room in Isthmus. This visit means that either M has changed his mind, not likely, or that Moneypenny and Q are going out on a limb for James Bond. While we have to admire this kind of support for a field agent, it is rarely found in a professional intelligence organization. So, yes, apparently Bond is a rogue agent in this film, but he is supported by a branch within his own agency and, more or less, a branch of the U.S. government's CIA. Of course, Desmond Llewelyn as Q was happy to have all the screen time in this film, his greatest exposure in any Bond film, but we suspect that M might be more than a bit perturbed to have his Q-branch head going into the field to support a rogue agent. Oh well, that roguish smile on Bond's face must be enough to change everyone's mind—at least it was enough for Moneypenny's. On the other hand, a smile from the lovely Caroline Bliss, who plays Moneypenny, might "move" two film critics we know very well too. It should be noted, now, however, that the greatest rogue agent in MI6's history is Silva, the former head of the Hong Kong office, from *Skyfall*. After spending an extended period in a Chinese prison, he escaped to destroy M's office and to make an attempt on her life and on Bond's. Silva had his reasons for being bitter, for he learned that M had traded him to the Chinese for six other agents. As far as M was concerned, when he ignored her orders to stop cyberterrorism on the Chinese, she treated him as just another rogue agent.

Global Positioning System.

People on the seven seas of this planet and people trying to find out how to get to the Bronx may all be using a Global Positioning System receiver in their hand, their boat or in their car. The USA has placed twenty-seven satellites into space (twenty-four are in operation; the other three are extras) in a fixed orbit around our planet at a cost of approximately $12 billion. Each satellite weighs from one-and-a-half to two tons, and circles the globe at a distance of approximately eleven thousand to twelve thousand miles. The receiver collects precise time and location broadcasts from as many of the geosynchronous orbiting satellites as available at any given time or location. A minimum of three satellites are required to resolve a position, with a fourth satellite able to resolve in three dimensions "altitude." From the data, software in the receiver extrapolates the most accurate location fix possible. A correction signal broadcast separately is used by more recent receivers as an after-thought to correct another error; this signal was introduced after the Bond film was released. (Thanks to Robert Loiacono, our intelligence operative at "E-Systems," for clarifying the process.)

In *Tomorrow Never Dies*, we see that Carver's plan to get a scoop to open his satellite network all hinges on Henry Gupta (Ricky Jay) hacking the GPS system to place the position of HMS Devonshire within Chinese national waters. Regrettably, we did not get to see Ricky Jay, sometime magician, doing his really lethal trick—tossing playing cards into watermelons from several feet away. Yes, a hurricane can drive a pencil through a board. Ricky Jay could toss a playing card into your throat, causing you to bleed out in ninety seconds. Why didn't they show this nouveau Oddjob trick in the film? Well, the playing cards just didn't look that lethal onscreen, but, trust us, they are.

EVERYTHING I KNOW ABOUT LIFE
I LEARNED FROM JAMES BOND

Tangled Web.

In ***Marmion***, Sir Walter Scott wrote, "Oh what a tangled web we weave/When first we practice to deceive!" Deception is part of the role of a secret agent, and James Bond has assumed many different identities or "covers" in the course of his various adventures. He has become David Somerset in ***From Russia with Love***, Mr. Young in ***You Only Live Twice***, Sir Hilary Bray in ***On Her Majesty's Secret Service***, Scaramanga in ***The Man with the Golden Gun***, Robert Sterling in ***The Spy Who Loved Me***, St. John Smythe and James Stock in ***A View To a Kill***. In ***Octopussy***, he takes on the identity of Colonel Luis Toro, Charles Morton, and James Bond, adventurer and fortune hunter. In ***Die Another Day***, he is Van Biert, a convict diamond smuggler and international arms dealer. Inventing and maintaining a cover identity is part of the tangled web 007 weaves to shield himself from his opposition and to put him into a position to accomplish his mission. Ideally, a cover identity should also protect the mission against the worst possible consequences of the secret agent's discovery. Dealing as it does with human beings, their relations to each other, with what they feel and believe, with their habits and impressions, their insights and their actions, cover is an art-form that James Bond strives to perfect but has never really mastered. His masquerade as Colonel Luis Toro is easily discovered by Toro himself; most of his other identities are also just as easily revealed. The best cover is one that contains the least fictional and the most plausible legitimate material. To be too precise in a cover story qualitatively increases the chances of repudiation by those who may already be suspicious of a newcomer. So James Bond continues to work hard at making deception a part of his job, not his lifestyle. 007 knows that he must deal honestly with those people in his life that matter, including M and Q, Miss Moneypenny and Bill Tanner.

Brainwashing.

In *Die Another Day*, James Bond is kept in captivity and receives brutal treatment for fourteen months. Had he received "brainwashing," a combination of sleep deprivation and programming from skilled interrogators who prey upon every physical and psychological weakness, as had Joseph Cardinal Mindszenty, he would have cracked. The Hungarian cardinal, who was convicted of treason by the communist government in 1949, was imprisoned and brainwashed until he was released during the Hungarian anti-communist rebellion in 1956. We note the blast of disorienting sound that appears when Bond slips into Dr. Alvarez's private office is often used as an aid to modern brainwashing and had been used in the brainwashing sequences in Sydney Furie's *The Ipcress File* (1965) with Michael Caine. Despite Bond's training, it was unreasonable to suppose that after fourteenth months of imprisonment and possible brain washing, any person could have kept the name of an American agent from his interrogators. Indeed, in the French Resistance during World War II, Resistance members were only expected to keep information to themselves for forty-eight hours. The real question to ask the U.S. intelligence chief Damian Falco was: Why did you give the name of an American double-agent to a British intelligence officer? Such information is rarely shared. We do applaud Bond for throwing away his cyanide poison pill years ago. Suicide should always be the very last resort. And it was in *Skyfall*, when Silva tells of taking the pill after months of torture in a Chinese prison, only to discover that, though it destroyed much of his facial structure, it was not lethal to him

EVERYTHING I KNOW ABOUT LIFE
I LEARNED FROM JAMES BOND

A View to Kill BR / US 1985, Photo by: Mary Evans/EON PRODUCTIONS/Ronald Grant/Everett Collection (10393603)

CHAPTER THREE

GADGETS AND ACCESSORIES FOR THE WELL-EQUIPPED MAN

> *He has a powerful weapon,*
> *He charges a million a shot,*
> *An assain that's second to none,*
> *The Man with the Golden Gun.*

—Lulu, *The Man with the Golden Gun* (1975)

In the final reel of ***On Her Majesty's Secret Service*** (1969), Major Geoffrey Boothroyd (Desmond Llewelyn), better known as Q, starts to lecture James Bond on his wedding day. But 007 interrupts him, saying, "This time, I've got all of the gadgets, and I know how to use them." This tongue-in-cheek exchange between the long-suffering Q and the 00-Agent who has destroyed most of his wonderful toys was meant to be a clever indictment of what had become a running joke in the series.

Exotic espionage equipment and extremely lethal accessories have always been very popular elements of James Bond's

EVERYTHING I KNOW ABOUT LIFE I LEARNED FROM JAMES BOND

literary and cinematic adventures; these items often prove critically important to Bond in climatic moments when the world is teetering on the edge of destruction. The early Fleming novels and subsequent screen adaptations were relatively free of gadgets and accessories for 007's use. In ***Dr. No*** (1962), Bond's sole gadgets were a Geiger counter, a Rolex watch with a radioactive dial, and a standard-issue semi-automatic pistol. In ***From Russia with Love*** (1963), Bond had a booby-trapped attaché case. The gadgets, however, assumed a higher, even spectacular profile in the 1964 film Goldfinger, and their success further encouraged Q-Branch to supply 007 with additional espionage equipment.

One of the major complaints that Sean Connery made about the series was that the films relied too heavily on gadgets, and downplayed Bond's natural resourceful ness. His complaint was not that far off the mark. Some of the later films relied on excessive amounts of gadgets and extremely outlandish accessories to save 007's Saville Row suits from shredding. Many of the Roger Moore films, in particular ***Moonraker*** (1979), made Bond more like an indestructible videogame character than the flesh and blood, devil-may-care spy of the Connery films. 007 relies on a laser gun instead of his trusty Walther PPK! Since ***Moonraker***, however, the producers have struggled to keep the gadgets to a minimum, relying on them only as the story's content demands, but alas, they reached an outrageous level with ***Die Another Day***. More recently, in the Daniel Craig films, Bond's gadgets are practically non-existent, and some fans prefer to have 007 rely on his wits rather than Q-branch. In fact, in the remake of ***Casino Royale*** and ***Quantum of Solace***, there has been little mention of Q and the special Quartermaster division of MI-6. In ***Skyfall***, however, a younger and geekier Q (Ben Whishaw) returns to give Bond a new Walther PPK and a radio beacon.

The new Q rejects any more exotic gadgets, except for the brand new Aston Martin DB-10 in *Spectre* (2015).

Despite what certain critics maintain, we love the gadgets and accessories that Bond carries in the movies. While most well-dressed men might add cufflinks or a pocket handkerchief to their outfit, 007's accessories are considerably more lethal. In fact, the well-dressed secret agent is never without certain gadgets, and James Bond proves in each of his dangerous assignments that they are endlessly useful, entertaining and fun. We know he's going to get out of trouble, but we are always bemused by his use of Q's gadgets!

Beretta.

For many years, James Bond's weapon of choice was a .25 caliber Beretta, a common weapon for Italian Army officers in WWII. A small and light weight weapon, the Beretta was inconspicuous, and easy to conceal inside a jacket or pants pocket. However, the handgun lacked firepower, and was prone to jamming. Most professionals considered the Beretta a woman's handgun because it was easy to carry in a purse. Although Bond liked the gun, it failed him on a mission (when he caught it in his clothes trying to draw it from his shoulder holster), and he spent six months in the hospital with bullet wounds. M insisted that his Beretta be replaced with the now legendary Walther PPK, and the "armorer" from Q-Branch trades Bond's sidearm for the new gun.

Walther PPK.

The Walther PPK was first introduced in *Dr. No* (1962) when Major Boothroyd, the armorer of MI-6, replaced James Bond's

.25 Beretta after the latter gun jammed on him. Ever since then, the Walther PPK has never left Bond's side, and has become legendary as the weapon of a secret agent. Its small size with a flat design makes it ideal for concealment and the 7.65mm caliber with a six round magazine pack a powerful punch, like "a brick through a plate glass window." The PPK was first marketed in the early 1930's, and saw action as the "Waffen" PPK carried by German officers in World War II. In the novels, Ian Fleming chose it as Bond's weapon after consulting with a weapons expert named Boothroyd. In both **Goldfinger** and **Moonraker**, Bond has little opportunity to use the semi-automatic pistol, and it stays mostly holstered in his Berns-Martin triple draw holster. In the more recent Daniel Craig films, which are meant to depict 007 at the start of his career, he carries the Walter PPK once again. In fact, when the new Q (played by Ben Whishaw) meets with Daniel Craig's Bond in **Skyfall**, the new Walther PPK which he presents to Bond may only be fired by Bond, an innovation that saves Bond's life.

Geiger Counter.

While investigating some rocks that Strangways collected from Crab Key in **Dr. No**, Bond uses a Geiger counter that Q-Branch has sent him, and determines that the rocks were radioactive. A Geiger counter is an instrument that can detect and measure radioactivity, and was invented by H. Geiger and E.W. Muller in 1928. Geiger counters are sensitive enough to measure Alpha waves, Beta waves, and Gamma waves, the three types of radioactivity.

Exploder Bag.

During his mission briefing with M in **Dr. No**, Bond is told that he will receive additional instructions in a self-destructing exploder bag when he reaches the airport. While we know that this meeting takes place at 3:00 AM, and that M is worried about Bond getting enough sleep for the mission, we're not quite sure how much sense it makes to send a brief case filled with explosives to Heathrow Airport. We would have almost preferred that Miss Moneypenny simply typed his additional instructions out in her office while Bond waited and caught a nap.

The Attaché Case.

Major Boothroyd (Desmond Llewelyn), the man from Q-Branch (or the Quartermaster Branch), presents Bond with a black attaché case which was being issued to all 00-agents as standard equipment in *From Russia with Love* (1963). Featuring an array of gadgetry that would become standard as the series continued, the attaché case came equipped with an easy-access throwing knife, a trick opener that triggered a tear gas canister, at least twenty rounds of ammunition, a folding lightweight AR-7 .25 caliber rifle with an infra-red scope, and fifty gold sovereigns. Talk about a getaway weekend in Las Vegas! 007 relies on all of the gadgets to get out of trouble, and carries the attaché case in future missions.

Lektor Cipher Machine.

This clever device in *From Russia with Love*, about the size of a portable typewriter, has its ancestor in the responses to the 1930's German ENIGMA machine, a device used to encode messages for radio broadcasts. By 1938, the Poles had created a machine to break the code. When the Germans changed procedures, the British designed another code-breaking machine.

EVERYTHING I KNOW ABOUT LIFE
I LEARNED FROM JAMES BOND

This machine gave the Allies a great advantage throughout World War II. [In the novel version, the Lektor was called the Spektor Decoding Machine, but that name was changed so that audiences would not confuse the machine with the criminal organization SPECTRE.]

Rolex Watch.

In the pre-credits adventure of *Goldfinger* (1964), a Rolex Submariner is beautifully spotlighted by James Bond's cigarette lighter, while Pussy Galore wears a Rolex GMT Master piloting Goldfinger's jet. As a man of style and substance, Bond wears the Rolex Oyster Perpetual Chronograph with silvered dial and expanding stainless steel bracelet. The watch is both classy and functional, and while its $3,500 price tag would bankrupt most Bond wannabes in that era, the well-dressed secret agent would not leave home without it. In subsequent adventures, Q repaired Bond's Rolex, and outfitted the wristwatch with a few lethal accessories. Pull the timing pin out, and the watch turns into a hyper-intensified magnetic field, capable of stopping a bullet at long range (or so Q claims). The bezel is also equipped with a diamond-cutting wheel which rotates at high speeds like a mini circular saw. At a critical point in his mission to stop Kananga's drug-smuggling operation in *Live and Let Die* (1973), Bond employs the watch with great success.

Dunhill-Ronson Cigarette Lighter.

Also, from the *Goldfinger* pre-credits adventure, Bond is shown using an oxidized Dunhill-Ronson cigarette lighter to illuminate his watch and to light a cigarette. Alfred Dunhill Ltd first manufactured what was called the Rolls Royce of cigarette lighters in the 1930's. The London-based manufacturer established a dictum that stated, "It must be beautiful, it must be the best of its kind, and it must last," and British royals, Winston Churchill, and many foreign dignitaries, were among the first to carry the Dunhill lighter. Ronson (known in its early days as Art Metal Works) produced the equivalent in the United States. After the Second World War, Dunhill-Ronson cigarette lighters were considered to be among the finest in the world. [Perhaps as a tip of the proverbial hat to the James Bond series, rival secret agent Derek Flint carries a Dunhill-Ronson cigarette lighter tricked out with eighty-two gadgets—"eighty-three if you wish to light a cigarette."]

Watch and Geiger Counter.

In place of his signature Rolex Oyster perpetual watch, James Bond wears a bulky stainless-steel diver's watch. Several times in *Thunderball* (1965), 007 relies on its hidden Geiger counter function to search for the missing atomic weapons on Largo's ship.

Camera and Geiger Counter.

This Geiger counter was built into the shell of a Nikon Nikonos underwater camera. If only Domino had kept a firm grip on it or packed it into a carrying case, she would not have had to endure Largo's torture. Oh well, no one had given her adequate training for espionage. She made her living just doing what came naturally.

Miniature Underwater Breathing Device.

The miniature breathing device was supposed to be good for

about four to five minutes. After the film was released, allegedly the U.S. Navy made an inquiry of EON Productions about the construction of this hand device, which saved Bond's life at least twice in *Thunderball*. Their response was along the lines of: "The device worked for as long as Connery could hold his breath." Alas, it was a miracle of film editing, rather than of miniaturized construction of an actual breathing device.

Radioactive Homing Pill.

Though James Bond had his doubts about the radioactive nature of the pill, he swallowed it before joining Largo's crew in disguise in *Thunderball*. It did enable Felix Leiter to locate Bond. One presumes, however, that this device passed gently. Thankfully, Q continued to perfect this device, and reduced the homing device to a piece of radioactive lint in *On Her Majesty's Secret Service*.

Bond's Q Suit.

When Evelyn Tremble (Peter Sellers) reports to Q-Branch in *Casino Royale* (1967), he is outfitted by an affected member of MI6 with a suit containing a plethora of useful gadgets. The gadgets include a poison capsule (located in the crotch), a combination switchblade and Geiger counter, an intercom, an infra-red camera and tape recorder, a Beretta in the buttonhole, and a mini-gun in the gusset. Should he need to go to the bathroom, Tremble/Bond must consult the instructions under the left lapel. Don't rush it, Tremble/Bond; that switchblade might be triggered by the wrong move.

Rocket Gun.

At Tiger Tanaka's ninja training camp in *You Only Live Twice* (1967), Bond is introduced to the rocket gun for the first time. He later carried a variation of this weapon in his second Caribbean adventure, *Live and Let Die* (1973). The Q-Branch of Japanese SIS had customized several rifles and pistols as rocket guns for use by Tanaka's ninja commandoes. What distinguished the weapons from standard military ordnance was special ammunition propelled by compressed gas. Using bullets with jet propulsion that exploded on impact, the modern ninjas had an advantage over Blofeld's security forces, and easily defeated the superior-numbered force. Bond first saw the guns in action at the ninja-training camp, and then, several missions later, used one of the gas pellets to "blow up" Mister Big.

Explosive Cigarettes.

"It can save your life, this cigarette", Tiger Tanaka boasts of his latest invention, an explosive cigarette. While James Bond may quip that he sounds "like a commercial," this innocuous-looking gadget actually saves 007's life when he is forced to watch Blofeld's television broadcast. This Japanese SIS-developed weapon contained a small rocket shell with penetrating explosive tip encased in an ordinary-looking cigarette. When lit, the device had a four-second fuse, and was accurate up to thirty yards. Ironically, Blofeld says, "It won't be the nicotine that kills you, Mr. Bond," but in fact the explosive cigarette is what leads to the destruction of his volcano hideaway.

EVERYTHING I KNOW ABOUT LIFE
I LEARNED FROM JAMES BOND

Throwing Stars.

Tanaka's ninja commandoes utilize razor-sharp throwing stars in their assault on SPECTRE's fortress. Small, light-weight, and extremely deadly in the hands of a martial artist, Bond is grateful when one throwing star hits Blofeld squarely in the hand, and throws off his aim.

Portable Safe-cracking Device.

James Bond carries the portable safe-cracking device in the breast pocket of his suit, and uses it to open the safe in Mr. Osato's office in *You Only Live Twice*. An invention of Q-Branch, the tiny device was about the size of a man's wallet, and had the ability to decipher the combination on any dial-locking safe. By attaching its magnetic censor to the metal surface of a safe, it had the ability to cycle through every possible code until the correct numbers were found. 007 must have misplaced the device after the mission was over because he must use a larger, clunkier model in Bern, Switzerland, for the same purpose.

Webley Mark VI .455.

In addition to the rocket guns, Tiger Tanaka's ninja commandoes also use Webley Mark VI .455 caliber pistols in their assault on Blofeld's volcano hideaway. The Webley six-shot pistol was a favorite weapon among British officers in World War I, and was carried into battle by none other than Winston Churchill. In the closing moments of *You Only Live Twice*, Blofeld picks up a Webley pistol, and uses it to kill Mr. Osato, then later threatens Bond with it. [007's rival Indiana Jones also relied on the Webley Mark VI in Indiana Jones and the Last Crusade (1989).]

Radioactive Lint.

In ***On Her Majesty's Secret Service*** (1969), when Q briefs M on the latest advancements in miniaturization, the Quartermaster shows him a piece of lint under a magnifying glass. The notion is that Bond or another member of the Secret Intelligence Service could place a piece of radioactive lint in an adversary's pocket, and then keep track of him at a distance. M does not seem to respond to the new offering from Q because his mind is thinking about the fact that 007 is missing.

Safe-cracking Machine.

In ***You Only Live Twice***, James Bond relies on a handy little device that he has secreted in his pocket to break into Osato's safe; but for some unknown reason, 007 has discarded this small accessory for a much larger one to break into Gebruder Gumbold's safe in ***On Her Majesty's Secret Service*** (1969). Has technology regressed between the two films, or are Swiss safes so much more difficult to crack? The bulky, safe-cracking device is delivered to Bond via crane, up to a balcony outside Gumbold's office, by Campbell (Bernard Horsfall). Bond then attaches a mechanical device to the tumbler dial on the safe, and sits back to wait while the machine manipulates the tumblers. The machine takes most of the hour to break into Gumbold's safe. When it finally succeeds in cracking the combination, Bond uses its handy photocopier to document papers on Blofeld's claim to his title.

Minolta Spy Camera.

Like his famous, real-life counterparts, James Bond relies on a Minolta Minox, 16mm miniature camera, to take photographs of import ant items and documents *in On Her Majesty's Secret Service*. 007 uses the camera to photograph a map of Piz Gloria and locations of where the "angels of death" are hidden.

False Fingerprints.

In *Diamonds Are Forever* (1971), when James Bond assumes the identity of smuggler Peter Franks, 007 relies on Q to provide him with not only his paper and plastic identification but also special latex fingerprints. Tiffany Case, just as smart as she was lovely, checks out Bond/Franks' fingerprints before she engages in any compromising conversation with him. Some suggest that the stickers are made by having the fingerprint imprinted onto latex sheets, while they are warm, and then sticking them on the subject with removable glue.

Finger Trap.

This Q gadget is placed close to the subject's holster in *Diamonds Are Forever*. When someone tries to frisk or lift his weapon, it clamps down on the opponent's hand. The sharp edges would do some damage and provide a distraction. Of course, Bond was far too clever to ever trip the trap himself after having a few drinks, unlike most of us.

Slot Machine Magnet.

Yes, Q used it successfully in *Diamonds Are Forever* by using his ring to control the revolutions per minute of the machine plus his computer knowledge. Of course, you don't see him pocketing any of those coins, do you? Criminals have used other devices in the past. Those who were not extremely clever and lucky, however, may be found in various prisons or may not be found at all. What's done in Las Vegas, stays in Las Vegas—in the old days they were sometimes buried in the nearby desert at night. Believe it!

Piton-firing Pistol.

In ***Diamonds Are Forever***, James Bond is lucky enough to have a piton-firing gun handy when he goes "mountaineering about" the Whyte House in Las Vegas. Unfortunately, two Blofelds are there and no Whyte. Deprived of his trusty Walther PPK, Bond somehow managed to keep his single-shot piton gun concealed. Unfortunately, when the wrong cat jumps the right way, Bond kills the duplicate Blofeld, instead of the smooth-talking Blofeld with the diamond-collared pussycat. For once, James Bond did not go for the big money.

Pulsar Time Computer.

While his Rolex is out for repairs, James Bond wears Pulsar's Time Computer, the world's first all-digital watch with a liquid crystal display and numeric read-out. Unlike the Rolex, this particular wrist watch does not appear to have any special accessories, and he quickly exchanges it for his trusty Rolex in ***Live and Let Die*** (1973).

Shaving Kit.

Inside his shaving kit in ***Live and Let Die***, Bond carries several of Q's assorted goodies, and uses several of them just after he has checked into his hotel room on San Monique. 007 removes the cover from his rather ordinary-looking hairbrush to reveal

EVERYTHING I KNOW ABOUT LIFE I LEARNED FROM JAMES BOND

a telescopic antenna and transmitter capable of sending both vocal and Morse-code communications. He also has a "bug" detector which allows him to find the listening devices that have been planted in his room, including the one at the head of his bed and one hidden in a statue. And while not necessarily a weapon, Bond employs his spray shaving lotion (along with a conveniently-lit cigar) as a flamethrower to kill the poisonous snake that dropped into his bath.

Shark Gun.

Reminiscent of the Rocket Guns from *You Only Live Twice*, the Shark Gun that Felix Leiter insists 007 bring to the island with him in *Live and Let Die* (1973) uses the same technology of compressed gas pellets that explode upon impact. Kananga confiscates the shark gun from Bond when he is captured, and then mocks him with the weapon by destroying a favorite couch and sending an overweight henchman flying to the floor. Later, 007 appropriates one of the bullets, and uses it to explode Kananga's already over-inflated ego. Without any set-up from Q, we're really not quite sure how the damned thing works, and suspect it was thrown into the mix at the last moment to lend credibility to one of the worst pieces of special effects in all of the James Bond films. Better to have thrown Kananga to the sharks!

Smith and Wesson .38 Revolver.

In *Live and Let Die*, the Smith and Wesson .38 caliber revolver is established as the standard CIA-issue weapon. Both Rosie Carver and Quarrel Jr. carry it. With a corrugated three-inch stock, no serial number, and limited to six shots, the handgun seems like a major step-down from the Walther PPK Felix Leiter carried in the earlier films.

The Golden Gun.

In the novel *The Man with the Golden Gun*, Francisco Scaramanga's weapon of choice was a customized 1911 Colt .45 caliber semiautomatic pistol with a gold finish. This large caliber pistol still has an unsurpassed reputation for a standard military pistol as a one shot "manstopper," even though its magazine holds seven rounds. In *The Man with the Golden Gun* (1975), the golden gun is a 4.2 mm single-shot pistol with a bullet about half the size of a 9mm round, a weapon only appropriate for a professional assassin who was a trick shot artist at age ten. Scaramanga's golden weapon was composed of elements put together by Calibri of London (a maker of cigarette and cigar lighters and men's accessories) such as: a barrel made from the housing of a Water man fountain pen (if Q had done it, it would have written too), a lighter (forming the firing chamber), a cuff link (providing the trigger), a cigarette case (as the handle of the gun), and a twenty-three karat gold bullet with a traceable amount of chrome, provided by Lazar of Macao.

Solex agitator.

As Alfred Hitchcock would call it, the solex agitator is the "McGuffin" of *The Man with the Golden Gun*, the thing that keeps the plot moving. It is the device that concerns every person in the film. In John Huston's *The Maltese Falcon* (1941), Sam Spade calls his McGuffin, the bejeweled statuette of a falcon covered in black enamel, a "dingus." Whatever you call it, James Bond is seeking the solex agitator throughout the film. After all,

EVERYTHING I KNOW ABOUT LIFE I LEARNED FROM JAMES BOND

Bond was searching for the solex agitator and its inventor before he even learns about Scaramanga's perceived threat. Any device which could translate ninety-five percent of the thermal energy of sunlight into electricity would be the most valuable device in the world. And it's only the size of a pack of cigarettes; it better be that size. Imagine the difficulty of Miss Anders carrying it around if it weighed as much as a desktop computer.

Solar Gun.

When Scaramanga goes to his solar gun and destroys Bond's very functional seaplane, we were surprised. Anything that fired at two thousand five hundred degrees Fahrenheit should cause the moisture in the air to sizzle. In any case, it certainly was a good weapon to have with a solar energy station to provide the "ammunition." Surprising as it may seem, American troops in the aftermath of World War II captured a German weapon designated a "sun gun," a prototype that would focus the energy from the sun into a devastating beam to down Allied aircraft. The principle of that gun is still in use in creating solar electricity today.

Ski Pole Rifle.

In the pre-credits adventure of *The Spy Who Loved Me* (1977), with Sergie Barsov and the Soviet assassins in hot pursuit, Bond swivels around on his skis, and raises one of his ski poles in an offensive maneuver. He takes aim, pulls the trigger on the handle, and fires the standard snow skiing pole like a rifle. The bullet from the end of the pole instantly kills Barsov. 007 turns back around, and skis for the edge of a precipice. Apparently, the ski pole rifle has only one shot, but in the hands of a trained assassin like Bond, he only needs a single shot.

Seiko Wristwatch.

With his Rolex presumably at Q Branch for additional repairs, James Bond wears a seemingly ordinary digital watch from Seiko. The wristwatch is far from ordinary, however. It contains a built-in satellite link, and types out printed messages from MI6 on a thin spool of tape. The cable 007 receives at the beginning of the movie requires him to "pull out" of his current mission, warming up in a log cabin with a beautiful Soviet agent. In *Moonraker* (1979), James Bond employs another Seiko watch to blow a hole in the ventilation system so that he and Holly could escape. The Seiko Exploding Watch comes with some plastique, a detonating cord, and a built-in detonator in the watch—just the thing for blowing up the lock on the door of the room beneath a space shuttle that is about to take off. Unlike the Seiko he carried on the *Moonraker* mission, Bond's Seiko wristwatch in Octopussy does not contain any high explosive packed in the shell. Instead the digital watch acts as a receiver for tracking the homing device planted inside a Fabergé egg. 007 uses the watch on several occasions throughout the mission to track the location of the egg.

Wrist Dart Gun.

Throughout the entire *Moonraker* (1979) mission, James Bond leaves his Walther PPK holstered (a first in the series!), and relies on other gadgets that he receives from Q, including the Wrist Dart Gun. We presume the gun, which he wore like a watch on his right wrist, employed highly pressurized gas. The tiny anti-personnel darts were cyanide-based (good for stopping Drax's heart); the armor-piercing dart probably used depleted uranium (to stop Drax's centrifuge controls).

Cigarette Case/Safe Opener.

We don't know how this X-ray device looks into the interior of the locking mechanism of a steel safe in *Moonraker*, and Q won't tell. But Bond used a similar device in *You Only Live Twice*, and the device kept getting better and better. We wonder if James Bond ever considered working as a jewel thief in Monaco on his vacations. No, that was Cary Grant in Alfred Hitchcock's *To Catch a Thief* (1955). Still, Cary with Grace Kelly might have been a mentor for Bond.

ATAC.

The ATAC or Automatic Targeting Attack Communicator was a high-tech encryption device used by the British Navy to send ultra-low frequency coded transmissions to nuclear submarines with target coordinates, firing data and launch codes. When the British spy trawler St. Georges accidentally struck a mine and sank off the coast of Albania in the Ionian Sea, the ATAC went down with it. MI6 was concerned that, in the wrong hands, the devicecould be used to order Western subs to attack friendly nations. Both the British and the Soviets launch missions to recover it from the bottom of the sea, but 007 is the one person who actually succeeds—only to have it taken from him by Kristatos. Shaped like a keyboard with a LCD panel, the ATAC represented one of the most dangerous devices in the world. At the end of *For Your Eyes Only* (1981), Bond throws the device over a cliff rather than let the KGB have it.

Crossbow.

Melina Havelock's weapon of choice is a crossbow in For Your Eyes Only. While crossbows have existed for centuries, they have not been used as a frontline combat weapon since the invention of gunpowder, though U.S. Special Forces have used the crossbow for night and stealth assaults. The crossbow fires a missile-like bolt with approximately the same range and accuracy of a typical long bow but with a great deal more force. The rather bulky weapon fires steel bolts and can drop a human target with the same kind of effect as a bullet. Melina uses the crossbow several times in the course of the adventure, and proves that she is just as deadly with the weapon as Bond is with his Walther PPK. In *Operation Kid Brother*, Neil Connery, Sean's kid brother, arms his men with bows and arrows, so that they make their final assault quietly.

JIM.

Named after Jim Jarrett (not James Bond), the JIM diving suit is known as a One-Atmosphere Armored Dive Suit (OMADS), and allows divers to work far deeper than normal scuba wear could. The pressurized suit and helmet protects divers from the effects of water pressure at depths nearly two thousand feet below the surface. While recovering the ATAC, 007 encounters Mantis Man, one of Kristatos' men wearing JIM equipment, and plants the ATAC's self-destruct charge on the back of his dive suit. The charge blows him to pieces, giving new meaning to the term "explosive decompression."

The Identigraph.

Q's latest toy, in *For Your Eyes Only*, is an experimental device known as the Identigraph that helps James Bond track down Emile Leopold Locque. By inputting the man's facial characteristics into the machine, the Identigraph checks databases of the Sureté, Interpol, Mossad, CIA, and the West German Police for a match. The device then prints out the suspect's image.

Walther P-5.

In *Octopussy* (1983), James Bond loses his beloved Walther PPK during the Tuk Tuk Taxi chase in Udaipur, India, and asks Q (Desmond Llewelyn) for a replacement. Later, behind the Iron Curtain in East Berlin, 007 captures General Orlov red-handed with the Kremlin jewels, and holds him at gunpoint with a Walther P-5. We can only speculate that Q didn't have any spare PPKs lying around, and gave Bond the next best thing. In the early 1970s, as a response to Heckler & Koch's superior-made P9S semi-automatic handgun, Walther re-designed its P-38 as the P-5. The barrel was shortened to 3.5 inches, and was supported at the muzzle as well as the breech for excellent accuracy with a fully-enclosed slide. The P5 shared the same type of swinging-link locking block as the P.38. Because the barrel returned to the same position each time it cycled, this type of lock-up was inherently accurate and deadly for a semi-automatic handgun. Bond returns to the Walther PPK for his next several missions, then later traded up to the Walther P-99, but found the Walther P-5 to be a very suitable alternative. [In the rival James Bond film, ***Never Say Never Again*** (1983), Sean Connery's 007 also carries the Walther P-5. Apparently, even though they were working on rival productions, Algernon (Alec Mc Cowen) and Major Boothroyd (Desmond Llewelyn) shared memos about how to equip 007.]

Fountain Pen.

While social scientists may debate whether the pen is indeed mightier than the sword, James Bond proves that his unique fountain pen is particularly lethal in the right hands. In Udaipur, India, Q outfits Bond with the eighteen-carat gold Mont Blanc Pen, which contains an assortment of useful tools and gadgets. Not only can 007 write coded messages with the fountain pen but he can also use the mixture of concentrated nitric and hydrochloric acid that is contained within to dissolve all metals. This particularly comes in handy when Bond must burn through the iron bars of his prison cell at Khan's Monsoon Palace to escape. The fountain pen also contains a bugging receiver (in the form of a removable earpiece) that allows him to eavesdrop on the bug he has placed in the Fabergé egg. An exquisite pen to satisfy that burning desire to eavesdrop or send poison-pen letters!

Lethal Rocket Pen.

Q told us that they were not finished working on the rocket pen. We had to admire the Union jack design that called our attention to the pen. But we must admit we were holding our breath until that warhead exploded that Fatima Blush could be quite a handful. Of course, some of us would have liked to have seen more of Barbara Carrera later in that film. As a matter of fact, some of us would have liked to have seen more of her at any time.

Tracking Device.

Looking for a tiny microchip on a dead agent? It is a good thing that Q is so versatile. That thing could hide under a postage stamp in *A View to a Kill* (1985).

EVERYTHING I KNOW ABOUT LIFE
I LEARNED FROM JAMES BOND

Bug Detector.

James Bond has a built-in "bug" detector in his electric shaver in "A View to a Kill." There is no need to share with Zorin or the KGB what he and Sir Godfrey might be doing. And a good microtape recorder plays the pre-recorded tape of Bond snoring, though we suspect Bond is so subtle that even his actual snoring is barely detectible.

Camera Ring.

Eat your heart out, Minox. Q has a camera built into a ring on James Bond's finger in *A View to a Kill.* "Is that Mr. Smythe waving his hands in the air?" No, you silly bad guy, it is James Bond putting you on record.

Better than Polarized Sunglasses.

With these sunglasses, James Bond can see through tinted windows and spy Max Zorin writing out a check to Stacy Sutton in ***A View to a Kill.***

Check Impression Copier.

By placing his copier over the blank check on top of Zorin's checkbook, James Bond discovers that Miss S. Sutton has just received a check for $5 million. That sort of money would pay for a lot of Beluga and Bollinger.

Cane Radio Controller.

Zorin uses his radio controller built into his cane to have an automated syringe inject natural horse steroids into his second-rate stallions for a first-rate performance on the racecourse. Alas, we all know that cheaters never win, at least, not in the long run against James Bond.

Sharper Image Lock Pick.

Yes, that card that James Bond used to flip the window lock at Stacey Sutton's mansion was a Sharper Image "lock pick." Or, maybe it was just a Sharper Image credit card (which would do that job just as well). In any case, Sharper Image put Roger Moore's face on their catalog that year. You've got to get the cash and the advertising where you can.

Robot Snooper.

Q was so proud of his Snooper, a robot dog with a television camera and satellite hookup that would let him know who was doing what anywhere in the world. But he was too much of a gentleman to let M know exactly what James Bond was doing in Stacey Sutton's shower at the end of *A View to a Kill* (1985). Good fellow, Q.

Walther WA-2000 Sniper's Rifle.

Like his trusty Walther PPK, James Bond turns to Walther to provide him with a reliable rifle in *The Living Daylights* (1987). The Walther WA-2000 Sniper's Rifle with infrared sight and telescopic lens was the state-of-the-art weapon for dealing with counter terrorist insurgents and Soviet assassins. When it came to ammunition, 007 had a choice between soft-nosed bullets or armor-piercing ones. Ultimately, Bond chooses the armor-piercing ones because he knows that most Soviet snipers wear body armor. Saunders, as the station head of V-Vienna, was responsible for smuggling the weapon into Bratislava, Czechoslovakia, but only James Bond had the training to use it. When the sniper appears at the window, Bond recognizes her as the cellist from the symphony he attended earlier. Noticing that she was only an amateur and "didn't know one end of the rifle from the other," 007 takes careful aim with the Walther WA-200, and merely shoots the gun out of her hand rather than kill her. He looked forward to using it again on a future assignment.

Keychain.

Q Branch provides James Bond with an ordinary-looking keychain that offered an incredible array of defenses in *The Living Daylights*. By whistling the first few bars of "Rule Britannia," the keychain would dispense a cloud of stun gas capable of disabling a normal person for about thirty seconds. 007 uses the stun gas to disable his prison guard long enough to escape from the Afghan prison. By whistling a wolf's call or "wolf whistle," the keychain would trigger a C4 explosive charge, capable of blowing a door off its hinges or blasting through a wall. Bond uses the device to explode a statue of Wellington on Brad Whitaker. And finally, the keychain was attached to lock picks capable of unlocking ninety-percent of the world's locks. 007 frees himself from his handcuffs with the pick lock.

Binocular Glasses.

James Bond also uses a pair of binocular glasses from Q Branch to spy on Koskov in Tangiers in *The Living Daylights*. The binoculars have a magnification of 10x, with a field of view (at one thousand yards) of two hundred and sixty-one feet.

Dentonite Toothpaste.

Do not look for this plastic explosive in your drugstore. If you find it, you might blow up stumps with it in your back forty acres, or, like James Bond in *Licence to Kill* (1989), blow a hole in a bulletproof window so that you can snipe at a bad guy, such as Franz Sanchez. We suspect Jaws may have mistaken Dentonite for real toothpaste, and that's the reason why he must wear the silver-plated dentures.

Signature Optical Scanner Camera/Rifle.

Disguised as a medium-format camera using 120 or 220 film, this custom-made rifle in *Licence to Kill* uses .220 caliber bullets (close to the American 5.56 mm or .223 caliber bullet used in the infantry's M16A2 rifle) and is designed as a sniper rifle, in this case to take out Franz Sanchez. It is a signature rifle, in that only James Bond can fire it due to an optical printer built into the handle. We do not believe, however, that James Bond can take any 16x20 pictures of moonlight landscapes in Yosemite, as the bullets go where the film should go, though Q may surprise us yet again.

Manta Ray Disguise.

If Milton Krest in *Licence to Kill* had focused very closely on that manta ray swimming beneath Wavekrest, he might have seen James Bond in his latest underwater camouflage gear. We like the way the ray flapped.

EVERYTHING I KNOW ABOUT LIFE I LEARNED FROM JAMES BOND

Rappelling Cummerbund.

Yes, when James Bond has to rappel down the exterior of Franz Sanchez's casino while wearing a tuxedo (what else for a casino), that's when James Bond really appreciates a rappelling cummerbund. Finally, someone has figured out what a cummerbund's function can be. Ironically, in the novels, Bond is somewhat contemptuous of cummerbunds as a piece of formal wear clothing, and claims that only the less fashionable KGB operatives wear them.

Broom Transmitter.

When that peon with the broom lifts it to his mouth in *Licence to Kill*, we see the aerial poking out of the straw. Yes, it is Q, out in the field reporting on the progress of Sanchez's convoy. Afterwards, Q tosses it aside. Probably, it is too heavy to take to the cocktail lounge.

Walther P99.

We were both glad to see James Bond give up his Walther PPK (accurate pistol that it is, its 7.65mm bullet is only roughly equivalent to the .32 caliber round) in favor of the Walther P99 in *Tomorrow Never Dies* (1997). The P99 holds 16 9mm bullets in its magazine; the Walther PPK only 6 bullets. There are optional tritium sights (glow-in-the-dark) for night or lowlight shooting scenarios. The P99 with a length of about seven inches is larger than the PPK, but, then, as Bond almost always wears custom-fitted clothes, he can get them tailored to prevent an imprint from his P99.

Ericsson Cell Phone.

Thanks to Q in *Tomorrow Never Dies*, not only can Bond flirt with Moneypenny on his cell phone, he can also use its scanner to read a fingerprint (or to reproduce one for a fingerprint identification locking system). Bond can use its remote-control device to control his BMW 750iL. Finally, he can blast things such as locks with its stun gun (also handy for any Doberman Pinschers trying to take off his arm). In addition, there is a clever lockpick built into the removable antenna.

Global Positioning System Encoder.

The standard USA GPS encoder was modified by Henry Gupta in *Tomorrow Never Dies*; a broadcast from it would deliberately mislead the British Navy into thinking they were in international waters when they really were within Chinese waters (though HMS Devonshire eventually settled into Vietnamese waters). We wonder if Gupta had a hand in designing our Boy Scout compasses too. They always seemed to be a little off.

Omega Seamaster Wristwatch.

Trust the cleverness of Chinese technology. Wai Lin had an Omega Sea master wristwatch in her stores in *Tomorrow Never Dies*. In James Bond's hands, it could help detonate a grenade to make Carver's stealth ship visible on the Royal Navy's radar. Good show, Commander Bond. In *Die Another Day* (2002), Bond uses the Omega's detonator, courtesy of Q, to blow up the C4 explosive lying beneath the diamonds, which results in Zao getting a diamond facial. Later in *Die Another Day*, Bond uses the Q-installed laser in his Omega to cut a hole in

EVERYTHING I KNOW ABOUT LIFE I LEARNED FROM JAMES BOND

a sheet of ice so that he can use his mini-underwater breather from *Thunderball* (1965) to gain surreptitious entry into the "diamond mine." In *Casino Royale, Quantum of Solace,* and *Skyfall*, James Bond wears a version of the Omega Seamaster Plan et Ocean. In *Skyfall*, he also wears an Omega Sea master Aqua Terra Mid-Size Chronometer in the London street scenes.

Video Camera with Uplink.

Carver may have thousands of reporters on his staff, but, thanks to modern technology, a video camera with an uplink to the U.S. satellites provides Bond with the ability to show M, the admiral and the Russian general what is happening at the arms bazaar on the Russian border. We like the fact, however, that James Bond did not appear in a trench coat here with a microphone in his hand and blow-dried hair. He is a man of action, not of words.

Lighter/Grenade.

It looks just like a small gold lighter in *Tomorrow Never Dies*. But when James Bond tosses it near some airplane fuel, it is a super explosive device, just the thing for closing down an arms bazaar.

Sonic Agitator Ring.

In *Die Another Day* (2002), Bond uses his high frequency ring to break the glass floor and escape Miranda Frost (since he was held at gunpoint, a trip to the men's room to escape the lady was out). It was also useful when he needed to blast the windshield of his Aston Martin to rescue the half-drowned Jinx. Rumor has it, the sonic agitator ring also covered Pierce Brosnan's wedding ring to his new bride, Keely Shaye Smith.

Heckler & Koch UMP-9.

Daniel Craig's James Bond carries a Walther PPK throughout ***Casino Royale*** (2006) and ***Quantum of Solace*** (2008), abandoning Brosnan's Walther P-99. But when he needs more firepower, Craig employs a suppressed version of a Heckler & Koch UMP-9, which is the same weapon depicted in the 2006 teaser poster. The weapon is chambered for 9x19mm (see the curved "banana" style magazine), and packs a walloping punch that few other similar automatics do. During the pre-credits car chase, James Bond uses the UMP to dispatch the last of Mr. White's henchmen.

CHAPTER FOUR

BOND GIRLS ARE FOREVER

For Your Eyes Only, can see me through the night.
For your eyes only I never need to hide.
You can see so much in me, so much in me that's new.
I never felt until I looked at you.

—Sheena Easton, ***For Your Eyes Only*** (1981)

Ever since Ursula Andress first emerged from the water onto that Jamaican beach in ***Dr. No*** (1962), the James Bond films have always featured some of the most beautiful women from around the world. From established actresses to photographic models, the women have each been alluring, sexy, and a bit dangerous in their own way. After all, how much fun would the films be without a James Bond girl or two or three? Ian Fleming's heroines, while clearly not paragons of virtue or champions of feminism, are nonetheless strong, independent, and often tragic figures. Rarely damsels in distress, the "Bond girls" tend to have their own hidden agendas, and demonstrate the surprising ability to survive in the world of 007.

Whereas the essence of the films—especially the beautiful Bond girls—has always remained the same, the character of 007 has had to adjust to the changing role of women in society. The world of today is considerably different from the swinging sixties or the pleasure-seeking seventies when James Bond indulged in promiscuous sex with three or four women per cinematic adventure. It is also different from the paranoid eighties or conservative nineties when HIV and AIDS had totally rewritten the rules for sexual relations, and 007's escapades as a womanizer ended (for a brief time) in monogamy. Today, James Bond is still active as a lover, having sex with as many obligatory Bond girls as humanly possible. But what he has noticed most of all is that women are so much more different now. With the changes from Connery and Moore to Dalton and Brosnan and Craig (with Lazenby included, for good measure), the producers have always shaken rather than stirred the formula up a bit, and broken all sorts of cultural and ethnic barriers by selecting the women 007 bonded. Everything that we know about women, we learned from James Bond. The novels and their cinematic counterparts have introduced us to women from all around the world, and taught us valuable lessons about them.

THE FEMININE MYSTIQUE

While some may choose to dismiss 007 as a womanizing misogynist, James Bond does truly love women, and he has spent a lifetime attempting to penetrate the mystery and mystique of what makes them who they are. The appearance of Major Anya Amasova, his opposite number in the KGB, in *The Spy Who Loved Me* (1977) presented 007 with his first, true equal out

EVERYTHING I KNOW ABOUT LIFE
I LEARNED FROM JAMES BOND

of all of the previous films. She is clever, resourceful, deadly, and more than a match for our favorite secret agent. The first in a new breed of Bond girls who were individuals in their own right, Anya also caused him to rethink all of his notions about women.

According to the novels, Bond learned his first lessons about women and love at a very young, impressionable age from Marthe de Brandt, the notorious madam and brothel owner who worked as a spy for the other side. At nearly twice his age, she taught him the finer points of lovemaking and secrets about women that few men knew. But when he was (mis)informed that she had betrayed him and England, he killed her. The famous scar on his cheek that he wears in the books happened in a car crash that he had arranged for her. Later in life, we are told that he fell in love with Vesper Lynd, a double-agent who killed herself, and he lived with Tiffany Case throughout several adventures, despite objections from his maid May. He was married only briefly to the Contessa Teresa di Vincenzo (Tracy) who was killed on their honeymoon by Blofeld and Irma Bunt. He may have also fathered a son named James with Kissy Suzuki. In the January 1997 issue of ***Playboy*** Magazine, author Raymond Benson's short story "Blast from the Past," a direct sequel to ***You Only Live Twice***, has 007 learning that he has a son.

And from his various missions, Bond formed certain other impressions about women. He learned to suspect women with cold lips, and with the exception of Tiffany Case, he didn't trust any woman with red hair. 007 discovered that most women possessed a dark side, and that, even if they appeared to be happy and well-adjusted, they really wanted to be bad. He found out that women seemed to rely more heavily on the opinions of others to gauge their self-worth, and yet just as easily dismissed compliments from men as "just being nice." So much more than men, they were very sensitive and in touch with their own inner feelings, but Bond discovered this sensitivity also made women vulnerable to all sorts of other influences. Interpersonal relationships with family, friends, loved ones, and co-workers, not to mention the intense pressure women put on themselves to be physically attractive and also successful in their careers, could affect women and their moods on a daily basis.

007 also discovered their predilection to pull a normal, well-adjusted man into an exclusive relationship only to spend years trying to change and "domesticate" him. In other words, they make him act more like the kind of guy they really wanted to marry. James Bond was pleased to learn that women craved sex as much as men did, but was also dismayed to discover they used sex as a kind of tool to manipulate men. All in all, Bond learned that women were unique and special individuals who possessed many wonderful qualities and many of the same annoying habits and frustrating characteristics that men did. He concluded that women were a mystery, even to themselves, and we can add very little to that.

For Your Eyes Only / US 1981.

EVERYTHING I KNOW ABOUT LIFE
I LEARNED FROM JAMES BOND

DAMSELS IN DISTRESS

In *On Her Majesty's Secret Service* (1969), James Bond charges into the fray to rescue Tracy from her self-destructive behavior on the beach, the two would-be assassins, and then later at the casino tables without thinking much about his own welfare. Bond is the archetypal hero who rescues damsels in distress, and has risen to the occasion on assignment after assignment. From the oldest melodramas to the cliff-hanging serials, the hero has always dashed to the rescue of the young, attractive woman who has been placed in a dire predicament by the villain. Damsels in distress are almost inevitably tied onto railroad tracks or chained to logs headed into the sawmill. But in the incredible world of 007, these damsels are rarely totally helpless, foolish, or ineffectual. Often they are femme fatales who place themselves into distress to attract the attention of James Bond, only later to turn on him. While Bond should have learned his lesson with the likes of Miss Taro, Fiona Volpe, and Helga Brandt, he still charges into the fray to affect a rescue. Not every woman in the Bond films or life, for that matter, is a damsel in distress who needs rescuing.

Honey Ryder.

Few entrances in motion picture history are as memorable as the one in which the first ever Bond girl, Honey Ryder (Ursula Andress), emerges from the sea in a skimpy white bikini, with a knife strapped to her belt, singing "Underneath the Mango Tree." Honey Ryder, who is known as Honeychilde Ryder in the novel, set the standard for all Bond girls to follow. She is extremely beautiful, sexy, a bit vulnerable, and innocent about the ways of the world. When she meets Bond for the first time, she draws her formidable knife, and asks him, "What are you doing here? Looking for shells?" 007 replies, "No, I'm just looking." At first, she is reluctant to trust him, and worries that he might steal her shells. Later, she comes to rely on him as they penetrate Dr. No's hideaway, and they are both captured and tortured by the madman. In the end, Honey surrenders to Bond's charms as they float away on the current. [Ian Fleming was so taken with the Swiss-born Ursula Andress that he made her a minor character in the novel version of *On Her Majesty's Secret Service*. Andress, whose singing voice was dubbed by Diana Coupland, would later appear as Vesper Lynd in the James Bond parody, **Casino Royale** (1967).]

Domino Derval.

Domino Derval (Claudine Auger) is another innocent caught up in the world of espionage and double-dealing. While she clearly demonstrates how clever and resourceful she is in dealing with the man who killed her brother, Domino is nonetheless a damsel who has been trapped by expensive jewelry and furs by Emilio Largo. When we first meet her, she pretends to be Largo's niece but is, in fact, his mistress. She is a very beautiful woman, and has used her beauty to obtain the better things in life from her wealthy benefactor. But the costs are much higher than she ever realized, and before she can get away, Domino has been implicated in the megalomaniacal villain's nuclear extortion plot. James Bond who treats her like a woman and not a whore is her only escape. [Julie Christie and Faye Dunaway both auditioned for the role of Domino, but ultimately it was awarded to Raquel Welch. Just prior to filming, Welch bowed out to appear in Fantastic Voyage, and Auger, who was Miss France in the 1958 Miss World Contest, stepped into the part.]

EVERYTHING I KNOW ABOUT LIFE
I LEARNED FROM JAMES BOND

Tracy.

Perhaps the strongest and most vulnerable of all the Bond girls, the Contessa Teresa di Vincenzo or Tracy (Diana Rigg) is also the only woman that James Bond truly loves and sadly, when she dies, mourns so deeply. In ***On Her Majesty's Secret Service***, Tracy flirts, despises, and ultimately wins Bond's heart, and when 007 asks to marry her, he has genuinely fallen in love with her. In the course of the novels, Bond had sexual relations with many different woman, but brought very few back home to London to live with him. First, he had a long-lasting affair with Tiffany Case from ***Diamonds Are Forever*** who lived with him through several novels, and later left to marry an American serviceman. Then, Tatiana Romanova left her home behind the Iron Curtain in From Russia with Love to be with Bond. And finally, in the first two films, 007 was involved with party-girl Sylvia Trench (Eunice Gayson). But he never loved them with his heart in the same way that he loved Tracy. She is a woman who has had a troubled past: she lost her mother at a very young age, and was over-indulged by her wealthy but distant father; she married the Comte di Vincenzo to spite her father, and then watched him die in his Maserati with a mistress. She has lived her life so long in the fast lane that she longs to put an end to her misery. When James Bond first spies her on the beach, Tracy is attempting to commit suicide. At first, Bond feels pity for her, and recommends to her father that she see a psychiatrist. But then, he grows to love Tracy for her indomitable spirit and her vulnerability as a woman. Sadly, the new Mrs. Bond is gunned down by Irma Bunt, Blofeld's sinister henchwoman, just moments after the Bond wedding. Later references in ***The Spy Who Loved Me*** (1977) and ***For Your Eyes Only*** (1981) reveal that James Bond has never gotten over her death. While several other actresses were considered for the part of Tracy, including Brigitte Bardot and Catherine

Deneuve, it's hard to imagine anyone but Diana Rigg in the role. [Diana Rigg played the leather-clad karate expert Emma Peel on TV's *The Avengers*, and was replaced on the show by fellow Bond girl Joanna Lumley.]

Solitaire.

In Ian Fleming's novel version of ***Live and Let Die*** (1973), Simone Latrelle (aka Solitaire) is described as a white fortune teller with a mixed racial heritage (possibly French and Haitian) who works for Mr. Big. Early versions of the script dropped any references to her Christian name, and made Solitaire a black woman with the power to foretell the future using Tarot cards. Mankiewicz specifically crafted the role for singer Diana Ross, but when the ethnicity of the two female leads was flipped, Ross was out and the search for a replacement first brought Catherine Deneuve and ultimately Jane Seymour to the part. In the final film version, Solitaire (Seymour) is a very naïve young virgin who serves Dr. Kananga just as her mother did before her; since it was Kananga who stripped Solitaire's mother of her powers, the implication is that he is possibly her father. Trusting in the cards, in particular the stacked deck that Bond uses, Solitaire surrenders to 007's sexual advances and trades her powers for a chance at love and freedom for her egotistical boss. Among the pantheon of Bond girls, Solitaire is a rarity. She was a woman who represented virginity, innocence and tremendous beauty.

Domino Petachi.

In the identical role that was played by Claudine Auger in ***Thunderball*** (1965), Kim Basinger plays the mistress of billionaire Maximillian Largo, Domino Petachi, in ***Never Say Never***

EVERYTHING I KNOW ABOUT LIFE
I LEARNED FROM JAMES BOND

Again (1983). When Domino allies herself with James Bond, her rich benefactor sells her into slavery to North African tribesmen. But never fear, 007 hurls himself into the fray, and saves the helpless innocent from a fate worse than death!

Kara Milovy.

A celebrated concert cellist, Kara Milovy (Maryam d'Abo) represented one of the next generation of Bond girls whose character was distinctly more complex than some of the bimbos of the Connery years. At first, she is merely a beautiful woman Bond spies at the symphony; but then later, 007 zeroes in on her with the scope on his sniper's rifle. Kara appears to be a Russian sniper who has been assigned to kill General Koskov. Defying orders to kill her, Bond shoots the rifle out of her hands only marginally injuring her arm. Like the original Fleming story, 007 knows that she is not a professional assassin, but only later discovers that Kara has been set up to shoot blanks in order to make Koskov's defection look real. Bond helps Kara escape from the KGB in Bratislava, and finds himself naturally attracted to her beauty and innocence when they reach Austria. But 007 has to keep reminding himself that she is not what she appears to be. After drugging him, Kara switches allegiances again, and helps Bond get free of his cap tors. For her help on the mission, Ms. Milovy is granted asylum to pursue her artistic talents. While some times slightly gullible and easily lead by Koskov, Kara is a courageous and brave ally to Bond. She shames Kamran Shah and his Mujahedeen forces to action against the Russian air force, and proves her metal in the epic battle that ensues. [Maryam d'Abo came to the attention of EON productions when she first auditioned for the role of Paula Ivanova in *A View to a Kill*. While she was wrong for the part of the Soviet agent, she returned to play Kara Milovy. Then, after her role in *The Living Daylights*, she produced a television special titled *Bond Girls Are Forever* (2003).]

REDHEADED WOMEN AND OTHER FEMME FATALES

While redheaded women are enjoying a new status as sex symbols, according to a recent 2004 Australian study, historically red heads have been seen as women with uncontrollable tempers and dangerous attitudes about mating. Redheaded women are more likely to be unfaithful and cheat on their partners than blondes or brunettes. Ian Fleming felt that redheaded women were more dangerous and deadly than their counterparts. These many common beliefs about redheaded women seem to describe the femme fatales Bond meets in *Thunderball* (1965), *You Only Live Twice* (1967), and other 007 adventures. But not all "bad" girls in the series are as easily identified by their hair color. Sometimes it's by their kiss. According to Fleming, women with cold lips are not to be trusted for they are likely to be agents of SMERSH. James Bond has learned the hard way that a willing partner in bed doesn't mean he can drop his guard. Beautiful women are sometimes more dangerous than guns!

Miss Taro.

James Bond is introduced to Miss Taro (Zena Marshall) when he meets with the Home Secretary at the Government House, and discovers that she has been eavesdropping on their

EVERYTHING I KNOW ABOUT LIFE I LEARNED FROM JAMES BOND

conversation by listening at the keyhole. 007 bullies her into accepting a dinner date. When Bond calls Miss Taro from his hotel, she gives him directions to her house at 239 Magenta Drive, but she has no intentions of going out on a date with him. As a confederate of Dr. No, she has secretly arranged for the three blind assassins to run Bond off the road to his death. Later, when James Bond shows up at her door, she is surprised; Miss Taro has just stepped out of the shower, and is wearing a towel. Hopefully, Bond will learn that women who have just come out of a bath or a shower are not necessarily clean. Bond does figure out Miss Taro's agenda, and after sleeping with her (and who wouldn't), he bundles her off into a waiting police car. By the way, the address Bond gives to the police "taxi" is 2171 Magenta Drive. We guess he gave the police the wrong address so that he would have enough time with Miss Taro to score.

Bonita.

Bonita (Nadja Regin), which means "pretty" in Spanish, is a treacherous cabaret dancer who lures Bond back to her room so that a waiting assassin can kill him in ***Goldfinger*** (1964). Fortunately, she kisses Bond with her eyes open, and he sees the approach of his assailant reflected in her eyes. James Bond has already learned on previous assignments that women with cold lips are deadly, and now he knows not to trust a woman who kisses with her eyes open. [Nadja Regin is one of the few actresses who has appeared in two Bond movies; she played Kerim Bey's girlfriend in From Russia with Love (1963).]

Fiona Volpe.

Fiona Volpe (Lucianna Paluzzi) drives 007 back to his hotel

at speeds exceeding one hundred miles-per-hour in her Mustang convertible, and delights in his obvious discomfort in *Thunderball* (1965). Pulling into the valet parking, Volpe quips, "Some men don't like to be driven." But Bond fires back, "No, some men don't like to be taken for a ride." By the end of the film, Paluzzi's redheaded mankiller was dead from shots fired by her own men but far from forgotten. She was among the early femme fatales in the Bond films and, as evident from her curvature, probably the most beautiful. She did not have to bat her eyelashes to get James Bond's attention, for foxes or vixens (which is what "volpe" means in Italian) always have a man's eye. After her sexual encounter with James Bond, Volpe was angry that he had made love to her for Queen and country, and was determined to get even. A woman scorned is no laughing matter. She might have gotten 007, if she had only realized that you shouldn't exchange quips with James Bond.

Lady Fiona McTarry/Agent Mimi.

The red-haired Lady Fiona McTarry/Agent Mimi (Deborah Kerr) is presumably the "redhead in his (007's) arms" in the title song of *Casino Royale* (1967). And like redheads in so many James Bond films, she is working for the opposition. Yes, she and her nine daughters (all SMERSH agents, too) are there to seduce Sir James Bond in order to corrupt his moral image of himself. But 007 shows such style and good breeding that, when Sir James reminds Mimi of her duties to society, she runs away to joins a convent.

Helga Brandt.

"Mr. Osato believes in a healthy chest," Helga Brandt (Karin Dor) reveals to Bond, thrusting her breasts at him in an obvious

EVERYTHING I KNOW ABOUT LIFE
I LEARNED FROM JAMES BOND

ploy to get his attention in *You Only Live Twice* (1967). We're actually disappointed that James Bond hasn't learned his lesson about redheads. Not only do they have terrible tempers, but they also have a tendency to work for the opposition. Italian-born Fiona Volpe, the deadly redhead from his previous assignment, should have been proof enough to Bond; no sooner had she finished making love to 007, she tried to kill him. The German-born Brandt is yet another red-haired femme fatale, and Dor plays her deliciously with equal parts of malice and sexuality. As a SPECTRE operative posing as Mr. Osato's secretary, Helga Brandt easily gets the upper hand on 007, and traps him in a falling plane. Of course, when Bond escapes, she is fed to Blofeld's piranha fish for her failure to kill the British agent. Hopefully, James Bond has learned his lesson about son about redheads. Not only do they have terrible tempers, but they also have a tendency to work for the opposition. Italian-born Fiona Volpe, the deadly redhead from his previous assignment, should have been proof enough to Bond; no sooner had she finished making love to 007, she tried to kill him. The German-born Brandt is yet another red-haired femme fatale, and Dor plays her deliciously with equal parts of malice and sexuality. As a SPECTRE operative posing as Mr. Osato's secretary, Helga Brandt easily gets the upper hand on 007, and traps him in a falling plane. Of course, when Bond escapes, she is fed to Blofeld's piranha fish for her failure to kill the British agent. Hopefully, James Bond has learned his lesson about redheads, and will concentrate on blondes and brunettes instead.

Angels of Death.

Ernst Stavro Blofeld's "Angels of Death," twelve women from around the world who suffer from some kind of allergy, have been brainwashed to spread "Virus Omega" in their host countries, and thus eliminate entire strains of plants and livestock in *On Her Majesty's Secret Service* (1969). Each of them was invited to the Bleauchamp Allergy Research Institute at Piz Gloria to cure their ailments, but their treatment, through hypnosis, turns out to be far worse than the cure. Ruby Bartlett (Angela Scoular), one of three women from the British Isles, and Nancy (Catherine Schell) from Austria are the first two women who make overtures to James Bond. In fact, Ruby gives Bond all the information he needs (her room number) with some lipstick on the inside of his kilt-clad leg . . . an uncomfortable experience to which 007 explains that he feels "a slight stiffness coming on." Eventually, Bond becomes intimately acquainted with each of them, including the Scandinavian girl (Julie Ege), the Chinese girl (Mona Chong), the Jamaican girl (Sylvana Henriques), the Indian girl (Zara), the American girl (Dani Sheridan), the Australian girl (Anoushka Hempel), the German girl (Ingrid Back), the Israeli girl (Helena Ronee), the Irish girl (Jenny Hanley), and the other English girl (Joanna Lumley). And then later, as the destruction of Piz Gloria ticks down, Bond captures each of their images on a spy camera so that they can be rounded up by International authorities. In the novel, the girls were from different parts of England, not the world. [Ruby Bartlett also played Buttercup, the youngest daughter of M, in the James Bond spoof *Casino Royale* (1967), and Joanna Lumley would replac her fellow Bond girls Honor Blackman and Diana Rigg as John Steed's partner on TV's *The Avengers*].

Bambi and Thumper.

While they sound like two cute and cuddly characters from a Disney cartoon, Bambi (Lola Larson) and Thumper (Trina

EVERYTHING I KNOW ABOUT LIFE
I LEARNED FROM JAMES BOND

Parks) are two *femme fatales* working for Blofeld in ***Diamonds Are Forever.*** They are holding Williard Whyte hostage in his own home. The two women are very deadly, and nearly beat James Bond to death. But of course, 007 gains the upper hand, and decides to teach them "breaststroke" lessons in Whyte's pool.

Naomi.

Following in the tradition of Miss Taro, Fiona Volpe, and Helga Brandt as a *femme fatales*, Naomi (Caroline Munro) plays the role of Stromberg's beautiful but deadly assistant in ***The Spy Who Loved Me*** (1977). She is ordered to escort James Bond and Major Anya Amasova from their hotel in Sardinia to Atlantis, and during the relatively short journey, she flirts with 007 who is posing as a marine biologist. When Bond remarks, "What a handsome craft. Such lovely lines." he isn't talking about a boat, but rather Naomi's curvy figure, which looks especially luscious in a bikini. After returning 007 and Triple-X to their hotel, Naomi is ordered to kill them, and certainly enjoys every moment of their dangerous cat and mouse game as she chases their Lotus with her armed helicopter. Like all *femme fatales* before her, Naomi is no match for James Bond. She dies in a fiery explosion when 007 fires a surface-to-air missile from the submerged Lotus at her helicopter. [Caroline Munro also played an uncredited Guard Girl in ***Casino Royale*** (1967), and starred opposite future Bond villain Christopher Lee in ***Dracula A.D.*** 1972.]

Fatima Blush.

In ***Never Say Never Again*** (1983), Barbara Carerra steps into the spiked heels of Lucianna Paluzzi's Fiona Volpe, and nearly steals the show as the movie's femme fatale, Fatima Blush.

Whenever that character is onscreen, all eyes tend to go toward her. It isn't just Barbara Carerra's physical presence, though the camera loves her every movement. When she wheels Jack Petachi through Shrublands dressed as a nurse, we focused on her. When she is water skiing in the Bahamas, her body fell into a pose we would associate with the ballet, rather than a teenager from Busch Gardens. You may remember how she joins James Bond in the cabin of her little cruiser, and they both strip quickly without any reservations. She is not shy, and she is deadly. That dance step she uses as she goes down the casino steps to kill Nicole is positively vicious in her merriment. She is not just a pretty face, but a memorable villainess who plots 007's demise. What a pity Bond's written endorsement of her incomparable charms and sexuality turns out to be so deadly!

May Day.

When we first saw May Day (Grace Jones) dressed in red at Ascot, we thought, "There is someone who would be out of place in the Ascot sequence from *My Fair Lady*. She is a stunner at five-ten-and-a-half." Whenever May Day appears in a scene in *A View to a Kill*, she commands every inch of the frame. We wonder what will happen next: will she slay him or sleep with him? As it happens, she does a little of both. It's not surprising that Grace Jones can captivate the camera. Though the native-born Jamaican studied theater at Syracuse University, she became a successful model in Paris. Her looks were just a bit too strong for most American magazines, but she could certainly wear clothes with the best of them. Andy Warhol was enamored of the tall Jamaican, and often escorted her as his date to various events. She was a regular at the fabled New York disco Studio 54 in the 1970's. She started a singing career in

1977. Her cabaret musical act, with leopards and lions, made for quite a cult following. Then, Grace Jones turned to acting. Arnold Schwarzenegger allegedly wailed that Grace Jones was just "too tough" during the shooting of *Conan the Destroyer* in 1984. Well, we don't think too many men would be eager to have a violent encounter with Grace Jones for real or on a film set either. And the way she jumped on top of Roger Moore for their lovemaking sequence, made us wonder who was in charge there. But, as long as you both get to the station, who cares who gets there first?

THE WOMEN OF GREAT BRITAIN

James Bond has tremendous respect for the women of the Britain Isles, and sees them as very loyal individuals who have contributed their femininity, domesticity, brilliance, assertiveness, and political activism to building a strong empire. In fact, he toasts Queen Elizabeth II in his office, and feels a certain pride in serving on *On Her Majesty's Secret Service*. Great queens like Elizabeth I and Victoria have shaped the history of Great Britain in a way that few other monarchs have. In World War II, nearly a hundred thousand women served in British women's forces as non-combatants, and over fifty women were parachuted behind enemy lines as secret agents by the Special Operations Executive; thirty-six "Jackdaws" returned. 007 may tease and flirt with Miss Moneypenny, but he still respects the job that she does in serving M in a way that goes beyond their office roles. And without his Scottish housekeeper, May, tending to his domestic needs, Bond would not have been able to save the free world as many times as he has. The women of Great

Britain may well have a stiff upper lip, but for Bond, their bodies are soft, luscious, and very desirable.

Sylvia Trench.

The character of Sylvia Trench (Eunice Gayson), whom Bond first meets across the card table at Le Cercle Club in ***Dr. No*** (1962), was supposed to have been a recurring character, her romantic intentions continually foiled by Bond's missions. But after a brief appearance in ***From Russia with Love*** (1963), her character was dropped from the series altogether. Trench was probably too sexually aggressive for James Bond, and therefore a liability. For instance, when we next meet her in ***Dr. No,*** she has broken into 007's bachelor pad, and slipped out of her clothes into one of Bond's pajama tops. Naturally, James Bond is surprised to find her there, playing with his golf clubs, and realizes that a woman like her might threaten his bachelor's taste for freedom. Even though her character was short-lived, Gayson has the distinction of being the only Bond girl to appear in two films as the same character. Ironically, the role of Sylvia Trench was first offered to Lois Maxwell, who instead went on to play the long-suffering Miss Moneypenny in thirteen other films.

Miss Moneypenny.

"Britain's last line of defense", according to James Bond, Miss Moneypenny (Lois Maxwell) was M's loyal and diligent secretary. For many years, this middle-aged, sophisticated woman has carried on a flirtatious relationship with Bond, but that innocent flirtation has never gotten her anywhere with the debonair secret agent. Still, despite warnings from her boss, Moneypenny pines away for him. While 007's flirtations might be mistaken as

EVERYTHING I KNOW ABOUT LIFE
I LEARNED FROM JAMES BOND

sexual harassment in today's world, he has always been able to keep his personal affairs separate from the workplace, and thus his relationship with Moneypenny has been an innocent one. Too bad. We have always thought that Moneypenny, who has no other first name than "Miss," would be an incredibly passionate lover for Bond. At the wrap party celebrating the end of filming of *Dr. No,* Ian Fleming approached Lois Maxwell with a compliment that echoes our sentiments: "I envisioned a tall, elegant woman with the most kissable lips in the world. You are her!" In *Skyfall,* Moneypenny (Naomie Harris) reveals that shaving James Bond with a straight razor does not have to be dangerous, but, we presume, quite an experience for both the female barber and the male associate. We are clearly looking forward to seeing more of her in the future.

Jill Masterson.

Jill Masterson (Shirley Eaton) works as Auric Goldfinger's paid escort, and helps him cheat at cards. After helping Bond foil his card swindling, she faces the billionaire's wrath, and dies from skin suffocation from being spray painted gold. Jill is clearly not the girl-next-door nor the little sister. She is blonde and very sexy in her black bra and panties. The fact that she works as an escort for money suggests that she is a woman of easy virtue, and falls as easy prey for a man like James Bond who treats her like a woman and not a whore.

Tilly Masterson.

Tilly Masterson (Tania Mallet) seeks revenge for the death of her sister Jill. Determined to kill Goldfinger, she follows him to Switzerland with the same AR-7 sniper's rifle Bond carried in

From Russia with Love (1963). At one point, while Goldfinger is stopped on a mountain road, she shoots at him using the single shot rifle but misses, nearly hitting Bond. Tilly never takes the time to get to know Bond, but instead lies to him about ice-skating at St. Moritz (when Bond clearly knows that there is no ice this time of season). In the novel, she is portrayed as a lesbian who prefers the company of Pussy Galore to the charms of James Bond, and whom Bond identifies as "one of those women whose hormones need straightening out." In the film, she loses her head to Odd-Job's deadly bowler before Bond has a chance to straighten out her hormones. The fact that she is all business suggests that Bond was better off leaving her at the garage in Switzerland.

Pussy Galore.

While it is hard to imagine a Bond girl with a more provocative name, Pussy Galore (Honor Blackman) is the most liberated and self-sufficient of all the early screen heroines, and more than a match for James Bond. In the novel, she is clearly a lesbian with a disdain for men altogether. In fact, she is described as having formed an underworld empire of lesbian thieves, burglars and assassins, known as "The Cement Mixers." Bond felt a certain "sexual challenge" in dealing with lesbians, and made fast work of swinging her back to heterosexual behavior. In the film, Blackman plays her as a strong-willed businesswoman who has little time for men, and not as a lesbian. Ms. Galore knows Judo and has skippered her own Flying Circus of female pilots. When Bond first turns up the charm, she responds with a Judo throw. Of course, she does eventually fall for James Bond's charms, and helps Felix Leiter and the U.S. government switch the gas canisters. Only Bond would be bold enough or foolish enough to

EVERYTHING I KNOW ABOUT LIFE
I LEARNED FROM JAMES BOND

think that he could straighten out a lesbian; perhaps the rest of us know better. [Honor Blackman played Cathy Gale on TV's *The Avengers*, and was replaced on the show by another future Bond girl, Diana Rigg.]

Patricia Fearing.

Patricia Fearing, that blonde nurse at Shrublands (played by Molly Peters in ***Thunderball***, 1965 and Prunella Gee in ***Never Say Never Again***, 1983), certainly had James Bond's attention, even if the health plan there did not. He almost has to die on the traction machine, however, before she will give him a tumble in the steam room. While Bond had a certain amount of blackmail in his approach, he certainly made up for it by massaging her ever-so-gently with a mink glove, certainly one step above the famed "a rubdown with a velvet glove" from the show tune "You're Just in Love." Later, she wants more of Mr. Bond's attention, but he seems a bit remote. Could she be too needy for our aggressive rough-and-tumble character? Apparently so, he surely didn't want to meet mom and dad.

Mary Goodnight.

The competent Mary Goodnight of the novel bears no relationship to the bumbling Miss Goodnight of ***The Man with the Golden Gun*** (1975). On the other hand, the lively, smiling Goodnight, played by Britt Ekland, does have a sting in her package. She turns Bond down for an evening's encounter while having dinner in Thailand. "Killing a few hours as one of your passing fancies is not one of my scenes," she says. Yet, hours later, she unexpectedly appears in his bedroom ready for a sex. Well, a lady has the right to change her mind. But then, with Anders (Maud Adams) about to enter Bond's bedroom too, we somehow find ourselves in a French bedroom farce, a genre we don't associate with Bond films. First, Goodnight is passed off as three pillows, placed in the bed for the occasional nearsighted assassin who may wander in. Then, Bond stuffs Goodnight in a walk-in closet for hours while he makes love to Anders, admittedly, on Bond's part, mostly to obtain the solex-agitator. Goodnight is furious for his treatment of her. Yet, at the end of the film, after causing the destruction of Scaramanga's island, she determines to do the nasty with Bond for several days as they wend their way back from mainland China to the next secure port. Though she articulates a feminist position in the middle of the film, she seems to be just another beautiful woman in a bikini by the end of it. Ah well, Bond will just have to deal with her.

Countess Lisl Von Schlam.

Lisl (Cassandra Harris) poses as an Austrian countess in order to gain James Bond's confidence, and learn his intentions for Milos Columbo, her lover in *For Your Eyes Only* (1981). With expensive tastes, she has enjoyed all of the luxuries of life, and traveled in the finest circles. But in reality, she is a party girl from Liverpool who has used her obvious beauty and charm to con men into supporting her expensive lifestyle. 007 plies her with a few drinks, and she quickly loses her upper-crust accent. Bond actually likes her, and is saddened when Lisl is ruthlessly killed by one of Kristatos' assassins. [Ms. Cassandra Harris was the wife of Pierce Brosnan, the future James Bond, and died regrettably several years after her appearance in the film.]

EVERYTHING I KNOW ABOUT LIFE
I LEARNED FROM JAMES BOND

Penelope Smallbone.

Ms. Moneypenny's new assistant, Penelope Smallbone (Michaela Clavell), catches the eye of James Bond just before he embarks on his new mission, but like Moneypenny (Lois Maxwell) herself only gets flowers and little more from 007. The role in *Octopussy* (1983) is somewhat comic, and suggests that she was being groomed as a possible replacement for "Britain's last line of defense," but the job must not have worked out. She has yet to re-appear in any of Bond's future adventures. [Michaela Clavell was the daughter of bestselling novelist James Clavell, who wrote *Shogun* and *Noble House*, the latter of which featured Pierce Brosnan in a television miniseries.]

Jenny Flex.

Jenny Flex (Allison Doody) is a villain, appearing whenever Max Zorin needs a lovely flunky to do something funky. We remember her in riding togs, trim, athletic, and waiting to be spanked with her own riding crop, although we prefer to avoid that sort of activity to save our energy for more unique endeavors. *A View from a Kill* was Allison Doody's first feature film, and the Dublin-born beauty has had a career in films and television ever since. You may remember her as Dr. Elsa Schneider in Steven Spielberg's *Indiana Jones and the Last Crusade* (1989), opposite former James Bond Sean Connery.

Caroline.

Caroline appears briefly in the first act of *GoldenEye* (1995) as a fictional SIS/MI6 psychologist sent by M (Judi Dench) to evaluate the readiness and stability of Pierce Brosnan's Bond. Played mostly for laughs by the capable British actress Serena Gordon, she is the first Bond Girl of the Brosnan era. Other than ordering 007 to stop chasing Xena's Ferrari, she has little to do with the plot. Her character is expanded upon in John Gardner's novelization.

Dr. Molly Warmflash.

Dr. Molly Warmflash is the second of three British women who work for MI6 seduced by Pierce Brosnan's 007. After James Bond is injured in the pre-credits sequence, the beautiful, attractive, and sexy physician diagnoses Bond with a dislocated collar bone and advises him to stay out of action. Not wanting to be taken off the active duty roster, Bond seduces her into clearing him as fit for duty. She tries desperately to resist, but ultimately Molly allows Bond to have his way with her. Serena Scott Thomas, sister of well-known Kristen Scott Thomas, essayed the role before reprising Dr. Warmflash in the 1999 video game of *The World Is not Enough* (1999).

Miranda Frost.

Miranda Frost (Rosamund Pike) in *Die Another Day* (2002) works for MI6 as an analyst, but as a gold medalist fencer who won her title at the Sydney Olympics, she seems to be the perfect agent to go undercover to track the billionaire industrialist Gustav Graves. Unfortunately, when James Bond goes under the covers with her, he discovers that she is actually a double-agent working against the British government. Beautiful and deadly, her name says it all. Rosamund Pike later took to the West End of London to headline the play *Hitchcock Blonde,* and won rave reviews from the critics for *Gone Girl* (2014). She is actually one of the few James Bond girls who has had a long, distinguished career on film, providing one great performance after another.

Vesper Lynd-1.

Vesper Lynd (Eva Green) made the transition from the novel to film *Casino Royale* (2006) with relatively few changes, unlike the character that Ursula Andress played in the 1967 comedy. Ian Fleming always maintained that Vesper's name was meant to be a pun on "West Berlin," and that she was based upon a real-life Special Operations Executive agent that he knew (named Christine Granville). In the novel, the character explains that she was born on a "dark and stormy" night, and that her parents named her "Vesper" after the Latin word meaning evening to commemorate the night. In the film adaptation, Vesper Lynd works in Section S, and is foisted upon Bond (Daniel Craig), much to his irritation, to assist him in his mission to bankrupt Le Chiffre. Of course, as in the novel, Vesper turns out to be a double-agent working for the bad guys. Fleming created a cocktail recipe in the novel, named the "Vesper martini," after Vesper's demise, that became very popular after the novel's publication, and gave rise to the famous "shaken, not stirred" catch-phrase, which was immortalized in the Bond films. The actual name for the drink (as well as its complete recipe) is uttered on screen for the first time in *Casino Royale* (2006). Vesper Lynd truly must have meant something to James Bond as he is still mourning her death as *No Time to Die* (2021) reveals in the first act.

Strawberry Fields.

Strawberry Fields may be "forever," but alas Agent Strawberry

Fields (Gemma Arterton), an MI6 field operative working at the British consulate at Bolivia, lives a very short life as a Bond girl in *Quantum of Solace*. Drowned in oil on the orders of baddie Dominic Green, her oil-covered body is found in a position reminiscent of Jill Masterson in Goldfinger, whose skin was painted with gold. The twenty-two-year-old British beauty is portrayed as yet another one of the gorgeous red-heads in the Bond films, but unlike so many of the others, she gives over her body to 007 without any strings attached. In real life, Gemma Arterton was born with an extra finger on each hand, a condition called polydactyl, but left a truly indelible impression with her lovely, wide-eyed turn as Agent Fields.

MATA HARI AND THE WOMEN OF EUROPE

Throughout the course of his impossible missions behind the Iron Curtain, in France, Italy, and Germany, James Bond has encountered many European women. Like their counterparts in Great Britain, 007 has admired their unique contributions to society and culture, and has never doubted their ferocity in completing an important assignment. In *Casino Royale* (1967), we learn that Sir James Bond (David Niven) had had an affair with one of the most nefarious women in European history, Mata Hari. Born in Holland as Magaretha Gertrud Zelle to a well-to-do Dutch shopkeeper and his Japanese wife, she attended a school for teachers, but was forced to leave for having sex with the headmaster. She married a Dutch naval officer, twenty years her senior, but left him and her two children

EVERYTHING I KNOW ABOUT LIFE
I LEARNED FROM JAMES BOND

after only a few years of marriage. In 1905, she moved to Paris, and posing as a princess from Java, became an exotic dancer with the stage name Mata Hari (which means "eye of the day" in Malay). She was also a courtesan who had many affairs with military officers and politicians. During World War I, she had an affair with a twenty-five year-old Russian pilot flying with the French, Captain Vadim Masloy. When he was wounded and she sought permission to see him in the forward hospital, the Deuxième Bureau manipulated Mata Hari into spying for them against the Germans. On an assignment in Spain, she met and had an affair with the German military Attaché, Major Kalle. Kalle knew that she was a spy, and sent a message to Berlin in a code that he knew the Allies had broken, saying that "H-21" (Mata Hari's code number) had revealed key information about a French troop deployment. In fact, she had remained loyal to France, but when the troops were massacred by the Germans, the Deuxieme Bureau was convinced that she had turned into a double-agent. Mata Hari was arrested, tried, convicted, and finally executed on October 15, 1917. Sir James Bond blames himself for her betrayal to French authorities, and subsequently retired from the British Secret Service. Not all the European women that Bond meets in his assignments are double-agents like Mata Hari, but he remains extremely vigilant in his dealings with them all the same.

Mata Bond.

In *Casino Royale* (1967), Sir James Bond reveals that he and Mata Hari had a daughter named Mata Bond (Joanna Pettet). When she steps out of the Asian temple in full regalia like her mother, she certainly gets every viewer's attention as she dances in her first sequence. Her character is a genetic natural for the role of female spy to determine who is killing the best spies of the major powers. When she worried that she could not do as good a job as her mother did in the information-gathering business, Sir James notes with an objective eye up and down her body, "Your mother took out two divisions. . . . You have more equipment than she had." She is a lively character, able to dance, converse with social equals and generate laughs while frantically running all over International Mother's Help in West Berlin at a "Tom & Jerry" cartoon's pace. Her career pretty much peaked with *Casino Royale*; thankfully, we have our memories.

Vesper Lynd-2

In *Casino Royale* (1967), Vesper (Ursula Andress) appears as a very modern assertive woman executive who, on the side, keeps up her espionage practice for SMERSH and, presumably, anyone else who can pay an exorbitant fee. Sir James Bond did not get her attention, in any case, until he offered a waiver of her tax bill of five million British pounds. Later in the film, it was glorious to watch her multi-tasking—seductively welcoming Tremble/Bond to her private quarters via intercom while dumping a body into the freezer and giving orders to her flunky almost at the same time. We so enjoyed her buying the Nelson statue, before the IRA could damage it in real life too. The woman was accomplished in whatever she did. Her costuming was creative, such as the feathered headdress she wore in her headquarters. It is hard to imagine any man saying "no" to her. On the other hand, once she had said "yes", you would have to worry about being dumped in the freezer if you did not suit her.

EVERYTHING I KNOW ABOUT LIFE
I LEARNED FROM JAMES BOND

Miss Caruso.

Miss Caruso (Madeline Smith) is the first Bond girl of the Roger Moore era in *Live and Let Die* (1973). During an assignment in Rome for the Italian Secret Service, Bond met Miss Caruso, and brought her back to his home on Kings Road in Chelsea. She is only one of two women (the other being Sylvia Trench) who have spent the night in Bond's bachelor pad; in the novels, of course, 007 actually allows Tiffany Case and then, later, Tatiana Romanova to live with him. Miss Caruso, who seems to have no first name, and Bond are both awakened by M, paying an uncharacteristic house call at 5:47 AM. While giving 007 instructions for his latest mission, M mentions that the Italian Secret Service is missing one of their agents, but before he can discuss it further, Bond distracts her with a cup of coffee. Later, Miss Moneypenny uses her incomparable talent at foreign diplomacy to avoid an international incident, and save Bond from an embarrassing situation. Miss Caruso is a very beautiful woman, and risks trouble with her superiors so that she can stay on with 007. [Madeline Smith debuted in the Hammer Films' *Taste the Blood of Dracula* (1970), opposite future Bond villain Christopher Lee, and appeared on an episode of *The Persuaders* in 1971 that was also directed by Roger Moore.]

Andrea Anders.

Andrea Anders (Maud Adams) is a desperate woman, the mistress of Francisco Scaramanga, a man who is not able to have a real relationship with any woman or any man. It is not surprising that she hates him. She is the one who has put this plot into motion by sending the golden bullet, inscribed with "007," to "M." Though he may have been the best-paid assassin in the world, Scaramanga was unable to keep his house in order. Therefore, he caused his own demise. We have learned, though the female may be the weaker of the species (but only in upper body strength), she is often just as deadly as the male. So why is she flirting with James Bond? Because he is the only man that Scaramanga fears. Maud Adams, who plays Anders, started off her career as a model. Her perfectly chiseled features gained her attention on the runways, but her acting career was rather minor. She was the only Bond girl to appear in three Bond films: the second female lead in *The Man with the Golden Gun*, the title role in *Octopussy* (1983) and as an extra in the crowd in *A View to a Kill* (1985).

Log Cabin Girl.

Never identified by name, the "Log Cabin Girl" (Sue Vanner) is yet another *femme fatale* out to stop 007 in *The Spy Who Loved Me* (1977). As a double-agent, she has been ordered by her KGB operatives to seduce James Bond and keep him otherwise occupied so that Sergei Barsov and his men can swoop down and kill the British agent. When 007 is ordered "to pull out immediately," she radios ahead to inform her allies of Bond's whereabouts. We're a bit surprised that she didn't use one of the trick cigarettes that Anya later employs to stop Bond from leaving, but alas, that's show business!

Corinne Dufour.

Corinne Dufour (Corinne Clery) first appears in *Moonraker* as the pilot bringing James Bond from the LAX Airport to Drax's French estate, which has been transplanted to southern California. She escorts Bond to Dr. Goodhead's office and then returns to her duties. In the evening, Bond drops by her bedroom, looking for information. One thing leads to another, and Bond and Dufour find themselves in bed. Corinne Clery was a very sensual actress. Her sexual allure was spotted quite early. Her third film gave her the lead in *The Story of O* (*Histoire d'O*) (1975), based on the erotic novel of Dominique Aury, a tale of sexual explicitness with bondage and other activities not seen on commercial television. Her career in French and Italian films plus European television shows has never ended. She seems to be one of those women whose appeal never wanes.

Linda.

After James Bond parachutes clear of the Land Rover wreckage in the pre-credits adventure of *The Living Daylights* (1987), he drops down on a boat passing below. Linda (Kell Tyler) is in the midst of complaining about the lack of a "real man" (among the playboys and tennis pros) with a friend on a cell phone call when he asks to use her phone. She is momentarily startled by his sudden appearance, but gains her composure enough to offer him a glass of champagne. Linda is a stunning brunette whose near-perfect body, accented by a skimpy black bikini, shouts sex appeal; she wants Bond, badly. After telling his superiors that he will report in one hour, 007 considers Linda's offer, and changes that estimate to two. Precious little is known about her character, other than the fact that Linda has been bored and disappointed by the other men that she has met while cruising on a yacht in the Mediterranean. She finds her "real man" in James Bond.

Professor Inga Bergstrom.

Professor Bergstrom (Cecile Thomsen) teaches Bond Danish at

Oxford University, though the image of a nude blonde woman somehow makes us forget that she's a teacher. The irony here is that Cecile Thomsen probably could teach Danish as she was born in Denmark, grew up there until she was 16, and now has an MFA in Dramatic Arts. She appeared in 1998 in Mark Christopher's *54*, about the famous New York nightclub, and has appeared in foreign films. Should we need a Danish coach or some acting lessons, we would be happy to approach Miss Thomsen first!

Séverine.

Séverine (Berenice Marlohe), the beautiful but doomed French seductress, makes a very sexy entrance in *Skyfall*. Though, as Bond observed on first meeting her, she had a Beretta Model 70 (.32 ACP) strapped to her thigh; she noted that he had a Walther PPK (.380 ACP) on him. They certainly were pretty evenly matched. We do wonder how James Bond got onto Silva's ship, which was well guarded, for the seductive shower sequence. We can only presume that that underwater training really paid off for 007. We were disappointed that Séverine was so quickly gunned down by Silva (Javier Bardem) and becomes the sacrificial lamb mid-way through the film. We would have much preferred to have seen a great deal more of her, but alas, the real Bond girl in *Skyfall* is Judi Dench in her last outing as M. Bond certainly had admiration for this M, perhaps because she was as tough as he was, yet she had a soft spot for him. She risked her career when she sent him back into action without passing his certification. And she was "man" enough to let him know it to his face. What a woman!

EVERYTHING I KNOW ABOUT LIFE I LEARNED FROM JAMES BOND

Lucia Sciarra.

The oldest woman (at age fifty) to play a Bond girl, or should that be a Bond woman, Italian actress Monica Bellucci brought a raw sensuality to the character of Lucia Sciarra, who was rumored to be a bisexual in early drafts of the script for ***Spectre*** (2015). The controversial actress from ***Irreversible*** was no stranger to fans who had fallen in love with her from the ***Matrix*** films and had played a Bond-girl clone in the James Bond spoof, ***Shoot 'Em Up***, opposite Clive Owen, the actor who should have been James Bond. We both loved Sam Mendes' choice of a mature woman playing opposite our favorite secret agent, and only wished that it had happened sooner. Actresses like Sharon Stone and Jessica Lange would have made excellent Bond girls had they not been ruled out for being too old, while we had to endure teenaged Denise Richards as nuclear scientist Dr. Christmas Jones. We actually didn't care that Christmas came twice because it was actually one too many times for Richards. Thank Mendes, for getting this one right!

Dr. Madeleine Swann.

French actress Léa Seydoux played Dr. Madeleine Swann, a psychologist working at a private medical clinic in the Austrian Alps, in ***Spectre*** (2015). Fans of the Bond series recall that the last time 007 was anywhere near the Alps, he was "guest" of Ernst Stavro Blofeld, the leader of SPECTRE, at a private medical clinic in Switzerland, specifically Piz Gloria. Blofeld was pretending to be a humanitarian working on a cure for allergies, which required a balance of chemistry and hypnosis. But of course his real plot was to use girls cured of their allergies to introduce a deadly strain of bacteria on the world. Is Dr. Madeleine Swann actually Blofeld's daughter, taking up where her father left off? In *No Time to Die* (2021), Swann is revealed to be Mr. White's daughter, and her connection to Blofeld remains a mystery. She has a daughter named Mathilde with 007.

THE WOMEN OF THE UNITED STATES

James Bond has encountered a number of American women in the course of his adventures, and has found some of them to be two-faced liars with their own hidden agendas. From Tiffany Case (Jill St. John) and Rosy Carver (Gloria Hendry) to Jinx (Halle Berry) and Paris Carver (Teri Hatcher), these women have given Bond some of his greatest thrills and presented him with his greatest challenges. Throughout most of the history of the Americas, women have had fewer rights and career opportunities than men. Women were also considered naturally weaker than men, squeamish, and unable to perform work requiring muscular or intellectual development. In pre-industrial America, domestic chores were relegated to women, leaving "heavier" labor such as hunting and plowing to men. When women won the right to vote in 1920, they increased their educational and job opportunities, and following World War II, they fought for and won the right to be treated as equals. However, with no more battles to fight, post-modern feminists sought to strip American men of their identities, and caused a backlash that is still being felt to this day. Agent 007 has always respected women, but does not care much for American women who seek to undermine his identity. So, when it comes to American women, he prefers to love them and leave them.

Tiffany Case.

If there ever was a hard case that 007 had to face, it surely is Tiffany Case (Jill St. John) in ***Diamonds Are Forever*** (1971). She got the name when her mother gave birth to her at Tiffany's jewelry store where mama was shopping for a wedding ring. Don't let that beautiful body in those mini bikinis and scanty dresses fool you. Of course, if you don't have too many beautiful women up close to the camera in a James Bond film, it pretty much requires that your leading lady have costumes consisting largely of thin air. But her voice! Instead of the husky, sultry tones of Italian or Russian or French women in heat, we get the rasp of an American princess with an axe to grind. Jill St. John is the first American Bond girl. You may not like the tone of her voice, but you have to admire the area surrounding her voice box and everything else below! While she doesn't dress for "the hired help," she is quite striking and memorable, the primary responsibility of every Bond girl. We think, however, that Tiffany Case deserves a spanking for being a naughty girl. We will flip a coin if we have the opportunity to administer the necessary discipline. But she'll have to wear a bikini bottom with a cassette stuffed into it.

Plenty O'Toole.

As James Bond observes, Plenty (Lana Wood), "of course," has plenty of frontage. The pulchritudinous professional companion has already ditched the mug she was with when he busted out at the tables of the casino. She was out for fresh meat immediately;

Bond was a likely candidate: attractive, well-dressed, loaded and ready to play. Lana Wood was attractive as well but a bit short. She spent most of her role in ***Diamonds Are Forever*** standing on a box somewhere. Lana was the sister of Natalie Wood. In John Ford's Western epic ***The Searchers*** (1956) Lana played the young Debbie Edwards, who was kidnapped by the Comanches. Thanks to ***Diamonds Are Forever***, Lana Wood has had much more than Andy Warhol's prescribed "fifteen minutes of fame." She will always be the woman on the box next to Sean Connery at the craps table or the beautiful brunette that gets thrown out the window at the Hotel Tropicana in Las Vegas. "I didn't know there was a pool down there," the underworld thug remarks to Bond." Thank goodness, for Plenty's sake, there was.

Dink.

Dink (Margaret Nolan) is plainly and simply a party girl who hangs out at pools waiting to be picked up by men in ***Goldfinger*** (1964). The fact that she lets Bond smack her on the behind and talk down to her suggests that Dink is either very, very naïve or simply used to being treated like sex object by men. [Margaret Nolan is also featured as the "golden girl" in Robert Brownjohn's opening and closing titles.]

Rosie Carver.

In addition to being Bond's first African-American lover, Rosie Carver (Gloria Hendry) is also the first in a long line of femme fatales who pretend to be loyal confederates only to turn out evil in the end. She begins ***Live and Let Die*** (1973) as a hapless, CIA-operative, assigned to 007 by Felix Leiter, but becomes a lot more than she first appeared. Her air of naiveté is nothing more than a clever ploy crafted to seduce and deceive James Bond. When 007 discovers her true nature, she becomes a liability to Kananga, and is killed. [In a fairly late draft of the script, the part of Rosie was written for a white actress, while the role of Solitaire was scripted for African-American singer Diana Ross. Following the reversal of roles, Ross lost interest in the part, and Florida native Gloria Hendry was hired.]

Dr. Holly Goodhead.

Lois Chiles, the five-foot-eight top shelf fashion model and experienced actress, was quite an eyeful, even though, at thirty-two years of age, she was considering at least a temporary retirement before she accepted the female lead in *Moonraker*. She had played significant roles in Sydney Pollack's *The Way We Were* (1973), Jack Clayton's *The Great Gatsby* (1974), Michael Crichton's *Coma* (1978) and John Guillermin's *Death on the Nile* (1978). She had not been seeking the *Moonraker* role. Indeed, she had turned down the role of Anya in *The Spy Who Loved Me* (1977). Lewis Gilbert just happened to be sitting next to her in an airliner while she was looking forward to getting some time away from the hustle of show business. The role of Dr. Holly Goodhead came to her, and Chiles made the NASA scientist into a full, three-dimensional character who spars with James Bond as his equal throughout most of the movie.

Bibi Dahl.

Sweet and seemingly innocent, Bibi Dahl (Lynn-Holly Johnson) is the ice-skating protégé of Aristotle Kristatos in *For Your Eyes Only* (1981). She wants to win the gold medal for ice-skating, and trains with Jacoba Brink for the next Winter Olympics. After meeting James Bond, she breaks from her rigorous training schedule, and attempts to seduce 007 in hotel room. Bond politely declines, as he is old enough to be her father, but offers to buy her an ice cream cone if she puts her clothes back on. Bibi Dahl may seem like a little sister, but she is always scheming. Not long after Bond's rejection, she sets her sights on the East German champion, Erich Kriegler. At the end of the film, when Kristatos' plurality is discovered, Bibi and her trainer Jacoba Brink find another sponsor in Columbo.

Stacey Sutton.

From the moment we saw Stacey Sutton (Tanya Roberts) at Zorin's garden party in *A View to a Kill* (1985), it was hard to keep our eyes off her. While May Day gets the bizarre and whacky award, Stacey Sutton receives the blonde bombshell trophy. At the party, she delivers a series of "put down" lines to James Bond, keeping her distance at all times. Later, when we learn of her heroic stand against Zorin, we appreciate her character as well as her obvious attributes. For the remainder of the film, however, she seems to be spending a great deal of time wailing, "Help me, James." Since Bond goes through three different aliases with her, it is just as well that she never uses his last name during these stressful periods. Tanya Roberts is a girl from the Bronx who studied acting under some of the best instructors who teach at the Actor's Studio. She did some modeling in New York, played one of Charlie's Angels on television, and took her clothes off in *The Beastmaster* (1982) and *Sheena* (1983). *A View to a Kill* was probably the peak film in her career.

EVERYTHING I KNOW ABOUT LIFE I LEARNED FROM JAMES BOND

Pam Bouvier.

Pam Bouvier (Carey Lowell) first appears as a tough shotgun-toting woman in a Bimini night club in *Licence to Kill* (1989). A CIA pilot who has gone undercover and is working her connections with the underworld, Bouvier is a good person to have at your back, as James Bond discovers when Dario gets knife-happy. The first conversation between them is far from pleasant. Bouvier is clearly a modern woman, emancipated, not the kind who totters about in high heels saying, "Save me, James! Save me!" As the film progresses, we see her taking chances and doing what has to be done to help out James Bond, who relies on Bouvier and Q, almost exclusively, for help in this film. After all, M has told him that officially he is not one of the "family." In Carey Lowell's real life, she probably has more in common with former Bond heroines in high heels than with gun molls. She was a model on the runways and on the covers of fashion magazines for New York's Ford Agency from her high school years, and is now married to actor Richard Gere.

Paris Carver.

In *Tomorrow Never Dies* (1997), Paris Carver (Teri Hatcher) has a billionaire husband, gets to travel all over the globe and stay in the best hotels, meet the most fabulous people and live a life of total luxury and leisure. But does that make her happy? No, she needs the love that only James Bond can bring to her life, the love of a man on the edge, an agent with a gun under his pillow ready to die for Queen and country. Of course, when she knew him, she was unacquainted with Elliot Carver. She was just a college student. But she always remembered the spy who loved her, the spy who, when she saw him years later, she slapped in the face. She is a proud woman, yet Bond's first instinct was not to take advantage of their former relationship. This is one of the few moments in James Bond's career when we see him emotionally vulnerable. His vulnerability and her beauty make it a memorable moment when the two finally bond.

Dr. Jones.

In *The World Is not Enough* (1999), Dr. Christmas Jones (Denise Richards) is clearly far too young for James Bond, like Bibi Dahl, but inexplicably very well-educated with a Ph.D. (in nuclear physics), like Holly Goodhead. Over the years, we've met plenty of well-educated women in Academia who were also strikingly beautiful, but we just don't buy Denise Richards in this role. We loved her in *Starship Troopers* as the cadet turned starship captain, but when it comes to Bond girls, we are hugely protective of those who have come before. Ms. Richards is simply miscast, and quite honestly, we don't care that Christmas comes twice. It's a lame joke, and an equally lame character.

Jinx.

Halle Berry's character Jinx in *Die Another Day* (2002) is a mystery woman wrapped in the enigma of the National Security Agency. When she first appears in the film, Jinx appears to be working against our favorite spy. Who can forget her entrance, however, with a knife hanging off her bikini-bottomed hip, just like Ursula Andress in *Dr. No*. But later, at Gustav Graves' ice palace, 007 learns that both of them are fighting the same megalomaniac from different sides of the ocean. James Bond saves Jinx's life, destroying Q's latest tricked-out car, and in return, she gives Bond his first onscreen orgasm. Seems like a worthwhile trade! [The exquisite Halle Berry was also the first Oscar-winner, for Marc Forster's **Monster's Ball** (2001), to become a Bond girl.]

THE WOMEN OF RUSSIAN

In the 1950's and 1960's, tourists were photographing Russian women, who all seemed to be on the heavy side. Their diet was primarily carbohydrates—bread, pota toes, and the usual starches—when the long lines to buy food were functioning. Obviously, the women of the upper and upper middle classes in the Soviet "classless" society were not being photographed by American tourists. In that era, rather than shopping among the Soviet debris of Moscow, the Russian elite were shopping in foreign countries to pick up their lingerie, such as the lacey garments that James Bond bought for Tania. Today, with the influence of European fashions and a varied diet, skeletal and statuesque Russian models sometimes appear on the runways of fashion houses in Paris, Rome and New York. Thanks to the mixture of ethnics in Mother Russia—Slavs, Germans, Mongols and other Asians, plus Scandinavians, and all of the Baltic states—Russia is a breeding ground for some of the most attractive women in the world, much like American women, and for the same reason. The most attractive women are often the most sexually active. Just as **From Russia with Love** (1963) had featured one of the first gorgeous Russian women, many of the other films in the series depicted them as stunning beauties who lust for 007's affections.

Probably the only downside to dating Russian women might be some of the memories and legends from World War II.

We know that Russian women fought in the front against the Nazis during what they called the Great Patriotic War; Russian women pilots shot down German fighters, bombers and transport planes; Russian women snipers took out German army officers on the Eastern Front; Russian women seduced German spies. So, yes, Russian women may be very attractive, but, just like drop-dead fashion models from Texas, they also might be able to make you food for worms at two hundred yards if you provoke them. So, as you jet off to the former Soviet Union and the promise of a beautiful Russian bride, think twice about checking under her pillow for a weapon or searching her shoes for a poison dagger.

Tatiana Romanova.

With her long blonde hair and exotic features, Daniela Bianchi represented our first glimpse behind the Iron Curtain at a Russian beauty as the female lead Tatiana Romanova in ***From Russia with Love***. Tania's mouth always seemed ready to break into a smile or swallow something big when we first see her in Bond's bed. Though she complains that her mouth is too big, in fact, her mouth is just perfect for a photographer's model: the points where her lips end line up exactly with the middle of her eyes. And though she says she was one inch too tall for the Russian ballet, at five feet, seven inches, she just might have made it. On the Orient Express, when his friend Kerim Bey has been killed, Tatiana is one Bond Girl who gets slapped, and then still tells James Bond that she loves him and cries over his rough, masculine treatment. The question is: Does she really love *him*, or does she only seek the promise of high fashion clothing and a life of leisure in London? Since a gentleman never tells, we'll never know.

EVERYTHING I KNOW ABOUT LIFE I LEARNED FROM JAMES BOND

Major Anya Amasova.

Clever, resourceful, and deadlier than most of her male counterparts, Major Anya Amasova (Barbara Bach) represents the first of a new breed of Bond girls who were distinctly more complex and enjoyed a greater range of freedoms than her predecessors. Her appearance as his opposite number in the KGB in *The Spy Who Loved Me* (1977) presented 007 with his first, true equal out of all of the previous films. Like Bond, Anya has never failed on a mission, and has earned the right to carry a license to kill enemies of her government. Codenamed Triple-X, she cleverly outwits and outthinks 007 on numerous occasions. After she learns that it was Bond who killed Sergei Barsov on his recent mission in Austria, Anya vows to avenge her lover's death by killing 007 when their mission is completed. Her only failing is that she easily succumbs to the charms of her British counterpart, and trades her desire to kill him for a glass of Dom Perignon champagne. Married in real life to Ringo Star, she can come bang our drums any day of the week.

Pola Ivanova.

There is one thing you can say about James Bond; he never lets business interfere with his personal pleasure. Sure, Pola Ivanova (Fiona Fullerton) works for the Russians in *A View to a Kill* (1985). That's no reason to not spend an evening in a hot tub with her. He is doing the right thing, as long as he manages to get hold of her tapes of Max Zorin's discussions with his underlings. The three dozen *red* roses he gave her last time must have had an effect on her this time too. Do you think he put them on his expense account? [Fiona Fullerton has had a varied and continuing career since she was fourteen years old. She appears on the stage, on TV and in films as well as working as a writer on satellite television.]

Natalya Simonova.

In Pierce Brosnan's first film in the James Bond franchise, *GoldenEye* (1995), Izabella Scorupco plays Natalya Simonova a computer technician who survives the attack on the titular satellite station. She allies herself with 007, and helps him stops a cyberattack on the world. Although she plays Bond's love interest, she's not as sexy as Xenia.

Xenia Onatopp.

In *GoldenEye* (1995), James Bond offers to buy Xenia Onatopp (Famke Janssen) a drink. He asks, with tongue firmly planted in cheek, "How do you take it?" And she replies, "Straight up . . . With a twist." That best describes the beautiful Russian agent who works for the Janus Crime Syndicate. Once a pilot in the Soviet Air Force, she now spends her time living life in the fast lane, and enjoying a good squeeze more than the average Bond girl. Her unique form of assassinations provides James Bond with a valuable link to the Russian secret weapons facility. When they later meet at the Grand Hotel in St. Petersburg, Russia, 007 practices "safe sex" with her. Later, in Cuba, they battle for one last pleasure. But on this occasion, Bond comes out on top of things.

THE WOMEN OF ASIA

Unlike their European or American counterparts, the Asian

EVERYTHING I KNOW ABOUT LIFE I LEARNED FROM JAMES BOND

women in *You Only Live Twice* and several other features presented James Bond with a few surprises, and we can learn much from their beauty, determination, and unbridled sexuality. When Tiger Tanaka invites 007 back to his home for an evening of rest and relaxation, Bond meets four Japanese beauties in white bikinis. "In Japan," Tiger tells him, disrobing, "men always come first; women come second." "I might just retire here," Bond says, looking over each of the women with a glint in his eye and lust in his heart. Throughout most of its history, Japan was a male-dominated society with women treated as little more than property by their husbands and fathers. Similarly, women in China and other Asian countries had few rights as individuals. During the Feudal period, women were elevated in poems and songs to a position of great adoration and desire, but their real-world counterparts suffered as second-class citizens with very little power of their own. Seemingly, the Geisha girl, who was similar in status to a European courtesan, was the only woman who could make choices for herself, even if they were very limited choices. Following World War II, Asian women made tremendous strides towards equality, but fell vastly short of their European or American counterparts. Today, many traditional women still follow the dictates of the past, and serve men without thought or consideration of their own needs and desires.

Aki.

"I think I will enjoy very much serving under you," Aki (Akiko Wakabayashi) whispers into Bond's ear while he is enjoying a relaxing massage in *You Only Live Twice* (1967). 007's Japanese guardian angel, Aki saves Bond's life on more than one occasion. At first, she seems to work for Dikko Henderson, and escorts

Bond to his residence in her Toyota 2000-GT convertible; later, she appears out of nowhere, and saves Bond from an assassin's bullet outside Osato Electrical and Engineering Company. Then Aki lures 007 to Tiger Tanaka's secret headquarters, with considerable ease we might add. She is very beautiful and sexy, and as a very traditional Japanese woman, she easily gives into Bond's sexual charms. Unfortunately, she meets an untimely end when a ninja assassin misses his target. [She appeared with her co-star Mie Hama in *King Kong Versus Godzilla* (1962).]

Kissy Suzuki.

"This is business," Kissy reminds 007 when he tries to make sexual advances during their honeymoon, and does not give into him until their mission has been fulfilled. While she is never actually called by the name Kissy Suzuki in *You Only Live Twice* (1967), Mie Hamma's character is credited only as Kissy in the end credits; Fleming named her Kissy Suzuki in the novel. An employee of Japanese SIS, she has worked to establish a cover as an Ama diving girl who makes her living diving for shells; how Tiger Tanaka came to assign her to that particular island and at that particular point in time is a completely different matter. Kissy is also the first girl that James Bond marries, albeit to establish his cover. She is not as beautiful as Aki, but also does not have "the face of a pig" that Tiger confesses to Bond. She is a very competent agent, and does her part alongside Tanaka's ninja commandoes to destroy SPECTRE's hidden rocket base.

Ama Diving Girls.

007, Tiger Tanaka, and his forces infiltrate the south end of the Izu Peninsula, southwest of the Kanto area, to hide among the local men who rely on Ama diving girls for their livelihood. In fact, Tiger's contact on the island, Kissy Suzuki, is herself a diving girl. Ama diving girls are trained from a very young age to dive into shallow water and reef areas to retrieve shellfish and other marine life that is used in gourmet seafood meals. Other than diving goggles (and a good pair of lungs), the girls use no special equipment to reach the lower depths, and the work is very hard and dangerous. Most work for a labor boss who pays them a minimum wage for long hours of diving. Not a popular occupation today, it reached its height just prior to World War II. Bond is especially grateful for Kissy's training, for when he sends her back to the island for Tiger's men, she eludes a deadly helicopter attack by swimming deep below the surface and holding her breath. Great lungs, not that James Bond would notice!

Ling.

"Darling, I give you very best duck," Ling (Tsai Chin) as the Chinese agent tells Bond in *You Only Live Twice* (1967). The double-entendre in her words is deliberate, and we're both still surprised the speech passed MPAA censors. While James Bond does admit to Henderson that he has never been to Japan before, 007 does have a discriminating pallet when it comes to kissing Asian women. He tells Ling that she tastes different from all other women, like Peking Duck is different from Russian Caviar. Bond enjoys her brazen sexuality, a quality that he notes in other Asian women, but later lies to Miss Moneypenny about whether he had sexual relations with Ling or not. Apparently, she was responsible for setting Bond up with the Chinese agent. We can just imagine what would have happened if 007 had filed a complete report!

Chew Mee.

Chew Mee (Francoise Therry) is swimming in Hai Fat's enormous pool in ***The Man with the Golden Gun*** (1975). When Bond refuses to join her, on the grounds that he has no swimming trunks, she replies: "I don't have them on either." She certainly looks like a cuddly teddy bear with no chance of drowning. If Bond did not have other business, he might have taken up her proposition. In any case, Ms. Therry had her moment of fame, which we all remember.

Wai Lin.

Wai Lin (Michelle Yeoh) is poetry in motion, but no flowery poetry by Wordsworth, rather her poetry is of the black bloodiness of Edgar Allan Poe. Wai Lin is a cocky street fighter. Remember the way she waved at James Bond as she literally walked down a wall outside of Carver's secret laboratory. And how about the way she cleaned up her office of several of General Chang's operatives in a hurry? True, Bond saved her life, but she had helped save both of their lives as she shifted while James rode their BMW motorcycle. And she was quite an eyeful, as well. Michelle Yeoh, born in Malaya, started out as a ballet dancer in London's Royal Academy of Dramatic Arts in her teens. The former Miss Malaya of 1983 went to Hong Kong in the 1990's and became a Hong Kong action star with Jackie Chan, among others. The group she fights in her office HQ was played by some of her Hong Kong action pals. She went on from ***Tomorrow Never Dies*** to star in another big hit, Ang Lee's ***Crouching Tiger, Hidden Dragon*** (2000), and more recently *Star Trek: Discovery* (2020).

EVERYTHING I KNOW ABOUT LIFE
I LEARNED FROM JAMES BOND

THE WOMEN OF THE MUSLIM WORLD

In *The Spy Who Loved Me* (1977), after Sheikh Hosein offers Bond a female companion for the night, 007 quips, "When one is in Egypt, one should delve deeply into its treasures," and goes off with one of the beautiful women in the sheikh's harem. Throughout most of its cultural and religious history, the Muslim world has been a male-dominated society with women treated as an inferior, oppressed minority by men. They had very few rights, and were considered the property of their father or their husband; they were restricted to their homes, and if they did appear in public, they were forced to cover their face and hair with a *hijab* (often translated as "veil) or scarf. They were not permitted to speak directly to other men; they were not allowed to read or seek educational advancement. They could not engage in any commerce or own any property. The prophet Muhammad in the **Qur'an** granted certain rights to women that made a vast improvement on their lives, but after the Prophet's death, the condition of women began to decline and revert back to what it was before. For centuries, women in Islam suffered many indignities and injustices at the hands of their male counterparts. In the twentieth century, however, as the women's movement emerged in the West, feminists from upper-class Muslim households began to speak out. The last two decades have witnessed many changes as a form of Islamic feminism has swept the Muslim world. Some women have cast aside their veils, and taken strides that, at any other time in history, would have meant death. But the majority of

Muslim women still follow the dictates of the past, and serve men without thought or consideration of their own needs and desires. Among the most beautiful women in the world, they have proved to be a very real challenge to 007 in several of his adventures.

Saida.

In ***The Man with the Golden Gun*** (1975), Saida proved that a woman's belly is well worth watching, and not because of an unexpected pregnancy. You will notice the predominance of men in the audience of the Beirut club where she performs. Obviously, Bill Fairbanks, 002, found her hard to resist. And even James Bond seemed to be appreciative of her navel as he nuzzled her stomach—even though his real goal was to steal her gold bullet, which had passed through Fairbanks and which she placed in her naval for luck. Carmen du Sautoy, who was ten years younger than her contemporaries in the film, was extremely provocative and sexy, and her belly dance is worth the price of admission.

Felicia.

When it comes to Bond girls, 007 is truly a lucky man! Not only does James Bond get to make love to them, but he always seems to have one on hand to take a bullet for him or an assassin's blow. In Goldfinger, Bonita is the perfect shield when an assassin suddenly appears in her room, and threatens 007 with a club; in ***Thunderball***, Bond takes Fiona Volpe for a spin around the dance floor, and she twirls right into a bullet meant for him; in ***Live and Let Die***, the scarecrows take aim at Bond but kill Rosie instead. So, we were really not too surprised when Felicia (Olga Bisera)

EVERYTHING I KNOW ABOUT LIFE
I LEARNED FROM JAMES BOND

offered to keep 007 entertained in *The Spy Who Loved Me* (1977) while they waited for her boss Aziz Fekkesh to return from the Pyramids, and she ended up taking a bullet from an assassin's gun that was meant for Bond. Beautiful and clearly delectable as a "dessert," Felicia has but a few moments of screen time to entertain and distract our favorite secret agent before her demise.

The Hareem.

For fans of the James Bond films, the traditional image of a hareem or harem conjures visions of a richly appointed hall filled with beautiful female slaves whose only mission in life is to serve the sexu al appetites of their master. That image is reinforced by scenes in which Mata Bond dances for her father in *Casino Royale* (1967) or in which Bond promises to "delve deeply into its treasures" when offered a sexy concubine for the night by Sheikh Hosein in *The Spy Who Loved Me*. In *The Living Daylights*, 007 leaps over a courtyard filled with beautiful women who constitute a harem, and worries that Kara Milovy will be sold into bondage as part of a lustful sheik's hareem. The Arabic word "hareem" refers to the living quarters reserved for wives, concubines, and female relatives in a Muslim household that were forbidden to male strangers. Through years of improper usage and pronunciation, the word became "harem" for Western tongues, and described a group of women, wives and concubines who lived in a polygamous household, and not the living quarters at all. From a purely pragmatic sense, the Muslim tradition relied on concubines kept as slaves and legally-wedded wives for reproduction. The hareem also emphasized the patriarchal nature of power. Muslim men needed sons to carry on the "hereditary" bloodline of their fathers, and they took many women to their beds in order to make certain they had sons. In the sixteenth and seventeenth centuries, slave "concubinage" was recognized as an equal form of reproduction, and then again, many women in the hareem would never even see the Sultan and would function purely as servants in the household. Today, in most Arabic countries, the traditions of the hareem have been mostly replaced by very traditional marriages, and the harem remains a vestige of the past that is still cloaked and shrouded in mystery and eroticism. We're certain that if Bond had had a choice in the matter he would have been born a Sultan in the 16th century with a very large hareem.

THE WOMEN OF INDIA

When James Bond follows the trail of the Fabergé Egg to India (and Kamal Khan) in *Octopussy* (1983), he encounters his first Indian woman at the hotel, and then discovers an entire island of women, many of whom are native to India. In the Hindu Shastras, or holy writings of India, a woman was described as the bond slave of her father when she was young, the bond slave of her husband when she was married, and the bond slave of her son when she was a mother. A woman's place in society was not the same as other human beings. She had no rights; she could not move or do anything else of her own volition. She was branded just like an animal. The ancient Hindu Codebook ***Manusmrati*** determined that women were to be placed on the lowest rung of humanity's ladder, on par with animals and slaves.

During prehistoric times, people worshipped the Mother Goddess Kali as the source of life and fertility, and then in

EVERYTHING I KNOW ABOUT LIFE
I LEARNED FROM JAMES BOND

the fifth and sixth centuries, with the publication of the ***Devi Mahatmya***, the worship of the feminine principle took on dramatic new dimensions. Kali was pic tured as a Nubian woman with four arms (later changed to six), one holding a sword and another holding the head of a demon she had slain; with the other two arms, she encourages her worshippers. For earrings, she wears two dead bodies, and for a necklace, a ring of skulls. She is naked, except for a girdle made of dead men's hands. Her eyes are red, her tongue protrudes from her mouth, and her fulsome breasts are smeared with blood. She stands with one foot on her thigh, and another on the chest of her husband. This was an extremely powerful image, particularly the dominance of the male figure, but the worship practices of this mother goddess did not help elevate women in society. They were still treated as a slave who had come into the world to cook food, wash clothes, and fulfill the sexual desires of their husbands. In recent years, certain efforts have been made to empower women, and to give them the same rights as men. But this has been slow in coming, and continues to be a source of controversy among those who stick to very traditional beliefs.

The only women who seem to have any sort of power in the Bond films are those that belong to the Octopus cult and Octopussy herself. In fact, on posters advertising ***Octopussy*** (1983), she is depicted as the Goddess Kali, with multiple arms holding Bond and other items from the film.

Octopussy.

With the exception of Pussy Galore, few other Bond girls have had such a provocative name. Octopussy (Maud Adams) is the most liberated and self-sufficient of all Roger Moore's leading ladies, and proves herself to be the very competent, strongwilled business owner of Octopussy's Traveling Circus. She has also built an underworld empire of female thieves, smugglers, and assassins, known as the "Octopus cult." She controls a heavily-guarded, floating fortress in which only women are allowed. Octopussy is grateful to James Bond for giving her father, Major Dexter Smythe, an "honorable alternative" to facing trial for treason and ultimately a firing squad, and suggests they team up as business partners. She is very attracted to 007, and sleeps with him, even though she doesn't fully trust him. Later, when Kamal Khan double-crosses her, Octopussy relies on Bond as well as her female assassins to exact revenge on her former business partner. [Maud Adams is the only actress to have starred as two leading ladies in Bond films. She previously played the ill-fated Andrea Anders in *The Man with the Golden Gun* (1975).]

Magda.

A member of Octopussy's Traveling Circus, Magda (Kristina Wayborn) seduces James Bond in order to acquire the real Fabergé egg that he cleverly switched for a fake at the auction. When 007 first spotted her at Sotheby's Auction House, he assumed that she was the lady who owned the "property," and tracked her and her companion, Kamal Khan, to India. Later, she proves to be a valuable ally during the assault on the Monsoon Palace. Magda is extremely beautiful, and has a deep sultry voice that reminds men of Lauren Bacall. She is also a performing magician, acrobat, and belly dancer.

EVERYTHING I KNOW ABOUT LIFE
I LEARNED FROM JAMES BOND

THE WOMEN OF GREECE AND TURKEY

James Bond has had the pleasure of knowing women from all corners of the globe, but in *For Your Eyes Only*, 007 meets his first Greek woman (in Melina Havelock), and discovers a whole new world of pleasure. During the classical period, people worshipped Greek goddesses like Aphrodite and Hera, and even built the Parthenon in Athens as a tribute to Athena, the goddess of wisdom and war, but their real-world counterparts suffered as second-class citizens with very little power of their own. Women had very few rights, let alone legal rights. They had no rights to vote or take part in political matters. Once a woman was married, her husband controlled all of her property, including property she might have inherited from her family. If they divorced, control and rights over any property went back to a woman's father or nearest male relative. She had no rights to wander around town, without a just cause; in fact, any respectable woman would not be seen in public.

The writer Simonides characterized women as animals, claiming they could not control their own sexual urges and had to be restricted for their own protection. Fellow author and playwright Euripides suggested in his Greek tragedy *Medea*, "if women didn't exist, then human life would be rid of all of its miseries." Most Greek men felt that women had but one purpose in life, and that was to produce children. Today, many traditional women in Greece still follow the dictates of the past, and serve men very faithfully without thought for themselves.

Melina Havelock.

In *For Your Eyes Only* (1981), Melina Havelock (Carole Bouquet) seeks revenge for the death of her parents. Determined to kill Hector Gonzales, she follows him to Spain with a crossbow, and shoots him with a single bolt while he is diving into a swimming pool. Her shot is perfectly timed, for it creates a necessary diversion that allows James Bond to break free of his captors. Half Greek, her vengeance also extends to the people who hired Gonzales in the first place, and, like the mythical Elektra, she is willing to sacrifice herself for that revenge. Melina Havelock is a very strong-willed character, courageous and highly intelligent. She is very different from most of the women that Bond meets, and he is very attracted to her. With her background as a marine biologist, she proves to be a valuable ally for 007 in recovering the lost ATAC from the wreck of the *St. Georges*. In the final assault on the villain's mountaintop hideaway, Melina lends her crossbow and deadly aim, and saves James Bond's life as he climbs to the top.

Elektra King.

"There's no point living, if you can't feel alive," Elektra King (Sophie Marceau) declares to James Bond when he is assigned by MI6 to protect her from a would-be assassin in *The World Is not Enough* (1999). Of course, 007 doesn't know until much later in his adventure that she planned her father's death and M's abduction in order to solidify her hold on vast oil resources near the Caspian Sea. Both Melina Havelock and Elektra King identify with Greek women like Elektra who "always avenge their loved ones," and relies on the mythological tale to justify her revenge against those who murdered her parents. Elektra,

EVERYTHING I KNOW ABOUT LIFE
I LEARNED FROM JAMES BOND

an alternative spelling of Electra, was a famous figure in Greek mythology whose acts of vengeance were celebrated in a tragic play (which bears her name) written in 410 BC by Sophocles. When her father King Agamemnon returns from the Trojan War with his new concubine Cassandra, her mother and his wife Clytemnestra, who has taken Aegisthus as her lover, kills Agamemnon and Cassandra in a fit of rage. Elektra hides her brother Orestes, fearing that her mother will kill him as well. Years later, Orestes returns as a grown man to take revenge together with Elektra. While Greek mythology provides the origin of Elektra, her story has formed the basis for many other literary works.

Vida and Zora.

Vida (Alicia Gur) is an acrobatic wild Gypsy woman ready to risk her life to gain the man of her choice. Zora (Martine Beswicke) has the same attitude but is a little larger in size. They were good picks for the fight sequence in *From Russia with Love* (1963). Off-screen, director Terence Young was egging them on, calling for "more legs, more legs." The actresses gave him what he wanted. The next day, when the chief sent the two wild women to see James Bond to choose which was to become the bride-to-be, presumably they gave him what he wanted, too. In any case, both women had many things in common offscreen as well. Both were beauty contest winners. Gur was Miss Israel of 1960 and a finalist in the 1960 Miss Universe contest with Bianchi. Beswicke won a "Miss Autoville" contest in Jamaica, sold the car she won in the contest, and went to London to study acting and to get into the film industry. She was in the opening credits of *Dr. No*, the feisty Zora in *From Russia with Love* and Bond's assistant, Paula, in *Thunderball*, a much larger role.

Despite the seeming personal viciousness in their fighting, as both Gur and Beswicke went to Hollywood and made careers in film and television afterwards, they were probably just playing themselves onscreen all the time.

OTHER UNFORGETTABLE BOND GIRLS

We would be remiss if we didn't mention several other Bond girls that are simply unforgettable. Several of them come from South American countries that 007 has briefly visited in his travels around the globe. One other hails from the Caribbean, and still another started life as a man.

Paula Caplan.

That tall Gypsy girl in *From Russia with Love* returned to Bondage in *Thunderball* as a Caribbean aide to James Bond. Ironically, this role is what Martine Beswicke was, a woman raised in the Caribbean (Jamaica) by British parents. Her sun tan, however, had suffered from her stay in London, so she spent two weeks in the Bahamas' sunshine getting that outdoor look. It is her capture by Volpe and company that leads to her suicide by cyanide capsule. She took her work very seriously. Would 007 bite his cyanide capsule? No, he would look for a way out.

Tula.

In *For Your Eyes Only* (1981), the tall brunette with the white string-bikini, lounging around the pool at the Hector Gonzales estate, was actually a transsexual named Caroline Cossey, or Tula. She was the first woman played by a former man in a Bond movie, and while she has no intimate scenes with 007, we still cannot understand what all the fuss was about. After the movie's release, the UK tabloid *News of the World* revealed that Tula was born Barry Cossey and had a sex-change operation when he was seventeen. The news that she was a transsexual disrupted her career as a fashion model, and caused problems later in life when she tried to marry. But with a body like that (!), we can certainly understand why James Bond would have given her more than a second glance.

Manuela.

Just how does one kill a few hours in Rio? With Manuela, of course! Manuela (Emily Bolton) is the sort of agent who is on the ball in ***Moonraker*** (1979). The Bond ally follows him from the airport in the car but introduces herself to him as his bartender in the presidential suite. The suite is so large that Bond observes he may need a cab if he gets lost. She knows how Bond likes his martini. And she is quite willing to wile away a few hours with the world's best known secret agent. The only criticism about her is that she sure can't handle a knife. When Jaws approaches her (he appears to be twice her size), she pulls a knife and stands there unmoving until he overcomes her. It would seem that if she could not handle a knife, a Walther PPK would be a smart substitute (or a Smith and Wesson .38 Ladysmith Revolver). Emily Bolton, who started her career as "June" Bolton, first appeared on the ***Space: 1999*** TV series as Operative Nine. She went on to do some British television and film work through the 1980's.

Lupe Lamora.

In *Licence to Kill* (1989), Lupe Lamora (Talisa Soto) is the most luscious Latina we have seen ever. OK, so she does not get along with her boy friend, Sanchez. Who could? So, she finds happiness in the arms of another man. What woman can live with a man who beats her with a whip, unless she is in one of De Sade's fantasies? In this film, Lupe shows that she can go and glow with the flow. James Bond appears. She can relate to him. Sanchez disappears. There's always the President of Isthmus. A girl's gotta' cope. Lupe is just one of those beautiful, sensual and seductive women who drive other women crazy (particularly Pam Bouvier) and always find a wealthy man to pay the bills. Well, if our Lotto number comes in, we'll call. Talisa Soto is actually a Puerto Rican woman from Brooklyn who has made good. She too has appeared on fashion magazine covers and is currently married to actor Benjamin Bratt.

Solange Dimitrios.

The first Bond girl introduced in the Daniel Craig films, Solange Dimitrios was the wife of Alex Dimitrios, an associate of Le Chiffre in *Casino Royale* (2006). Bond seduces her for information, but fails to save her from Le Chiffre who has her tortured and killed. Her death made her the first sacrificial lamb in the series, but clearly not the last.

Camile Montes Rivero.

In *Quantum of Solace* (2008), Camille Montes Rivero (Olga Kurylenko) is a Bolivian national that Bond first meets in Haiti, where she has her sights set on killing General Medrano.

EVERYTHING I KNOW ABOUT LIFE I LEARNED FROM JAMES BOND

Medrano was responsible for murdering her entire family when she was a girl, and in the great tradition of Bond heroines, 007 saves her from Dominic Greene, an assassin who eventually plans to kill her. She never hooks up with James Bond, but stands by his side as a powerful ally as Bond takes on those responsible for Vesper's death. *Maxim* magazine named actress Olga Kurylenko as "the hottest Bond girl ever," and showcased the Ukrainian beauty on its Dec. 2008 cover.

Estrella.

Stephanie Sigman, best known for her role in the American crime drama ***The Bridge***, played the mysterious femme fatale Estrella in the pre-titles opening set in Mexico for ***Spectre*** (2015). After shortchanging us with Bond girls in ***Skyfall*** (2012), EON Productions more than makes up for that oversight with plenty of gorgeous but dangerous beauties in ***Spectre*** and ***No Time to Die*** (2021).

Nomi.

Nomi (Lashana Lynch) is the new 007 in ***No Time to Die***. Ending years of speculation whether a woman would ever play the titular role in a James Bond film, the London-born actress became 007 after Daniel Craig's Bond retired. In Jamaica, Nomi informs Bond about Valdo Obruchev and Project Hercules, and warns him not to interfere. Unlike Bond, she is an agent who follows instructions, and her professionalism clashes with Bond's devil-may-care attitude. They do eventually come to respect each other, and Nomi as Bond's new ally gives him back his 007 codename and helps him save Madeleine and his daughter. Lynch is a beautiful woman, and moviegoers may remember her as Ms. Marvel's gal-pal from *Captain Marvel* (2019).

Paloma.

No Time to Die's Paloma (Ana de Armas) is James Bond's CIA contact in Cuba. There, she helps Bond penetrate a secretive gathering of the evil organization, SPECTRE. The meeting turns out to be a trap meant to kill Agent 007, but when things don't go the way SPECTRE planned, Bond and Paloma make a daring escape. Their banter and the incredible fight choreography as they shoot their way out provides a delightful highlight for the long, almost incomprehensible plot. Unfortunately, she is gone as quickly as she came, but Paloma's time on screen reimagines the notion of a Bond Girl.

For Your Eyes Only BR / US 1981, Photo by: Mary Evans/ EON/Ronald Grant/Everett Collection (10393335)

CHAPTER FIVE

SEX AND RELATIONSHIPS—007 STYLE

Nobody does it better
Makes me feel sad for the rest. Nobody does it half as good as you.
Baby, you're the best!

—Carly Simon, *The Spy who Loved Me* (1977)

Ian Fleming single-handedly transformed the protagonist of popular spy and detective fiction from the dark, brooding, middle-class private eyes of Raymond Chandler and Dashiell Hammett to the elegant, sophisticated, gentleman secret agent James Bond 007. He dressed his socially astute character in the finest suits and made him clever and witty, athletic and debonair, dangerous and heroic. In affecting this transformation, he made Bond sexually irresistible to women, and populated his novels with dozens of beautiful girls who were ready, willing, and able. The films, in turn, followed suit, and Sean Con nery brought a wry, self-deprecating, winking sex appeal to his performance as 007. By virtue of sheer charisma, Connery transformed James Bond from a man's idea of what women desire into a woman's idea of what they hungered for in a man. "Mr. Kiss Kiss Bang Bang" was born: the tough guy with a sensitive streak, equally at home kissing the blonde bombshell or shooting the bad girl at point-blank range. Women wanted to love him, and men wanted to be him.

The Spy Who Loved Me BR / US 1977 Photo by: Mary Evans/EON PRODUCTIONS/Ronald Grant/Everett Collection (10341379)

For the adolescent male growing up in the 1950s and 1960s, 007 was everything that we were not. We knew that James Bond's vast range of skills and knowledge was only matched by his clever resourcefulness in dealing with each new challenge that came his way. But what we envied most was how his approach with women succeeded every time with such little effort. We wanted to be just like James Bond! We wanted to be suave and debonair, with every beautiful woman swooning at the very mention of our names. And now as middle-aged adults, looking back over the years, we both realize how Bond helped define our understanding of what it meant to be a man, particularly at a time in our culture when the roles of men and women were becoming so fractured and confused.

EVERYTHING I KNOW ABOUT LIFE I LEARNED FROM JAMES BOND

Not only did each James Bond adventure teach us important lessons about life, but 007 also taught us how to succeed with women in terms of sex, dating, and relationships.

Dating.

For the first time in the film series, James Bond takes a woman (Kara Milovy) out on a date in *The Living Daylights* (1987). Yes, we said it, a date! Even before their formal date begins, 007 helps Kara pick out something special to wear. He then escorts her to the opera at the Musikverein Concert Hall in Vienna, and progresses to romance her on several amusement rides (including the Reisenaad Big Wheel) at Prater Park. We were surprised in looking back over the films that our favorite secret agent did not have more experience with dating. The closest thing to a real date was a boating outing he had with Sylvia Trench in *From Russia with Love*. Most of the women Bond has known have caved in very easily to his sexual charms, and he has not had to "wine and dine" them first, like the rest of us mere mortals. So, in an actual life lesson about dating, we felt let down by 007—until his date with Kara. Dating, as an age-old ritual, is the process of socializing and spending time with one person to determine if she or he is the right one for a committed relationship. Conventional dating rituals, like going out to dinner, seeing a movie, or meeting for coffee or a drink, provide couples with the time to explore the other person for commonalities and differences. Most people employ a three-date ritual, and don't proceed beyond three dates if the other person is not right for them. The first date is usually the coffee date, in which the two people meet for an hour and chat and gain an initial feel for each other; sometimes they may not want to proceed beyond the first date. If there is potential, then the second date is typically longer, and involves an activity or two, like dinner and a movie. Again, if the potential is there, they may move to a third date in which they may spend more time together doing mutual activities. The three most usual choices for what to do on a date are dinner, a movie, and a public event such as a sports game or concert. Those activities often give the couple several hours of time to enjoy each other's company, and to communicate with each other on a wide variety of personal and philosophical topics. By relying on familiar or shared activities, couples have a chance to bond. Bond himself presumably takes Kara to dinner before the opera, and then, while they are enjoying themselves at the amusement park, he kisses her for the first time. The first kiss is very important, for it sets the tone for the rest of the relationship, and even if the relationship is to continue. The kiss should be soft and gentle, not a peck and certainly not open-mouthed and forceful. Ideally, the lips should linger together for a moment, with the unspoken suggestion that there is more to come. Sex is something that comes much, much later in the dating process. One should also be aware that men and women think about dating differently. For some men, dating is often simply a means to an end.

Not surprisingly, women want the same thing as men, but they also want to make sure they are not used in the process. We were reminded recently by a woman in both our lives (our agent!) that women want sex just as much, maybe even more than men, but that it takes a little more psychological commitment and the reassurance that they will not be thought of as "whores" for their desire for sex. Of course, that is a huge shift from the thinking of the fifties and sixtiess, the era when James Bond came into our lives, and today. The twenty-first-century sees women in a different light. They want sexual freedom and also want to be loved. While we would rate 007's date with

EVERYTHING I KNOW ABOUT LIFE
I LEARNED FROM JAMES BOND

Kara a huge success for the eighties' male, we know that James Bond can do better today. Daniel Craig's interpretation of a more modern 007 may well help dissipate Bond's outmoded, chauvinistic approach to love and relationships, and establish more complicated and thus more realistic relationships with his leading ladies in the new millennium. After all, Craig's relationship with Madeleine Swann in *Spectre* (2016) and *No Time to Die* (2021) is clearly a very modern one . . . one that future James Bond movies may wish to adopt and emulate.

For women, dating is another means for social interaction which may lead to a sexual encounter if she feels comfortable in the relationship. James Bond has a way of assuring women of his complete attention and concern. We would rate 007's date with Kara as a huge success.

Courting.

While James Bond has certainly had sexual relations with more than his fair share of women, he has rarely courted them and almost never has fallen in love. The singular exception in the half-dozen short stories, thirteen novels, and twenty-odd films is the Contessa Teresa di Vicenzo or Tracy (Diana Rigg) from *On Her Majesty's Secret Service* (1969). She becomes the love of James Bond's life, and, when she is taken from him in a brutal act of violence, he weeps for her in a way that he never does for any other woman. In fact, nearly a dozen years later, as shown in *For Your Eyes Only* (1981), he is at her gravesite still mourning her death. We can learn much from James Bond when he treats a woman like a lady and courts her with a style worthy of the great courtiers of history. In courting Tracy, he flirts, talks, listens, and makes friendship an integral part of their relationship. He takes her horseback riding, walks with her in beautiful gardens, strolls with her on an isolated beach, and takes her window-shopping. Bond uses every opportunity to kiss her delicately or put his arm lovingly around her, but he never moves their relationship horizontal. He even selects a song of their own, "We Have All the Time in the World." Bond knows that when a woman is courted, she feels special and safe. In making her feel special and safe, Tracy just opens herself up to him even more, showering him with more admiration, respect and appreciation for even the smallest things he does for her. He feels like a winner because she makes him feel that everything he does is terrific. And so he continues to court her and do even more for her because he wants to continue to make her happy. In courting, he vies for a woman's attention, so she doesn't have to question if she's the dessert. He loves her for who she is, and not just for her body parts. The courting ritual is one that is rarely seen in the James Bond films, but when it happens in **On Her Majesty's Secret Service**, you see a side of 007 that is truly special.

Sex.

With the rising popularity of Hugh Hefner's *Playboy* magazine, the importation of saucy European films, and the introduction of new forms of contraception in the late 1950s and early 1960s, the notions of sex and reproduction were, once and for all time, separated from each other. Sex was finally accepted as a form of recreation in the United States, and discussed very freely and openly abroad. Enter James Bond. In both the novels and the film series, Bond is portrayed as a sensualist, unencumbered by romance or obligation. Agent 007 makes love with many gorgeous women who are equally interested in sex for its own sake. He is both an icon of the sexual revolution and the literary embodiment of sexual freedom. Bond does not view recreational sex as wrong. He feels no guilt, and enjoys sexual relations, detached and free of consequences. He is not a misogynist. His female partners are never victims, but rather welcome his sexual advances as equals in their own right. For that matter, the Bond girls are empowered icons of the sexual revolution as well. Some women even use their sexuality as a tool for manipulation, seduction, and power. In the mid-80s, when HIV and AIDS was a relatively new threat, Bond exchanged his promiscuity for a single partner and "safe sex" in several of the films. But, alas, this was short-lived, and by the 1990s, Agent 007 had returned to enjoying sexual relations with multiple partners. From Honey Rider and Pussy Galore to Elektra King and Miranda Frost, James Bond usually sleeps with two to three women per movie. Ironically, he is only seen having an orgasm for the first time with Jinx (Halle Berry) in *Die Another Day* (2002).

Lover's Lessons.

In *Live and Let Die* (1973), the first time in the film series, James Bond deflowers a virgin (Solitaire), and finds himself needing to explain the lessons of lovers to her. Both of us found that amusing until we realized just how ill-defined the whole notion of love was in any of the movies. One of the things that we have always admired about Bond is his sexual prowess. He enjoys sexual relations with lots of women, and does not hide his enjoyment of sex behind any pretenses or false hypocrisies of political correctness. For the most part, 007 comports himself like a modern-day Casanova or Don Juan, and relies on his superior art of seduction to score with two to three women (and sometimes more) per adventure. However, we don't think that gives him a license to love. In fact, Bond's discourse (to Solitaire) on the lessons of love is like the Big Bad Wolf giving Little Red Riding Hood lessons on the proper etiquette for unwelcome dinner guests. When 007 informs her that lovers "have no secrets," are together "till death" or thereabouts, and don't go off "half-cocked," we find his words of advice truly ludicrous. Especially lover's lesson number four, which is to "follow the scarecrows." James Bond may well have started us thinking about the lessons of lovers, but we ultimately learned that love is so much more than that. Eli Sternberg, a well-renowned psychologist and psychotherapist, suggested that perfect or consummate love is comprised of passion, intimacy, and commitment. 007 certainly understands passionate love, which is physical attraction and the desire for sexual interaction. At times, he may have also known true intimacy, which is that sense of emotional closeness and warmth. But Bond has made only one commitment to a woman to love her in spite of difficulties and problems, and it is unlikely he will ever again commit to one woman alone. So, in terms of love, James Bond knows romantic or chivalric love, and is simply incapable of anything more than that. Thankfully, we have the capacity to love fully, and the life lesson here is to discard all lover's lessons in favor of loving each other with our heart, mind and soul.

May–December Relationships.

Not long after meeting James Bond in *For Your Eyes Only* (1981), Bibi Dahl attempts to seduce 007 in hotel room. Bond politely declines her advances, believing that she is too young for him, but offers to buy her an ice cream cone instead if she agrees to put her clothes back on. While we were surprised by 007's incredible self control, considering that he has succumbed

EVERYTHING I KNOW ABOUT LIFE
I LEARNED FROM JAMES BOND

to the charms of other younger women—Dr. Christmas Jones, Miranda Frost and Strawberry Fields are three that come immediately to mind—we realized there was an important life lesson here. May–December romance represents the common expression we use in our society to describe an age-disparate relationship. The expression draws upon an implicit analogy between a person's age and the time of the year, with "May" referring to the younger partner who is in the Spring of life, and "December" referring to the older partner who is in the Winter of life. In many non-Western cultures, age-disparate relationships are common. Older men who have spent a lifetime establishing themselves in business or with their careers will choose women many years younger than themselves as wives to start their families. Historically, unequal pairings were quite common, even in Western cultures. Many men in positions of prestige or power have taken young women as their lovers or wives. At the same time, certain women of influence have also sought out the sexual favors of younger men. Frequently, arranged marriages and situations involving mail-order brides feature older men and younger women. From their study of age-disparate relationships, psychologists and social scientists have concluded that older partners search for a way to maintain their youth while their younger partners find someone who is financially secure enough to guarantee or increase their status within the society. Naturally, some view age-disparate relationships as aberrant or even perverse; they frown on dirty-old-men who chase nubile young cuties or chastise attractive youthful women as "gold diggers" who latch onto rich older men. And extreme disparities in sexual relationships, particularly those that might involve an underage male or female with an adult figure, are denounced as pedophilia. Mary Kaye Letourneau went to prison for an affair that she had with one of her students. We think May–December relationships are acceptable as long as both parties are mature enough to know and honestly communicate what they want and need from the other person involved. As for 007, we are concerned that, if he continues his trend for dating younger and younger women as he continues to age, he will be dating sperm and unfertilized eggs in a few years.

A Gift for Flowers.

While spying on Melina in the snow-covered village of Cortina in *For Your Eyes Only* (1981), James Bond stops in a florist shop, and orders a dozen lilies. Moments later, after sending a wouldbe assassin crashing through the front window of the shop, 007 instructs the salesgirl to send the lilies to the funeral. Earlier in the film, Bond leaves a dozen red roses at his deceased wife's gravesite. As a worldly gentleman, he has often demonstrated that he has a real gift for knowing what flowers to send for all the right occasions. The tradition of giving flowers to loved ones, friends, and family members is one that is revered all around the globe. While the most common reason to give flowers is to express romantic love, people celebrate birthdays and holidays by giving flowers, bouquets, and floral arrangements. A simple flower is sometimes all that most guys need to break the ice on a nervous first date. Special holidays like Valentine's Day are really incomplete without some kind of floral arrangement. Flowers express joy, romance, passion, appreciation, or sympathy in a way that is unmatched by any other gift. Of course, knowing the right flowers to give is just as important as remembering to give them. When Bond orders lilies at the florist shop, he must know that something fatal is about to happen. Lilies are available in a wide range of colors, but the most common variety is the white lily, which is a symbol of purity and innocence. Most often associated with Easter, white lilies are normally used to commemorate funerals or celebrate weddings. The yellow lily symbolizes happiness and gratitude, and is given as a form of thanks. Carnations, the longest lasting of all flowers, are the flower of choice for many professional florists. They are used to complement other flowers, often small roses of the same color, in a mixed bouquet. Due to the wide variety of colors, carnations are a very versatile flower. Pink carnations are popular on Mother's Day; white carnations adorn wedding bouquets and sympathy wreaths, and red carnations express love and affection. Like carnations, irises come in a rainbow of colors, and are another popular choice because of their strong fragrances. Once a symbol of faith for the ancient Greeks, the iris has been adopted by the French nobility as the Fleur-de-lis. Irises are given to friends and acquaintances, but never to lovers. The rose alone is the symbol of love and desire. In Ancient Greece, Aphrodite first presented a rose to her son Eros, the god of love, and ever since then, roses have cornered the market for denoting love. But we should also point out that only red roses mean love; pink roses signify friendship; yellow roses symbolize respect, and white roses signify innocence and silence. Naturally, Bond leaves red long-stemmed roses for Tracy. Knowing the right flower and when to give it is a lesson well learned.

The Scent of a Woman.

In *On Her Majesty's Secret Service* (1969), when James Bond meets Tracy in his suite at the casino to fulfill her financial obligation to him, he notices that she is wearing L'Heure Bleue perfume, and remarks that it is an unusual scent for a business transaction. Bond knows much about women, including perfumes. The perfume L'Heure Bleue, which means "blue hour" in French, was first introduced in 1912, and was reputedly inspired by the gentle bluehued twilight of a pre-World War I Paris. Third-generation perfumer Jacques Guerlain conceived L'Heure Bleue for the sophisticated woman, and it became the landmark scent of 1912 among women of wealth and power. In creating the scent, he combined passionate florals with musk, vanilla, and aromatic woods. The resulting floral scent is romantic, sensual and bewitching, much like the subtle pastel hues of Paris at twilight. A two-and-a-half oz. Eau de Parfum Spray of L'Heure Bleue perfume costs $100.

Sex in Zero Gravity.

We all enjoyed seeing James Bond and Holly Goodhead floating in zero gravity at the end of ***Moonraker***, though we did wonder how that sheet covered them instead of floating away. We may even have fantasized more than a bit about the things we could do in zero gravity, things, for example, that only people in the Kama Sutra seem to be able to do on Planet Earth. We are reminded, however, that gravity is not such a bad thing at times. For example, a good pelvic thrust might send your companion across the room as well, perhaps, as into ecstasy. One proposal is to create some special clothing with four leg holes that two people, interested in each other, could wear. Presumably, depending on the position you wished to undertake or the type of sexual stimulation you prefer, you could have several types of sexual workout wear. Perhaps they would be color-coded. "Honey, not the blue again. We're always doing the blue. Let's make this an orange night, huh? We could start out with a little yellow." On the other hand, it might take you both quite a while to change sexual workout wear. You might (gulp) lose your

EVERYTHING I KNOW ABOUT LIFE I LEARNED FROM JAMES BOND

focus. Oh, well, we'll postpone these considerations until we climb into a space shuttle.

Sex and the Sea.

In ***Thunderball*** (1965), James Bond and the lovely Domino make it at the bottom of the sea with SCUBA gear intact and a great wave of bubbles hitting the surface. After all, you can't be gnawing on someone's mouth or other appendage and breathing through your SCUBA gear as well. Certainly, there will be lots of bubbles. They might even be ticklish. It could be fun, if you can hold your breath. Of course, Bond seems always to leave the ladies satisfied, no matter what. On the other hand, if the subject of your desire would not like seawater as an intimate part of the experience, perhaps an evening *by* the sea would be the way to go. Perhaps you'd like a late night or very early morning, with the surf pounding on the glistening sand, a sound enhanced by your heavy breathing, her heavy breathing, and the call of tropical birds in the distance. We think you get the idea. A little beach cottage with an open window with the moonlight streaming in could be fun too. And a cold bottle of Tattinger in the bucket might inspire another go-round.

The Tango.

James Bond executes the perfect tango with Domino (Kim Basinger) in ***Never Say Never Again*** (1983), and very literally steals her away from her megalomaniac lover, Maximillian Largo (Klaus Maria Brandauer). Some people call the tango "the dance of love," but it certainly started as the dance of sex. The origins of the tango were in the brothels on the south side of Buenos Aires, Argentina, in the 1880's. The women who worked in the brothels included immigrants from the Mediterranean countries, Germany and Poland, and the women liked having live bands in their workplaces. The men who patronized them were working class—gauchos, butchers, factory workers, etc. Cuban influence on the dance and on the music was heavy, hence the African as well as Mediterranean roots. From the academies of Buenos Aires to the streets, the tango became the rage at cafes. By 1904, it was performed at the Opera Theatre in Buenos Aires. The apache, the gangsters of Paris, were performing dances to tango music by the late nineteenth century, but their apache dances had a little more edge—sometimes, both parties drew knives during the dance. And then there is Hollywood. After making several so-so films, Rudolph Valentino made his breakthrough in Rex Ingram's *The Four Horsemen of the Apocalypse* (1921). Entering a sleazy dance floor in Buenos Aires, Valentino, dressed as a gaucho with a whip on his arm and a knife through his belt, tangoed his way to stardom. The tango became more socially acceptable in the twentieth century, a great dance for the triumphant posturing of both sexes. We believe if you both aren't having a good time, why do it again?

Aphrodisiacs.

When James Bond orders a bowl of conch chowder in *Thunderball* (1965), the lovely Domino corrects him, claiming the dish has no aphrodisiac effect. Bond, of course, replies that he just likes conch chowder. Do aphrodisiacs really work? That is, do things you ingest tend to make you or your sexual companions just a little more randy, a little more ready to do the wild thing? Well, some of them do. We think it was Dorothy Parker who said: "Candy is dandy, but liquor is quicker." Chocolate gives people a feeling of satisfaction, sort of a substitute for love

EVERYTHING I KNOW ABOUT LIFE I LEARNED FROM JAMES BOND

and sex. But if you have the substitute, why would you bother with sex? No, though oysters and other sea food are often mentioned as aphrodisiacs, the most likely substances to turn you on are alcohol or marijuana and marijuana's derivatives—hashish, bhang, etc. Why these substances? Because they tend to remove inhibitions. Whether it's a classic aged Burgundy from your grandparents' cellar or a joint rolled in a Zig-Zag paper by a college classmate, alcohol and marijuana cause individuals to let the fine print of responsibility go and live in the pleasure of the present. Of course, good sources of protein such as seafood certainly are useful in creating stamina in the male. Probably, the best approach for sexual activity is the classic one—a dinner in a first-class restaurant with a good wine list—perhaps a bottle of Dom Perignon, if your budget permits it; or Möet & Chandon's more reasonably priced White Star; or even Korbel's "Natural" for the American young fellow with exquisite taste. Just eat lightly and keep the lady smiling throughout the event. And be ready to say "yes" if she suggests a drink at her place later, even if it's coffee. You want to be awake for the main event. Well how about Spanish Fly (cantharides, part of the dried remains of the blister beetle)? Does it work? It works on bulls, which get an irritated urinary tract when the product is excreted. Does it work on cows? It's too dangerous. Yohimbine (a crystalline alkaloid from the bark of the yohimbé tree), does it work? Only in toxic doses. In other words, stick to dinner and fine wine. It works for James Bond; it can work for you. Trust us.

Virgins and Virgin Sacrifice.

007 actually relies on trickery to get Solitaire into bed in ***Live and Let Die*** (1973), and then after she has sacrificed her virginity to him, he continues to pump her for information about Kananga's

operation. This is a manipulative side of Bond that we haven't seen before, and we're really not sure we like it. He does eventually confess to stacking the cards against her, but we're not convinced that makes everything all right. Later in the film, even though she is no longer a virgin, Solitaire is offered up as a virgin sacrifice to Baron Samedi. In literature and mythology, virgins have always been a symbol of purity and innocence that are offered to the gods in exchange for good fortune. Hindu beliefs found that ultimate power from the Goddess Kali still rested in the murderous magic of a virgin sacrifice, while Athena, the virgin goddess from Greek mythology, could only be appeased by the sacrifice of a willing virgin. Virgins and those recently deflowered require a great deal more care and feeding than what happens to dear Solitaire in *Live and Let Die*. Most women are nervous and afraid of their first time making love. More than likely, they want to give themselves to someone whom they love deeply and passionately. They are concerned if they will do well, if they will satisfy their man, and if it will hurt. In Solitaire's case, she is also worried that she will lose her powers to foretell the future. After sex, some women have feelings of happiness and euphoria, while others experience discomfort and sadness. And most guys compound a woman's negative feelings by acting thoughtlessly or indifferently. At least, 007 had the good sense to stay with her afterwards. He does spend the night, and he also encourages her to discuss what has happened; some women won't want to talk about it until much later. Bond also takes Solitaire to do something spontaneously the next day to show that he still cares about her. This is another plus. We certainly don't advocate virgin sacrifice, and are honestly appalled that 007 sacrificed a perfectly good virgin to get ahead with his mission. But we are also realists and know that is a rite of passage for most young people. We recommend honesty and communication, then great lovemaking.

EVERYTHING I KNOW ABOUT LIFE
I LEARNED FROM JAMES BOND

Marriage.

Throughout the twenty-five films in EON's James Bond series, 007 marries only once, in *On Her Majesty's Secret Service* (1969). Statisticians may argue that Bond actually got married twice, but his marriage to Kissy Suzuki (Mie Hamma) in *You Only Live Twice* (1967) was part of his cover, and had little to do with love. When he marries the Contessa Teresa di Vincenzo or Tracy (Diana Rigg), he has genuinely fallen in love with her. In the course of the novels and the films, Bond has had sexual relations with many different woman, but brought very few back home to London to live with him. First, he had a long-lasting affair with Tiffany Case, *Diamonds Are Forever,* who lived with him through several novels, and later left to marry an American serviceman. Then, Tatiana Romanova left her home behind the Iron Curtain in *From Russia with Love* to be with Bond. And finally, in the first two films, 007 was involved with party-girl Sylvia Trench (Eunice Gayson). But he never loved them with his heart in the same way that he loved Tracy. Bond grows to love Tracy for her indomitable spirit and her vulnerability as a woman, and when he proposes to her in the snow-covered barn in the Alps, he really wants to share his life with her and her alone. Sadly, the new Mrs. Bond is gunned down by Irma Bunt, Blofeld's sinister henchwoman, just moments after the Bond wedding. Later references in *The Spy Who Loved Me* (1977) and *For Your Eyes Only* (1981) reveal that James Bond has never ever gotten over her death. Perhaps, like James Bond, there is only one true love of our lives, and when you find it, you will know that it is right.

JOHN L. FLYNN AND BOB BLACKWOOD

Homosexuals and James Bond.

In *Skyfall* (2012), the movie's multi-layered villain Silva (Javier Bardem) not only reveals that he has "mommy issues" with Judi Dench's M but also flirts with James Bond (Daniel Craig), who quips "What makes you think this is my first time?" As much as we'd like to agree with our gay friends who say that 007's quip means that he's homosexual or, at the very least, bisexual, we just don't see it. Bond is merely toying with Silva to buy himself enough time to think of a plan of escape. In the earlier James Bond films, homosexuals are played mostly for laughs, particularly in the two gay assassins, Mr. Wint (Bruce Glover) and Mr. Kidd (Putter Smith), in *Diamonds Are Forever* (1971) or the characters of Q (Geoffrey Bayldon) and Q's Assistant (John Wells) in *Casino Royale* (1967). In the novel *Goldfinger*, both Pussy Galore and Tilly Masterson are lesbians, while the film version flirts with the question but fails to deliver an answer. Similarly, there is some question about the sexual proclivities of Rosa Klebb (Lotte Lenya) in *From Russia with Love* (1963), but likewise they go unanswered. As James Bond turns sixty in the year 2022, we'd like to see other LGBTQ individuals in future Bond films but not merely as assassins or clothing designers. Silva is a step in the right direction. In *No Time to Die* (2021), Bond and Moneypenny (Naomie Harris) make a surprise visit to Q's apartment, and find him (Ben Whishaw) making dinner for a male companion who he met on a dating site. Whishaw who is openly gay had previously played gay characters, and had been lobbying the Bond team to include a gay character, as reported by Newsweek. But a gay or bi James Bond? Unless he's played by Rupert Everett, Julia Roberts' gay boyfriend in *My Best Friend's Wedding* (1997), we have serious doubts if anyone else could pull it off. Besides Ian Fleming would likely turn over in his grave.

EVERYTHING I KNOW ABOUT LIFE
I LEARNED FROM JAMES BOND

Playboy magazine.

While James Bond waits for the safe-cracking machine to break into Gumbold's safe in the solicitor's offices in ***On Her Majesty's Secret Service*** (1969), he discovers the February 1969 issue of *Playboy* magazine hidden surreptitiously among several other newspapers and magazines. He picks up the magazine, and thumbs through the pages, presumably to read the articles. (By strange coincidence, this issue features a short story by Irwin Shaw titled "Whispers in Bedlam," and 007's mission to apprehend Blofeld is codenamed "Operation Bedlam.") Later, Bond steals the centerfold, and we see just a flash of centerfold Lorrie Menconi on his way to the elevators as Gumbold returns from lunch. For years, the fictitious lifestyle of James Bond and *Playboy* magazine have been linked as a nearly synonymous cultural force. Every man in the world wants to be 007, and many feel that by reading the magazine they can acquire the styles and tastes *and women* of James Bond. This link was first established in the March 1960-issue in which author Ian Fleming introduced *Playboy* readers to his character James Bond in his first short story entitled "The Hildebrand Rarity." The relationship between Fleming and *Playboy* continued as the magazine later serialized a new Bond adventure each year (up until Fleming's death), and published ten Bond-related pictorials. Today, *Playboy* still publishes Bond's adventures as written by Raymond Benson, and features extensive pictorials from each of the Bond films. We can think of no better way to celebrate the beauty and mystique of women than in the pages of James Bond's favorite magazine.

What is James Bond's Secret?

Calm. Cool. Relaxed. Those simple three words describe James Bond's relaxed confidence, and reveal the secret why he is so successful with women. The rest of us have to struggle to achieve the relaxed confidence that comes so naturally to Agent 007. When you lack confidence, as we all do in some way or another, you have to fight to keep up a good appearance. Very often, we have to call upon a great deal of personal energy just to keep up the "act" of confidence, and then it feels artificial; like we're not "being ourselves." Women can sense that in a way that defies all reason or explanation. Without knowing the basic rules of engagement (and yes, this is a military operation), most men stumble into the arena of women and fall flat on their faces. Some persist by simulating confidence in the form of arrogance or male bravado, but that never really works. Others just give up or grab the first ugly woman who comes along and marry her. We must all remember that James Bond did not gain his relaxed confidence overnight. Confidence is something that is built over time with a great deal of perseverance and repented failure. Each time you fail, you must continue trying until you succeed. The success you receive from each task not only builds confidence but also makes you more relaxed, cool, and calm when you face that task again. Relaxation starts with physical presentation. James Bond often takes things very slowly and methodically. Slow down, and pace yourself. Cool down, and find a place within yourself that anchors all of your nerves and nervousness. Never let the opposition see you sweat. And finally, take control of your emotions, and remain calm. Remember that most women still count on men to maintain control. Some Alpha males, particularly those in a business like James Bond's, always control their emotions. They are also not afraid to show emotion if and when the situation arises, but they are never provoked to have an emotion by another person. Bond never shows his fear. He always remains calm, cool, and relaxed, and such confidence always rewards him with success. It works for him!

CHAPTER SIX

JETPACKS, BOBSLEDS, AND AUTOMOBILES

Hey driver, where we going?
I swear, my nerves are showing
Set my hopes up way too high
Living's in the way we die.

—A-Ha, ***The Living Daylights*** (1987)

The James Bond films have always been known for their exciting cars and fantastic vehicles. However, it wasn't until the third movie, ***Goldfinger*** (1964), when Bond drove a tricked-out car that the official Bond signature car came into being. Afterwards, it was a foregone conclusion that 007 would have a unique vehicle for each of his adventures. To most Americans in the early sixties, cars were a symbol of status and an outward sign of wealth and privilege, something the Europeans had known for years. The producers of the Bond movies wanted to link their hero with that image of elegance, sophistication, style, and performance, and chose some of the finest vehicles in the world for his rides. For Sean Connery, that car was always the Aston Martin DB5; for Roger Moore, the Lotus Esprit, and for Pierce Brosnan, the BMW Z-3 Roadster. We love the fact that Daniel Craig's Bond has given the Aston Martin another test drive. Throughout the course of the films, the Broccoli family has been keenly aware that, since the early sixties and in the decades that followed, one out of every seven jobs in the United States was connected directly or indirectly to the automotive industry.

Goldfinger, 1964

Our knowledge of cars and our fondness for vehicles of all kinds stems primarily from our love of the James Bond films. In our own family-styled vehicles, with Bond music playing on the car radio, we've imagined driving each of 007's cars and boats and moon-buggies. We've also raced along the European countryside on the Orient Express or blasted off in a jetpack over France or piloted a one-man gyrocopter in Japan or barreled down a Swiss mountain course in a bobsled! The cars and vehicles of the Bond films continue to tickle our imagination, and we can't wait to discover what unusual forms of transportation our hero will next use.

Sunbeam Convertible.

In ***Dr. No*** (1962), James Bond relies on the 1962 Sunbeam Convertible to travel the back roads of Jamaica on his way to Miss Taro's house, and expertly maneuvers it to evade the three blind assassins in their hearse. The 1962 Sunbeam was a small, two-seater sports car convertible with sleek, stylish lines, which a man of elegance and sophistication, like Bond, would have chosen as his weekend getaway car. While it contained no special modifications from Q-branch, the sports car proved to be very maneuverable on the twisty roads of Jamaica.

Hearse.

Dr. No's three blind assassins drive a black, 1930 La Salle Hearse. No other vehicle in the world invokes a sense of dread, death, and destruction the way a hearse does in a motion picture. Each time the hearse appears in ***Dr. No***, people die. The very grim vehicle first appears when the three blind assassins gun down Strangways outside the Queen's Club, then again when Strangways' secretary dies, and finally, when the hearse is trying to run James Bond's Sunbeam off a cliff. Ultimately, 007 prevails and sends the hearse and its three occupants plunging to an explosive and horrible death.

Dragon Tank.

Dr. No relies on the myth of a fire-breathing dragon to protect him from the locals on his island fortress. But James Bond discovers this so-called "dragon" is actually a custom-built armored tank, painted with "eyes" and "teeth" to look like a dragon. After they penetrate Dr. No's outer defenses, Quarrel,

Bond and Honey Ryder came under attack by the tank. During the one-sided struggle, Quarrel is killed by the tank's flamethrower cannon, and Bond and Honey are captured and taken to Dr. No's headquarters.

Bentley Mark IV Convertible.

Although the cinematic James Bond will be forever associated with the Aston Martin DB-5, his literary counterpart preferred a Bentley to just about any other car. In *Casino Royale*, he drives a four-and-a-half litre Bentley with an Amherst Villers supercharger. Built in 1930, James Bond is said to have purchased the battleship-gray convertible coupe in 1933, and kept it in storage throughout the Second World War. Although it was badly damaged in *Casino Royale*, Bond's Bentley was repaired so that he could drive it during his *Moonraker* mission and then later in *Thunderball*. The Bentley Mark IV Convertible makes its first onscreen appearance in *From Russia with Love* (1963) and is driven extensively by Sir James Bond in *Casino Royale* (1967). Apparently, there were no lethal devices in this classic car with the exception of 007 himself. It did have a mobile telephone, however, and it spoke of great style wherever it was driven.

Aston Martin DB5.

Perhaps the most famous of all the James Bond cars, the Aston Martin DB5 was the first car in the film series to be modified and fitted with a lethal array of gadgets from Q Branch. In 1964, each Aston Martin was handmade at the factory, one vehicle at a time, and was considered a first-class luxury car well before it made its cinematic debut in *Goldfinger*. James Bond actually preferred the 1933 Bentley convertible, which he had driven for a number of years, but later became very fond of the DB5, especially after its gadgets saved his life several times. The silver birch Aston Martin sports car was outfitted with tire shredders which could be extended from the hub, bullet proof windshields, a retractable bullet shield which emerged from the trunk, revolving number plates (BMT 216A, 4711-EA-62, LU6789) which were valid in all countries, retractable dual machine guns mounted below the headlights, oil slick and smoke screen dispensers, an early form of GPS tracking system, and an ejector seat for ejecting unwanted passengers. Also fitted but never used in the film were a set of extendable front bumpers, a device which threw dozens of nails from the rear light, and an arsenal of weapons under the driver's seat. Bond used most of the gadgets during the course of his mission, but he was particularly fond of the tire shredders. They allowed him to flatten the tires on Tilly Masterson's car, so that he could meet her by "accident." Regrettably, Bond smashed the Aston Martin when he was trying to elude Goldfinger's men, and Q has never quite forgiven him for it. In 1963, the Aston Martin Company, which is now owned by Ford, loaned Eon Productions a prototype DB5 for filming. All of the now-famous gadgets were dreamt up by Guy Hamilton, Paul Dehn and Richard Maibaum and were built into the prototype by special effects wizard John Stears at Pinewood Studios. Ultimately, after Stears had completed his unique modifications, the producers had to pay for the Aston Martin, but with the huge success of the film, both at the box office and for EON Productions, the company never had to spend money on another car again. A second car, also loaned by Aston Martin, was used by the second unit for filming when the primary was not available. Despite Peter Hunt's superior editing, film geeks can tell the two apart by the different housing for the license plates and by a gold reflector plate near the front air-intake panel. Two additional cars were supplied by Aston Martin for publicity when it became clear what a tremendous success the film was. The Aston Martin DB-5 makes two fan-pleasing returns to the film series in *Tomorrow Never Dies* (1997) and *Casino Royale* (2006), and returns for its last hurrah in *Skyfall* (2012), and then inexplicably, *No Time to Die* (2021) when it once again is called to save Bond's life.

Rolls Royce Phantom 337.

While most fans of the film *Goldfinger* remember the Aston Martin DB5, two other famous cars made their debuts in the motion picture—Auric Goldfinger's Rolls Royce Phantom 337 and Tilly Masterson's Ford Mustang. Like the Aston Martin, the yellow and black Phantom 337 was also a classic luxury automobile, with less than one hundred produced by Rolls Royce worldwide. The vehicle, which reeked of European old money, was unique in that it featured a closed cabin for passengers and an open cabin for the driver. Auric Goldfinger used the car to smuggle gold, in place of its armored plating, from one country to the next. Even Bond was impressed when he saw the Rolls at the Stoke Poges Country Club.

Ford Mustang Convertible.

The less expensive Ford Mustang was first introduced in April 1964, and the yellow convertible, which was driven in the film *Goldfinger* by Tilly Masterson, was the vehicle's first appearance in a major motion picture. Following Goldfinger to Switzerland, Tilly attempts to assassinate the nefarious villain with a single rifle shot to avenge her sister Jill's death. However, her accuracy, and her car, let her down when she "runs into" Bond and his Aston Martin DB5. Double blow-out—the tires must have had a defect of some kind.

Bell Textron Jet Pack.

In *Thunderball* (1965), Bond blew off Colonel Boitier's château with the Bell Textron Jet Pack strapped to his back, and jetted into the history books with his short onscreen flight. One year earlier, at the 1964 World's Fair, U.S. Army pilot Bill Suitor demonstrated the jet pack for the first time, and Cubby Broccoli thought that 007 should use one in the next Bond film. Consisting of two tanks filled with propellant and a turbine thruster, the jet pack could reach six-hundred feet and stay aloft for four minutes. Of course, it was large, and it really couldn't fit into the trunk of Bond's Aston Martin DB5, but who noticed? We're both still waiting for a functional jet pack to hit the shelves at Walmart, as Bond said in *Thunderball*, "No well-dressed man should be without one."

BSA Lightning Motorcycle.

Fiona Volpe's BSA had a gold colored body and fuel tank plus a rocket launcher on both sides of her motorcycle. She certainly had no trouble matching speed with Count Lippe's car. And she certainly had control of her vehicle, as we saw when she dumped it into a lake in *Thunderball*.

The Disco Volante.

Emilio Largo's ship in *Thunderball* was a hi-tech yacht, a combination of a hydrofoil with a very high speed and a shell, armed with machine-guns and a large naval gun, which had to be jettisoned so the hydrofoil could speed away. The hydrofoil was fairly inexpensive, a used ship bought cheaply, but making it into the Disco Volante was a challenge. Only a couple of bolts held it together. The moviemakers were lucky they weren't filming during the tropical storm season.

Little Nellie.

In the first film in the series that James Bond does not drive a car or a truck, 007 does pilot one of the most popular vehicles produced by Q-Branch. The aerial version of Bond's beloved Aston Martin DB-5, this small one-seater autogyro packs a punch that Blofeld's helicopter pilots will not soon forget in *You Only Live Twice* (1967). "Little Nellie," nicknamed by her father Q, arrives in Japan in four large alligator bags, and is quickly assembled into a nine-and-a-half-foot long, two hundred and fifty-pound gyrocopter. It comes equipped with heat-seeking air-to-air missiles, left and right forward-firing rocket launchers, rear-firing dual flamethrowers, smoke screen dispensers, dual machine-guns, and aerial mines. It has a maximum altitude of eighteen thousand feet, and is perfect for recon missions into hostile territory. The real gyrocopter was invented by Ken Wallis, and he doubles for Sean Connery in most of the aerial sequences filmed in Japan and Spain.

Toyota 2000 GT.

In *You Only Live Twice*, Aki drives a white, 1966 Toyota 2000 GT, two-seater convertible with modifications from Japanese SIS. The special modifications include a small color television and surveillance monitor, an FM transceiver, a hidden voice-activated tape recorder, a video cassette deck (installed in the glove box), and several other counterintelligence options. With a top speed of two hundred and thirty kilometres-per-hour, the trendy little sports car is perfect for zipping through the streets of Tokyo. Aki rescues Bond from assassins outside Osato Enterprises, and uses one of her car's gadgets to call in a special "air drop" when she is unable to shake them on the highway to Kobe.

Bird 1 Spacecraft.

Blofeld's Bird 1 Spacecraft was a large reusable, chemical-reaction rocket that took off like a conventional Saturn V rocket, and returned to Earth with its payload like a space shuttle, landing upright on four retractable legs like a lunar-excursion module. The spacecraft stands sixty-six feet tall, and when fully fueled with liquid oxygen, weighs approximately 3,000 tons. Half of its overall length was a cargo bay which, when split open into four equal parts, was capable of swallowing another space capsule whole. Piloted by two SPECTRE astronauts, Bird 1 seizes both an American Gemini capsule and a Russian Soyuz capsule in geo-synchronous orbit. Thankfully, Bond was able to destroy the spacecraft before it could seize a third capsule in *You Only Live Twice* (1967).

Aston Martin DB-S.

In *On Her Majesty's Secret Service* (1969), in an effort to link their new James Bond (George Lazenby) to the legacy left by Sean Connery's Bond, Albert R. Broccoli and Harry Saltzman dressed him in the same Saville Row suits, equipped him with the same Walther PPK and Rolex watch and outfitted him with the newest model Aston Martin, the Aston Martin DB-S.

EVERYTHING I KNOW ABOUT LIFE
I LEARNED FROM JAMES BOND

Silver-gray in color, the sporty two-seater has no obvious high-tech modifications beyond a hidden compartment for holding the sniper rifle Bond carried in *From Russia with Love* (1963). But the DB-S is fast and maneuverable, and serves Bond well as he chases Tracy's Ford Cougar on a highway on the coast of Portugal. Later in the film, he drives the Aston Martin DB-S to M's home at Quarterdeck and to the College of Arms in London. Still handmade at the factory, one vehicle at a time, the DB-S was considered a first-class luxury car only affluent gentle-men (and secret agents) could afford.

Ford Cougar.

Tracy's red convertible, which she refers to as her big M, is a very rare 1969 Mercury Cougar CJ428 convertible supplied by the Ford Motor Company to *On Her Majesty's Secret Service* (1969). The producers selected the Ford convertible as a subtle homage to the 1964 ½ Mustang convertible that Tilly Masterson drives in *Goldfinger* (1964). In fact, Bond's accidental meeting with Tracy along the winding road in Portugal mirrors, in many ways, his meeting with Tilly along a similar winding road in Switzerland several years earlier. Tracy's Cougar is bright red, with mag wheels and excellent speed and agility. Later in the film, when Bond and Tracy are being chased by Blofeld's henchmen, she drives her car into a demoli tion derby at a local ice arena, and easily outmaneuvers their Mercedes. Of course, the American-made sports car is no match for a European blizzard, and they are forced to abandon the car in a Swiss barn. Thank providence that Tracy had the good sense to have an optional ski-rack installed on her trunk, and she brought two sets of skis and poles.

Mercedes Benz.

Irma Bunt and the rest of Blofeld's henchmen travel in a black, classic Mercedes Benz. Not as fancy as Bond's Aston Martin DB-S, the Mercedes Benz has always represented tradition and elegance. Since 1886, the company has been one of the world's most successful automotive companies, and most Americans view the Mercedes Benz as a car for the wealthy. The classic Mercedes from the film is virtually indestructible, and thus, it should come as no surprise that Blofeld and his cinematic counterparts usually rely on the vehicle (in classic black) as a weapon of death and destruction.

Bobsled.

In an early version of the script for ***On Her Majesty's Secret Service*** (1969), Bond was originally going to chase Blofeld down the bobsled course, sitting on a shovel, but thankfully cooler heads prevailed. Now, when the head of SPECTRE escapes the destruction of Piz Gloria in a two-man bobsled, James Bond jumps into a sporty, orange and white bobsled in pursuit. Eventually, the two adversaries end up in the same sled, and are forced to duke it out for control of the cable-rudders and hand-brake.

1971 Red Mustang Fastback.

The 1971 Mustang Fastback was one of the largest that Ford built. The standard engine for the Mach 1 was a 351 Cleveland V8 with 285 bhp, but a 330 bhp model was also available. You will note that it handled beautifully in the fast turns both in and out of the parking lot when Bond was pursued by the sheriff's motorized posse in ***Diamonds Are Forever*** (1971).

EVERYTHING I KNOW ABOUT LIFE
I LEARNED FROM JAMES BOND

Moon Buggy.

James Bond had learned about the satellite with the diamond laser that would be threatening the planet. He then had to leave in a hurry. Yes, they were doing a dry run about exploring the moon. Bond grabbed the first thing available, a moon buggy. Luckily, the desert terrain around Las Vegas resembled the surface of the moon, making the buggy a good choice vs. the sedans of the Willard Whyte security force. Nevertheless, the original Moon Buggy wheels had to be replaced as they came off during the chase rehearsal.

All-Terrain Vehicle.

Obviously, the sedans were not going to catch the moon buggy. Cleverly, the security force turned to three-wheeled ATV's to catch the elusive James Bond. In 1970, Honda brought to U.S.A. the first three-wheeled, all-terrain vehicles. They were just the thing for really rough broken ground, but, even so, the riders would occasionally take a spill. Thank goodness James Bond was there to take advantage of a rider who did.

Bathosubmarine.

The bathosubmarine was a special mini-sub created for Blofeld's use in ***Diamonds Are Forever*** (1971). Bond seized control of the crane that was lowering the bathosubmarine to the ocean and used the sturdy vehicle, designed to take deep underwater pressures, to destroy the control room that was manipulating Blofeld's satellite with its diamond laser.

Hang Glider.

Bond literally drops in on Kananga's mountain-top hideaway on San Monique using a conventional hang glider in *Live and Let Die* (1973). In 1973, the extreme sport of hang-gliding took flight when the first American-built delta wings appeared over ski resorts in the French Alps. Because it was relatively novel, the producers decided to add hang-glid ing to their new 007's repertoire of skills. Movie-goers were thrilled by the spectacle of James Bond cutting the cable-tow to Quarrel's boat and gliding safely to land on his hang glider's delta wings. In the years between 1973 and 1980 hang-gliding became a huge sensation in Europe and then throughout the world. So much so, that, when Bond's high-flying exploits in a hang glider take him over Iguacu Falls in Brazil six years later in *Moonraker*, the stunt almost seems rather routine.

Double-Decker Bus.

In order to escape the corrupt law enforcement officers on the payroll of Dr. Kananga in *Live and Let Die* (1973), James Bond steals a double-decker bus from a small village on the island of San Monique, and drives it under a very low bridge. Meanwhile, 007's one and only passenger Solitaire hangs on for dear life in the back of the bus. The double-decker bus is a motor vehicle designed with two levels to accommodate more passengers. Originally employed as part of the Greater London public transportation system, they are extensively used throughout England, Hong Kong, Singapore, and other cities in the former British Empire. These buses are also popular as tour buses visiting tourist attractions in most of the major cities in the world. The double-decker bus that Bond commandeers is the Routemaster, a specific model that was first introduced in London in the early 1960s and has become something of an icon. The bus features an open-rear platform for passenger entry and exit, while the driver occupies a cab that is totally isolated from the passenger section. We're not satisfied the top would sheer away as easily as it does in the film, but the sequence is still memorable. Besides who wants to see James Bond stuck in a bus under a low bridge? That would be as bad as listening to the Beatles with earmuffs on!

Glastron Boats.

Called Stingers, the two Glastron speedboats that James Bond pilots through the Louisiana bayou in *Live and Let Die* have a top speed of two hundred miles-per-hour and can jump one hundred and fifteen feet in the air, which is the world record. After narrowly escaping the crocodile farm, 007 steals a red and white speedboat with an outboard engine, and races along the swampy mashes just outside Sidell, Louisiana. Further down the river, at a dead end where Sheriff J.W. Pepper has cornered one of his assailants, Bond begins to run out of water. Determined to keep on going, 007 launches his boat into the air, jumping not only the road bank but also Pepper's patrol car. The stunt is an impressive one for the record books, and sets the bar pretty high for any future boat chases. Later, Bond is forced to trade his boat for a faster one, and dukes it out with a far superior inboard with chromed pipes and exhaust. [The speedboat chase was originally written for *Diamonds Are Forever*, with Bond pursuing Blofeld on Lake Meade.]

AMC Matador.

Cinematically, it must have been a good year for American Motor Corporation's publicity department. Not only was James Bond driving an AMC Hornet in *The Man with the Golden Gun*

(1975), but Scaramanga had a flying Matador, and we don't mean a Spanish toreador with a gold American Express card. When Bond in the Hornet pulled up to what looked like an old barn/factory building, out the back door went Scaramanga and Nick Nack in their Matador with a wing assembly and an airplane engine with a propeller on the top. Someone actually had developed a car plane by 1975, but it did not look anything like a regular vehicle in its over-the-road unit. What we did enjoy, however, was Miss Goodnight opening the trunk in mid-flight because she thought the car had stopped. Evidently, she must have been almost deaf. Otherwise, the airplane engine at work would have been creating a roaring sound and causing the entire structure to vibrate; perhaps she thought it was a noisy air conditioning fan.

Bond's AMC Hornet.

When James Bond teases J.W. just before he makes the leap across the river from the half-demolished bridge, we were too impressed by the sight of the stunt vehicle spiraling through the air to laugh in ***The Man with the Golden Gun*** (1975). Apparently, Cubby Broccoli had seen the stunt performed in a car show in the U.S.A. Later, after getting a computer visualization that employed some information from the National Safety Council, they did the stunt in one take. W. J. Milligan, Jr. was the stunt coordinator. "Bumps" Willard did the jump. Everyone on the set was amazed. The Hornet they used for the jump was no stock car. It had been rebuilt and rebalanced to ensure that it could make the jump in one piece.

Bond's RC-3 Seabee Seaplane.

Bond's seaplane was a small, short-bodied "pusher" seaplane

which cruised at one hundred and seventeen miles. When we see the pleasure that Scaramanga takes in destroying the beautiful little flying boat, we are reminded again that this man likes to destroy things, as well as people. Now, when was the last time you were offended by a seaplane? We rest our case.

Scaramanga's Chinese Junk.

Scaramanga's (and later, Bond's) junk was a classic Chinese junk in the Hong Kong mode. Its exterior allowed it to blend in with the traffic on the South China Sea, though junks have crossed the open water of the Pacific Ocean, on occasion. Inside the junk, however, we see all the comforts of home to a European—an engine to drive the junk and to provide electricity, a master bedroom with electronic communication devices, a large bed, and, definitely, a refrigerator to keep the champagne at the proper temperature.

Lotus Esprit.

One of the things that had been lacking in the two previous films was a signature car for James Bond. 007 had driven or piloted a double-decker bus, numerous boats, a factory-new Hornet (right out of the showroom), a plane, a Chinese junk, and a hang-glider, but nothing specifically designed for him by Q Branch. With the deliberate attempt to make Roger Moore's Bond more like that of his predecessor, the filmmakers decided to put him behind the wheel of a tricked-out Lotus Esprit. Like the Aston Martin DB-5 before it, the Lotus Esprit was modified and fitted with a lethal array of gadgets from Q Branch. In 1977, the Lotus Esprit was one of the finest and most expensive luxury sports cars in the world, and made its cinematic debut in *The Spy Who Loved Me*. James Bond actually preferred his 1933 Bentley convertible, but had settled for the Aston Martin DB-5 because of its ingenious gadgets that had saved his life. The pearl-white Lotus Esprit had the capability to transform into a submarine, and was outfitted with retractable wheels (with extendable covers to protect the wheel cavity) fins and rudders for navigation below the sea, a convertible dashboard which doubled as a submarine control system, radar and nautical guidance equipment, metal blinds, retractable propeller units, and a periscope. Its defensive systems included surface-to-air missiles, underwater mines, oil slick, rear-mounted concrete sprayers, harpoons for close-quarter underwater combat, and a self-destruct system. Also fitted, but never used in the film, were the revolving number plates, which were valid in all countries; the single number plate "PPW 306R" served 007 throughout his mission. Q personally delivered the Lotus Esprit to Bond on Corsica, and warned him to be careful with the car. 007 ignored him. Through no fault of his own, however, the car sprung a leak during his reconnoiter of Atlantis, and Bond was forced to make an impromptu "landing" on a heavily-used beach. Sales of the Lotus Esprit nearly doubled after its appearance in the film, and prompted filmmakers to bring it back four years later. Nicknamed "Wet Nellie" (after the Little Nellie helicopter in *You Only Live Twice*), the Lotus returned in *For Your Eyes Only*. After the release, demand for the Lotus surged to the point that new customers had to be placed on a three-year waiting list.

Lotus Esprit Turbo.

Just as the Aston Martin DB-5 was the signature car of the Sean

EVERYTHING I KNOW ABOUT LIFE
I LEARNED FROM JAMES BOND

Connery Bonds, the Lotus Esprit was Roger Moore's signature car. Ironically, Melina's French-made Citroen 2CV, not the Lotus Esprit, runs rings around a couple of pursuit cars when the Lotus deploys its self-destruct system in *For Your Eyes Only* (1981). Q does manage to put all of the pieces back together, and give the Lotus a new paint job. Due to the popular success of the Lotus Esprit, Q-Branch modified a later model of the vehicle for Bond's use. The White Lotus Esprit Turbo featured double-red pinstripes, alloy wheels, and a self-destruct system packed with four one-pound packs of C4 explosive. 007 follows Hector Gonzales to Madrid, and parks the car just off the main road into the hitman's Spanish estate. When his guards attempt to gain illegal entry into the vehicle, the Lotus explodes into a million tiny little pieces (and takes a couple of bad guys with it). Later in the mission, Bond shows up in Cortina, Italy, with a red-colored version of the same car, equipped especially with a trunk-mounted skirack. James Bond had nothing but praise for his new sports car, and while he still prefers the Aston Martin DB-5 for his own personal use, he is always pleased to take the Lotus out for a spin.

Wet Bike.

The wet bike makes its first appearance on film when James Bond needs a speedy transport to Atlantis in *The Spy Who Loved Me* (1977). This seated-version of the very popular Jet Ski was the first of its kind in the world, and launched a whole new industry for water sports' fans and the public at large. Made from a fiberglass, the wet bike contained lots of safety features that made it ideal for weekend enthusiasts. It had an automatic engine cut-off valve, an anti-capsizing mechanism, two wide-body skis, and a Jet Ski engine that could travel up to sixty miles an hour. Delivered to the *USS Wayne* by Q Branch, Bond was able to quickly assemble the bike, and rescue Anya from Stromberg before the torpedo attack destroyed Atlantis.

Gondola/Hovercraft.

Venice was built on a series of islands to avoid the attention of Lombards and other raiders during the fifth century A.D. and following centuries. The city was built on a total of one hundred and eighteen separate islands. To connect these islands, you must travel over four hundred or more bridges. There is no point in trying to drive an automobile through Venice, though you might be able to do it with a lightweight motorcycle (a vehicle considered, but rejected, for James Bond in 1979's *Moonraker.*) You could not get the car over most of the bridges. But there is nowhere in Venice that you could not get via a gondola, a shallow draft boat without a keel. It requires an art to pole a gondola down the many canals of Venice. To have an inboard motor in your gondola requires some effort. To also have a hovercraft built into a gondola seems almost impossible to anyone but Q. It should be noted, however, that the *Moonraker* tech crew started with parts of several gondolas when creating and maintaining Bond's gondola. To put it simply, James Bond is hard on his vehicles. But we did enjoy the reaction of the people in Saint Mark's Square when he cruised by them. He is the most visible secret agent, but we like him for it! If you are wondering how they propelled that gondola through the square, don't start looking for a tow rope. Stay with the illusion.

Glastron Speedboat/Hang Glider.

Glastron Corporation made the speedboats that appear in ***Live and Let Die***, ***The Man with the Golden Gun***, and *Moonraker*.

EVERYTHING I KNOW ABOUT LIFE
I LEARNED FROM JAMES BOND

The firm, originally based in Austin, TX, in 1956, was the first large-scale manufacturer of fiberglass runabouts in the world. The boats run from fourteen feet to twenty-four feet. Glastron has built over three hundred sixty thousand of them since its founding. It has built some with deep-vee Aqua Lift hulls. It built twenty-six speedboats for *Live and Let Die*, and the stunt people destroyed seventeen of them doing stunts—the largest stunt being a world record jump of one hundred and ten feet. In *Moonraker*, they designed a custom boat which inspired the Glastron/Carlson Scimitar, a twenty-thre-foot model with removable tinted roof panels, a safety glass windshield, power seats, a center console and an overhead switch panel. Surprise! It was selected Boat of the Year by *Powerboat* magazine. It did not, however, have a hang-glider on the top. So keep your Scimitar away from Niagara Falls and other dangerous spots unless you have a one-man jetpack stashed in the galley.

Drax's Moonraker Space Shuttle.

When Cubby Broccoli decided to go with *Moonraker* and its 1979 release, he wanted a match between his Moonraker and NASA's shuttle Columbia, which first flew in 1981. As you can see by the dates of the film's release and the Columbia's first flight, Broccoli wanted to capitalize on the publicity building for the first flight. Broccoli was trying to get "science fact" into his film. Both vehicles consisted of an orbiter vehicle attached to solid rocket boosters and an external fuel tank. Rockwell International made the Columbia. Some of the footage of *Moonraker* was shot at Rockwell International facilities in Palmdale, California, and at the Vehicle Assembly Building at Cape Canaveral, Florida. The Columbia shuttle weigh four-and-a-half million pounds, was one hundred and fifty feet high and twelve feet around its cylindrical area. Unlike Drax's special vehicle, none of them had a laser in the nose to destroy satellites. And if Drax had not been too cheap to make an extra shuttle for his program, James Bond would not have been any the wiser about Drax's nefarious plot.

Neptune Submarine.

Bond and Melina Havelock use the deep-sea submersible, two-man submarine to travel to the extreme depths of the Mediterranean Sea to salvage the wreck of the *St. Georges*. The Neptune submarine comes complete with robotic pick-up arms and an airlock chamber for deep-sea divers. Ideal for marine archaeological research, 007 discovers the craft is also a formidable weapon in the hands of an expert mariner like himself.

Citroen 2CV.

When Bond's Lotus Esprit Turbo is destroyed by henchman, 007 must rely on Melina Havelock's bright yellow Citroen 2CV to escape pursuers on a narrow Spanish road in ***For Your Eyes Only*** (1981). The French-made car was designed for city driving and short jaunts in the country, not racing bad guys. Bond pushes the car to jump over several obstacles, including some olive trees, and rolls the car not once but twice in order to elude his pursuers. Eventually, 007 manages to outsmart the henchmen, and uses their turbo-powered engines against them. At the end of the chase, Melina doesn't seem to mind that her bright yellow Citroen 2CV has been battered and bruised. She survives and thrives!

EVERYTHING I KNOW ABOUT LIFE
I LEARNED FROM JAMES BOND

Acrostar Mini-Jet.

At just under twelve-feet long, the Acrostar Mini Jet is the world's smallest jet aircraft. Powered by a micro-turbo TRS-18 single jet engine, the plane is capable of speeds of over three hundred miles per hour, and has the maneuverability to manage a ninety-degree roll in very tight quarters. It also had the capability of climbing to thirty thousand feet with a climb rate of two thousand eight hundred feet per second. The Acrostar's retractable wings are ideal for small storage areas. During the course of his mission in *Octopussy*, James Bond pilots the jet out of the back of a horse trailer (where it has been hidden by the fake hind quarters of a horse), and sets out to destroy the hangar where an experimental aircraft is housed. After narrowly escaping one heat-seeking missile, he is closely tracked by another. Unable to shake the persistent missile, Bond dives into the hangar, and flies straight through, out a very narrow exit. The missile explodes on impact with the ground, destroying the hangar and all its contents. The Acrostar Mini-Jet was one of only two in existence, both owned and operated by stunt pilot Corkey Fornof. [This pre-credits sequence was originally planned for *Moonraker*, but was later shelved as too dangerous.]

The Nene Valley Steam Train.

007's dramatic struggle aboard Octopussy's Traveling Circus train was filmed on the Nene Valley Steam Railway in Peterborough, near Cambridgeshire, England. The NVR is a standard gauge railway which runs for seven and a half miles from Peterborough, through the haunted Wansford tunnel, to Yarwell Junction. Steam trains (like the NVR and the Orient Express) were once the stuff of legend, and have a unique appeal to rail enthusiasts all around the world. The very first passenger train along the Nene Valley departed Peterborough at seven o'clock on Monday, June 2, 1845, and ran continuously for one hundred and twenty-seven years until British Rail ended the service in 1972. James Bond has not traveled by steam train since his adventure in Istanbul in *From Russia with Love* (1963).

Crocodile Submarine.

James Bond relies on a crocodile submarine, built by Q-branch, to spy on the waters surrounding Octopussy's floating palace. This full-size replica of a crocodile with an outer fiberglass hull covered in authentic crocodile skin is designed for one man to lay flat inside the hull and look out through the mouth of the beast. With opening and closing jaws, the crocodile submarine is powered by a quiet electric motor that propels its fake tail through water.

Rocket-assisted Motorcycle.

Q started with a basic Yamaha XJ 650 Turbo black motorcycle. It has 653cc, seventy-three horsepower and a top speed of one hundred and twenty-seven miles per hour. Then Q added a rocket-assist so that Bond could leap over blocking cars, as he does in *Never Say Never Again* in the race alongside the waterfront. The rocket-assist is particularly valuable when you link it to a diagonal ramp, as Bond does when he uses the rising back door of the truck to jump over some of his former pursuers in their sedans. Thank Her Majesty for the skill of Q. How would James Bond get out of these tight spots without Q's foresight? In *No Time to Die*, 007 uses the Tiger 900 and Scrambler 1200 Triumph motorcycles for the film's key stunt sequences.

EVERYTHING I KNOW ABOUT LIFE
I LEARNED FROM JAMES BOND

ST-7B One-Man Transporter.

We saw James Bond in a jet pack escaping from SPECTRE hoodlums after eliminating their cross-dressing boss in *Thunderball* (1965). In *Never Say Never Again*, however, we see James Bond and Felix Leiter using the U.S. Navy's ST-7B OneMan Transporters to attack SPECTRE opponents. We always like to see Bond on the attack. And when we see Bond and Leiter blasting from the depths of the sea in missiles which turn into a type of one-man jetpack, we were thrilled. We would like to use one of them during rush hour.

Bond's Renault Half-taxi.

We enjoyed following James Bond's path with the commandeered Renault taxi in *A View to a Kill* (1985). It went downstairs; it drove atop a bus. It slipped under barriers; it frightened people on the Parisian boulevards. It suddenly became topless. Then, it continues on only two wheels. He runs up a heck of a bill for damages, as M is not hesitant to tell him. We can only say that if we could buy a Renault automobile that could, out of the dealer's showroom, stand up to that kind of assault, we would gladly buy it immediately.

Bond's Iceberg Boat.

Q put together a camouflaged boat for James Bond in *A View to a Kill* (1985), thanks to a mass of fiberglass. Since it is intended to pass as a small iceberg, it would have to float on top of the water. It does not have visible windows; if it did, it could not pass as an iceberg. If it is a submersible, which we suspect, it would need to jettison the fiberglass iceberg camouflage before proceeding underwater. Regardless of its construction, it certainly provides a cozy nook for some cozy nooky.

Aston Martin Volante.

After putting Roger Moore's 007 behind the wheel of the foreign-made Lotus Esprit for two missions, the producers decided to return to Aston Martin of England for Timothy Dalton in *The Living Daylights* (1987). They wanted to link their new James Bond to the same tradition of style, elegance and sophistication that had once been associated with Sean Connery's 007. In the intervening years, Aston Martin had become a subsidiary of the Ford Motor Company, and while the cars still represented some of the finest vehicles in the world, they were no longer hand-produced one at a time. Not as famous as the DB-5, the Aston Martin Volante was especially modified and fitted with a similar lethal array of gadgets from Q Branch. The gun-metal black, 1986 Aston Martin V8 sports car was outfitted with a cutting laser mounted in the port and starboard hubcaps, bullet proof windshields, retractable ski outriggers for snow driving, retractable tire studs for more traction while driving on snow and ice, a rocket booster, a guided missile system consisting of two stinger missiles hidden behind the fog lights and a targeting display, a full frequency car radio, and a self-destruct system. Bond used most of the gadgets during the course of his mission, but he was particularly fond of the cutting laser; it allowed him to cut a police car in half during a car chase. Regrettably, Bond smashed the undercarriage of the Aston Martin when he was trying to leap over a cement barrier at the border, and subsequently crashed into a snow bank. 007 was forced to abandon his car, setting the self-destruct before moving on. And to think that Q (Desmond Llewelyn) had just given the vehicle a new coat of paint! The Aston Martin DBS V8 Vantage appears in the film as a coupe and as the soft-top Volante version.

EVERYTHING I KNOW ABOUT LIFE
I LEARNED FROM JAMES BOND

Audi 200 Quattro.

James Bond also drives an Audi 200 Quattro in *The Living Daylights* that Saunders (Thomas Wheatley) has requisitioned from Station V-Vienna. Stone-gray metallic in color, the Audi 200 Quattro serves Bond well as he delivers General Koskov to the Trans-Siberian Gas Pipeline Station, and then makes his own way out of the country. While driving in the car with Saunders, Bond says memorably, "If he [M] fires me, I'll thank him for it."

HH-65A Dolphin Helicopter.

We never imagined lassoing another aircraft in mid-air and towing it home, but James Bond does just that with the help of the Coast Guard's HH-65A Dolphin Helicopter (which weighs around nine thousand pounds and has two gas turbine engines with a top speed of one hundred and sixty-five knots) in *Licence to Kill* (1989). Try it sometime when you have nothing to do but risk your life at two thousand feet or, alternatively, to play another round of Russian roulette. If you radically change the point of balance in a light single-engine airplane, the engine will stall out. Then, with the proper copter, you can tow it home. We prefer first class seats in a Boeing 747, thanks.

Cigarette Café Racer.

Whenever James Bond gets in a bar fight in Bimini, he has his Cigarette Café Racer docked by the bar. "Cigarette" boats earned their name from the cigarette smugglers who used them to bring untaxed cigarettes into France and Italy post-World War II. They were faster than any country's patrol boats and big enough to carry a light but profitable cargo. A thirty-five feet long Cigarette Café Racer TD built in 1994, powered by twin 540 Hawk engines (six-hundred fifty horsepower each), will reach eighty-two miles-per-hour on a calm sea. If you have to ask about the cost of owning and maintaining one, you can't afford it (asking price of $130,000, used, plus marriage to a relative of an oil sheik to keep it running).

BMW Z-Series.

In *GoldenEye* (1995), James Bond drives the BMW Z-3 Roadster with the top down along the shoreline, and catches some warm tropical rays with the requisite Bond girl at his side. In *The World Is not Enough* (1999), Agent 007 was again behind the wheel of a convertible in the BMW Z-8 Roadster. For both films, the producers went with the very popular and affordable luxury cars from the German automobile manufacturer in an effort to establish their new James Bond (Pierce Brosnan) with his own signature car and to reap millions of dollars in product placement from their new films. For several years, John drove the limited James Bond edition of the BMW Z-3 Roadster. **BMW 750iL Sedan.** Q turns this car over to James Bond garbed as an Avis representative in *Tomorrow Never Dies* (1997). Some think it is a V-8; it is really the larger 5.4-liter V-12 engine model with rear wheel drive, ABS and four disk brakes. The standard models include remote control interior monitoring anti-theft protection, as well as audio anti-theft protection. Q made a few modifications, however, with James Bond's needs in mind. They include: twelve STS missiles mounted under the sunroof, remote control drive and ignition via Bond's cell phone, electric-shock and tear gas dispenser security systems, cable cutters that rise from the BMW logo on the hood, re-inflatable tires (try to buy these at your Firestone dealers, ha!), machine-guns (not used this time), bulletproof glass and body armor, and droppable caltrops (spikes) for shredding tires. Luckily, Mr. Bond has never been in the bank-robbing business. He would be hard to stop on a fast road. The cost without Q's modifications would run about $100,000.

BMW R1200C Motorcycle.

James Bond and Wai Lin were certainly born to be wild in *Tomorrow Never Dies*. If you feel that you were also born to be wild, you could hit the road in a BMW R1200 Cruiser Classic motorcycle, a heavy machine designed by BMW for the open road. It will feel free to take on the Harley-Davidson motorcycles but with a European difference. BMW had never made a highway cruiser motorcycle before, but, since one out of three motorcycles made are cruisers, BMW thought it should enter the market. The Boxer engine is a two cylinder, four stroke 1170 cc engine with fuel injection and a five speed gearbox. The top speed is one hundred and four miles-per-hour. It is a heavy bike at over five hundred and sixty pounds with the tanks full. The cost to you is about $15,000. It does corner better than other cruiser motorcycles, something that James Bond and Wai Lin must have appreciated as they sped down alleys and over rooftops.

Stealth Ship.

What a clever device the stealth ship was in *Tomorrow Never Dies*! The low-level stealth ship was painted black, was similar to a catamaran in design, had some sort of device to mask radar detection, and contained at least one surface-to-air missile as well as a Cruise missile firing tube. It contained a Sea Drill for demolishing ships and, like all of Carver's offices, a host of closed-circuit cameras and large screen monitors. The ship's design was similar to that of a U.S. Navy stealth boat model that the producers obtained in the USA.

Aston Martin V12 Vanquish.

The producers of *Die Another Day* (2002) turned to Ford International, which now owned Aston Martin, to produce a British-made car for their next film. Very much like the famous Aston Martin DB5, the Aston Martin V12 Vanquish provided James Bond with the usual array of gadgets and accessories, and saved him from dying until another day. The V12 Vanquish has a forty-eight valve, 5935cc V12 engine, with a top speed of one hundred and ninety miles-per-hour. It reaches sixty miles per hour in under five seconds. In ten seconds, it reaches one hundred miles per hour. Its Q-installed equipment includes missiles behind the grill, automatic target-seeking shotguns in the upper hood, twin machine-guns in the front, an ejector seat, tires with spikes that retract and the ability to project an image on all sides to grant it near-invisibility from a distance.

Jaguar XKR.

Take away the invisibility factor, and Zao's Jaguar XKR is a good match for Bond's Aston Martin Vanquish. The Jaguar is a thirty-two valve, 4196 cc V8 engine. Its speed from zero–sixty miles per hour is 5.2 seconds with a top speed of one hundred and fifty-five miles per hour. The Jaguar carries rockets in its door panel, dual machine-guns at the grill, a Gatling gun mounted on the rear plus mortars mounted on the trunk. Of course, for the chase sequence on the lake in *Die Another Day*, both the Aston Martin and the Jaguar contained Ford V8 engines coupled with special all-wheel drive units so that they could both drive and stop on the ice. We'd take either car for a visit to our rowdy relatives.

Aston Martin DB10.

The Ford Motor Company International designed the Aston Martin DB10 especially for *Spectre* (2015), the latest Aston Martin in the film series to be modified and fitted with a lethal array of gadgets from Q Branch. The car was unveiled "as the first cast member" by director Sam Mendes at an official press launch of the film on the 007 Stage at Pinewood Studios on December 4, 2014. Shortly after its unveiling, fans had the chance to inspect the DB10 at the *Bond in Motion* exhibition at the London Film Museum in Covent Garden, London. One of ten models of the DB10 produced for the film was caught on video racing around Blenheim Palace, one of the movie's many locations, on February 11, 2015.

Aston Martin DB5 lives again!

In *No Time to Die* (2021), the Aston Martin DB5 from *Goldfinger* (1964) makes a rare curtain call in the precredits sequence. After his beloved DB5 was turned into Swiss cheese by Silva's men at the end of **Skyfall**, James Bond (Craig) drives the repaired DB5 on a thrilling chase through the narrow streets and alleys of Matera. 007 can't save the spy car from being shot-up again, but does manage to get his passenger Madeleine to her train. Can you imagine what the Carfax Report on the DB5 must look like!

CHAPTER SEVEN

COUTURE: HOW TO DRESS LIKE A SECRET AGENT

See him move through smoke and mirrors,
Feel his presence in the crowd,
Other girls they gather round him,
If I had him I wouldn't let him out.

—Tina Turner, ***GoldenEye*** (1995)

Throughout the film series, James Bond demonstrated that he was always on the cutting edge of fashion, wearing some of the finest clothes designed and tailored for a man of action. From Anthony Sinclair of Saville Row and Cyril Castle of Mayfair to Douglas Hayward and Bermans & Nathans of London, 007's couture ranged from the elegantly formal to the very casual. Regardless of what the "look" was, contemporary men took note, and made Bond's style their own. As always, James Bond reflected the changes in clothing styles without going to any extremes. He always appeared as a well-dressed man for any social situation.

EVERYTHING I KNOW ABOUT LIFE
I LEARNED FROM JAMES BOND

Nearly every man has the fantasy to be James Bond, but with these few, practical pointers about couture, even those of us who don't stand a chance to fill the shoes of 007 can still dress like our favorite secret agent.

THE COUTURE OF SEAN CONNERY.

Thanks in large part to director Terence Young, who was himself a bon vivant, James Bond became a man of culture, refinement and sociable tastes. One of the first things that Young did during pre-production on **Dr. No** (1962) was take Sean Connery to his tailor on Saville Row, in London, and have him fitted with several suits from Anthony Sinclair. Connery was, after all, very rough, and Young was determined to transform this former coffin-polisher and bricklayer into a star. At the time, Sean Connery was not used to wearing suits, and Young made him wear the suits around the clock, even to bed, so that he would feel totally natural in them. Young wanted James Bond to reflect the style of a gentleman with good taste and breeding, and nowhere in the series of films is this more apparent than in the couture Bond wears in **Dr. No** (1962) and **Goldfinger** (1964). His business suits had a slim look that came to be called the "Conduit Cut," and were embraced by men all over the world who wanted to look just like James Bond. The lightweight wool suits, with the single-breasted two-button look, were mass-produced in navy, gray and a very subdued Glen Urquhart check. In Steven Spielberg's **Catch Me If You Can** (2002), Leonardo DiCaprio's Frank Abagnale has a suit tailor-made to match the one Connery wears in **Goldfinger**.

James Bond's adventure in the Far East also brought some changes to his traditional Western couture. While he still wears gray flannel suits tailored by Anthony Sinclair of Saville Row, he also adopted some of the traditional wear of his Japanese hosts. And for the first time in the series, 007 wears his naval uniform in *You Only Live Twice* (1967). East or West, the couture of James Bond always reflects the style of a gentleman with impeccable taste and superior breeding.

The Tuxedo.

In *Dr. No* (1962), when we are first introduced to James Bond at Le Cercle Club in London, he is wearing a black dinner jacket and matching wool trousers. He also wears a tuxedo on two occasions in *Goldfinger* (1964), a black dinner jacket for his meeting with Colonel Smithers and a white jacket for his after-hours rendezvous with Bonita. And then again, he wears a black dinner jacket and matching wool trousers in *Thunderball* (1965) and *Diamonds Are Forever* (1971). The tuxedo as worn by James Bond was invented by Pierre Lorillard of Tuxedo Park, New York, in 1886, as a less formal but still elegant option for men used to wearing a white tie and tails.

Suits.

When James Bond first arrives in Kingston, Jamaica, in *Dr. No* (1962), he is wearing a gray flannel, two-button, single-breasted, double-vented suit. Anthony Sinclair of Saville Row, London, exclusively tailored this suit, as well as others designed for the early films. Sinclair created the "conduit cut" of Connery's suits which emphasized a slimmed-down waist, single-breasted, two-button look. The tailor also chose lightweight one hundred

EVERYTHING I KNOW ABOUT LIFE I LEARNED FROM JAMES BOND

percent wool fabrics in navy, shades of gray, and a subtle Glen Urquhart check. His gray, lightweight wool, three-piece suit serves him well when he visits Goldfinger's stud farm in Kentucky, and maintains its crease and holds up nicely in the battle for Fort Knox. He also wears his signature suit for his trek behind the Iron Curtain in *From Russia with Love* and his sojourn in Japan in *You Only Live Twice* (1967).

Shirts.

For his assignment in the West Indies, Bond wears custom-designed shirts from Turnbull & Asser, London. His dress shirts feature turn-back cuffs (ones with buttons, so that Bond can easily change them without bothering with troublesome cufflinks), and are tailored in the very respectable colors of white and pale blue. For his late-night rendezvous with Miss Trench, he wears a heavy white silk shirt without pleats. Later in *Dr. No*, Bond sports a light blue polo shirt for his excursion to Crab Key.

Ties.

With his black tuxedo, James Bond wears a thin, double-ended black satin tie that he ties himself; he would never be caught dead in a clip-on or pre-tied ties. For his business trips abroad, Bond wears a black knitted silk tie with his gray flannel suit, and uses the regular round-over-through knot; he distrusts men who wear Windsor knots as they are characteristic of SPECTRE. and SMERSH.

Shoes.

James Bond hates shoelaces, and generally selects shoes that are comfortable and easy to slip onto his feet. For formal wear, he always chooses the pump over the more traditional patent-leather oxford. The pump is a low-cut slip-on made of patent leather with a dull ribbed silk bow in front. While the oxford is clearly the more popular to many men who consider the pump effeminate, the pump is nevertheless the choice of the more sophisticated dressers. When he's not dressing in pumps for a formal affair, Bond prefers black moccasin shoes that are lightweight, comfortable, and stylish.

Hosiery.

James Bond, as the well-dressed secret agent, prefers hose that is made out of sheer silk; when that is not available, he settles for semi-sheer lisle and cotton. He does not like fine wool or nylon blends. The choice of color depends largely on the color of 007's trousers. This means black socks for black and gray trousers or dark blue socks for navy trousers. He never ever wears white or multi-colored socks.

Pocket Tees.

When James Bond is dressed formally for an elegant affair or for a business meeting, he always wears a properly folded (all points showing) white, hand-rolled linen handkerchief in his breast pocket. Silk may be more elegant, but lacks the body of linen to hold its points when folded. Many of his contemporaries may prefer to match the color and design of their pocket tees to their ties, but Bond always settles for the more traditional look.

EVERYTHING I KNOW ABOUT LIFE I LEARNED FROM JAMES BOND

Vests and Cummerbunds.

While formal styling demands that the waistband of a man's formal trousers never be exposed, Bond despises cummerbunds, and refuses to wear them with his tuxedo. On certain occasions, he may select a formal vest with shawl lapels and a deep V-shaped front in the same fabric of the dinner jacket, but Connery's Bond will not be caught dead in a pleated cummerbund. Of course, Timothy Dalton's rappelling cummerbund in *Licence to Kill* (1989) enabled him to set up a shot against Sanchez. In the novels, Bond considered cummerbunds with formal suits to be stylishly incompatible, and left them to KGB operatives who had no sense of style.

Business Attire.

At M's office, James is wearing a navy tropical wool suit with a small gray fedora hat. His white shirt has folded French-style button cuffs used on all of his shirts throughout the rest of *From Russia with Love*. His navy-blue tie is also plain with no pattern; there are no patterns on any of his ties. His white, silk handkerchief is showing approximately five-eighths of an inch with the edge parallel to the top of his pocket. In *Thunderball* (1965), Bond wears a three-piece, dark gray, two button wool suit. The suit jacket is formal in detail with inset pockets, buttonhole lapel and four button pocket handkerchiefs appear for Bond in this film, though others—M, Largo—sport them. At Shrublands, Bond favors a medium brown jacket with a cream-colored shirt and a plain dark brown tie.

Casual Wear.

Even when he is dressed casually, Bond sports the look of class.

In the famous golf game with Goldfinger, he wears a tailored sports shirt, a Cashmere V-neck sweater, and slacks. The hat that he wears while playing golf or the blue terrycloth jumper he dons at poolside seems like a fashion faux pas. While "punting" with Sylvia Trench, Bond wears white swim trunks, fully lined with a small snap pocket. His blue and white checked, long sleeve shirt is made of fine cotton, probably Sea Island.

Swimwear.

In the Bahamas, Bond wears light blue swim trunks with a black belt; later, he adds a tropical coral short sleeve shirt in *Thunderball* (1965). It is the same shade of coral favored by John Wayne in many of his Western neckerchiefs. Coral shirts and neckerchiefs reflect a rosy pattern of light upon the face and neck. In a beach appearance with Domino, Bond wears a red check short sleeve cotton shirt with matching swim trunks. Domino is very fetching in her black and white bikini, that Claudine Auger had a hand in designing. 007 also wears two colors of wetsuits; when he infiltrates Largo's men, he wears a black wetsuit; when he joins the Marines in their assault on Largo's forces, he wears an orange wetsuit.

Japanese Kimono.

During his downtime in *You Only Live Twice* (1967), James Bond wears a kimono, which is the traditional clothing of Japan. Kimono styles have changed significantly from one period of Japan's history to another, and today, many different types of kimono are worn by men, women, and children of all ages and classes. The cut, color, fabric, and decorations of a kimono may vary according to the sex, age, and marital status of the wearer, the season of the year, and the occasion for which the kimono is worn. For example, red kimonos made from a high quality of silk are often worn by retired men who are no longer responsible for their actions.

Ninja Outfit.

When James Bond infiltrates Blofeld's volcano hideaway in *You Only Live Twice*, he is wearing a gray ninja outfit similar in design to those worn by the commandoes at Tanaka's training school. The traditional ninja outfit is known as a "shinobi shozoku." Made of 100% cotton, the uniform set consists of special trousers, a shirt-jacket, and head-piece. The trousers are made with double waist ties plus additional ties at the knees and ankles. The shirt-jacket features gauntlets on the sleeves to cover the hands and forearms and has a hidden shuriken pocket. The head piece comes in two parts, including a hood and mask, both with ties. In addition to the uniform set, ninjas wear high "tabi" boots which have a splittoe feature designed to improve the foot's gripping ability.

British Naval Uniform.

James Bond wears the uniform of a British Naval Commander in only three adventures, including *You Only Live Twice* (1967), *The Spy Who Loved Me* (1977), and *Tomorrow Never Dies* (1997). Inspired by the fictional exploits of Horatio Hornblower, 007's uniform features a navy-blue, double-breasted jacket with two rows of gold buttons that can be worn either open or closed. He also wears navy-blue trousers, a white hat, white shirt, and black tie.

JOHN L. FLYNN AND BOB BLACKWOOD

THE COUTURE OF GEORGE LAZENBY

In the first five films of the series, Sean Connery as James Bond appeared in some of the finest suits and hand-tailored clothing in the world. And while 007 sported the occasional fashion faux pas, like the light-blue jumper in *Goldfinger* (1964), his couture was always first-class. After Connery left the role in 1967, and the frenzy to find his replacement began, George Lazenby wisely bought a Rolex watch, got a haircut to match Connery's, and purchased a Saville Row suit tailored exclusively for him by Anthony Sinclair. So, when he got his chance to audition for Harry Saltzman, he strolled into the producer's office attired like 007. Most everyone involved in the series recognized their audience would only accept a new James Bond if he looked and dressed the part. In ***On Her Majesty's Secret Service***, Lazenby *is* James Bond. He wears tailored suits, the Turnbull & Asser shirts, and the black knitted silk ties. His formal attire, while still very traditional, comes with a few updates.

Suits and Jackets.

Like Terence Young, director Peter Hunt was also a stylish dresser, and had most of his clothes tailored for him by Dimitrio (Dimi) Major of Fulham, London. When a former fashion model was hired to play James Bond, Hunt felt the character of 007 needed a more fashionable look, and took George Lazenby to Major. Suits, sport jackets and blazers still had the same "conduit cut" that had been popularized by Connery, but they also had wider lapels and pocket flaps that showed a younger, hipper look. The louder checks and brighter colors also revealed a Major departure from the gray flannel suits of the past.

Kilt.

When 007, disguised as Sir Hilary Bray, arrives for his first dinner at Piz Gloria, he is wearing the tartan kilt of the Black Watch, a short-waisted tuxedo jacket, a frilly formal shirt, and leggings that match the kilt. Later, Bond surprises Ruby Bartlett when he removes the kilt during their after-hours rendezvous, and he isn't wearing any underwear. The tartan kilt, one of the most recognizable cultural traditions of the Highland Scots, is in fact a development by English and Scottish tailors in the nineteenth century for noblemen, and not a historical tradition that has been handed down from generation to generation from the "Highlanders" of the tenth and eleventh centuries. The kilt, or philabeg in Gaelic traditions, was a speckled or partially-colored garment worn with a belt that took the place of trews (or trousers) for many of the early peoples in Scotland and Ireland. Certain clans did aspire to create a uniformity of design for their members, and weavers combined certain colors in their wools to create stripes and checks, known as setts, to identify a clan, family, or regiment. But it wasn't until 1618, when Sir Robert Gordon of Gordonstown insisted that all of the plaids worn by his men be uniform, that a formal system of tartan kilts was established. The kilt itself was nothing more than a six-foot tall piece of wool cloth that was gathered at the waist by a belt. In the 1800's, this belted plaid, as it was called, was replaced by a kilt that had traditional pleats sewn permanently into place, with an upper torso of cloth that could be separated from the lower when it became convenient. During the reign of Queen Victoria, nobles began wearing tartan kilts as a statement of their position and title, not as a fashion. Even to this day, as seen in the film, kilts are worn by the aristocracy.

Formal Shirt.

At the casino and then later at Piz Gloria, James Bond wears his first frilly shirt. Popular in the late sixties and early seventies, formal shirts made with frills were worn by young men who opposed the traditional plain-front shirts of their father's generation. By 1977, this style of shirt had lost its popularity, and was replaced by shirts with pleats. Naturally, this newer, hipper version of James Bond followed the fashion trend of his day. But his frilly shirts were still tailored in heavy white silk, of course!

Ski Wear.

In the novel ***On Her Majesty's Secret Service***, James Bond shops at Lillywhites in London for the appropriate and sensible clothing to wear while on his mission to the colder regions of Switzerland. He selects a comfortable but old-fashioned type of ski-trouser in smooth cloth that contours to his upper body with suspenders; on top, he relies on a lighter jacket for ease of movement; underneath, he relies on long, ugly, cotton and woolen pants and vests to keep him warm. In the film version, Bond takes whatever is available to him from Blofeld's stores, selecting a one-piece, union suit in light blue and a cable-knit turtleneck. Following the release of the film, the slopes were covered with men in light-blue union suits.

EVERYTHING I KNOW ABOUT LIFE
I LEARNED FROM JAMES BOND

THE COUTURE OF ROGER MOORE

In an effort to distance themselves from the Connery films and attract a younger audience, the producers discarded most of Bond's familiar couture, including his ever popular tuxedo, and dressed Moore in some very youthful outfits. The classic tailored suits by Anthony Sinclair of Saville Row were exchanged for the contemporary stylings of Cyril Castle of Mayfair. The results are less than satisfying. Ironically, Ian Fleming himself favored Roger Moore over Sean Connery back in 1962 to play James Bond because of the former's sophistication and sense of gentlemanly style. We wonder what Ian Fleming would have thought, had he lived to 1973, of dressing his gentleman agent in denim from Levi-Strauss or leisure suits from Mayfair.

During the Roger Moore years, James Bond's sense of style and traditional elegance in couture seemed to take a back seat to whatever was the latest fad in men's clothing. The leisure suit, for example, was a pop ular item among younger men for a period of approximately two to three years in the middle seventies, and yet Roger Moore was still wearing leisure suits in *Moonraker* (1979) when the style had already gone the way of the dinosaur. But instead of looking forward for new fashion trends, the designers looked backwards, and selected couture that 007 had worn before. The retro-look suits of Bond reflects the style of a gentleman with great taste. In *For Your Eyes Only* (1981), Moore's 007 replaced all of the leisure suits in his closet with a more traditional style designed by Douglas Hayward. He eventually returned to wearing tuxedos for formal occasions. But even as his Saville Row tailor began cutting more traditional suits and jackets for the stylish secret agent, Moore continued to defy fashion conventions by donning one outlandish outfit after another. In *Octopussy* (1983), he wore a clown outfit and a gorilla suit.

Suits and Jackets.

James Bond replaces his dark-blue and gray flannel suits that were exclusively tailored for him by Anthony Sinclair of Saville Row, London, for a tropical worsted brown suit and an alpaca light tan suit tailored by the reputable Cyril Castle of Mayfair, London. Both of these suits, as well as others designed for the later films, are single-breasted with double-vents in the back for ease of movement. Castle who had worked with Moore on *The Saint* and *The Persuaders* decided to discard the "conduit cut" of the Connery years in favor of a more contemporary style. Moore's Bond wears fewer suits, preferring contrasting sport jackets and slacks in colors that favored brown and tan, which favored his blond hair, as opposed to black and gray.

Shoes.

007 still wears his favorite black moccasin shoes, but now they are made out of alligator skins instead of real leather. Ironically, alligators and crocodiles almost make a meal out of our favorite secret agent in *Live and Let Die* (1973).

Levi-Strauss Jacket and Slacks.

We never thought we'd see the day when James Bond was reduced to wearing a pair of Levi's jeans and coordinating jacket for an assignment, but then 007 appeared at his Sans Souci breakfast table in *Live and Let Die*, drinking orange juice, wearing a light

EVERYTHING I KNOW ABOUT LIFE I LEARNED FROM JAMES BOND

blue-coordinated set. He appears very stylish in the clothes, but we all know that's not really the sort of thing 007 wears. James Bond is a gentleman, and would not have been caught dead in the kind of common wear that Fred C. Dobbs from *Treasure of the Sierra Madre* or Indiana Jones would have worn.

Overcoat and Gloves.

When James Bond first arrives in New York in *Live and Let Die* (1973), he is dressed in an overcoat and gloves. Admittedly, the colder seasonal temperatures dictate warmer wear, but 007 looks like a secret agent the way he is dressed. Why not take out an advertisement in a local men's magazine? Or better yet, wear a sandwich board that reads, "I am a British spy." Clever disguise, Bond, even in Harlem!

Business Attire.

Bond chooses a blue-gray with white pin-striped, double-breasted suit, complimented by a red tie and white shirt in *The Man with the Golden Gun* (1975). This is the "mod" era; it is reflected in the wide lapels on the suit, large collars on the shirts and wide ties. The shirt is definitely the French button cuff style, and Bond's fingernails are manicured with clear polish and buffed. Lest you think the manicure makes Bond too chi chi, do recall that the stunt men frequently say that Roger Moore could really throw a punch. Later in *The Man with the Golden Gun* (1975), Bond sports a light gray suit jacket with European side vents. His white shirt features French button cuffs offset by a navy-blue silk tie with black shoes. Both the jacket cuffs and the pants have a slight "mod" flare. He wears no handkerchief in his pocket. The jacket has flap pockets, and the overall styling trumpets the leisure suits that he would wear in subsequent adventures. The jacket cuff is buttoned facing out on both seams causing the flare.

Formal Dinner Wear.

For dinner with billionaire Hai Fat in *The Man with the Golden Gun* (1975), Bond wears a white double-breasted Euro-cut tuxedo jacket with white buttons. His pleated tuxedo shirt has French button cuffs, a black silk bow tie, black slacks, and black shoes. There is one button on each jacket cuff and a slight flare to the pants. Unlike the formality of the white tuxedo jacket Connery first wears in *Dr. No* (1962), this white dinner jacket is very casual and sporty. For those fashion victims out there, the white dinner jacket is generally worn from mid-April through Labor Day, for afternoon affairs, or in warmer, tropical climates.

Afternoon Brunch.

James Bond dons a gray and red, windowpane plaid, European cut jacket with two buttons and patch pockets to dine with Scaramanga in *The Man with the Golden Gun*. His trousers are black with a slight flare. The jacket has two buttons on each cuff, and the cuffs are flared out, as in most of the other jackets in this film. Bond has buttoned both of the front buttons of his jacket, probably to show the lines of the plaid to their best advantage.

British Naval Uniform.

In the second of three appearances (thus far) in the series, James Bond wears the uniform of a British Naval Commander. Navy-blue in color, the double-breasted jacket features two rows of

EVERYTHING I KNOW ABOUT LIFE I LEARNED FROM JAMES BOND

gold buttons that seem inspired by the fictional exploits of Horatio Hornblower. 007 trades his white shirt and black tie for a more utilitarian black turtleneck. He also leaves the white officer's hat at home, and relies on a ball cap with scrambled eggs on the brim instead in *The Spy Who Loved Me* (1977).

Tuxedo.

For his meeting with Max Kalba at the Mojaba club in *The Spy Who Loved Me* (1977), Roger Moore's James Bond wears his first formal wear tuxedo. Timeless and classic, he wears a double-breasted, four-button, notch-lapel black dinner jacket and matching wool trousers from After Hours Formal Wear. With his tuxedo, he wears a heavy white silk shirt with pleats, and a large, black solid bow tie. Later, when he meets with Aristotle Kristatos in *For Your Eyes Only* (1981), Bond sports his signature black wool tuxedo jacket and matching trousers. The trousers are naturally pleated for ease of wear and comfort, and secured by suspenders (not a belt). Under his tuxedo jacket, he wears a heavy white silk shirt with pleats, and a large, black solid bow tie. His shirt is finished off with plain black studs and cufflinks.

Ski Wear.

For the ski wear he dons in Austria in *The Spy Who Loved Me* (1977), James Bond has already made a stop at Lillywhites in London to purchase the most appropriate and sensible clothing for the colder regions of the Alps. He selects a comfortable but old-fashioned type of bibbed ski-trouser in nylon storm-dry material that contours to his upper body with suspenders; on top, he relies on a heavyweight parka with a fur-insulated hood; underneath, he wears fleece-lined thermal-wear pants and vests to keep him warm. In this case, yellow seems to be the color of choice for the outerwear. Later, when he takes to the slopes in Cortina in *For Your Eyes Only* (1981), Bond wears a heavyweight, insulated parka in royal blue, a comfortable ski-trouser in nylon with suspenders, and a white, cable-knit turtleneck sweater.

Basic Black Spy Wear.

After hours, James Bond wears a black silk shirt and black flared slacks, black leather belt and black shoes. His shirt appears to have standard cuffs rather than the French button cuff of Bond's dress shirts. This is undoubtedly the sort of outfit he wears when he anticipates a burglary or wants to play ninja.

Leisure Suit.

In both *The Spy Who Loved Me* (1977) and *Moonraker* (1979), James Bond wears a leisure suit which was a popular item among younger men for a period of approximately two to three years in the middle seventies, but had since fallen out of fashion. The four-button jacket, which resembles a shirt with its wide-open collar, flap pockets, and turned-up jacket cuffs, has a decidedly European cut. Worn with matching trousers and an open-necked shirt, with the collar folded over the jacket's collar, this "look" characterized Roger Moore as James Bond 007.

Carnival Clothing.

Bond wears a cream-colored suit—European cut—with a silk café au lait shirt with large Mod collar worn unbuttoned for the Carnival in Rio during *Moonraker*. His two button (both mother of pearl) jacket has four buttons on the cuffs and slanted patch pockets. His trousers are flared. His breast pocket handkerchief matches the shirt. He carries the "standard issue" black briefcase. This man is ready for a party with any level of society.

Mountain Climbing Apparel.

Considering that James Bond's parents died in a mountain climbing accident, we were surprised to see 007 so eager to scale the supposedly insurmountable rock face to reach the monastery of St. Cyril in *For Your Eyes Only* (1981). But then, that's so like Bond! For the ascent, 007 relied on Boreal climbing shoes that were ideally suited for rock climbing. He also wore a pair of Cappuccino full-length climbing pants, and a Prana fleece top; both allowed him an easy and complete range of movement. The rest of his gear included a climbing harness, helmet, pick, carabineers, chalk and chalk bag, ropes, slings, crash pad, a camming device, quickdraws, and pitons.

Deep-Sea Diving.

Unlike his previous excursions diving under the water, in which he wore a wet suit made of neoprene rubber, James Bond must rely on a dry suit to explore the wreck of the *St. Georges* in *For Your Eyes Only*. 007 knows that divers at extreme depths lose body heat sixty times faster underwater than on land, because water conducts heat much more efficiently than air does. To stay warm in water where the temperature drops below 10° C (50° F), he and Melina Havelock wear dry suits to keep from freezing. Unlike a wet suit, which traps a thin layer of water the diver's body heats, Bond's yellow-colored dive suit is entirely waterproof, made of materials that keep him completely dry and warm. Of course, 007 also knows that they will need a special mixture of oxygen and helium in their breathing tanks because "air would be useless at that depth."

Suits.

James Bond replaces his dark-blue and gray flannel suits that were exclusively tailored for him by Anthony Sinclair of Saville Row, London, with three different suits—a three-piece in gray pinstripe, an alpaca light tan suit, and a safari jacket and trousers—tailored by the reputable Douglas Hayward of London in *For Your Eyes Only*. All of these suits, as well as others designed for the later films, feature two buttons and double-vents in the back for ease of movement. Hayward was a former partner of Dimi Major, who dressed Lazenby, and had established a reputation for created beautifully tailored suits that reflected a traditional style. Even to this day, Moore's suits have a classic touch that never seem dated.

Clown Outfit.

We thought we'd never see the day when James Bond dressed up like a clown (or a gorilla, for that matter) to evade detection, but in *Octopussy*, he puts on white greasepaint, a red nose, floppy shoes, an oversized hat, and a multi-colored suit with bow tie to infiltrate the circus tent. What next! Does 007 don a dress, hose, and high-heals to penetrate a harem in drag? Hey, wait a minute, that's really not such a bad idea.

Gorilla Suit.

Yes, we still can't believe this one either! James Bond puts on a fur jumpsuit with attached shoe covers, fur hands, and a mask to hide in the prop room as a gorilla. *This never happened to*

EVERYTHING I KNOW ABOUT LIFE I LEARNED FROM JAMES BOND

the other fellow! We think it would have served to teach 007 an important lesson about fashion sense had Gobinda managed to lop off the gorilla's head with his sword in the tension-filled scene from ***Octopussy*** (1983).

Formal Wear for Ascot.

In *A View to a Kill* (1985), James Bond and his MI6 associates are in the appropriate attire for the grandstand at the Royal Ascot races: a medium gray morning coat (with split tails), matching gray trousers, matching gray top hat with black band, a gray silk tie, white shirt, white carnation in his buttonhole, and gray suede leather gloves. His slightly darker gray vest has rounded lapels. The men are wearing gray suede gloves. Binoculars are the customary accessory. Ladies usually wear hats, as Moneypenny does, just as they do at the American Kentucky Derby.

Riding Clothes.

James Bond's riding clothes are predominantly in earth tones in *A View to a Kill*. His light brown tweed Euro-cut jacket has two flap pockets on the right, one on the left. His white shirt has a large collar with a pale yellow knit tie. He carries a riding crop, wears a brown English riding cap, dark brown jodhpurs and below-the-knee brown English riding boots. His riding gloves are a medium brown, just between his coat and his jodhpurs in color.

JOHN L. FLYNN AND BOB BLACKWOOD

THE COUTURE OF TIMOTHY DALTON

Timothy Dalton's Bond trades the leisure suits that characterized the Roger Moore years for more traditional suits and sports clothes. In an effort to get back to the rough-and-tumble James Bond of the Connery years as opposed to the "mod" stylings of George Lazenby or the hippest fads of Roger Moore, the producers spent more money, and built their gentleman secret agent a complete wardrobe, starting with Bermans & Nathans of London. In *The Living Daylights* (1987) and *Licence to Kill* (1989), his couture ranges from the elegantly formal to the very casual with many changes of clothing in between.

Suits.

Dalton's James Bond wears suits that were exclusively tailored for him by Bermans & Nathans, 40 Camden St. London, NW1, and he prefers his jackets single-breasted, with three buttons and double-vents in the back for ease of movement. His slacks are made from a lightweight wool or flannel, and feature pleats for greater comfort. He also wears a threepiece navy pinstripe suit, and a checkered wool jacket with plain-colored slacks. Dalton's 007 struggles to keep his ties tied and his shirts buttoned, and appears to be a secret agent more concerned with getting the job done than keeping himself as finely attired as the other Bonds.

EVERYTHING I KNOW ABOUT LIFE
I LEARNED FROM JAMES BOND

Tuxedo.

007 wears his black Giorgio Armani tuxedo several times in the course of *The Living Daylights* (1987); once, when he first spies Kara Milovy at the symphony; then, a second time at the opera, and finally, at the end. Modern looking yet very classic, he wears a single-breasted, two-button black dinner jacket and matching wool trousers. With his tuxedo, he also wears a heavy white silk shirt with pleats, a large, black solid bow tie, and matching pleated cummerbund. Yes, we know that Bond thoroughly despises cummerbunds, but somehow that information didn't get to the costume designers when they were dressing Timothy Dalton. One very unique feature of his tuxedo jacket is its Velcro-like closure at the collar, which allows Bond to cover his white shirt for late-night surveillance.

Black Jumpsuit.

For the training exercise on Gibraltar in *The Living Daylights*, James Bond wears a black, tactical jumpsuit. With its superior durability and comfort, the jumpsuit is the one most popular items of couture Q Branch offers SIS agents. Constructed of a black, color-fast seven and three-quarter-ounce, poly-cotton cloth blend, it is totally machine washable and fade resistant. The jumpsuit features nine pockets, including two zippered front chest pockets, two front slash pockets, two zippered rear hip patch pockets, two thigh cargo pockets with diagonal zipper closure and one calf cargo pocket—each ideal for securing gadgets and other spy accessories. Other features include a pleated bi-swing back for ease of movement, double-reinforced knees for durability, adjustable two-ply cuffs with concealable Velcro closures, and a heavy-duty two-way zipper front closure for easy access or removal. 007 looks especially smashing in the black tactical jumpsuit, and is clearly ready for action.

Formal Wedding Attire.

James Bond and the other groomsmen at Felix Leiter's wedding in *Licence to Kill* (1989) are in formal dress indeed—gray morning suits. The gray tuxedo top with split tails has a matching vest with a gray striped tie, white pleated dress shirt, gray top hats, gray trousers and a white carnation. The shoes and socks are black.

THE COUTURE OF PIERCE BROSNAN

James Bond's impeccable sense of style had been restored in the clothing designed for Timothy Dalton. So, when Pierce Brosnan was pressed into Bondage, the tailors on Saville Row began cutting more traditional suits and jackets for the new 007. The producers of the series felt that Bond's choice of clothing should be immaculate, even for casual wear, and when Brosnan stepped out in his Brioni Tuxedo in *GoldenEye* (1995), his style was the blueprint of dressy menswear. Most fans agreed that Pierce Brosnan was a man's man; in his films, he combined the grace and elegance of a man who had seen it all and still enjoyed every minute of it. We don't blame you for wanting to dress like Pierce Brosnan. We all wanted to be in his shoes (and clothes) and have the opportunity to play James Bond 007 on the big screen for once in our lives!

EVERYTHING I KNOW ABOUT LIFE I LEARNED FROM JAMES BOND

Tuxedo.

Since 1995's *GoldenEye*, Pierce Brosnan's 007 has been fighting the world's most dangerous villains in tailored Brioni suits. The benchmark of Italian tailoring, Brioni suits and formal wear are what power-brokers like Donald Trump wear to corporate affairs. The jackets are characterized by the wide shoulders and narrow waists, and the matching trousers are pleated for ease of comfort. In several of the Brosnan films, Bond wears a black, one-button, single breasted wool tuxedo with peaked silk grosgrain lapels and five-button shawl lapel vest—a 1930's style making a comeback. Ready-to-wear suits run from $3,600 to $5,500, and the custom-tailored from $4,000 to $24,000. It's no surprise they're favored by power players. Brosnan's Bond is one of the slickest dressers out there in his tailor made Brioni suits and has women the world round fainting at the mere mention of his name.

Business Suits.

James Bond's clothing was influenced by costume designer Lindy Hemming in her choices from the Italian firm of Brioni's master tailor Checchino Fonticoli. In *GoldenEye* (1995), Bond wears a lightgray, pin-striped wool suit, and in *Tomorrow Never Dies* (1997), he favors a midnight blue silk-wool blend three-piece suit—both with accentuated shoulders and slightly narrowed at the waist with European pleats at the side and flap pockets. His brown silk tie with black dots is set off by a white shirt. Bond wears black oxfords and a silver watch. For the street, he wears a light brown cashmere overcoat with classic lines in the same shade as his tie.

Action Wear.

In several of the Brosnan films, James Bond is literally dressed to kill in outfits styled by Uncle Sam rather than Checchino Fonticoli. In **GoldenEye** (1995), he wears a khaki-green commando suit with matching vest and trousers to penetrate Alex Trevalyan's satellite base in Cuba. In **Tomorrow Never Dies** (1997), Bond is dressed to pass as a terrorist at the bazaar near the Russian border; his brown leather jacket, army fatigues, army boots, and black turtleneck shirt actually make him seem rather stylish as an international terrorist rather than a member of the British Secret Service.

British Naval Uniform.

For only the third time in the series, James Bond wears the uniform of a British Naval Commander. In **Tomorrow Never Dies** (1997), Bond's uniform reveals a GSM (a medal for campaigns that have no special decorations—such as Northern Ireland), the Rhodesia Media (for its transition to Zimbabwe), the Distinguished Service Cross and the Order of the British Empire, an award sometimes given to civilians as well as distinguished soldiers. Bond also has wings indicating his experience in High Altitude Low Opening (HALO) parachuting. James Bond has seen action both in the service and in the Secret Service. 007's uniform features a navy-blue, double-breasted jacket with two rows of gold buttons that can be worn either open or closed. He also wears navy-blue trousers, a white hat, white shirt, and black tie.

EVERYTHING I KNOW ABOUT LIFE
I LEARNED FROM JAMES BOND

THE COUTURE OF DANIEL CRAIG

Even though Daniel Craig has played the role of James Bond five times, including **Casino Royale** (2006), **Quantum of Solace** (2008), **Skyfall** (2012) **Spectre** (2015), and **No Time to Die** (2021), he has brought very little of Pierce Brosnan or Sean Connery's impeccable sense of style with him. In fact, many critics have referred to Craig as a brute, the "brunt instrument" of MI-6 that Ian Fleming initially imagined, with little sense of style or dress. He may well be initially less fashionable than some of the actors who have played 007, but that does not mean that Daniel Craig lacks a style of his own. We also must acknowledge that, in the films that have featured Craig as James Bond, he has portrayed the famous British agent in the early stages of his career. He has yet to learn much about fashion, and thus his style is one that reflects a man who cares little about couture. In *Skyfall* we do see some improvement. Perhaps Bond's new boss, Gareth Mallory (Ralph Fiennes), can take him down to Saville Row, and show him a thing or two about men's fashion.

Action Wear.

In *Casino Royale*, Craig's famous blue swimsuit is La Perla Grigioperla Lodate from its Spring/Summer 2006 collection. The blue polo shirt worn by Bond in the Bahamas and then later, the long sleeved polo worn in Venice at the end of the film was made by Sunspel, a very small British company that traces its heritage back to 1860. Sunspel recently supplied the couture for **Tinker,**

Tailor, Soldier, Spy (2011), featuring Gary Oldman. The two different types of sunglasses that 007 wears were trademarked by Persol. Craig's Bond wears several leather jackets in his films. In *Casino Royale*, his leather jacket is Armani. Costume designer Lindy Hemming found it in LA for $4000. Since they needed twenty-five of them, Hemming was able to work out a better price for the lot. In *Skyfall*, while recovering from his gunshot, Bond wears a Levi's Vintage Clothing 1930s leather jacket.

Business Suits.

In the Turkey sequence of *Skyfall*, Bond appears quite dapper in a Tom Ford light gray suit with a white shirt and white straight-line pocket handkerchief and Crockett and Jones Tetbury chukka boots. The Omega Seamaster Planet Ocean on his wrist compliments his ensemble. Just the thing for a high speed chase in Turkey. On the streets of London, however, his suit is a darker gray, his shirt is blue and his shoes are Crockett & Jones Highbury three-eyelet calfskin with rubber soles. Tom Ford designed many of Bond's clothes in *Quantum of Solace*, *Skyfall*, and *Spectre*, then outfitted Daniel Craig again for the fourth consecutive time as James Bond in *No Time to Die*. Ford worked with costume designer Suttirate Anne Larlarb on 007's wardrobe with mostly made-to-measure tailored clothing. For instance, the beautiful dark-blue wool-silk check O'Connor notch lapel jacket and tailored trousers Craig wears is Tom Ford at his best. Ford accessorizes Bond with a sky blue poplin collared shirt and a dark blue diagonal silk tie. According to Ford, "James Bond epitomizes the Tom Ford man in his elegance, style, and love of luxury . . ." In an effort to dress to impress, like 007, fans routinely spend thousands of dollars to buy a jacket or tie from Tom Ford.

Tuxedo and Dress Wear.

Ford, Brioni, Turnbull and Asser, and Lobb Shoes, distinct brands that have had a long history and affiliation with the Bond films, provided the tuxedo and dress wear that Daniel Craig wears in his five outings as James Bond.

CHAPTER EIGHT

MAKE MINE A DOUBLE-0 SEVEN

Darling, you've won,
It's no fun,
Martinis, girls and guns
It's murder on our love affair.

—Sheryl Crow, **Tomorrow Never Dies** (1997)

In the Ian Fleming novels as well as the motion picture series, James Bond shows that he is a man of sophisticated tastes by the kind of food that he orders and the kind of drinks that he consumes. We all know that he prefers his vodka martinis shaken and not stirred, and that he consumes yogurt, green figs, and Turkish coffee for breakfast. We can certainly admire his tastes, even if those things are not quite to our liking. While Bond's encyclopedic command of little-known facts and knowledge may irritate those closest to him, like M and Q, his flawless knowledge of the best wines, champagnes, foods, and cigarettes make 007 an icon of class. From Dom Perignon Champagne to Mooreland's cigarettes, James Bond defines a certain elegant

EVERYTHING I KNOW ABOUT LIFE I LEARNED FROM JAMES BOND

taste that only gentleman possess. Even when he is traveling abroad, 007 reveals that he is "exceptionally cultivated" for a European. But would you be surprised to know that Bond's taste for the good life has changed significantly with each of the actors who have played Agent 007?

Throughout the Sean Connery films, we could always count on James Bond ordering a vodka martini, shaken not stirred, or consuming a bottle of Dom Perignon, properly chilled, or sending for Beluga Caviar from north of the Caspian Sea. But with the departure of Connery following ***Diamonds Are Forever*** (1971) and the takeover of Roger Moore in ***Live and Let Die*** (1973), Bond's consumption of the good life took a detour down a temperate path. Moore's Bond never orders a medium dry vodka martini, shaken or otherwise, drinks Bollinger champagne instead of the favored Dom Perignon, and smokes cigars instead of cigarettes. We had to wonder if M had finally restricted Moore's diet or sent 007 back to Shrublands for more "purging of free radicals." Still Bond does manage to enjoy a few guilty pleasures, even if they are only implied. In ***The Spy Who Loved Me*** (1977), Anya actually orders Moore's Bond his first medium dry, vodka martini. Then, in ***Octopussy*** (1983), as she finishes her glass of champagne, Magda says, "I need refilling," and Bond remarks, "Of course you do." Not only did we love the wonderful double-entendres that made up the humor in the series but we also discovered that the food and drink 007 gets to sample in the Roger Moore films were closer to our own tastes.

When Timothy Dalton took over for Roger Moore in 1987, his Bond made the extraordinary seem ordinary in his choice of food and drink. He chose only the best, even if it meant he had to make a special trip to Harrod's in London to find the top brands in the world. And with his sexual escapades somewhat curtailed by the changing mores of the day, his James Bond wastes little time drinking favorite alcoholic beverages as a kind of consolation prize. Pierce Brosnan's Bond was also fond of good food and drink, and spared no expense being the international sophisticate that he is to share some pleasant moments with a glass and a lady. And finally, when Daniel Craig's young and inexperienced Bond is offered a vodka martini, shaken not stirred, he replies, "Do I look like I give a damn?" Perhaps, like a good wine or a bottle of Dom Perignon, Craig will grow more refined with age. He may simply need to take our advice about the lifestyle of a gentleman secret agent. On the other hand, we do note that, according to *Entertainment Weekly*, Sam Mendes, the director of ***Skyfall*** (2012), transported the bartender from London's Savoy Hotel to correctly create Craig's martini in the sequence at the Macau casino. Bravo!

Tomorrow Never Dies BR / US 1997 MICHELLE YEOH, PIERCE BROSNAN, TERI HATCHER, Photo by: Mary Evans/EON PRODUCTIONS/Ronald Grant/Everett Collection (10344986)

Absolut vodka.

When traveling abroad, vodka is more portable and less explosive than champagne, as James Bond discovers in several of his adventures. Absolut vodka is a Swedish vodka, first exported in 1979 and now one of the world's ten leading brands of spirits.

EVERYTHING I KNOW ABOUT LIFE
I LEARNED FROM JAMES BOND

Absolut, produced from Swedish wheat, was created with a new method of distillation using rectification by Lars Olsson Smith in 1879. Rectification involves passing the crude spirit through a number of columns, each designed to remove a different group of impurities—such as solvents, fusel oil, methanol and another column to concentrate the spirit. Absolut claims it is the purest vodka ever produced, hence the fewest isomers, therefore the least likelihood of hangovers. We suggest that you accept the company's claim, but avoid that fourth drink . . . unless, of course, you're alone.

Bacardi on the Rocks.

In *The Spy Who Loved Me* (1977), Major Anya Amasova's signature drink is Bacardi on the Rocks, a rum. Made with Bacardi Carta Blanca, the cool crystal look of rum mixes in a clear glass of ice cubes to give it a class all its own. She likes the sweet, distinctive taste that is usually not as strong as whiskey but still packs a punch. Usually served with a slice of lemon, the drink is as distinctive and memorable as Agent Triple-X.

Beer.

James Bond is really not a beer drinker. When 007 catches a ride with the German couple in the Volkswagen in *Octopussy* (1983), he is offered wurst and a bottle of beer, and he gracefully declines, saying, "Danke schön, sehr freundlich" ("Thanks already, you're very friendly"). Generally, Bond prefers fine wines and hard liquor to beer. Hard as it is for us to believe, 007 drinks Löwenbräu in both *Goldfinger* and *The Living Daylights* (having one and two beers respectively). On both occasions, he drinks his Löwenbräu with schnapps. In *Skyfall*, we do see

Bond drinking Heiniken while recovering from his gunshot wound; then again, in *No Time to Die*, Heiniken is served to Felix Leiter and Logan Ash at the bar in Jamaica, while Bond orders a scotch at the bar. In the original novels *The Man with the Golden Gun* and *Dr. No* as well as its feature film, Red Stripe lager is the beer of choice.

Bollinger Champagne.

With the belief that no other sparkling wine (regardless of vintage) comes close to the *grandes marques* of champagnes, James Bond dumped his preferred Dom Perignon 1953 vintage in favor of the more-expensive Bollinger champagne. Founded in 1829 by Jacques Bollinger of German origin, the Bollinger Champagne house remains a family-run business in an industry that is dominated by giant corporations. During the twentieth century, Madame Lily Bollinger was well known for using a bicycle to oversee all aspects of the champagne's production. The company produces less than a million bottles a year, and each bottle sells for more than $250 a bottle (compared to $150 per bottle for Dom Perignon). The Bollinger family still uses oak for fermentation and applies a "Charter of Quality" hand-stamp on each bottle. A vintage designated the Grande Année, or "Great Year," is released only for exceptional years. Known for the quality of its grapes (which are primar ily from its own vine-yards), Bollinger has been awarded the Royal Warrant by seven British monarchs since 1884. 007 definitely prefers his Bollinger champagne slightly chilled, with two glasses. Thank God for expense accounts, for that's the only way this civil servant can afford it! The literary James Bond first encountered Bollinger in *Diamonds Are Forever* when Tiffany Case arranged to have a quarter-bottle sent to his cabin on the *Queen Elizabeth*. In

Moonraker, 007 expressed a preference for the 1969 vintage of Bollinger, but when the champagne is being served by a beautiful woman, he does not put up much of a fuss. In *Die Another Day*, he takes the trouble to order the Bollinger 1961, if there is any available. "Cheers!" Or should we say instead, "Bottoms up." To celebrate the release of *Spectre*, Bollinger produced a 2009 bottling which has been dedicated to the Bond Limited Edition exclusively. In *No Time to Die*, Bond and Madeleine each have a glass of Bollinger champagne beside their bed in the hotel in Matera.

Bombe Surprise.

A forerunner of Baked Alaska, Bombe Surprise was a big hit in Victorian France and England, but it did not have to explode, except in the guests' mouths. A frozen white coffee ice is covered with an elaborate meringue. The ice is filled with sponge cake steeped in syrup, a fruit brandy or perhaps some other goody—e.g. finely sliced fruit with fruit brandy. Mr. Kidd was right; it would not be a *surprise* if he told what was in it. Otherwise, it might be a Princesse Marie de Orleans Surprise Bombe with maraschino syrup on the sponge cake. To our knowledge, however, none of the great chefs of Europe ever served a *Bombe Surprise* filled with *plastique*, as it is served by Mr. Wint and Mr. Kidd in ***Diamonds Are Forever*** (1971).

Bourbon.

At the Fillet of Soul restaurants in New York and New Orleans, Bond orders a bourbon and water neat (without ice). Basically, 007 prefers hard liquor, like Old Grand-dad, Harper's, or Walker's Deluxe Bourbon, to beers, sherries or port brandies.

Bourbon, which is the most popular variety of corn whiskey, is distilled with corn comprising between fifty-one percent and seventy-nine percent of the mash grains (including barley and usually rye), and made only in the United States. The term "sour-mash" refers to the process of collecting leftover liquid from the primary source of distillation with a subsequent mash for quality control. In the books, Bond fills his glass half-full of ice, adds three-fingers of bourbon, and then swills it around to cool it and break down the ice. But in *Live and Let Die*, 007 orders his drink "neat" or without ice, and the bartender reminds him "that's extra, man."

Brandy.

During his late-night meeting at the Bank of England, Bond is offered a "rather disappointing" brandy by Colonel Smithers in *Goldfinger* (1964). M does not know what to make of the drink, but Bond identifies it as a "thirty-year-old Fine indifferently blended with an overdose of Bon Bois." To the uninitiated, brandy is distilled liquor (at less than one hundred and ninety-degree proof) from fermented juice, mash, or wine of fruit, and has a taste, aroma and characteristics that are very distinctive. When brandy is derived exclusively from one variety of fruit, it is designated by the name of such fruit. Cognac is the most famous of brandies and comes only from within a particular region of France. Bon Bois is a Cognac region known for its lime and clay soils. So, when Bond says the brandy has "an overdose of Bon Bois," he is not only saying that it is a very strong cognac but he is also criticizing how it was blended. Later, M sniffs the brandy to see what the fuss is all about, but cannot tell the difference.

EVERYTHING I KNOW ABOUT LIFE
I LEARNED FROM JAMES BOND

Breakfast.

While traveling to exotic foreign lands, such as Istanbul in *From Russia with Love* (1963), James Bond sometimes orders "green figs, yogurt and coffee 'very black'" for his 9:00 AM breakfast. We know he wants to wake up quickly, but we are astounded that he can maintain his body mass and energy levels on green figs and yogurt alone!

Caviar.

In *On Her Majesty's Secret Service* (1969), Bond orders a bottle of champagne (Dom Perignon, of course!) and caviar from hotel room service to be sent to Tracy's room, in advance of his romantic, late-night rendezvous. 007 is not able to savor the treat with the Contessa because of an unfortunate "gate crasher," but he does take a taste. Caviar, which is in fact tiny fish eggs, is a rare luxury product, with the best of the best being Beluga Caviar from North of the Caspian Sea. Beluga Caviar is big and tender, colored black to gray, ideal on blinis, crackers, or baked potatoes. Naturally, nothing tastes better than caviar accompanied by Dom Perignon '57. Please Note: We have discussed the best caviar, Beluga, before, but we must warn our readers that problems with the sturgeons in the Caspian Sea have caused the cost to go up on all Russian caviar—and the quality to be a bit uncertain. Rumors of the Russian mafia's involvement are rife. So, be sure to buy from a reputable dealer. The other types of common Caspian Sea caviar are Osetrova or Ocietra caviar and Sevruga. Be advised that the Iranians also sell Caspian Sea caviar, Caviar Astara— from Karaburun or Asetra sturgeon, close to the Osetrova in color and quality. We actually wouldn't be surprised to learn that Zukovsky (Robbie Coltrane) was behind this nefarious plan. He had after all acquired a company that harvested Beluga Caviar in *The World Is not Enough*. There are also sturgeon caviar sources from a number of other locations, including farm-raised Sterling caviar from California. Whatever your source, figure one ounce per person and enjoy it; you have earned the luxury.

Cigars.

In *Live and Let Die* (1973), James Bond also trades his Morland cigarettes, which he had made for him from a Balkan and Turkish mixture, for cigars. In the Fleming novels, 007 dismisses individuals who smoke cigars as dope-smugglers or assassins, and yet the producers have their new James Bond lighting up hand-rolled Monte Cristo cigars. A mild, full-flavored cigar with a well-rounded taste and good burning qualities, Bond seems to enjoy the flavor that blends sweetness, cedar, woody notes, nuts, and the strange taste of pine. The cigars cost the producers over $7,000 for this one film. Later, in *Die Another Day*, Pierce Brosnan's 007 enjoys a "Romeo y Julieta" cigar from Cuba.

Claret.

James Bond quite properly trips up the assassin in *Diamonds Are Forever* (1971), when Wint-wearing the chain of a sommelier or cellar master—does not know that a claret is a British term used to describe a red Bordeaux, such as the Château Mouton-Rothschild offered with his dinner. True, most Americans do not use this term, but a sommelier on a cruise ship should have some awareness of British wine terminology. The contemporary Bordeaux region contains some of the finest winegrowing areas in the world with individual vineyards, called châteaus, that produce the best wine. The château bottles its own wine;

those that are best are called *crus classés* or grand cru. In 1855, Napoleon III created the "Fine Wine Index" when he rated the Bordeaux wines from one to five. He took as his base the quality and prices paid for each château's wine over the previous century. The only change occurred in 1979, when Château Mouton-Rothschild was upscaled from a second growth wine to a first growth wine or grand cru, along with Château Lafite-Rothschild. Considering the particularly French nature of the wine snobbery in this area, we cannot presume that the mention of Château Mouton-Rothschild in the 1971's ***Diamonds Are Forever*** could have been a factor in the upgrading of this smooth and delicate red wine. On the other hand, it surely did not hurt. In any case, the red Bordeaux that we customarily purchase is usually a mix of Cabernet Sauvignon and Merlot grapes, the cabernet for the flavor and the merlot for the fruitiness. More individual research and sampling seems called for in this area. Perhaps everyone should purchase a summer cottage in the Bordeaux region, or, if your French is beyond repair, perhaps the Napa Valley of California. At least one California vineyard speaks of a "California Claret."

Conch Chowder.

James Bond orders conch chowder as a kind of aphrodisiac in ***Thunderball*** (1965) as a means to defrost the lovely but cold Domino, but she dismisses his food order as a myth. Conch chowder, and yes, it's pronounced "conk," is made from a shellfish (or sea snail). True conchs feed on small particles of plants found in warm water. The queen conch (Strombus gigas) is sought from Brazil to the tip of the United States. Its shell is about a foot long and has a pink whorl. We believe the word "chowder" came from the French "chaudière" ("pot"), possibly from Breton fishermen who fished the Grand Banks opposite eastern Canada. New England or Boston chowder features milk or cream; New York chowder has a tomato base. Conch chowder, a tomato base chowder spiced with dried peppers, allspice and other delights, is a favorite in Key West and throughout the islands. Conch is not related to garden-variety snails. The French started eating those little ones during Medieval sieges, after everything else was gone, including the cats. Douse your snails with warm white wine, a touch of garlic, butter and parsley, and you'll eat them as much as 007 does.

Dates? Sheep Eyes?

In *The Spy Who Loved Me* (1977), Sheikh Hosein offers Bond several traditional Bedouin delicacies as part of his duty as a host, but 007 declines them without incident; Bond simply doesn't have a stomach for sheep's eyes. According to the **Qur'an**, the Prophet Muhammad never criticized any food he was invited to partake, but ate only the food he liked and left the food that he disliked. That's an excellent piece of advice for Westerners whose taste buds may be unaccustomed to sheep eyes or monkey brains.

Dom Perignon Champagne.

In a moment of anger, during his dinner meeting with Dr. No, James Bond grabs a bottle of champagne, and threatens to smash it in a pointless show of force. Dr. No says, "That's a Dom Perignon '55. It would be a pity to break it," whereupon Bond replies, "I prefer the '53 myself . . ." James Bond does prefer to drink the 1953 vintage of Dom Perignon champagne. Considered to be the best champagne of the giant Möet et

EVERYTHING I KNOW ABOUT LIFE
I LEARNED FROM JAMES BOND

Chandon Champagne house, Dom Perignon is named after the famous monk, who was influential in the development of champagne into the sparkling wine we know today. Dom Perignon made its debut during the late 1920s. Helped in part by the James Bond film series, this extremely well marketed brand has developed a well-earned and widespread reputation in countries all around the globe. Like any truly good champagne, the brand is expensive, with the price per bottle running well over $150. The literary James Bond first drinks Dom Perignon in *Moonraker*, when he has two bottles of the '46. In the films, this fine champagne is best associated with Sean Connery, as Roger Moore's Bond preferred to order Bollinger champagne. Connery's Bond prefers to drink the champagne properly chilled, and chides Jill Masterson in ***Goldfinger*** for her lack of taste, explaining, "My dear girl, there are some things that just aren't done, such as drinking Dom Perignon '53 above the temperature of thirty-eight degrees Fahrenheit. That's just as bad as listening to the Beatles without earmuffs!" And while he prefers the 1953 vintage, 007 drinks a glass of the 1959 in ***You Only Live Twice*** (1967), the 1957 in ***On Her Majesty's Secret Service*** (1969), and shares a bottle of the 1952 with Anya in ***The Spy Who Loved Me*** (1977).

Five-star Hennessy Brandy.

In ***Goldfinger***, James Bond was "disappointed" by the brandy served during his meeting with Colonel Smithers, so when he sends the St. Bernard dog off to secure him a brandy in ***On Her Majesty's Secret Service***, he insists the brandy be Five-Star Hennessy, of course! This is the finest brandy in the world. Started in 1774 by Richard Hennessy on the right bank of the River Charente in France, eight generations of the Hennessy family have built up what is now the finest collection of brandies available on the market. Five-Star Hennessy is a brandy that literally rates five stars on a scale of one to five in terms of its quality; the brandy tends to be a wonderful blend, nurtured to maturity by successive generations of the same family of cellar masters. It is smooth, full-bodied, and long-lasting on the palate. When ordering a brandy like James Bond, nothing can beat a Five-Star Hennessy! Of course.

Foie Gras de Strasbourg.

As James Bond indicated by his listing of exquisite foodstuffs to Patricia Fearing in *Never Say Never Again* (1983), foie gras de Strasbourg (from Alsace) is regarded as the best goose pâté in the world. The geese (yes, sometimes ducks and chickens are used for their individual pâté but geese are best) are kept in a restricted area, forcefed food and are then harvested for their three-pound livers. The fresh goose-livers are cooked down to a paste, flavored with wine and aromatic herbs and combined with truffles and shavings of veal. There are variations in this process; foie gras (fat liver) is also produced in Toulouse, France. When serving the foie gras, avoid bread. Serve it on little Melba toasts, as Bond does, or on very thin, buttered toast points. The flavor is everything, and it can be the prelude to some other delightful, lip-smacking good things.

Greek Brandy.

While we thought we'd never see the day, James Bond actually refuses a drink he is offered in *For Your Eyes Only* (1981). In Columbo's office on board his yacht, the Greek smuggler grabs two glasses and a decanter of the Greek brandy Metaxa from his well-stocked bar. He declares, "By tomorrow, we'll be good friends. Let us drink to that." But 007 refuses his drink. Only later, after the two men have flexed their proverbial muscles, does Bond accept a second offer, and clinks his glass with the Greek toast, "Yasou." Thank God, we were really starting to get worried about him, but maybe he just didn't want to drink until he knows the smuggler is a friend.

Glüwein.

At the ice rink in Cortina d'Ampezzo, Italy, when Aristotle Kristatos first meets Bond, he offers 007 a mug of Glüwein in *For Your Eyes Only* (1981). James Bond accepts, saying "That's a very good idea. Thank you." Unlike most wines that are meant to be served chilled or at room temperature, Glüwein is a spiced wine that tastes best when served warm. A carafe of the wine rests on a small heater at the table, and instead of elegant wine glasses, several small mugs kept the beverage warm. Hot punches like mulled wine and Glüwein are perfect for winter cheer. Fortified wines like Sherry and Port also make warming aperitifs.

High Tea.

In *From Russia with Love* (1963), James Bond makes it an order that Tania must have "tea" on the Orient Express to keep their cover as a proper English couple. To have "high tea" at 6:00 PM with assorted sweet treats may be a bit late by English time (4:00 PM would be more likely), but in the Balkans, when dinner is served well after 8:00 PM, one has to rough it.

Bourbon and Branch Water.

Disguised as Sir Hilary Bray in *On Her Majesty's Secret Service* (1969), James Bond orders a bourbon and branch water to drink instead of his usual Vodka martini, shaken not stirred. 007 himself would never order a drink like this as he prides himself on being a gentleman of good taste, and assumes (perhaps wrongly) that a stuffy old professor like Bray would not be knowledgeable about worldly matters. Bourbon and branch water harkens back to eighteenth century America where explorers and émigrés were accustomed to mixing alcohol with water that might have been contaminated. Branch water is nothing more than water from a fresh running stream or "branch" of a stream, and bourbon is a type of whisky. The drink order shows a lack of sophistication, and is meant to throw suspicious people off the track of Bond. After all, if 007 had ordered his trademark vodka martini, shaken not stirred, Blofeld would have spotted him immediately. We should point out that Bond does suggest, "The bourbon and branch water is rather splendid here in Kentucky" to Pussy Galore in *Goldfinger* (1964), but we think he is merely appealing to "her maternal instincts" when he does.

Jim Beam Bourbon.

In *The Living Daylights* (1987), Felix Leiter grabs a bottle of Jim Beam Bourbon, and pours Bond a drink. We've already established that 007 prefers hard liquor, like bourbon, to beers, sherries, or port brandies, but we didn't know that he was a fan of Jim Beam Bourbon. Made from the highest quality ingredients, Jim Beam is an American standard for bourbon, found in almost every American Jim Beam's eight-year-old Jim Beam Black is distinctive for its great finesse and subtle nuance, never light or heavy, but rather a mellow mix of spirits that is perfect in every way. Fans claim to drink Jim Beam not only to taste its full bourbon character, but also for its rich American heritage.

Mimosas.

At 007's hotel room in Venice, James Bond and Tatiana enjoy breakfast on the veranda in *From Russia with Love*. They appear to be eating a very hearty meal of bacon, eggs, and sausage, and they are drinking orange juice. Inside their suite, Bond has a bottle of champagne (possibly Taittinger) and vermouth (possibly Cinzano) sitting on a table. More than likely, they are drinking mimosas, which is a combination of champagne, sometimes vermouth, and orange juice.

Mint Julep.

In the film version of Goldfinger, Bond is offered a drink at Goldfinger's stud farm in Kentucky, and knows that his mint julep should be tart "but not too sweet." The mint julep was probably first introduced in Georgia or Virginia, but upscale residents of Kentucky take credit for its popularity as the official drink of the Kentucky Derby. While bartenders will continue to debate whether to serve the drink with leaves in or leaves out, straw or no straw, crushed, layered, or muddled, Bond is served a mint julep with shaved ice, sour mash bourbon, sugar, and mint (not peppermint or spearmint) leaves in.

Mojito.

While James Bond is searching Cuba for Lao in *Die Another Day*, he shares the most popular rum-based highballs with Jinx, a mojito. Not a very strong drink, a mojito is made from five ingredients: white rum, sugar (traditionally sugar cane juice), lime juice, sparkling water and mint. The original Cuban recipe uses spearmint or *yerba buena*, a mint variety very popular on the island. Its combination of sweetness, refreshing citrus and mint flavors tend to complement the potent kick of the rum, and have made this clear highball a popular summer drink, especially for those who have just come in from a swim at the beach.

Morland Cigarettes.

James Bond routinely smokes sixty cigarettes a day in the novels and about half as many in the films. Shortly after completing his assignment in the pre-credits adventure, he lights up a cigarette, and inevitably his cigarette of choice is one specifically made for him by Morland's of 83 Grosvenor Street in London. A Balkan and Turkish mixture with three gold bands at the butt end of the paper, the cigarettes had a higher content of nicotine than the over-the-counter brand, and were considered a luxury item.

Omelets.

As Mr. Bond will testify, there's nothing like knocking about a crowd of thugs to work up an appetite in *A View to a Kill* (1985). Though Stacey can't cook, she can eat. Bond proves that a man who can improvise—such as a quiche des cabinet (read a quiche made from whatever is available)—can win a lady's heart and defeat legions of short-sighted bad guys. Bond's quiche requires several eggs (hence the "omelet" reference), strips of red and green peppers, some cheese—perhaps a Monterey Jack, since this is California—maybe a few black olives, perhaps some farmer's or ricotta cheese, a smattering of herbs plus salt and pepper all into a quiche pan lined with thin pastry and then into a four hundred-degree oven for about forty-five minutes for baking. Insert a knife blade in the center of the quiche until it comes out clean. Serve with a chilled California rosé and enjoy the results. As to whether "real men don't eat quiche," we take pride in noting that any stunt man who ever had a punchout sequence with Roger Moore did not look forward to it, regardless of the pay.

Oysters.

At Kissy Suzuki's home on Ama Island in *You Only Live Twice*, when she and Bond sit down to eat the meal her friend has prepared, 007 forgoes the oysters. He knows that they are wasted as an aphrodisiac because Kissy will not sleep with him. Raw oysters have long since been regarded as a kind of organic sex food. In the second century A.D., the Roman playwright Juvenal described the wanton ways of women after ingesting wine and eating "giant oysters" in one of his satires. Many Western and Eastern cultures around the world have also documented oysters as an aphrodisiac, but little scientific proof exists beyond the fact that oysters are very nutritious and high in protein. One additional hypothesis suggests that, since the oyster resembles the "female" genitals, they are a sexual stimulant. Regardless of the truth or myth behind oysters, Bond pushes them away at Suzuki's dinner table.

Peking Duck.

Peking Roasted Duck is a delicacy served in well-cut slices in China, and James Bond has tasted the best of this famous duck at the Quan Ju De restaurant in Beijing, China. When Bond is visiting the brothel in Hong Kong in *You Only Live Twice* (1967), Ling offers 007 "the best duck," but we're pretty sure she was not talking about food. Peking Roasted Duck is prepared in several stages: First, the specially fattened, grain-fed ducks are slaughtered, then rubbed with spices, salt and sugar. Next, their bodies are kept hung in the air for some time. Finally, the ducks are roasted in an oven, or hung over the fire till they become brown with rich grease perspiring outside. The meat is served in well-cut slices with cucumbers and shallot bars.

Quail's Eggs.

The eggs of the quail are about one-third the size of hen's eggs. You may have noticed that James Bond has a dozen of them in his bag in *Never Say Never Again* (1983). Bond also has quail's eggs at his Hong Kong Hotel in *Die Another Day* (2002). Quail's eggs have random patterns of color, something like a Pollock painting. You can boil them for two–four minutes and eat them warm, dipping them into a little salt, perhaps just a tiny bit of pepper, accenting them with pieces from a rich dark chocolate bar (don't forget chocolate when you are with a woman). Texture and flavor are everything when you are having an intimate dinner.

Raki.

While Kerim Bey may dismiss it as "filthy stuff" in *From Russia with Love* (1963), Turkish raki, an anise-flavored liquor, does pack a punch that James Bond is not going to dismiss. Raki, which is more popularly known as "Lion's Milk," is made from grapes, figs or plums. Due to the anise, it becomes milky white when water is added. Considered Turkey's national drink, raki has been produced for at least four-hundred years, and is best when served cold. Most people consider it similar in taste to the more popular Greek Ouzo, though perhaps not as delicate in flavor. Bond uses the raki to disinfect Kerim Bey's gunshot wound, and then takes a healthy swig, merely for medicinal purposes.

Rum.

While not a beverage that James Bond often consumes, he has been known to drink a Bacardi on the rocks from time to time. In *Dr. No* his confederate Quarrel drinks rum before departing for the island of Crab Key, and when Felix Leiter gets a whiff of his foul breath, he suggests that Quarrel breathe on the rumored Dragon to render it harmless. Rum, a spirit initially made by Spanish colonists from the juice of sugar cane plants in Puerto Rico in the 1500's, is not only the Caribbean beverage of choice but also one of the leading alcoholic products sold in the world. Many people enjoy the slightly sweet distilled liquor over ice or mixed with their favorite soft drink, like Coca-Cola. Bacardi has been producing and distributing rum throughout the world since 1862. Returning to his house with Nomi in *No Time to Die*, Bond pours himself a glass of Blackwell Rum; later, while talking to the new 007, he pours a glass of Johnny Walker Black Label. Sometime later, after escaping from SPECTRE, Bond pours he and Paloma another glass of rum, presumably Johnny Walker. His consumption of rum in the movie makes us rethink earlier comments about Bond's tastes.

Rum Collins.

In *Thunderball*, Largo offers and James Bond gratefully accepts a rum collins. They were drinking rum collins made from white rum, probably with a dash of bar sugar, a squeeze of lemon juice and a splash of club soda—lemon or lime slice for garnish. You can make a rum collins from either white or dark rum, but, if you pick a white rum, make it Bacardi or a Jamaican white rum like Appleton. Both of these white rums have a full flavor that 007 and Ian Fleming would have approved and appreciated. Another flavorful rum cocktail is a mojito. In ***Die Another Day*** (2002), Bond shares a mojito with Jinx on a Cuban beach. His cocktail has light rum, a lime wedge, mashed mint leaves, a touch of sugar and a splash or two of club soda. It's a great cooler with a full-flavored rum; you'll need a cooler with a girl like Jinx.

Saké.

While on Tiger Tanaka's private subway train (which has a small bar), a woman brings Bond and Tanaka cups of saké. After 007 thanks her in Japanese, he takes a sip, and comments, "I like saké ... especially when it's served at the correct temperature, 98.4 degrees Fahrenheit, like this is." Saké, the traditional drink of Japan, is a beverage fermented from rice, water, yeast, and a mold known as "Koji-kin," or "koji" mold. Most Westerners dismiss saké as a kind of rice wine because its flavor and taste seem closer to a wine than any other beverage, but in fact saké shares a kinship with beer because it is fermented from a grain. The alcohol content in saké is generally between fifteen percent and seventeen although it is definitely not a distilled beverage like gin or vodka. According to the Saké Association of America, saké can be warmed only from ninety-eight to one hundred and four degrees Fahrenheit; any hotter would destroy it; of course, saké can also be enjoyed chilled. 98.4

degrees is the proper temperature, at least as far as James Bond is concerned.

Sashlik.

The word "sashlik" is Armenian, and means "grilled." It is used to describe the finest beef (in the case of this dish prime rib *au jus*) cooked on skewers as in ***Diamonds Are Forever*** (1971). In the past, it was cooked on sabers over a campfire from freshly liberated steers, but it is so hard to find a good saber these days. If the cook overcooked the sashlik in previous centuries, he often was required to eyeball the sabers up close and very personal.

Salade Utopia.

Utopian salad is made from broccoli, cauliflower, celery, cucumbers, etc., over mixed greens with hummus and hot flat bread; it carries on the middle-Eastern theme of the sashlik served in ***Diamonds Are Forever***.

Scotch.

At Puss Feller's nightclub in ***Dr. No*** (1962), Bond and Leiter drink glasses of Scotch, which is a form of whisky. Haig and Haig, produced by John Haig and Company, Ltd., is frequently the Scotch of choice in the Fleming's novels, and is a particular favorite of Felix Leiter. The CIA agent drinks two Haig and Haig whiskies on the rocks in ***Casino Royale***, and Bond joins Leiter for several in ***Live and Let Die***. The Haig family has been producing whiskies since 1627. The higher priced "Pinch" Haig and Haig (informally called "dimple Haig" in Great Britain) was first created in the early 1890s. In ***Skyfall***, Silva offers Bond some fifty-year-old single malt whisky, saying that it was Bond's favorite and his too. We are familiar with twenty-five-year-old and thirty-year-old Macallan in the U.S., but the fifty-year-old must be reserved for the British elite and the occasional international terrorist with an unlimited income.

Sherry.

M was correct that ninety-nine percent of sherry is not identified by a vintage year. James Bond was also correct in that all sherry starts with an original wine, often dated from one hundred years before the date of bottling—hence the 1851 date for the original sherry that was featured in the fine beverage he was sipping in Sir Donald Munger's office in ***Diamonds Are Forever*** (1971). After fermentation, the new wines are from twelve to thirteen percent alcohol; they then are fortified to over fourteen percent alcohol and aged for blending. The best barrels are fortified to over fifteen percent alcohol, resulting in *fino* sherry. The other barrels became *oloroso* sherry or others and are fortified to over seventeen percent Most of the sherry goes into the *solera* process, though, recently, some producers have returned to the practice of bottling a small amount of single vintage sherry, known as *añadas*. For the *solera*, picture three rows of wine barrels—five on top, six in the middle, and seven on the bottom. Each year, roughly a third of the wines are bottled from the bottom row. They are topped off by wine from the middle row. The middle row is topped off with wine from the top row. The top row is topped off with new wines. The best sherry is produced by the vintners with the best palate and nose for blending. A new wine may take from five years to one hundred years to go through the *solera*. Most sherry, therefore, is identified not by a vintage year but rather by its type, from the

EVERYTHING I KNOW ABOUT LIFE
I LEARNED FROM JAMES BOND

dry (at fifteen percent alcohol) *fino, manzanilla, amontillado* to the more full-bodied and sweeter (from seventeen to eighteen percent alcohol) *oloroso, palo cortado, pale cream, cream* and *Pedro Ximénez*. Sherry has been produced for centuries in the area around Jerez, Andalucía, Spain. A first century B.C. Greek writer of geography noted that vines were brought to Jerez by the Phoenicians in 1100 B.C. The Romans appreciated the wine grown there too. Although the Arabs—who had kingdoms in Spain from the eighth to fifteenth centuries—were forbidden to drink wine by Islam, some of them indulged in the wine of Jerez anyway. Jerez wine became corrupted in English to "sherry," a wine mentioned in Shakespeare's plays—e.g. Sir John Falstaff's "sherris sack."

Siamese Vodka.

"Ugh! Siamese vodka?" Bond remarks, after downing a shot in Mr. Osato's office in **You Only Live Twice** (1967). For connoisseurs of the good life, like James Bond, only Russian vodka will do. He prefers Stolichnaya vodka, but will settle for one of the better American brands, such as the triple-distilled Smirnoff vodka, based on an 1860 Russian recipe, in **Tomorrow Never Dies** (1997), if that's all that is available. He despises all other vodkas, especially an inferior one produced in a country with no history of fine spirits.

Stuffed Sheep's Head.

While dining at Kamal Khan's Monsoon Palace in **Octopussy** (1983), James Bond is offered a rare Indian delicacy, stuffed sheep's head. 007 is revolted by the meal glaring at him from his plate. In gastronomic horror, he watches Khan twist out one of the creature's eyeballs and gloriously pop it into his eager mouth. Bond refuses to partake claiming he "loses his appetite when he's stared at." Our favorite secret agent may well be a gourmet when it comes to food, but he has no stomach (or head) for this traditional New Year's Day feast.

Turkish coffee.

Bond orders his Turkish coffee "medium sweet," or "*mezza, mezza*" in the Middle East during ***From Russia with Love*** (1963). The coffee is served in small cups and is very strong with the grounds filling up half of the cup. Its high caffeine content will wake you up and keep you there for hours. It is seemingly identical to Greek coffee, but it lacks the mellowness of a real Italian-roasted *espresso*. We know from the novel version of ***From Russia with Love*** that Bond likes coffee, and in fact brews his own coffee from a Chemex Coffeemaker. Later, in 1973's ***Live and Let Die***, when we get a rare tour of 007's flat, we learn that Bond has an espresso machine. He fixes M a cappuccino who subsequently comments, "Is that all it does?!".

Vodka Martini.

No other beverage has been as closely associated with a fictional character as the dry vodka martini, shaken not stirred, has been associated with James Bond. In the very first novel ***Casino Royale*** by Ian Fleming, Bond orders a dry martini by telling the bartender that it is made with "three measures of Gordon's, one of vodka, half a measure of Kina Lillet. Shake it very well until it's ice-cold, then add a large thin slice of lemon-peel. Got it?" He then asks for it to be served in a "deep champagne goblet." Bond calls the drink a "vesper" after the

EVERYTHING I KNOW ABOUT LIFE
I LEARNED FROM JAMES BOND

beautiful double-agent Vesper Lynd who tried to kill him. Traditional martinis (as opposed to the vodka martini) are made with gin, dry vermouth and either an olive or a lemon peel, and then stirred, not shaken. A contemporary vodka martini completely substitutes vodka for the gin, but in Bond's case, he adds them both together, making a powerfully lethal drink. Then, in requesting that it be shaken and not stirred, his drink tends to be colder, sharper, and less oily tasting to the mouth. Most martini drinkers would find James Bond's idea of a perfect martini—the "vesper"—far too distasteful. In *Dr. No* the bellman mixes 007 a "medium dry vodka martini" with Smirnoff Red vodka moments after Bond has checked into his room; later in the mission, when Bond discovers that his room has been compromised, he puts the Smirnoff Red aside, and pours himself a straight glass of vodka from Smirnoff Blue (which has a higher proof) that he has kept secretly in his hotel room drawer. We all know that James Bond prefers his medium-dry vodka martini shaken not stirred, but for some unknown reason, Dikko Henderson gets it wrong in *You Only Live Twice* (1967). After 007 is introduced to the Head of Station at his home outside Tokyo, Henderson mixes two martinis, using Stolichnaya vodka he acquired from the doorman at the Russian embassy and Martini and Rossi dry vermouth. He hands Bond the martini, asking, "That's stirred, not shaken . . . that was right, wasn't it?" Bond politely but wryly replies, "Perfect. Cheers." We wonder if Henderson missed the memo that was circulated by Miss Moneypenny! Thank God, 007 is gracious enough to drink the lethal concoction even when Henderson stirs instead of shakes, otherwise it might have been his knife in Henderson's back.

Whisky.

In the later films, whisky appears to be Bond's drink of choice. He drinks Talisker Whisky in *The World Is not Enough* (1999) and *Die Another Day* (2002) on several occasions. Even M (as played by Judi Dench) enjoys a glass or two. In *SkyFall*, M, James Bond, and Silva (Javier Bardem) all drink a fine whisky, known as The Macallan, a Sherry Oak whisky. The year varies from scene to scene, but ultimately, Silva cracks open a vintage Macallan that is fifty years old to celebrate Bond's fiftieth anniversary in film, or so it would seem.

Wine.

At the casino restaurant in Corfu, James Bond again seeks out Kristatos, and they agree to dine together in *For Your Eyes Only* (1981). After they place their dinner orders with the waiter, the Greek tycoon recommends "a white Robola wine from Kefalonía," his home place, but 007 disagrees with his choice. "Well, if you'll forgive me," Bond replies, "I find that a little too scented for my palate. I prefer the Theotaki Aspro." Once again, 007 proves that he clearly knows his wines. The Theotaki Aspro is a white wine produced in Corfu that has a far more pleasant aroma. For the record, white wines are ideal for fish and fowl, while red wines enhance any red meat.

Wine Traditions.

As a basic rule of gourmet tastes, red wine is drunk with red meats and white wine is drunk with fowl and fish. Today, however, many wine drinkers are more adventuresome. They may try a light red wine—perhaps Beaujolais-with a fish that

EVERYTHING I KNOW ABOUT LIFE
I LEARNED FROM JAMES BOND

has a strong taste—e.g. salmon. And some hearty Chardonnays might seem appropriate with veal or roast pig. But her Majesty's secret agents had enough trouble without alleged officers drinking a heavily flavored Italian red—a Chianti, which means a wine predominantly from the excellent though spicy Sangiovese grape—with a light fish dish, such as grilled sole. A British captain who drank red wine with fish would soon be isolated in the mess and would be unable to rise beyond his rank, unless he saved the life of the queen. If Captain Nash in *From Russia with Love* (1963) had been a lieutenant straight from Sandhurst with red spots akimbo, he might make such a mistake once, if his father were a Member of Parliament or a belted earl. By the way, though the waiter suggests it, no "white Chianti" exists. There are white wines grown in the wine region near Lucca in Tuscany where Chianti is king, but there are no "white Chianti" wines. It is a contradiction in terms. Despite the incredible emphasis placed on wine "correctness" in the U.S. these days, we recommend that you should always drink what you like.

Yuck, indeed!

When James Bond was entertaining Miss Goodnight at a Thai restaurant, the waiter had the presumption to bring them a bottle of Phu Yuck-Thailand '74 by T. Eanand Products Co., Bangkok. Not surprisingly to say, it did not go over well, though Bond did like the dress that Miss Goodnight was wearing—"not too many buttons." We think that had the waiter picked a better wine, things might have moved along a bit faster for Bond and Goodnight in *The Man with the Golden Gun* (1975).

CHAPTER NINE

GAMBLING AND OTHER SPORTING GAMES

When you were young and your heart was an open book,
You used to say live and let live.
(You know you did, you know you did, you know you did)
But if this ever-changing world in which we live in
Makes you give in and cry,
Say live and let die!

—Paul McCartney & Wings, ***Live and Let Die*** (1973)

The James Bond of the Fleming novels was a sporting man who enjoyed playing Chemin-De-Fer at his private club in London or golf at the Royal St. Marks in the English countryside. He didn't know chess or backgammon, and would probably have dismissed both of them as being too intellectual for his tastes. But on his way to the big screen, 007 changed. He was no longer simply a gamesman who enjoyed an occasional round of baccarat or golf; he became an expert at every conceivable

EVERYTHING I KNOW ABOUT LIFE I LEARNED FROM JAMES BOND

game. In movie after movie, James Bond has demonstrated that he not only knows how to play but can also beat any opponent with his superior skills and talents.

We do not pretend to be experts, but we have certainly learned a thing or two watching 007 gamble and play other sporting games. And we have learned something about the world's gambling meccas.

Spanish poster for *Casino Royale* (1967) illustrated by Robert McGinnis © Columbia Pictures International

Backgammon.

Backgammon is one of the oldest games in existence, with origins dating back possibly five thousand years to the ancient Egyptians. Documentary evidence suggests the ancient Greeks and Romans also played. The game that we know today was refined and developed in Great Britain in the seventeenth century by noblemen, which is also the time it acquired the name "backgammon." Like Chess and Go, backgammon is more of a strategic game of skill than a game of luck. The random element of luck is certainly involved, but a champion player also uses the laws of probability, intuition, imagination and psychology to outwit his opponent.

Backgammon is an obstacle race between two armies of fifteen men (also known as checkers or stones) each, moving around a track divided into twenty-four dagger-like divisions known as "points" according to rolls of the dice. Each player attempts to bring his own men home before his opponent does, hitting and blocking the enemy men along the way. In the 1920s, a doubling cube was added to the game so that players and non-participants could wager on the outcome. Backgammon enjoyed a huge resurgence in the 1970s, then again in the 1990s with the popularity of the Internet. Even though Kamal Khan trounces the Major with loaded dice in ***Octopussy*** (1983), and then 007 intervenes and beats him with his own dice, winning is not all in the wrist. Players can learn the basics of the game in less than five minutes, but winning consistently takes a lifetime of study.

Blackjack.

Blackjack is a very popular game that originated in sixteenth century France as "vingt-et-un" (twenty and one), hence its other name "21." It acquired the English name "blackjack" because the player who held the Ace of Spades (a Black spade) and the Jack of Spades (a Black jack) as the first two cards would be paid out extra, and the gambler's penchant for easy rhymes took over. The object of the game is to get as close to twenty-one without going over or "bust." While James Bond has certainly played a few hands of Blackjack in his career, he prefers the very similar themed-game, Chemin-De-Fer, for its European elegance and sophistication.

Chemin-De-Fer.

When the character of James Bond (as played by Sean Connery) is first introduced to cinema audiences in the opening scenes of

EVERYTHING I KNOW ABOUT LIFE
I LEARNED FROM JAMES BOND

Dr. No he is playing cards at his club in London. He has consistently beaten his opponent Sylvia Trench, and she continues to raise the stakes. At first, it appears as if they are playing Blackjack because there are so few cards dealt to each player, but when we count up the numbers on each of the cards, they don't amount to twenty-one. Bond is actually playing Chemin-de-fer. Chemin-de-fer, which derives from the French for "railroad," is the most popular gambling card game in Europe, and is a present-day variation of the Italian "baccara" which Charles VIII introduced to France in 1490. Like its counterpart Baccarat, which differs only slightly, Chemin-de-fer is a game of chance in which two or three cards are dealt to up to twelve players and the winning hand is the one that comes closest to but does not exceed a count of nine. The objective of the game is to predict whose hand—the one holding the "shoe" (which contains multiple decks of cards) or the player's hand—will be closer to the value of nine. Players can also bet on the possibility of a tie. The "shoe," which is controlled by the person known as the Banker, passes from individual to individual during the course of the game, depending on who is winning the significant portion of the bets. The game of Baccarat is very similar, with the one exception that the casino or "house" controls a single standard deck of fifty-two cards and players bet against the house. In this regard, Baccarat is similar to Blackjack played in American casinos, and the casino operators take all of the risk. Chemin-de-fer or Baccarat is a far more cultured game than Blackjack, and identifies a cosmopolitan gentleman.

Craps.

In **Diamonds Are Forever** (1971), James Bond plays craps, and wins $50,000 on two throws of the dice in a Las Vegas casino.

According to Plenty O'Toole, 007 handles dice "the way a monkey handles coconuts." Games of chance involving "dice" have been around since the dawn of civilization. The earliest dice were probably shaped from animal bone or carved from wood; Roman soldiers tossed pig knuckles onto their shields more than two thousand years ago in a game some called "bones," an early forerunner of craps. Muslim traders in Europe adopted the Legionnaire's pastime of "throwing the bones" by adding small, numbered cubes called "azzahr." At some time during trade with Europeans in the Middle Ages, this dice game came back across the Mediterranean, and was played by the French and English. The French called their game of chance "hasar" or "hazard," while the English preferred the term "hazard." With the discovery of the New World, French trappers brought the game to the Americas, and the game became simplified as "creps," the Cajun spelling of crabs in Louisiana. English speakers simply called it "craps." Today, craps is one of the most popular games in any casino. Craps tables are easy to spot on the casino floor for they are often filled with large crowds and a single dice thrower, known as a shooter. The shooter throws a pair of dice to establish a Point, and then people bet whether the shooter can repeat the Point before a seven is rolled. Shooters can keep rolling as long as they don't score a seven in order to score the Point. Totals of two (snake eyes), three (cross eyes) and twelve (box cars) are called craps, but a total of seven or eleven is called a natural. For a beginner, the best way to start playing craps is to place a Pass Line bet on the first roll. A seven or eleven will make you an immediate winner, paying one-to-one. If a Point is established, then the Pass Line bet will pay one-to-one if the Point is repeated before a seven. You may not win $50,000 like James Bond, but you'll have a great deal of fun.

EVERYTHING I KNOW ABOUT LIFE
I LEARNED FROM JAMES BOND

Domination.

The popularity of video games persuaded the makers of *Never Say Never Again* (1983) to substitute a 3-D, holographic game named "Domination" for the matching scene in *Thunderball* in which Bond (Connery) and Largo (Adolfo Celi) play cards. Domination is played very much like Risk, except the opposing generals have nukes they can fire at each other's territories. The opposing generals also suffer electronic shocks through the handgrips on the game board. Naturally, Bond bests his opponent after inititally loosing the first round. So now, Bond not only has to be good at most casino games but also video games as well.

Golf.

Bond challenges Goldfinger to a game of golf at Stoke Poges Country Club in Buckinghamshire, England, wagering a shilling a hole; that wager is eventually raised to five thousand pounds. They agree to play by the strict rules of golf, which include certain penalties for lost balls and playing the wrong ball. During the game, Bond cleverly switches Goldfinger's Slazenger one golf ball with a Slazenger seven after he catches the billionaire bullion dealer cheating. Goldfinger fails to notice the switch and, in turn, must forfeit the match when he plays the wrong ball. Golf represents a game closely associated with the James Bond films, primarily because of this famous duel between Bond and Goldfinger, but also because Sean Connery was an avid golfer. Golf evolved from a family of stickand-ball games played throughout the British Isles during the Middle Ages, and is often attributed to the Scots because the first-known rules of the game were recorded in Edinburgh. The earliest known reference to golf comes from King James II of Scotland, who in 1457, issued a ban on the game because it kept his archers from their practice. From an etymological point of view, the word "golf" derives from an Old Scots term "golve" or "goff," which meant club. For the record, Bond uses a Penford Hearts golf ball, plays with American Ben Hogan's clubs, and prefers the Royal Saint Marks just outside London.

Las Vegas, Nevada.

The neon-lit "Strip" in Las Vegas provides a gorgeous backdrop for ***Diamonds Are Forever***. From its inception, Las Vegas promised its visitors the thrills of easy money, available sex and privacy. "What happens in Vegas stays in Vegas," so the natives say. The man who put Las Vegas on the map was not a Spanish friar seeking souls, such as Father Junipero Sera who maintained missions in Los Angeles and San Francisco. Rather, it was Bugsy Siegel, the enforcer for the New York mob's moneyman, Meyer Lansky. In 1945, Siegel, after making friends and overseeing rackets in Hollywood, found a desert town in Nevada with legal gambling and prostitution with a straight shot to Los Angeles. Siegel built the Flamingo Hotel and Casino and made Las Vegas a mecca for people following that dream wherever that dream will lead them. In turn, Siegel soon received bullets for breakfast because of his skimming the construction funds provided by the East Coast mob. By the 1960's, Las Vegas had become a tourist attraction with Hoover Dam, Lake Mead, the Death Valley National Park and more gambling and sin than you could shake a Freudian symbol at. Frank Sinatra, Dean Martin and Sammy Davis, Jr. brought "The Rat Pack" to Las Vegas in the late 1950's and early 1960's. In turn, the Rat Pack attracted the nouveau riche from all over the country and even

EVERYTHING I KNOW ABOUT LIFE
I LEARNED FROM JAMES BOND

some of America's first families—e.g. Senator John F. Kennedy, who became entangled with Judith Campbell Exner, more than an acquaintance of Chicago mob boss Sam Giancana. Las Vegas was where everyone was making connections. Following the clean-up of mob influence in the late 1980's, Las Vegas became bigger than ever with major corporate investments in hotels and casinos plus a dominance of Mormons, rather than Mafia members, in the running of the hotels and casinos. Adjacent to mining, commercial and military areas, today Las Vegas is the fastest growing metropolitan area in the country. Should we decide to move abroad upon retirement, we just might keep a winter home in Las Vegas to remind us of what we are missing.

Macau, China.

The Casino de Macau was an excellent place for Scaramanga's mistress (Maud Adams) to be transacting business in *The Man with the Golden Gun* (1975), as there are too many casinos and tourists throughout Macau to attract attention. Twofifths of Macau's economy is based on tourism and gambling today, and Macau is always inviting more tourists. Some of the Europeans come because of the influence of the Portuguese, who first visited the site, near Hong Kong, in the early sixteenth century. During World War II, Macau with its Portuguese governor was declared a neutral zone, thus becoming a haven for Chinese and displaced European citizens and various intelligence services. In December of 1999, Macau came under the governorship of mainland China, but it remains a free port and now has an international airport. If you are visiting Hong Kong to meet that tailor who can make you some handmade suits quickly, consider one of the many ferry rides to Macau and try your luck at the casinos. In

Skyfall, Daniel Craig's Bond plays the game of Sic bo (or dai siu) at the Floating Dragon Casino in Macau.

Monte Carlo.

James Bond has made many trips to gamble and meet with dangerous opponents; in his most recent visit, as chronicled in ***GoldenEye*** (1995), 007 met Xenia Onnatop, and stumbled across an international plot to destroy the economy of the world with a space-based weapon. Monte Carlo is the central city of the one of the smallest, independent countries in Europe, the Principality of Monaco. Located by the Mediterranean Sea, Monte Carlo is known for its dream-like gardens, its athletic and cultural events, and its high-stakes gambling. In 1997, Monaco celebrated the 700th anniversary of the Grimaldi Family Dynasty. Its tradition of elegance and sophistication continues to this day.

Roulette.

In ***Casino Royale*** (1967), the roulette wheel turns into a lethal machine gun, and goes spinning all over the casino when James Bond (David Niven) and his British forces assault SMERSH's headquarters. Derived from a French word meaning small wheel, the origins of the game "roulette" are not very clear. Some sources hold that Blaise Pascal, a seventeenth century French mathematician invented the roulette wheel, while others contend the game originated in China and was brought to Europe by Dominican monks who were trading with the Chinese. In either case, the roulette wheel became very popular in the eighteenth century when Prince Charles, the reigning monarch of Monaco, introduced gambling to his small country as a way of resolving the enormous financial obligations of his subjects. The roulette wheel gained a great deal of popularity in the United States during the California Gold Rush, and has been a regular fixture at casinos ever since. The major difference between the American roulette Wheel and its European counterpart is that the American version contains thirty-eight numbers including zero, double-zero and one to thirty-six, while the European version has only thirty-seven numbers, with a single zero. Having two zeros (zero, double-zero) gives the house a 5.26% advantage. In other words, for every $100 a gambler bets, the house will make $5.26 in profit. In Europe, the profit is half as much. The game is played simply enough. Players place different colored chips on desired position on the table in an attempt to predict where the ball will land after the Roulette wheel is turned and the ball comes to a complete stop. Once the bets are made, the dealer spins the wheel, and waits for the wheel to stop. Players who bet on the winning number are rewarded highly, those betting on colors less so, while players who bet on numbers or colors other than the winning number and color lose their chips to the casino.

Slot Machines.

Charles Fey developed the first commercially successful slot machine in his San Francisco machine shop in 1896. Made of cast iron with three internal reels, a slot for taking in coins and an external lever for activating the machine, it quickly became a staple of saloons, gambling houses and even a few retail stores. Today, no casino would be complete without the gleaming rows of the one-armed bandits. In ***Diamonds Are***

Forever (1971), Q (Desmond Llewelyn) manages to cheat the Las Vegas casino by using a ring that generates an electromagnetic field that controls the revolutions per minute of the slot machines. In fact, we see him do this to several machines in a row. Now, before you buy that ticket to Las Vegas and fill your pockets with horseshoe magnets, consider this factor. If you hit a jackpot on more than one machine in a row in a very limited time frame, don't you think that someone in the casino might question your incredible luck? Believe it; someone would. Consider that every dealer, casino employee, and player engaged in games of chance is monitored by television cameras. So, too, the slot machines are monitored. That is not to say that you can't rig a slot machine. In 1998, four people were arrested, allegedly having won more than $6 million by rigging slot machines at Nevada casinos in 1996, including the Rio and the Luxor. In the past, some of that alleged 1998 crew used such things as keys, wires, magnets and other devices to rig slot machines. In addition to cash, the alleged crew won several luxury automobiles from the Stardust and other casinos. The alleged leader of the ring was a computer expert. He would tamper with the machine and leave the casino. A conspirator would win the jackpot. His 1998 arrest was due, in part, to a confidential informant. In other words, you need at least two people, one of whom is terribly clever with electronic and computer devices. If you want a larger score, you need more than two people. At that point, you all have to keep your mouth shut, not spread about the money nor cause attention to come to yourself. Then, simply look over your shoulder for the rest of your life, not only for the casino's corporate security personnel or their informants, but also for the FBI.

EVERYTHING I KNOW ABOUT LIFE I LEARNED FROM JAMES BOND

Texas Hold'em.

While we never expected to see James Bond give up Chemin-de-fer or Baccarat to play a game of Texas Hold 'em, he does just that in the remake of *Casino Royale* in 2006. Texas Hold'em is a popular form of poker in which two cards are dealt down to each player, and the remainder of the cards are turned up for all players to make a poker hand. Interestingly, in this game, a hand with a pair of eights is called an "Octopussy," the name of both a James Bond short story and movie. A hand with a pair of eights is actually seen in the movie. The poker cards, chips, and plaques featured in the movie were manufactured by Cartamundi, and were available for a short while as replicas of the movie props from Cartamundi.

World Champion Chess.

In *From Russia with Love* (1963), Kronsteen has the perfect plan to destroy James Bond and embarrass the British Government, and he goes about executing his plan like the grandmaster chess player that he is. World Champion Chess is highly regarded all around the world, but in particular the former Soviet Union. Boris Spassky, born in 1937 in Leningrad, U.S.S.R., became an international master of chess in 1953 and junior world champion and grandmaster in 1955. In 1960, he defeated David Bronstein for the U.S.S.R. Championship in Leningrad. The ending of this famous match is shown with Kronsteen (Sheybal) playing Spassky's game in the movie. Spassky became a world champion when he defeated another Soviet, Tigran Petrosian, in 1969. A courtly and public figure, Spassky was set to continue the Russian domination of the world of chess. But in 1972, the American Bobby Fischer defeated Spassky in Reykjavik, Iceland, ending thirty-five years of Russian championships. While Spassky returned to Mother Russia, allegedly in disgrace, he still appears occasionally to play in international competitions and make some money. Bobby Fischer, on the other hand, seems to be having problems relating to the world and, after his victory, had not granted a public interview for over thirty years. Just because you won, it doesn't make you a winner, as Kronsteen learned.

CHAPTER TEN

EVILDOERS AND THE EVIL THAT MEN DO

Goldfinger.
He's the man, the man with the Midas touch.
A spider's touch.
Such a cold finger.
Beckons you to enter his web of sin
But don't go in.

—Shirley Bassey, **Goldfinger** (1964)

Since the debut of **Dr. No** in 1962, James Bond has had to fight an array of memorable villains and their equally memorable henchmen. Many James Bond villains have tried to liquidate our hero, but few have come close to killing off the world's most famous secret agent. After nearly being drowned in a radioactive pool by Dr. No, inches from being emasculated by Goldfinger's industrial laser, placed on a shark's dinner menu by Emilio Largo, or diced and sliced into little pieces by Franz Sanchez,

007 has survived it all. Early villainous schemes were fairly modest, from plots to kill James Bond to extortion attempts to control technology. But with each new production, the schemes have grown larger and bolder, and 007 has been forced to keep pace. World domination has always been a favorite of megalomaniacs like Ernst Stavro Blofeld, Karl Stromberg, and Sir Hugo Drax. But even modest plots like controlling the world's oil supply or creating a monopoly in the microchip industry have caused the world to teeter on the brink of disaster, and required Bond to save the day. Ian Fleming was well aware that every great literary hero had to fight an equally great villain. Without the larger than life villains and their grand schemes of world conquest, the books and the film series would not have been as much fun.

Spanish poster for *Dr. No*, 1963 © United Artists

EVERYTHING I KNOW ABOUT LIFE
I LEARNED FROM JAMES BOND

THE SEAN CONNERY VILLAINS

The nature of the James Bond villains has changed through time. While the many villains in the Sean Connery films have sought to dominate the world with their nefarious schemes, their goals have seemed quite fantastic. Dr. No seeks to disrupt U.S. rockets fired from Cape Canaveral; Goldfinger wants to irradiate the gold supply at Fort Knox so that his holdings will increase tenfold. Ernst Stavro Blofeld tries several times to provoke the world's superpowers, and nearly succeeds in starting World War Three in *You Only Live Twice* (1967). Naturally, the world's greatest secret agent, in the guise of Sean Connery, relies on his clever resourcefulness and wealth of little-known facts to defeat them every time. One of the most famous and sinister of all of the James Bond villains and his equally infamous henchman make their debut in *Goldfinger* (1964), and set the standard for all of the films that followed. Every villain who sought to dominate the world and every larger-than-life henchman who obeyed his command would be compared favorably or not with the pair from the third James Bond adventure.

Dr. No.

The first of James Bond's many enemies, Dr. Julius No (Joseph Wiseman) was a sinister and clever villain who sought to dominate the world by controlling missiles launched into space. Much like his literary counterpart, Dr. No was the unwanted child of a German missionary and a Chinese girl who had risen to power in the Tong underworld. Now, as a confederate of SPECTRE (**Sp**ecial **E**xecutive for **C**ounter Intelligence,

Terrorism, Revenge, Extortion, the "*and*" is omitted), Dr. No has no allegiances to any country. He is ruthless, domineering, and makes it clear to James Bond that his brilliant criminal brain is superior to everyone else. The mad doctor's unique physical trait are two powerful steel hands that have replaced those amputated in an accident working with radioactive materials. In 1962, at the time when the film was being cast, author Ian Fleming recommended his nephew Christopher Lee for the role of Dr. No, but the producers dismissed him as being a B-grade horror film actor (Lee had played both Dracula and the Frankenstein monster in a series of horror films produced by Hammer Films). Ironically, Lee would later play Scaramanga, the titular character in ***The Man with the Golden Gun*** (1975). Fleming also asked friend and playwright Noel Coward to play Dr. No, and Coward turned him down with a telegram that read, "Dr. No? No! No! No!" Ultimately, Broccoli and Saltzman settled for stage actor Joseph Wiseman who was clearly not Asian but still managed to carry off the role. At one point, however, an early draft of a screenplay by Wolf Mankowitz and Richard Maibaum depicted Dr. No as a capuchin monkey that perched on the shoulder of the actual villain, Buchfield. Thank goodness they discarded that effort for a more straight-forward approach.

Rosa Klebb.

Rosa Klebb (Lotte Lenya) is memorable for her ferocity in ***From Russia with Love*** (1963). Who can forget the underlying menace of her comment to Tatiana, "You are a fine looking girl." Whether she is threatening the lovely Tatiana Romanova with death (repeatedly), or caressing fellow female Tatiana like a predatory lion would caress a young antelope, Klebb is ruthless and domineering. She has no long-term personal interest in her; Tatiana just must do what she is told to do. But it is in the action sequence in the Venice hotel that Klebb is most memorable. When her gun is knocked from her hand, she does not hesitate for a moment. She is all business, shoe kicking determinedly for James Bond's leg. All she needs to do is scratch him; the venom will do the rest. She fails because Bond's *machismo* has triumphed over her lethal threats. Let's hear it for the boy! [In the novel version, Klebb finds her target, and sends Bond down for the count.]

Donald "Red" Grant.

In *From Russia with Love* (1963), Donald "Red" Grant (Robert Shaw) is a homicidal paranoid being employed as an executioner by an organization of extortionists (SPECTRE). We see him stalking Bond throughout Istanbul, from the Gypsy camp, through Sancta Sophia (now a mosque; it was once the great cathedral of the Byzantine Empire), and finally on the Orient Express. At no time do we see him showing any serious interest in women or in men (for that matter), except in the killing of them. His prolonged fight with Bond in the cramped railroad compartment is memorable. Bond almost met his match that day. Thankfully, the better businessman always has a well-organized attaché case. Grant may not be carrying Odd-Job's bowler or wearing Jaws' metal teeth, but he is one of the most lethal of all of 007's adversaries.

Goldfinger.

While his name may sound like a French nail polish to James Bond, Auric Goldfinger (Gert Fröbe) was a crazed, eccentric megalomaniac who was willing to kill sixty thousand people and plunge Western economy into the dark ages in order to increase his stock in gold. Obsessed with gold, Goldfinger was quite possibly one of the richest men in the world, and had holdings in Great Britain, Switzerland, and the United States. Much like his literary counterpart, Auric Goldfinger appeared as an overweight man in his fifties whose charming façade and amiable demeanor hid the ruthlessness of a killer. His most inspired and daring plan, Operation Grandslam, meant that he had to make an uneasy alliance with various Mafia families and the Red Chinese in order to become richer and more powerful. In the novel, Goldfinger actually tries to steal the gold from Fort Knox; in the film, his plan is far more deadly and destructive. In the climax of the movie, Bond fights Goldfinger for possession of his golden gun; the gun is discharged, depressurizing the cabin of a small jet, and Goldfinger is sucked out the window to his death. The name Goldfinger was taken by Fleming from the Hungarian modernist architect Erno Goldfinger. Among other things Erno Goldfinger designed London's Trellick Tower, built in 1968. [Unable to speak any English, Gert Fröbe's voice in Goldfinger is dubbed entirely by Michael Collins. The producers also considered bringing Fröbe back as Goldfinger's brother in ***Diamonds Are Forever***, but that idea was thankfully discarded in the early drafts of the script.]

Odd-Job.

The most famous henchmen in the Bond series, Odd-Job (Harold Sakata) was the fanatically loyal, mute Korean servant of Goldfinger. He dressed in the traditional uniform of a manservant, including a bowler hat which was ringed with a razor-sharp blade, and did whatever he was told to do. In addition to

EVERYTHING I KNOW ABOUT LIFE
I LEARNED FROM JAMES BOND

his roles as a chauffeur, bodyguard, and golf caddy, Odd-Job was a cold-blooded killer. Asian by birth, he relied on the ancient deadly arts of his ancestors, including judo and karate, to kill his victims. When Bond gets trapped inside the vault of Fort Knox with Odd-Job and discovers his physical strength is no match for the powerful Korean, 007 uses a stray live electrical cable to electrocute him. [The character of Odd-Job is satirized in *Austin Powers: International Man of Mystery* by the presence of Random Task (Joe Son), another mute Korean manservant.]

Emilio Largo.

When you see a black eye patch, you either think of a pirate or that series of magazine advertisements from the mid-twentieth century featuring the terribly well dressed "Man in the Hathaway Shirt." With Largo (Adolfo Celi), a man of hot temper and a lack of judgment, we think "pirate" every time. True, he can put together a festive front on occasion. Largo is vulnerable, however, to Bond's advances on his mistress, Domino. Largo is conscious that Volpe feels free to tell him off. He even tortures Domino, just because she prefers Bond's honesty to his treachery in killing her brother. We think if any Bond villain deserves the title "male chauvinist pig," it would be Emilio Largo. But enough with political correctness! Any man who would wipe out Miami, Florida, is just guilty of overkill. We seriously doubt whether he could ever become a member of any respectable London Club. Serves him right!

Vargas.

In *Thunderball*, Largo's henchman Vargas doesn't say anything, doesn't love anyone, doesn't smoke, and doesn't drink any alcohol. The tall, thin, fairly competent man must have some faults. Oh, yes, kidnapping and murder come to mind. He is the ever-present right hand to Largo. He shadows Domino with his other thugs closely behind. He grabs Paula when it is appropriate. He was about to eliminate James Bond, but, James Bond helps Vargas understand that a real man can have a few vices. At least, it seemed apparent to us that he got the point.

Ernst Stavro Blofeld 1.

For several James Bond adventures, notably ***From Russia with Love*** (1963) and ***Thunderball*** (1965), we have been teased with the image of a faceless man petting a white, Persian cat as the head of SPECTRE. Finally, in his first frontal shot in ***You Only Live Twice*** (1967), Blofeld appears in the form of actor Donald Pleasence with a very nasty scar across his right eye. In addition to the ubiquitous cat, he sports an octopus ring on his right hand, and wears clothing fashioned after Chinese leader Mao Tse Tung. He does look truly villainous, and reacts to Bond (and all others who oppose him) with hostility and menace. Originally, British thespian John Werich was cast as the head of SPECTRE, but he was fired after filming only a handful of scenes because the producers thought he was not menacing enough; in point of fact, he looked like Father Christmas. Pleasence, a long-time character actor, was cast instead. Various options were tried to make him look truly menacing, including a hump and a limp; eventually, Broccoli and Saltzman settled for the scar. In ***You Only Live Twice*** (1967), the terribly scarred Blofeld (Donald Pleasance) escapes at the end (just like Dracula, always back from certain death). In Switzerland, the new Blofeld (Telly Savalas) in ***On Her Majesty's Secret Service*** (1969) even murders the lovely bride (Diana Rigg) of James Bond (George Lazenby) as they were about to start their honeymoon. It doesn't get much more personal that that. What a shock for James Bond (Connery) to discover, therefore, not one, but, two Blofelds (Charles Grey) in Willard Whyte's penthouse in **Diamonds Are Forever** (1971). It's not exactly a "double your pleasure, double your fun" situation. If only James Bond had brought a double-barreled piton gun; he could have taken them both out. In any case, we do admire Blofeld's cleverness, but we do dislike his wardrobe. A Mao suit? And when he escaped in drag, can you believe a frilly blouse with a severe pants suit accessorized with a garish outsized diamond bracelet? That outfit screams: "Look at me; I'm a female impersonator." He wore better clothes as "No Neck" in the ever popular, gender-bending and transvestite-triumphant **Rocky Horror Picture Show** (1975). Certainly, Max von Sydow in **Never Say Never Again** (1983) was the most elegant Blofeld. Keep in mind, however, that von Sydow had played both Jesus Christ in **The Greatest Story Every Told** (1965) and Satan, the Prince of Darkness, in **Needful Things** (1993). Von Sydow was good, but he would never appear quite as menacing as the faceless figure from the earlier Bond films who did horrible things to people while stroking his cat. [Anthony Dawson, who played Professor Dent in **Dr. No**, played the faceless Blofeld in **From Russia with Love** (1963) and **Thunderball** (1965).] After Roger Moore's Bond sends Blofeld plunging down a chimney at an industrial plant on the outskirts of London, presumably to his death, in the opening credits of **For Your Eyes Only**, Christoph Waltz returns as the man behind the SPECTRE ring in **Spectre** (2015).

Hans.

Hans (Ronald Rich) in **You Only Live Twice** is Blofeld's muscle-bound bodyguard who is entrusted with the key to the exploder button. Like Odd-Job, Hans is incredibly strong, and capable of snapping James Bond in two pieces. 007 is able to defeat Hans by using his strength against him, sending him to his death in the pool of piranha fish.

Bambi and Thumper.

Those two girls, Bambi (Lola Larson, an Olympic gymnast) and Thumper (Trina Parks, a statuesque dancer), would have been fun at any party. It's too bad James Bond had to visit them during their professional Blofeld-bodyguard party. They certainly made quite determined bouncers, but they probably would have attracted too much of the wrong sort of attention working at any New York nightclub. Jimmy Dean, the country and Western singer and breakfast sausage king, notes that the most frequently asked question he gets about the film is, "What were Bambi and Thumper like?" Regrettably, they were gone before he came to the set. In any case, we would prefer to meet the ladies for dinner at "21" or the new "Studio 54" in New York, rather than at the dojo.

THE GEORGE LAZENBY VILLAINS

Like the final two Connery films, George Lazenby comes face-to-face with his archrival, Ernst Stavro Blofeld. Ian Fleming was well aware that every great literary hero had to fight an equally great villain, and while the pages of his novels are filled with wonderfully drawn villains like Goldfinger and Sir Hugo Drax, there was only one archrival for James Bond. Sherlock Holmes may have had his Moriarity; Nayland Smith his Fu Manchu, or

EVERYTHING I KNOW ABOUT LIFE I LEARNED FROM JAMES BOND

Superman his Lex Luther; but 007's destiny was forever linked to his struggle with Blofeld.

Ernst Stavro Blofeld 2.

In his second of three on-screen appearances, Ernst Stavro Blofeld (Telly Savalas) seems to have adopted a polite, almost genteel personality, soft and very well spoken; but under the façade, he remains sinister and intimidating in *On Her Majesty's Secret Service* (1969). He is much like the white Persian cat he strokes, seemingly docile and elegant on the outside, but with deadly claws and fangs on the inside. While still obsessed with world domination and power, he seems to have traded one set of priorities for another. No longer content to demand one million dollars for his services (Perhaps he has learned a lesson from Dr. Evil?), Blofeld plans to extort a full pardon for his previous crimes and claim the title "Comte de Bleauchamp," which is the French form of Blofeld, from the United Nations in exchange for a virus which would render the world's food supply sterile. Apparently, Blofeld survived the destruction of his volcano lair in *You Only Live Twice* (1967), healed the scar on his face, and used the two years between films to build an extraordinary mountain fortress in the Swiss Alps without anyone in the world noticing his activities. He still rules SPECTRE (the **Sp**ecial **E**xecutive for **C**ounter Intelligence, **T**errorism, **Re**venge, and **E**xtortion) with an iron fist, but no longer relies on underlings like Dr. No, Rosa Klebb or Largo to carry out his instructions. Instead he remains very hands-on, working alongside his scientists in the lab or brainwashing the "angels of death" himself or chasing 007 on skis or in a bobsled. Blofeld has also taken a page out of Bond's playbook, and fancies himself a world-class lover, romancing Tracy and offering her a place in his new world order. (In his other cinematic appearances, Blofeld seems asexual, and makes no advances on Tiffany Case or any of Bond's other romantic conquests.) He is also a powerful man who trades blows with Bond in the climatic struggle on the bobsled course, not at all the figure we see in ***You Only Live Twice*** (1967) or ***Diamonds Are Forever*** (1971). Nonetheless, Ernst Stavro Blofeld remains one of Bond's most treacherous enemies.

Irma Bunt.

Irma Bunt (Ilse Steppat), Blofeld's personal secretary, is a cold hearted, authoritative, humorless woman with the instinct of a killer in ***On Her Majesty's Secret Service***. Strongly resembling Rosa Klebb, she caretakes the female patients at the allergy clinic with a latent homosexuality that is often violent and tyrannical. When Bond, disguised as Sir Hilary Bray, meets her at the train station, he asks Bunt if she is from a nautical family. The word "bunt" refers to the swollen or baggy part of a sail. She finds his query "interesting," but declines to answer. She is also Blofeld's aide in bringing about his plan to release walking time bombs into society in the form of beautiful young women. Bunt soon puts an end to Bond's amorous antics with Blofeld's bevy of beauties, and finally ends 007's hopes and dreams when she callously guns down his wife just minutes after their wedding. She remains at large, a deadly enemy.

THE ROGER MOORE VILLAINS

With the change in emphasis from Connery to Moore, the kind of villains that James Bond faced in his adventures also changed. Ernst Stavro Blofeld along with his SPECTRE organization was presumably dead and buried on an oilrig off the coast of Baja California. The Cold War had reached its apex during the Connery years, and was beginning to wind down with the Russians no longer viable targets. And with the end of the war in Vietnam, the threat of communism spreading throughout Asia was no longer a topic of conversation. So Albert R. Broccoli and Harry Saltzman had to find other kinds of enemies for Bond to fight. In the first of the Roger Moore films, 007 battles black hoodlums and the world's greatest assassin. But after the disappointing box office receipts for *The Man with the Golden Gun* (1975), the producers went back to the tried and true formula of a megalomaniac obsessed with world domination.

Mr. Big/Kananga.

In the Fleming novel *Live and Let Die*, Mr. Big is characterized as the most powerful criminal mastermind in the world. He is also head of the Black Widow Voodoo Cult, and a high-ranking agent in the Soviet murder organization SMERSH. He plots to sell the seventeenth-century pirate Black Morgan's treasure to finance a Soviet spy network in the United States. Most of that very interesting background material is discarded in favor of a fairly flat, stereotypical gangster who as Mr. Big (Yaphet Kotto) controls a band of street thugs and hooligans in Harlem in *Live and Let Die* (1973). Dressing in loud, multi-colored ethnic clothing, he looks more like a second-rate pimp than a criminal mastermind. Without the vibrant duds and cheap latex mask, he is equally uninteresting as Dr. Kananga, the Prime Minister of the Haitian-like country of San Monique. Even his scheme of flooding the American drug market with free heroin is not much of a plan compared with those of his fellow megalomaniacs from the other

James Bond adventures. Mr. Big/Kananga is actually kind of a low-rent villain that does not offer much of a threat to 007. Now, if Mankiewicz had demoted the Prime Minister to a secondary role and teamed Mr. Big and Baron Samedi as the one person who could not die, then Bond might have had a challenge. Just think of the possibilities if James Bond had been forced to fight a Terminator-like figure with voodoo connections! [The character of Dr. Kananga is actually named after Ross Kananga, the crocodile hunter and owner of the crocodile farm. Kananga appears briefly in the film as Bond's stunt double for the alligator walk.]

Tee-Hee.

Named for his wicked laugh, at least according to Fleming, Tee-Hee (Julius Harris) is Mr. Big's number-one henchman in *Live and Let Die*. He appears in the film as a tall, balding, and muscularly-built man with a mechanical steel hook as his right arm. Apparently, he got a little careless with a crocodile named Albert, and lost his right arm to the deadly predator. In the novel, Tee-Hee gets to break Bond's little finger during an interrogation scene, but his cinematic counterpart is not as fortunate. At the end of the film, after most of Mr. Big's men have been killed or rounded up, we are a bit surprised that Tee-Hee shows up in Bond's cabin on the train. Other than revenge, he has no real motivation, and, let's face it, after what he's been through, Tee-Hee would be far better off tangling with alligators than 007.

Francisco Scaramanga.

What we know about Scaramanga, The Man with the Golden Gun, we learn from his enemies—James Bond and Andrea Anders—much like what we know about Genghis Khan we learned from his enemies—the Chinese, the Persians, the Turks and the Europeans. Scaramanga's father was a ringmaster in a circus traveling through Europe, possibly of Cuban birth. His mother was English; she worked as a snake charmer. From age ten, Scaramanga worked as a trick shot artist. At fifteen, he was working as a gunman in the real world. He was soon recruited by the Soviet KGB who trained him in Europe to become an overworked and underpaid assassin. In the late 1950's, he went independent. By the 1970's, he was earning $1,000,000 a hit and killing his targets with a golden bullet from his custom-made, gold-plated 4.2 mm pistol. Scaramanga is tall and dark. No photographs are available of him, though his fingerprints are on file with the Central Intelligence Agency. We see him with only one beautiful girl friend, and, apparently, he only makes love before and, possibly, after he kills his target. He eats the best of food, as Nick Nack is a graduate of the French chef's school, the Cordon Bleu. Scaramanga dresses well, usually in white suits with gold accessories. He has a state-of-the-art home on an island claimed by mainland China that contains the most advanced solar power station in the world.

Nick Nack.

In *The Man with the Golden Gun* (1975), Nick Nack (Hervé Villechaize) serves Scaramanga as a gourmet chef and manservant. In addition, though small in stature, he is a killer. He sets up the shooting gallery for Scaramanga and even handicaps his own boss, knowing all the while that he will inherit the island if his boss dies. He is a very confident man. James Bond does not quite have the heart to do away with the tiny killer at the end of the film and instead hangs him in a cage from the mast of his Chinese junk.

Karl Stromberg.

One of the world's most powerful industrialists, Karl Stromberg (Curt Jurgens) in **The Spy Who Loved Me** (1977) sought to destroy the world by instigating a full-scale nuclear war between the United States and Soviet Russia, and then to rebuild a more perfect world dominated by him under the sea. The megalomaniacal recluse fancied himself a modern-day Captain Nemo with his own fleet of high-jacked nuclear submarines and his very own Atlantis. Situated off the coast of Sardinia, Italy, Atlantis contained everything that he needed to support life under the sea. The base included living areas, extravagant dining rooms, huge aquariums, research laboratories, helipads and shipping docks. Like Dr. No's island nation of Crab Key and Blofeld's volcanic hideaway in Japan, Atlantis was to have been the centerpiece of an underwater kingdom, where Stromberg could rule his subjects with an iron fist and still live in luxurious exile. His dream must have seemed so close that he could nearly grasp it with his web-fingered hands, but thanks to 007 and Triple-X, his nightmare was brought to a fitting end. [In an early version of the script, SPECTRE. was responsible for high-jacking the nuclear submarines under the directorship of a villain named Stavros. In an effort to avert any legal problems with Kevin McClory, who had co-written the plot of **Thunderball** with Fleming and introduced the character of Blofeld and the organization of SPRECTRE, all of these references were dropped. Stavros became Stromberg, and his organization became a multi-million-dollar corporate empire instead of a collection of masterminds and assassins.]

EVERYTHING I KNOW ABOUT LIFE
I LEARNED FROM JAMES BOND

Jaws.

Jaws (Richard Kiel), with his menacing steel teeth and seven-foot tall frame, was the ultimate villain's henchman. Remarkably strong and practically indestructible, Jaws withstood physical attacks from 007 that would have killed or permanently disabled any normal bad guy. Whether he was dropped out of an airplane without a working parachute, offered up as a delicious entrée for a hungry shark, driven into the roof of a house, thrown out of a speeding train, plummeted down over a dangerous waterfall, or forced to freefall from space, Jaws always got right back up, brushed himself off, and continued with his mission. His most distinguishing characteristic, and what gave him his nickname, was his razor-sharp teeth that could chew through almost everything. He lacked personal skills, and while not quite mute, could only manage to speak a few simple words at a time. In the novel by Christopher Wood, he was born to Polish parents, recruited into a special branch of the Russian KGB, and has the name Zbigniew Krycsiwiki. [Jaws was so popular in *The Spy Who Loved Me* that he made a return appearance in *Moonraker*.]

Hugo Drax.

When we first see Hugo Drax (Michael Lonsdale) he is playing a classical piece of music on a grand piano in a room that puts the interior furnishing of the White House to shame. Drax is a French billionaire whose upper-class breeding makes him a European intellectual. He finances his own space program so that he can feel superior to all of his contemporaries and has plans to build a master race of humans that only he will control. He probably is the most heinous villain in the Bond films as he intends to kill at least 99.99% of the human population. Drax doesn't need their money, just their planet. But we know that, at least, Hugo Drax has a highly developed sense of humor. That's more than you can say about that little German/Austrian monster that died ranting in his bunker. Allegedly, when *Moonraker* was to be a totally British production, James Mason was offered the role of Drax. But when it became necessary to do a $32 or $34 million co-production, French actors—such as Lonsdale, Corinne Clery and others—were needed to get French funding. [Michael Lonsdale has gone on to great success in many French films and European TV series. One of Lonsdale's more recent English-language films was James Ivory's *Jefferson in Paris* (1995).]

Aristotle Kristatos.

In the original screenplay, Aristotle Kristatos (Julian Glover) is characterized as the most powerful criminal mastermind in Europe, and a confederate of the Soviet Union's KGB. During the Second World War, he supposedly fought against the Germans, for which he received a medal from the British, and then later, fought the Communists in Greece. In reality, he was a double-agent during the war, and took credit for courageous deeds carried out by his rival, Milos Columbo (Topol). When James Bond first meets him in *For Your Eyes Only* (1981), Kristatos pretends to be a cultured gentleman who enjoys the finer things in life. He is well-dressed, polished, the mirror-image of 007. He also appears to be working selflessly for his ice-skating protégé Bibi Dahl. But beneath the façade Kristatos is a devious and intelligent criminal who is involved in smuggling, theft, and extortion. He plans to sell the ATAC to the Soviets and to destroy his rival at the same time. Aristotle Kristatos is actually a kind of low-rent villain that does not offer much of a threat to 007. Once Bond

EVERYTHING I KNOW ABOUT LIFE
I LEARNED FROM JAMES BOND

discovers his true identity, he makes quick work of him and his smuggling organization. The smuggler's plan is, after all, not very large. [Julian Glover played an almost identical role as Donovan in *Indiana Jones and the Last Crusade* (1989).]

Emil Locque.

Thanks to Q's Identigraph machine, Bond learns that Emil Leopold Locque (Michael Gothard) is a convicted felon who escaped from his prison cell by strangling his psychiatrist in *For Your Eyes Only*. He appears as a rather ordinary-looking man with wire-rim glasses, not at all the image of a ruthless assassin. Intelligent, calm and quietly confident in his demeanor, he enjoys killing. Locque works as a contract killer for Kristatos, and uses the sign of the "dove," which is actually Columbo's trademark, as a way to throw off suspicion. When James Bond discovers that Locque has killed his friend Ferrara, 007 chases him down, and ruthlessly kicks his car over a cliff with Locque still behind the wheel.

Kamal Khan.

A former Afghan prince exiled to the Monsoon Palace in Udaipur, India, Kamal Khan (Louis Jourdan) partners with General Orlov and Octopussy to smuggle stolen Russian artifacts across international borders in *Octopussy* (1983). But his real intentions are much darker and more nefarious. In exchange for smuggling a nuclear bomb onto a U.S. Air Force Base, Khan will not only profit from the Kremlin jewels but also eliminate a partner who has begun to question his motives. With no love lost for any of his associates, he stops at nothing to gain his fortune. Khan indulges in gambling (using loaded dice), sports (preferably man-hunts), and rare Indian delicacies (like stuffed sheep's head). With a background in International Law, he makes a formidable enemy for most civil servants, but not for James Bond. [Louis Jourdan, a long-time friend of Cubby Broccoli, was previously considered for the role of Sir Hugo Drax in *Moonraker* (1979).]

General Orlov.

General Orlov (Steven Berkoff) is characterized as an aggressive, hot-tempered, power crazed Communist hardliner who wants the Soviet Union to invade Western Europe in *Octopussy*. In fact, his fictional character is actually based on a composite of several real-world generals who drew up plans in the early eighties for a Soviet invasion of Europe. When General Gogol (Walter Gotell) and some of the more moderate members of the Kremlin dismiss his views as reactionary, Orlov plots with Kamal Khan to detonate an atomic bomb on a US Air Force base in West Germany, making it look like an accident. With no one to blame for the atomic mishap, public outcry will bring about unilateral disarmament, and Soviet tanks will then easily cross into Western Europe, crushing all opposition. Orlov sees himself as a patriot, but in fact he has lost his mind. As soon as Gogol learns that Orlov has been stealing the jewels from the Kremlin Art Repository to finance his maniacal scheme, he chases him to the West German border. But when Orlov crosses illegally into the West, he is gunned down by the border guards.

Gobinda.

Like Odd-Job, Tee-Hee, and Jaws, Gobinda (Kabir Bedi) of *Octopussy* is yet another big and tough henchman who speaks very little English but has a larger-than-life presence. They must have all attended the same school for henchmen together! He is the personal man-servant of Kamal Khan and follows the orders of his master, even when that means fighting Bond on top an airborne plane. Gobinda's most unique feature is his formidable stare. He was head of security for the Monsoon Palace, and managed Khan's palace staff; he was also an important link in the pipeline that smuggled jewelry across international borders, and he participated in placing a nuclear bomb on board Octopussy's Traveling Circus Train. In this final fight with Bond, Gobinda is struck in the face by the plane's antenna, and plummets to his death.

Max Zorin.

Max Zorin (Christopher Walken) is a product of eugenics experiments the Nazis were conducting during World War II in *A View to a Kill* (1985). His pregnant mother was shot up with steroids by a mad scientist, Hans Glaub (aka Dr. Mortner), in a Nazi concentration camp. The experiments did produce some high I.Q. children, but they all turned out to be psychotic (which can be a real effect of an overdose of steroids). Dr. Mortner and his kiddies vanished behind the Iron Curtain when the Soviets took over East Germany, and Zorin emerged as a KGB spy with his father-figure physician still in tow. Zorin became so crazy, he dumped his KGB connection. Like the Irish Republican Army, the KGB often lives by the slogan "Once in, never out." In any case, we believe that one should never make an enemy of a man like General Gogol, who has a habit of surviving the worst situations in the Soviet Union without the help of the Western intelligence agencies. Zorin thought he was a superman; Zorin attempted a psychotic victory and failed. General Gogol would never have approved such a stunt; that is why he was going to give James Bond the Order of Lenin. We doubt he would wear it on his Royal Navy uniform, however.

Scarpine.

Though May Day catches your eye as the statuesque executioner of Zorin's organization, Scarpine (Patrick Bauchau) is the organization's security director. He sizes people up, reports to the boss and takes care of whatever business needs to be done, however ghastly. Patrick Nicolas Jean Sixte Ghislain Bauchau was born in Brussels and raised in a number of places, educated in modern languages at Oxford. [Bauchau caught the last wave in the French New Wave cinema in the late 1960's and has had a healthy career in films and TV on the continent, the UK and in the USA.]

THE TIMOTHY DALTON VILLAINS

Because the villains in the Roger Moore films had gone so far over the top (and very literally into outer space), the producers of the James Bond series felt a more realistic approach was necessary. In *The Living Daylights* (1987), the role of villain is divided between General Georgi Koskov and Brad Whitaker. Unfortunately, neither character is large enough or eccentrically sufficient to fill the shoes of Auric Goldfinger or Dr. No. They are pretty much the run-of-the-mill bad guys with none of the dramatic flair of Francisco Scaramanga or the sadistic evil of Maximillan Zorin. Necros, on the other hand, makes a very convincing henchman. In *Licence to Kill* (1989), Franz Sanchez was also nothing more than a run-of-the-mill drug lord, not unlike the character Robert Davi played on the television series *Wiseguy* (1988).

General Georgi Koskov.

Charming but ruthless, General Georgi Koskov (Jeroen Krabbé) thinks nothing of setting his girlfriend Kara up to be killed or betraying his country to turn a profit in *The Living Daylights* (1987). The deceitful and two-faced Soviet general is in business for himself, and cleverly plays both sides of the Cold War. At first, he pretends to be a peace-loving man who has been trapped like a sacrificial pawn in the battle between the USSR and Great Britain; but then later, we learn that he is the mastermind behind the plan to buy large amounts of raw opium and turn the profit into purchasing illegal arms from Brad Whitaker. Koskov feigns friendship with Bond, but just as easily arrests the secret agent for Pushkin's "murder." He is prepared to dote on his mistress and give her all manner of expensive gifts, but, when necessary, Koskov just as easily signs her death warrant. 007 has rarely ever dealt with a villain who has so many different faces and personalities.

Brad Whitaker.

Brad Whitaker (Joe Don Baker) is an American arms dealer who pretends that he is an expert military tactician in *The Living Daylights*. Expelled from West Point Military Academy for cheating, he spent a short stint as a mercenary in the Belgian Congo before working with various criminal organizations to help finance his first arms deals. Whitaker fancies himself a military leader, and has surrounded himself with wax figures of all the great military leaders in history, including Napoleon, Caesar, and Genghis Khan; the unique feature of each of his wax figures is that they all carry his facial features. Obsessed with military tactics, he also enjoys re-playing famous battles with toy soldiers and various other gadgets in his "hobby room." Apart from his games, Whitaker has also surrounded himself with his own personal military force, and sees Koskov as one of his generals. His opium-smuggling operation and arms deals seem rather second rate when they are compared with the elaborate plots of previous Bond baddies. [Joe Don Baker returned as Bond's CIA contact Jack Wade in *GoldenEye* (1995) and *Tomorrow Never Dies* (1997).]

Necros.

A humorless, highly-trained, cold-blooded killer, Necros (Andreas Wisniewski) literally represents death; in fact, his name derives from the Greek word for "dead." He was once a Soviet agent with KGB affiliations, trained as an assassin for special operations, but now works exclusively for General Georgi Koskov. Although a fairly attractive man, Necros is known to use a great number of disguises and many different techniques of killing. He seems to enjoy listening to rock music on his personal Walkman radio, particularly "Where Has Everybody Gone" by The Pretenders, playing a couple of times throughout the film when he kills his victims. Necros uses the cord from his Walkman to strangle his victims, and seems to enjoy strangulation in general. Like Odd-Job and Jaws before him, he proves to be a menacing opponent for James Bond.

EVERYTHING I KNOW ABOUT LIFE I LEARNED FROM JAMES BOND

Franz Sanchez.

How can you describe a man like Franz Sanchez (Robert Davi)? Well, he was man enough to wear a pink shirt and get away with it, at least on his vacation. He was brutal to his girlfriend, a monster to his employees, and he was hard on his tanker trucks. You have to give him credit for consistency. He had the ability to survive in a sea of sharks by having the biggest smile with the largest set of teeth. Why did he believe James Bond when Bond talked him into believing Krest and others were going to betray him? We suspect that a man who talks so often about loyalty probably suspects that no one is really loyal to him. And, possibly except for Krest (though he was trying to have a freebee from Lupe) and Dario (who was too young to have ambitions of becoming El Jefe), Sanchez was right. In an international ring of drug lords, it is hard to always keep your back against the wall. The only good thing about Sanchez was that if Sanchez gave his word, he kept it. He could have fed Killifer to the sharks and kept $2 million. On the other hand, if he had a reputation of not keeping his word, he might lose a lot of business.

Dario.

Dario (Benicio Del Toro) is a young swine, ready to cut into a man or woman if the opportunity presents itself. There is a maniacal joy in his eyes when he does it too. This man really enjoys his work; we all should have this passion for our chosen profession. [Benicio Del Toro was twenty-one years old when he made *Licence to Kill*. Today, he is an Oscar winner for his supporting role in *Traffic* (2002) and one of Hollywood's hottest actors. *Licence to Kill* was only his second film.]

JOHN L. FLYNN AND BOB BLACKWOOD

THE PIERCE BROSNAN VILLAINS

With the departure of Timothy Dalton, Albert R. Broccoli and his son-in-law Michael Wilson and his daughter Barbara Broccoli sought to return the James Bond films full circle back to the glory days of Sean Connery. They first hired the right actor to play 007 in popular heartthrob Pierce Brosnan. They equipped him with all manner of gadgets and cars. They paired him with the most beautiful women in the world, and, finally, introduced him to larger than life villains and their henchmen with the same weight as those who had appeared in earlier films. *GoldenEye* (1995) and the films that followed restored our faith in the James Bond series. **Alec Trevelyan.** Alec Trevelyan (Sean Bean) may be James Bond's most difficult opponent because he is a 00-Agent just like Bond, and he knows all of his rivals' moves like they were his own. At the beginning of *GoldenEye* (1995), 007 and Alec Trevelyan penetrate a chemical weapons facility with orders from MI6 to destroy it. Alec is supposedly killed by General Ourumov, but surfaces many years later as the head of the Janus crime syndicate. The son of Cossacks who worked for the British against the Germans in World War II, his parents were betrayed to the Russians, and killed before his eyes. He never forgave that betrayal, and plotted to rob the Bank of England of huge amounts of cash before destroying the nation's capital with the GoldenEye Satellite. Bond is forced to kill him before he can initiate his ruthless plan.

EVERYTHING I KNOW ABOUT LIFE I LEARNED FROM JAMES BOND

Elliot Carver.

Elliot Carver has just about everything most men would desire in *Tomorrow Never Dies* (1997). He owns a successful international news business—an international newspaper, magazines, a TV satellite network, etc. He has a beautiful wife, who did seem to care for him. We recall her defense of him when Paris Carver was first talking to James Bond. She was putting Carver first, until her passion was aroused. That slap was just her way of saying, "Hi there, James. Back in town?" He had hurt her feelings, and she wanted to hurt him. Once that old business was over, she slowly started to heat up for a man, like her husband, who was very busy and had many responsibilities. Bond was unfinished business, and she was determined to see what she had missed. We suspect that Elliot Carver was spending most of his time promoting his businesses. He had his beautiful trophy wife. No man could touch her without facing his handpicked thugs. You will notice he himself never approached James Bond in an outrage. Rather, he used his "boys" to cool off Bond's ardor. Well, that approach might work with the casual Casanova, but it has never worked with James Bond. If you want him to go away, you have to kill him or give him what he wants. He made the most serious mistake that any man (and it usually is a man) in the public eye can make: he started believing his own publicity. He thought he could not only cover the news better than anyone else, he could even create the news. Who better that Elliot Carver to do it? He loves bad news. After all, the bad news was never about him, at least not until he had that little boating "accident" off the coast of Vietnam. Sic transit gloria mundi (Thus passes the glory of the world). Elliot Carver forgot that, despite his wealth and power, he was only a man, not a god, not an emperor, just a man.

Mr. Stamper.

Yes, but for every villain in a James Bond film who does not get to engage in sex or personal violence, there are ten Stamper henchmen who are very nasty. He is large. Stamper (Götz Otto) in *Tomorrow Never Dies* has white hair, like "Red" Grant (Robert Shaw) in *From Russia with Love*. He is massively muscled. We loved the sight of him machine-gunning the sailors who managed to escape from HMS Devonshire. It was like something from a World War II film after a warship was torpedoed by a U-boat, though truthfully we do not remember that particular atrocity as being commonplace. Anyway, Stamper was shooting the sailors with ammunition that would be used by Chinese Migs in order to blame the Chinese for this horror, not just for fun, though he seemed to be enjoying it. We liked Bond dropping a missile on Stamper's foot to hold him in place on the stealth ship. He deserved at least a hot foot.

Colonel Tan-Gun Moon/Gustav Graves and Zao.

We loved the opening sequence with Colonel Tan-Gun Moon (Will Yun Lee) punching out his anger-management coach in *Die Another Day* (2002). That says it all about him. He is a rich, spoiled brat. After his transformation into Sir Gustav Graves (Toby Stephens), he is a very rich, spoiled brat, thanks to a fortune in conflict diamonds he acquired by bartering away his country's military equipment. Always trying to oneup everyone, Graves meets his match at the point of James Bond's sword, and we're sure we weren't the only ones who enjoyed seeing him put down. The only person that Moon/Graves shows any affection for is Zao (Rick Yune). After all, Moon/Graves kills his own father in cold blood. There really isn't any particular woman

EVERYTHING I KNOW ABOUT LIFE I LEARNED FROM JAMES BOND

in Moon/Grave's life, but we say, "Don't ask. Don't tell." And as we play the movie over in our minds, it seems that whenever Moon/Graves is really challenged, Zao has to do the heavy lifting. The diamond-studded dude is a good driver as he proves on the frozen lake. Zao, like James Bond, is used to operating on his own. Zao is a terrorist's terrorist, just as Bond is a spy's spy. Take away Zao, and we think Moon/Graves might be just another rich kid.

Mr. Kil.

When James Bond meets Mr. Kil (Lawrence Makoare) in ***Die Another Day***, we get the usual banter:

Mr. Kil: I'm Mr. Kil.

James Bond: Now there's a name to die for.

The six-foot-four, barrel-chested Mr. Kil almost takes out both Jinx and James Bond with Graves' diamond mine industrial laser outfit; luckily, Jinx is good in a bad situation—although when she's bad, she's better. Mr. Kil is the strong silent type of villain, like Vargas and many others in Bond films. But he is skillful in creating menace. [If you saw the ***Lord of the Rings*** trilogy, you saw Makoare in heavy makeup or a helmet as three arch villains—Lurtz, leader of Saruman's Uruk-Hai orcs, in ***The Fellowship of the Rings***; Gothmog, leader of Sauron's orcs in ***The Return of the King***; and the Witch King, who is cashiered by Eowyn's sword and her hobbit helper in ***The Return of the King***.]

JOHN L. FLYNN AND BOB BLACKWOOD

THE DANIEL CRAIG VILLAINS

One of the most distinctive features of the villains in the recent James Bond films featuring Daniel Craig is just how uninteresting and common they are. Gone are the days of flamboyant figures like Goldfinger, Largo, and Blofeld in favor of true-to-life figures from the real-world of espionage. Instead of larger-than-life villains bent on world domination, the bad guys in the most recent films are bankers, corporate executives, and corrupt government officials. These post-modern villains inhabit a world in which terrorists crashed planes into the World Trade Center Buildings and killed millions of innocents with weapons of mass destruction. They are, in fact, a reflection of the real evil that citizens of the world face as they watch their hard-earned savings evaporate with the collapse of the world financial markets as fat cat bankers and executives get even fatter.

Le Chiffre.

The third incarnation of Le Chiffre (as played by Mads Mikkelsen) is quite unlike his counterparts (Peter Lorre and Orson Welles) in the other two adaptations of *Casino Royale*. This particular characterization finds Le Chiffre as a banker who services many of the world's terrorists. He is a mathematical genius and chess expert, and uses these skills when playing poker. He tortures Bond, as in the novel, and corrupts the beautiful Vesper Lynd. He is ultimately killed by Mr. White and his associates.

EVERYTHING I KNOW ABOUT LIFE
I LEARNED FROM JAMES BOND

Dominic Greene.

In *Quantum of Solace*, actor Mathieu Amalric plays Dominic Greene as a wealthy businessman who, as the leading member of Quantum, pretends to be working for a charity that supports the environment and the promises of better world order. His character seems to reflect the distrust that most moviegoers have of big business and "green" technology, and is truly a villain ripped from the news headlines of 2008.

Silva.

In *Skyfall* (2012), Daniel Craig's James Bond faces his most interesting and deadly villain to date in Silva (Javier Bardem). The movie's multi-layered villain not only reveals that he has "mommy issues" with Judi Dench's M, but he also flirts with James Bond (Daniel Craig). Bardem, a very subtle actor, also shows Bond that Silva knows what it is like to be out in the cold and invites Bond to join him in more than just a sexual encounter. Silva is the only villain who has risen to a high position, head of the Hong Kong bureau, under M's direction. His hatred/love for M has led him to direct the force of his attack solely upon M and her operation. He is quite successful in his efforts, even escaping from M's imprisonment. It is not until Bond takes the helm and moves the site of the action to his estate in the Scottish Highlands that the geek-mad Silva, without extensive electronic support, starts to make mistakes. However, Silva has been trained to be a deadly assassin, like Bond himself, and will stop at nothing to get his revenge on M, but he is defeated in a very strange, almost nineteenth century environment.

Ernst Stavro Blofeld 3.

During the Sean Connery years, Ernst Stavro Blofeld was James Bond's most formidable villain; he ran SPECTRE with an iron fist, and was not unlike Moriarty, whom Sherlock Holmes described as "the Napoleon of crime." Blofeld remained hidden from view in the first two Bond films, then later ***Thunderball*** (1965). We'd see him stroking a white Persian cat, and wearing a SPECTRE ring. When he finally did come out from behind the shadows, Donald Pleasence, Telly Savalas, and Charles Gray played Blofeld ***You Only Live Twice*** (1967), ***On Her Majesty's Secret Service*** (1969), and ***Diamonds Are Forever*** (1971), respectively. With Irma Bunt, he killed James Bond's wife Tracey, and maintained secret bases all around the world, including inside a volcano. Bond destroyed several of his doubles, then later, Roger Moore's Bond cast him down a chimney, presumably to his death. He remained dead and buried until EON Productions resurrected him for Daniel Craig's Bond, with a twist. Blofeld (as played by Academy-Award winner Christoph Waltz) was a surrogate brother to 007, apparently raised by a man named Oberhauser who taught the young James Bond to ski after Bond's parents died in a climbing accident. Blofeld became the source of Bond's "pain" working in the background, building SPECTRE. After he is captured and jailed, Blofeld relies on a bionic eye to maintain his control over SPECTRE.

Mr. Hinx.

All supervillains need a worthy henchman at their side, and in ***Spectre*** (2015), actor, wrestler Dave Bautista plays Mr. Hinx, the iconic henchman following in the tradition of Oddjob and Jaws.

EVERYTHING I KNOW ABOUT LIFE I LEARNED FROM JAMES BOND

Lyutsifer Safin.

In *No Time to Die* (2021) Lyutsifer Safin (as played by Oscar-winner Rami Malek) is an anarchist, terrorist leader, self-proclaimed scientist and assassin who desires to kill Blofeld and destroy the SPECTRE organization. Apparently, members of his family were talented chemists, and routinely supplied poisons to SPECTRE. They oversaw production at an island manufacturing facility called "The Poisoned Garden." When Lyutsifer Safin was a young boy, Blofeld sent Mr. White to kill his entire family with their own dioxin chemicals during a banquet in their honor. The sole survivor of the poisoning, Lyutsifer was left facially disfigured and forever traumatized by Blofeld's treachery. Forced to wear a mask, Safin plots against SPECTRE. First, he orders his men to steal Obruchev's nanobot technology (also known as Project Heracles), and then he uses it to exact his revenge upon Blofeld and SPECTRE. Later, he turns his attention to using the nanobots to subjugate the world. The Poison Garden and the backstory of Shatterhand (presumably changed to Safin) is borrowed from elements in Ian Fleming's original novel *You Only Live Twice* (first published in 1964). Much of the plot of the novel was jettisoned by EON Productions, and a whole new plot involving the theft of spacecraft by SPECTRE was created to make the 1967 film.

CHAPTER ELEVEN

THE WORLD ORDER—SIMPLIFIED

The World Is not Enough
But it is such a perfect place to start my love
And if you're strong enough
Together we can take the world apart my love.

—Garbage, **The World Is not Enough** (1999)

Ian Fleming's contribution to popular literature and postwar Western culture cannot be overstated. In creating his incredible world of James Bond, Fleming placed his characters smack dab in the middle of the Cold War at a juncture where the real world and the fictional world collided. Today, authors like Tom Clancy, John Le Carré, and Len Deighton routinely use topical references to add verisimilitude to their work, and they all have Ian Fleming to thank for pioneering that style of writing. Of course, what Fleming knew of the "world order" was filtered through his real-life experiences working as a spy for British

EVERYTHING I KNOW ABOUT LIFE
I LEARNED FROM JAMES BOND

Intelligence during World War II and at the beginning of the Cold War with the Soviet Union. His interweaving of fact and fiction is as much fun as the novels or movies themselves.

Though neither of us have ever had the pleasure of visiting the former Soviet Union, both of us feel like we know Russia and its former axis of evil because James Bond did the legwork for us. In particular, that "leg" work has included introducing us to a number of women with Eastern European ancestry! But more to the point . . . all we know about politics, political ideologies, and the "world order" we learned from the valuable information in the James Bond films.

World Domination.

World domination is a recurrent theme in the James Bond films, with most of the villains ambitiously plotting one nefarious scheme or another to control the entire planet. Though it is debatable whether our world, as complex and diverse as it is, could ever be successfully "dominated" by a single figure in this way, the concept of world domination has long been the dream of megalomaniacs. In the first film, Bond tries to provoke Dr.

No by decrying, "The same old dream. Our asylums are full of people who think they're Napoleon. Or God." But Dr. No does not react to his provocation. He does not see himself as a megalomaniac, even though his plan to topple U.S. rockets in order to control the high ground of space is an exercise of such power that only a megalomaniac could have conceived it. Like others throughout history before him, many had tried and failed to dominate the world. Caesar, Alexander the Great, and Genghis Khan had goals of world domination, and were only limited by transportation technologies and their knowledge of geography. French dictator Napoleon Bonaparte succeeded in conquering large portions of Europe, and is often considered to be the quintessential world conqueror. The popular board game *Risk*, subtitled "The Game of Global Domination," is largely based on the campaigns of Napoleon. But Napoleon did not conquer the entire world. Similarly, Adolf Hitler had ambitions of controlling the whole world, but the best that his Nazi regime could manage in World War II was dominance over most of Europe. During the Cold War—the time when Ian Fleming was writing the novels—most Western powers believed the Soviet Union had a plan for world domination. And as domino countries like Cuba, North Korean and Vietnam fell to the communists, the United States and its allies struggled to contain the totalitarian regime. Ironically, hard-line communists in the Kremlin and Beijing felt that it was the United States that had a goal of world domination. The pursuit of power and especially the economic costs and human sacrifice that the exercise of such power often requires are not generally congenial to democratic instincts. Today, the idea of world domination finds more credibility in science fiction as the sinister ambition of the story's villain than in the reality of our global village. Of course, that does not stop villains in the James Bond films from trying. Ernest Stavro

EVERYTHING I KNOW ABOUT LIFE I LEARNED FROM JAMES BOND

Blofeld, the head of SPECTRE, would try to conquer the world several times as would many of his predecessors and counterparts. Oh, and one more thing, if you do plan to threaten global domination and demand the world powers pay you a ransom, charge more than one million dollars. That's often a mistake megalomaniacs, like Dr. Evil from the Austin Powers' movie, make.

Russia and the Soviet Union.

Russia has always been something of a mystery, a place in history with thousands of miles of bleak steppes and thousands of dour Slavic swordsmen. Even the word "Russia" is of unknown origin, though it may be Scandinavian. In fact, we must thank the Swedes, the Danes and the Norwegians for opening trade routes between Scandinavia and Russia, down the river systems, through the steppes, all the way to Constantinople, now Istanbul. While they were traveling, these hardy Norsemen brought red hair to the steppes. Did you know that Genghis Khan had red hair? The first people that came to Russia were called Rus, perhaps as early as 3000 B.C. These early peoples left a rich and vibrant culture, not unlike the civilizations of the ancient Eskimos. Archeological evidence shows that they were great hunters of reindeer, seal, birds, and walruses. Many sites with ancient dwellings and homes have also shown what hardy and stalwart peoples they were. While most of Europe languished during the Dark Ages, the period of the Kievan Russian Empire (868–1698) showed much growth and learning; unfortunately, the Mongols and Tatars destroyed most of what had been built during that period. In 1698, during the start of the Imperial Period, the House of Romanov emerged, and Peter the Great Westernized part of Russia. Peter's Westernization of

Russia culminated in the destruction of the autocracy by the Socialist Revolution of 1917, and civil war plunged the nation into bloody conflict. After 1917, the Communist Party maintained the Empire as the Union of Soviet Socialist Republics. The USSR fell in 1991 and dissolved into fifteen nations, though many still answer to Moscow.

The Cold War.

The Cold War began as soon as the hot war with the Nazis ended in Europe in 1945. The Red Army entered Germany and the rest of Eastern Europe with the intent of completely dominating the political structures. They succeeded in establishing more or less puppet governments everywhere in their sphere of influence. In 1948, when the Russians challenged the Allies by closing the land routes to Berlin. The Allies which included American, British and French forces airlifted supplies to the starving and cold Berliners for eleven months. During this struggle, Wall Street wizard Bernard Baruch coined the phrase "Cold War" to describe the standoff between the Soviets and the Allied forces. The struggle intensified from 1948 to 1953 when the Americans formed NATO, which led to a unity of the West European, Canadian and American forces vs. the Warsaw Pact countries of Eastern Europe, which coalesced in 1955. Throughout the 1950's, American school children were often given drills on what to do if Soviet intercontinental ballistic missiles were launched at the USA. The drills consisted of squatting under your desk, while the class wiseguy always suggested you should "Kiss your ass goodbye." In the 1980's, American pressure brought about the collapse of the Soviet Union's economy and the desire of both sides for détente led to the end of the Cold War. In a number of the James Bond films, the Cold War gave SPECTRE the opportunity to play both sides (NATO and the Warsaw Pact nations) against each other, so that SPECTRE could emerge as a new world power. The moviemakers used SPECTRE as the villain to lessen the tensions between the two superpowers and to eliminate blacklisting of James Bond films in Eastern Europe.

Capitalism Versus Communism.

The ideological differences that once separated the Soviet Union from the West, Agent Triple-X from James Bond, are best explained as a difference between two competing theories for world dominance, Capitalism and Communism. In fact, the beginnings of the Cold War were deeply rooted in this competition for power in the new world order as well as the general mistrust between the United States and Russia that followed World War II. Both nations formulated policies designed to limit the expansion of the other. The foreign policy of the West, known as containment, attempted to contain the spread of Communism to smaller, third-world countries, while the Soviet Union's policy, known as expansion, tried to free suppressed peoples around the globe by introducing world Socialism. Neither policy was necessarily right or wrong, but ultimately led to conflicts in Southeast Asia and Central America. The fundamental difference between Capitalism and Communism fueled those conflicts. Capitalism is a system of beliefs that limits the government's role in a person's individual freedoms, and assures private citizens the rights to own property and goods, trade, and act without coercion. Communism, on the other hand, curtails this economic right by making every individual equal, and somewhat eliminates personal wealth and the resulting class system that allows owners to treat workers as slaves. Both claim to be economic systems that are more favorable to elevating the status of the common man, but history has already proven that Karl Marx's system does not work. In the middle-1970s, when the movie takes place, the diplomatic tension between nations had reached a fever pitch, and we were teetering on the precipice of nuclear war. Films like *The Spy Who Loved Me* (1977) showed the world that the Western powers and the Soviet Union could work together in peace and were a factor in warming the chill of the Cold War.

East and West.

During the scene in *Dr. No* (1962) in which the villain reveals his plans, James Bond demands to know if he is working for the East or the West, and Dr. No replies: "East, West, just points of the compass, each as stupid as the other." In 1962, the world was clearly divided between East and West, with the communist regimes of China, North Korean, Vietnam and their Russian supporter on one end of the spectrum vs. the constitutional democracies of Europe, the United States and Canada on the other. But that divide actually goes well beyond simple political ideologies. Historically, the East has always embraced metaphysical beliefs, while the West has always represented secular ideas. The East was spiritual, while the West was material; the East was intellectual, while the West was cultural. The East was viewed as dark and mysterious, while the West was wild and untamed. While these stereotypes hold very little meaning today, they were what drove us as a people, and formed most of the prejudices that kept us from living in harmony. Dr. No may well have been right about one thing: East and West are just points on a compass and should not determine how we view our counterparts on the other side of the globe.

EVERYTHING I KNOW ABOUT LIFE
I LEARNED FROM JAMES BOND

Vietnam.

Whenever we hear the Charlie Daniels' Band playing "Still in Saigon," we remember hearing the war news and wondering if our friends would ever survive. The Vietnam of *Tomorrow Never Dies* (1997) has a history with many Americans, Australians and other citizens of NATO countries. For some, the war in Vietnam actually began for thirty-five Americans in 1950 when the French asked for military and economic assistance from the United States, and the U.S. Military Assistance Advisory Group (MAAG) arrived in Saigon on August 3, 1950. After the French forces were defeated at Dien Bien Phu in 1954, and France was forced to withdraw from the Indonesian country, the CIA established a military mission. Fighting between the Communist North and the Democratic South began in 1956. The actual war with Vietnam broke out following the Gulf of Tonkin Incident when the U.S. Destroyer *Maddox* was attacked by two North Vietnamese torpedo boats in 1964. The first American combat troops entered in 1965. Eight years later, after tens of thousands of U.S. servicemen were killed, the Americans withdrew, and the war ended. Not long afterwards, the South fell to the North, and Vietnam became a Communist country. Forty years later, we find it hard to believe that Vietnam has a vibrant economy that is driven partially by tourism. Today, the formal name of Saigon is "Ho Chi Minh City." Today's Saigon is all business. By the end of the 1980's, the old communist party central planning was gone. Market economy is the name of the game. The Vietnamese turned to the richer countries in their area—Thailand, South Korea, Japan, etc.—for investors. Multinationals who wanted hard workers—often well educated, at low wages-came quickly; Coca Cola and others opened factories in the city. The economic growth rate was around eight percent; inflation was low. When the Southeast Asian boom slowed in the late 1990's, the Vietnamese government gave concessions to foreign companies to increase their support. Money talks; politics quibbles. Vietnam signed a bilateral trade agreement with the USA in May 2002 and is coping. In fact, next to China, it is the fastest growing economy in Southeast Asia. Just like most countries in Southeast Asia, Americans, British, French, and Australian tourists are welcomed. Special tours are available for veterans who wish to revisit some of the scenes of their struggle. In *Tomorrow Never Dies* (1997), James Bond and Wai Lin are taken as prisoners to Saigon, and forced to deal with Elliott Carver and his new legions of armies, the outlets of the mass media.

NATO.

In *Thunderball* (1965), Major Francois Derval was a French NATO officer assigned to a Vulcan bomber containing two atomic bombs. Derval's authorizing organization, NATO (North Atlantic Treaty Organization), was founded in 1949 as a Western European and American/Canadian force protecting Europe against the more numerous Soviet and Warsaw Pact armies occupying parts of central and all of Eastern Europe. By 1957, American bombers and nuclear weapons were based in Western Europe. As the Cold War continued, NATO envisioned a "flexible response" strategy in hopes that a war starting in Europe would not lead immediately to a planet-wide nuclear attack. NATO still exists with strong leadership not only from the Americans and British members but also from the French and German. Its Eastern European counterpart, the Warsaw Pact, however, ended in 1991 with the end of the Soviet Union.

EVERYTHING I KNOW ABOUT LIFE
I LEARNED FROM JAMES BOND

United Nations.

Like Alfred Hitchcock's *North by Northwest* (1959), which was a forerunner of the James Bond films, *Live and Let Die* (1973) begins with a mysterious murder at the United Nations in New York. The term "United Nations" was first coined by President Franklin D. Roosevelt on January 1, 1942, when representatives of twenty-six nations pledged to fight together against the Axis Powers of Germany, Italy and Japan. Following the Second World War, delegates from fifty countries met in San Francisco to draw up the United Nations Charter. Those representatives discussed proposals worked out by the representatives of China, the Soviet Union, the United Kingdom and the United States several months earlier at Dumbarton Oaks in United States. The United Nations officially came into existence on October 24, 1945, when the UN Charter was ratified by a majority of the nations, including China, France, the Soviet Union, the United Kingdom, and the United States. Like the League of Nations before it, the United Nations was an organization conceived to arbitrate conflicts between nations in order to prevent war. In *Live and Let Die*, delegates from Honduras, Russia, the United States, the fictional island nation of San Monique, and others debate the issues of the day, while an assassin works behind the scenes to kill the delegate from Great Britain.

MAD—Mutually Assured Destruction.

MAD or Mutually Assured Destruction, which first appears in *You Only Live Twice* (1967), was a policy from the Cold War era that dictated any use of nuclear weapons by either the United States or Russia would result in the destruction of both the aggressor and the defender. The policy assumed that each superpower possessed enough weaponry to destroy the other and that either side, if attacked for any reason by the other, would retaliate with equal or greater force. Both the United States and the Soviet Union believed that the exchange of nuclear weapons would bring about the other's total and assured destruction, and potentially any allies as well. Since neither side was irrational enough to risk its own destruction, neither side risked a first strike as they knew the other would launch on detection of that strike. The result was a stalemate or "Cold War" that lasted nearly thirty years, and brought about a hair-trigger peace between the superpowers. In *You Only Live Twice*, Blofeld plots with an unnamed Eastern power (possibly China) to destabilize the peace, and to usher in a new-world order after the United States and Russia have annihilated each other. Of course, like most madmen of his day, he fails to account for horrible aftermath of a nuclear exchange, including the deadly radioactive dust that would settle in clouds and seed the planet with death or the resultant nuclear winter which would kill off most of the animals and plants. Karl Stromberg in *The Spy Who Loved Me* (1977) plots a similar doomsday scenario, but at least he has made arrangements for his people to survive in an underwater city after the world is destroyed. One of the life lessons that we learned, and a wise recommendation to future madmen, is the need to preserve the natural order of plant and animal life first before launching Armageddon.

Unilateral Disarmament.

In *Octopussy* (1983), General Orlov is concerned that the old men who run the Soviet Union are giving away their nuclear supremacy to the West, and plots to detonate a nuclear bomb on a U.S. Air Force Base to force the United States, through negative world opinion, into unilateral disarmament. Fortunately, 007 stops the bomb from detonating. During the Cold War, many pacifists in the United States and around the globe argued for unilateral disarmament, saying that if all counties had no strong military forces, then no one would feel threatened and the world would be a safe one in which to live. With no significant nuclear weapons at its disposal, no one nation could dominate another militarily. But that notion of pacifism presupposed that every nation in turn would agree to unilaterally disarm itself, and that every nation could be trusted to do so. The reduction of arms, while an incredibly lofty and idealist goal, may not be practical in the world in which we live, or the world that is presented in the latest James Bond adventure. We live in a world in which nations mistrust each other, and with that sense of mutual suspicion, it seems unreasonable to assume that any one nation would honestly comply with a total disarmament policy because that nation would be vulnerable to the others that would not. Intelligence-gathering techniques, as evidenced by the war in Iraq, have not increased sufficiently to the level of sophistication that would be needed to verify a fully disarmed enemy. Consequently, the case for unilateral disarmament as a means to world peace is a myth propagated by naïve or far too trusting people who do not fully understand the world as it exists. James Bond never disarms and is very literally a weapon of peace. That is a lesson well-learned.

Détente.

As far back as *From Russia with Love* (1963), the James Bond films have always exploited the tension between the rival superpowers. But as those tensions in the real world began to ease, thanks to increased diplomatic, commercial and cultural contact and a genuine desire to negotiate and talk, a few films have made détente the centerpiece of the story. In *Octopussy* (1983), a Russian general sought to unravel the whole process of détente by detonating a nuclear device at an airbase. In *The Living Daylights*, another Russian general tried to derail détente for his own political and financial gain. This relaxing or easing of tensions between rivals can be traced back to the 1970s (and possibly further). Since the detonation of the first Soviet nuclear bomb in 1949, the East and West had been locked into a struggle for world dominance, the Cold War. Both escalated an arms race in an attempt to secure a military advantage over the other, thus fostering the fear that another world war, again with Europe in the cross-hairs, was a distinct possibility. The events of the Cuban missile crisis not only brought the world to the brink of a nuclear war but also showed the two sides that an arms race was not a solution. By the 1970s, both sides were motivated by a desire for peace because clear superiority of nuclear arms was no longer a viable foreign policy objective in the nuclear weapons arena. Eventually, détente and the collapse of the Soviet economy led to the end of the Cold War.

Diplomacy.

With a termination order signed by M against General Pushkin in *The Living Daylights* (1987), James Bond practices a rather unique form of diplomacy when he forcibly enters the Soviet general's room and negotiates an assassination pact. 007 does indeed shoot Pushkin on the last day of the conference in Tangier, but he shoots him with the foreknowledge that his quarry is wearing a bullet-proof vest with squibs rigged to explode blood with each bullet strike. Ultimately, Pushkin lives, and Bond has carried out his assignment without arousing

EVERYTHING I KNOW ABOUT LIFE
I LEARNED FROM JAMES BOND

hostility between the two men or their two respective governments. With his license to kill, 007 is the blunt end of the Secret Intelligence Service MI6. When he is given orders, he is expected by his superiors to carry those orders out without question. Rarely, if ever, does Bond get to rely on his skills as a diplomat. But he does know, according to Harold Nicholson, the seven virtues of being a diplomat: truthfulness, precision, calm, good temper, patience, modesty, and loyalty—many of the qualities that we have come to admire in 007. First and foremost, James Bond does know that MI6 and the rest of the British armed forces are the instruments of foreign policy, and not its master. He knows that diplomacy must be divested of an avenging spirit, and that diplomats must look at a political hotspot from all points of view, not just their own. He must be willing to compromise on issues that are not vital, and must be willing to give up unenforceable rights for substance of real advantage. He accepts that diplomats must never put themselves into a position from which they cannot retreat without losing face and from which you cannot advance without grave risks. And finally, Bond knows that good diplomacy is more a matter of style of action than the action itself. With his many years of experience as an enforcer, 007 also feels that he would make a great diplomat, and has proven it as well.

Weapons of Mass Destruction.

Goldfinger intends to contaminate the gold supply of the United States by detonating a small-scale atomic bomb inside the vault at Fort Knox, Kentucky. The bomb was built and supplied to Goldfinger by the Red Chinese national Mr. Ling. The core of the weapon was a combination of cobalt and iodine, which enabled the device to initiate a small-scale nuclear explosion. With a radioactive half-life of fifty-eight years, Western economy would be in chaos for decades. In 1964, at the time when the film was made, atomic bombs were usually huge bulky items, not at all like the one housed in a steel case about six feet long, by three feet high, with the timing device built right into the case. Like a terrorist, Goldfinger threatens to detonate the device at the Polaris submarine pens at New London, Cape Kennedy, or the White House, if his plans are thwarted. Today, atomic bombs are small enough to fit into a brief case, and represent one of the greatest threats to world peace. From the James Bond films, we have learned to cut the red wire before the green wire in order to disable an atomic device. If that fails, wait for an expert in nuclear physics to switch off the "on" button, preferably before the clock ticks down to 007 seconds.

Blood Feud.

In *From Russia with Love* (1963), Kerim Bey tells Bond that he regrets that the Gypsies, his hirelings, have reached a blood feud with the Bulgarians, the Russians' hirelings. This private warfare is quite common in Asia and in some areas of Eastern Europe, such as Montenegro in Yugoslavia. The Sicilians call it vendetta. For example, when the Japanese forces bombed Pear Harbor, they killed a young Sicilian man who was aboard a US ship anchored in the harbor. Since war had not been declared before this act took place, the young sailor's five brothers in Chicago, who were upstanding citizens otherwise, declared vendetta, joined the U.S. Armed Forces, and did their best during World War II to kill as many of the enemy as possible. Often, blood feuds are caused by the initial shedding of blood, but not always. The Hatfield–McCoy feud that was fought in the late nineteenth century in Kentucky and West Virginia

EVERYTHING I KNOW ABOUT LIFE
I LEARNED FROM JAMES BOND

allegedly started over the theft of a McCoy pig by a Hatfield. That feud was not officially declared over until the middle of the twentieth century. In any case, to return to *From Russia with Love*, the Bulgarians always had a lively interest in Istanbul since it was called Constantinople, a city where their armed might on the nearby European mainland helped raise many Eastern contenders to the Byzantine throne. The Gypsies, on the other hand, are to be found throughout Europe. The Gypsies (a shortened English term for "Egyptians," which popular misconception gave as their ethnic base), more properly called Roma or Romanys, originated in northern India, which they left around 1000 A.D. In their wanderings through Europe, they have often existed on the edge of the law, as they rarely owned property. Their traditions of handling their own problems can be seen in *From Russia with Love*, where the two women must fight hand-to-hand to resolve who shall marry the man they both love. They would never go to court to resolve a problem. For example, a few years ago in Rome, a young man on the back of a motor scooter grabbed a woman's purse. The woman buttonholed a nearby carabinieri and asked him to do something. The soldier/policeman said, "I can't arrest him. He's a Gypsy. You'll be gone, and he'll never come to court." Since the law cannot touch a Gypsy, you might as well make friends with him. Some of them, such as the French guitarist Django Reinhardt, are great musicians. Others dance the flamenco beautifully in Spain. Today, moreover, some Gypsies have left the traditional occupations of fortune-telling and car or horse trading. They exist in the anonymity of America's large cities, putting in forty hours a week, speaking English and raising their children to be good citizens. Farewell, crystal ball; hello, mortgage insurance.

JOHN L. FLYNN AND BOB BLACKWOOD

Siamese fighting fish.

Ernst Stavro Blofeld lectures Rosa Klebb about Siamese fighting fish, likening the two fish that fight and tear each other apart to Britain and the Soviet Union. Siamese fighting fish, *Betta Splendens,* are about two-and-a-half to three inches in length at their full growth. They live from two to three years, but the males cannot live together as they tend to fight too much. In this respect, they resemble the members of SPECTRE, who often are menacing, particularly to those outside their organization. We never see SPECTRE members partying together on Friday nights. In any case, the colorful Siamese fighting fish, which can have all the colors of the American flag, originated in the shallow waters of rice paddies, ponds and rivers with slowly flowing streams in Thailand (once-called Siam), plus other Southeast Asian countries and China. Since they originated in a tropical climate, they are kept warm—even going over eighty degrees Fahrenheit. If the water temperature falls below seventy-five degrees Fahrenheit, they get sluggish, something like Americans after a snowfall. In **From Russia with Love** (1963), Blofeld identifies with the particular Siamese fighting fish that waits until one fish has triumphed over another before attacking the tired winner. Yes, SPECTRE is hoping both the NATO allies and the Warsaw Pact members will destroy each other so that SPECTRE can triumph over both. Blofeld's lecture is one that we can learn much about life; the smart competitor is one that waits until his competition has exhausted itself besting other competitors before competing. If you look carefully at Blofeld's aquarium, however, you will note that there is a glass wall between that "waiting" fish and the two fighters. If it were not for that wall, the three fish would go at each other all at once. Siamese fighting fish, with their special breathing organ, need to breathe air from the surface of the water. They may be a lot closer to humankind than you thought!

Nuclear Extortion.

The second big "E" in SPECTRE stands for "extortion." That's what Largo was doing to the NATO countries. He threatened an atomic attack on a major city in the USA or Great Britain unless a payment of $280 million in diamonds was made. The possibility of nuclear extortion was certainly in the air in 1965. It was a factor in the establishment of the Nuclear Non-proliferation Treaty of 1968 signed by the USA, the United Kingdom, the Soviet Union and fifty-nine other states, which vowed not to assist states not possessing nuclear explosives to either get them or to create them on their own. This treaty certainly had a dampening effect on the growth of nuclear weapons, though India in 1974 and Pakistan in 1998 both conducted nuclear tests. Some observers say that only the doctrine of Mutual Assured Destruction (MAD) kept the peace during the India-Pakistan stand-off in May 2002. One example of a sort of successful nuclear extortion is evident in North Korea. North Korea has developed the ability to produce atomic weapons, using equipment it purchased from other nations. In effect, it is demanding financial support of its authoritarian regime in return for not selling nuclear weapons, as well as the missiles which it has been selling to terrorist groups. The USA had already supported that regime in 1994 when North Korea promised not to develop nuclear weapons. In return, for allegedly stopping the completion of its nuclear reactors, a total of twelve countries plus the European Union—with the USA as primary sponsor—provided North Korea with five hundred thousand metric tons of fuel oil annually since 1994. These oil shipments stopped in 2002 when the North Koreans started talking again about creating nuclear weapons.

Bacteriological Warfare.

Ernst Stavro Blofeld plans to use twelve women who have been brainwashed at his allergy clinic to introduce harmful bacteria (Virus Omega) into the food supply and livestock of their various home countries if the International community does not meet his demands in *On Her Majesty's Secret Service* (1969). Until very recently, bacteriological or "germ" warfare was considered the stuff of science fiction, and never treated seriously by anyone in the mainstream. The Protocol for the Prohibition of Poisonous Gases and Bacteriological Methods of Warfare, which was signed and ratified by the world powers in Geneva on June 17, 1925, assured everyone that the use of harmful gases and bacteria as weapons of mass destruction would never be tolerated by the international community. However, with the rise of certain terrorist groups in the last few decades, the threat has become a very real one again. In 1995, a group of terrorists known as Aum released nerve gas in Tokyo's subway system, killing twelve persons. During the first Persian Gulf War in 1991, Iraq fired missiles containing Anthrax, Aflatoxin, and Botulinum against Allied targets, and Saddam Hussein used poisonous gas against his own people to quell a potential uprising. Germ warfare has actually been around for centuries, and is one of the oldest weapons of mass destruction. Lord Jeffrey Amherst, the commanding general of British forces in North American during the French and Indian Wars (1754–1763), sent smallpox-infested blankets and handkerchiefs to Chief Pontiac's forces during their siege of Fort Pitt (Pittsburgh) in 1763. The smallpox started an epidemic among Pontiac's tribesmen that totally decimated their forces. Today, smallpox has been replaced by deadlier toxins like Anthrax, Ebola, Influenza, and Botulism. Governments are also concerned with toxins, poisonous products, and microorganisms that cause harm to produce and domestic livestock. While Blofeld's Virus Omega was purely fictional, other deadlier germs which can cause worldwide pandemics with very large death tolls are still waiting to be unleashed.

The Master Race.

In *Moonraker* (1979), Sr. Hugo Drax (Michael Lonsdale) boasts about creating a "master" race with the help of science, and repopulating the Earth after he has destroyed all of mankind. We have heard this boast before, and it always turns our stomachs. As the nineteenth century turned into the twentieth, many European thinkers, particularly Friedrich Nietzsche, were talking about the Ubermensch (the superman). No, this was not the figure in blue tights that comes from the planet Krypton to protect the American way, but rather a blending of philosophy, myth, and eugenics as epitomized by the English writer Edward Bulwer-Lytton in his 1871 science fiction novel *The Coming Race*. Bulwer-Lytton's supermen would be imbued with psychokinetic power, and would forge a world in which only the strong and powerful would survive. Well, as a sort of fantasy, one can enjoy what one wants. Unfortunately, SS Leader Heinrich Himmler, the number two man in the Nazi government, took the concept of the "master" race, which he had learned from a crackpot racial theory, very seriously. As a member of the Thule Society, Himmler believed the northern Europeans were a remnant of the super race of humans who had survived the destruction of Atlantis. Himmler inculcated an ethos in the SS which led to the formation of the Ahnenerbe Forschungs und Lehrgemeinschaft (Ancestral Heritage Research and Teaching Society) in 1935 which resulted in the Nazi search for the "Aryan" homeland in places such as Tibet and western and southern Russia. These Nazi archeological expeditions gave fruit for thought to Steven Spielberg for his ***Raiders of the Lost Ark*** (1981) and ***Indiana Jones and the Lost Crusade*** (1989) films, which provided thrilling entertainment for millions. Another mystic concept in Himmler's twisted psyche led to the designation of the castle at Wewelsburg, near the Teutoburg Forest where the Teutons defeated three Roman legions, as a sort of Camelot for SS officers who would eventually possess the Holy Grail. In Himmler's mind, the SS would provide the breeding stock for this "master" race, a mix of the genetic stock of the Teutonic Knights, from their good old days when they were killing Slavs and Russians, via contemporary Nazis. Himmler's more "scientific" approach to prove the superiority of the pale-skinned, fair-haired northern European types over the "mongrel" mixed-race folks from eastern Europe led to a number of horrible "experiments" in SS-guarded concentration camps during World War II. It is ironic that the mixed-racial stock of the Allied forces defeated the "Aryans" of Himmler's ideal "master" race and saved the world.

Mujahedeen.

Literally translated from Arabic, the word "mujahedeen" means "strugglers"; the root word "mujahid" therefore refers to someone who exerts effort or struggles. The most well-known and feared "strugglers" were the opposition cells that fought against the Soviets during the occupation of Afghanistan between 1979 and 1989, as seen in ***The Living Daylights*** (1987),

EVERYTHING I KNOW ABOUT LIFE
I LEARNED FROM JAMES BOND

and the civil war that followed in the wake of Soviet withdrawal. These Mujahedeen were financed, armed, and trained by the CIA. Afghanistan's resistance movement proved to be a highly effective guerilla force that struck Soviet troops without warning, and then retreated very quickly into the wilderness. Virtually all of its war was waged locally, with each cell or group segmented from the larger whole. After the Soviets withdrew, some of the Mujahedeen fought Taliban groups in a civil war that led to their ouster from power in 1996. More recently, the term has been pirated by Al Qaeda to describe the guerilla fighters fighting American troops in Iraq. James Bond comes to rely on Kamran Shah and his Mujahedeen forces when they break the truce and attack the Soviet airbase in *The Living Daylights*.

The Golden Triangle.

After Bond and Kara are "rescued" by Kamran Shah and his Mujahedeen forces in *The Living Daylights*, 007 discovers that his new allies have dealings with opium smugglers known as the Snow Leopard Brotherhood. While the Snow Leopard Brotherhood is a totally fictitious organization, the locale is a very real one. The Golden Triangle, which includes Afghanistan, Iran, and Pakistan, was once dominated by Afghanistan's enormous opium industry—the largest in the world. During the rule of the Taliban, authorities officially denounced the drug trade to the world, but continued to tolerate it in private. In fact, they relied heavily on taxes from the drug trade for revenue. Afghan warlords and remnants of the Mujahedeen also reaped huge profits from illegal poppy cultivation. In 1999, Afghanistan's total output of opium was over 1600 tons, followed by smaller numbers of tonnage in

Pakistan and Iran. After U.S. forces removed the Taliban from power and initiated free elections in 2004, the drug trade fell off significantly. Today, in some of the more remote spots of Afghanistan and Pakistan, warlords still conduct business like the Snow Leopard Brotherhood. Moreover, the country of Iran still acts as a "safe house" for these warlords and the heroin destined for Europe.

Drug Cartels.

The world has changed since James Bond first appeared in ***Dr. No*** (1962). We do not need villains who are members of secret criminal organizations to threaten the world. Today, thanks to the Columbian cocaine cartels and the Mexican equivalents, we have villains of criminal organizations who flaunt their wealth and enjoy a certain amount of immunity from prosecution. At the time that ***Licence to Kill*** (1989) was released, Pablo Escobar's Medellin cartel of Columbia was the primary drug cartel illegally exporting cocaine to the USA and elsewhere. Today, Columbia has at least two smaller caterls handling the business after a crackdown on the Cali cartel and its successor, the Norte Del Valle cartel. Agents still purchase coca leaves from Columbian, Bolivian and Peruvian farmers which is processed in remote areas into powdered cocaine. Then, the members of the cartel deliver the drugs at a wholesale price, sometimes directly, sometimes through Mexican middlemen or others, to their street salesmen—usually ethnic criminal gang members. As of 1999, street prices were around $10,500–$36,000 per kilo, depending on purity and availability. The upper class snorters of powdered cocaine paid from $20–200 per gram. Crack cocaine, manufactured by heating cocaine powder with baking soda, was sold at about $5–10 per hit. Its users are usually people with low self-esteem at the bottom end of the market. Because of the money they make, the Cali cartel members boughtships and airplanes, bribed government officials at the highest level, employed the best lawyers that money can buy, plus they bought protection from revolutionary fighters in Columbia and paid for paramilitary forces in Columbia to guard their operations. In 1996, the Cali cartel was taking home $4.5 billion annually from their drug sales according to DEA records. In 2003, the U.S. cocaine market was estimated at $35 billion at street prices, exceeding the revenues of a number of U.S. corporations—such as Starbucks. The Mexican smugglers, who were often used as middlemen by the Cali cartel, have now set up some of their own distribution networks in the U.S. market to sell the cocaine they receive for delivering the Columbian cocaine, as well as their own locally produced marijuana, heroin and methamphetamines. South American heroin and Mexican "mud" have encroached on the Golden Triangle product for over fifty percent of the U.S. heroin market. Heroin sells at $85,000–$185,000 a kilo, but large quantities are difficult to obtain without risk. While marijuana is much cheaper and more available, at prices from $500-$10,000 per kilo, its transportation and distribution costs are very high, cutting into the profit margin. The greatest problem that the Columbian and Mesican cartels have today is laundering the drug money. In the 1960's and 1970's, drug retailers would appear at banks in the United States with large quantities of money, dump the cash into accounts, and then have the money transferred back to Colombia or to offshore banks in the Caribbean or to European banks. Today in the U.S., putting more than $10,000 in cash into an account raises a red flag. Off-shore banks are now the depositories of choice.

Hong Kong.

Hong Kong is one of the most populated regions of the world within its four hundred and twenty-two square miles, though most of the people are on the thirty-five square miles of Hong Kong Island and its neighboring islands. The British influence began after it fought a war with China for the right to sell opium to the Chinese in 1840. The British had to have their tea, old sock, and didn't want to pay an exorbitant sum for it. They needed to be able to peddle a product that the Chinese would want. Besides, Hong Kong harbor is the largest natural harbor in the area. The British returned governorship of Hong Kong to China on July 1, 1997. Though there has been some friction, Hong Kong still thrives as a free-trade port, a good place for industry and financial institutions to profit and to have a modernizing influence upon mainland China, its number one customer. Today, stock traders throughout the world consult the Hong Kong stock market and foreign-exchange market on a daily basis.

North and South Korea.

During the Cold War, tensions between the United States and the Soviet Union led to the division of Korea in 1948 and the establishment of two separate governments, each with its own ideology. South Korea chose a pro-Western democratic government, while North Korea followed the Communist ideals of the Russia and China. The first major conflict of the Cold War occurred when North Korea invaded South Korea on June 25, 1950. The United Nations intervened when it was clear the militaristic North Korean forces would overwhelm the South, and dispatched troops, primarily from the United States, to back

EVERYTHING I KNOW ABOUT LIFE
I LEARNED FROM JAMES BOND

South Korea. The Soviet Union and China countered with military advisors from Russia and millions of Chinese troops. After a number of key military engagements which saw the balance of power shift from the North to the South and then back again, and massive numbers of casualties among Korean civilians, the war reached a stalemate. An armistice in 1953, which was never signed by South Korea, split the peninsula along the demilitarized zone near the original demarcation line. No peace treaty was ever signed, resulting in the two countries remaining technically at war. Now, almost sixty years later, the two sides remain antagonistic towards one another. Our favorite MI6 agent finds himself squarely in the middle of that hostility in *Die Another Day*, the twentieth film in the EON series.

Quantum.

In both *Casino Royale* (2006) and *Quantum of Solace* (2008), "Quantum" is name of the shadowy terrorist organization that seeks to control the world's markets and industries. Clearly, Quantum seems poised to be the new SPECTRE., which was a fixture of the early Connery films. While it appears that Daniel Craig's Bond may have destroyed the organization, Quantum, according to producer Barbara Broccoli, will be featured much more prominently in future storylines.

Silva.

Silva (Javier Bardem) in *Skyfall* is a rogue agent who is selling his organization and his cyber-terror skills to the highest bidder. He has his own island near Hong Kong, where he has frightened off all of the former residents. His actions are linked to Patrice, his agent who is pedaling a list of undercover MI6 agents in various terrorist organizations. In a sense, Silva is the most dangerous villain because he certainly is the most knowledgeable of all of MI6's secrets. Furthermore, in the initial *Skyfall* Turkish sequences, we see the film opening with James Bond being shot. We rarely see Bond this vulnerable, and never, we believe, in the very start of a film. Certainly, in the opening of *Never Say Never Again*, we see Sean Connery's fifty-three-year-old Bond being sent to a health club to sweat out his aches and pains, but that is hardly a bullet in the chest. It seems that Daniel Craig's Bond is now being seen in the context of real, international terrorism by actual organizations that have huge amounts of money at their disposal and deadly intentions toward the corporate worlds of the U.S., Great Britain, and Europe. Craig's Bond is less glitter when facing Silva and more "down home," and his home in the Highlands proves to be a damn hard one to enter uninvited.

SPECTRE

As the Cold War was coming to an end and SMERSH seemed less viable as a global threat, SPECTRE emerged as the International threat against world peace. SPECTRE's acronym said it all: the **Sp**ecial **E**xecutive for **C**ounterintelligence, **T**errorism, **R**evenge, and **E**xtortion—"the four great cornerstones of power headed by the greatest brains in the world." Blofeld became its leader, and various plots against the great world powers, like the United States, Great Britain, Japan, Russia and China, became the basis of the Bond films, including nuclear and bacteriological warfare.

CHAPTER TWELVE

A–Z: 007'S ENCYCLOPEDIC KNOWLEDGE OF EVERYTHING

> *Diamonds are forever,*
> *Sparkling round my little finger.*
> *Unlike men, the diamonds linger; Men are mere mortals who*
> *Are not worth going to your grave for.*

—Shirley Bassey, ***Diamonds Are Forever*** (1971)

Better than an encyclopedia and certainly a great deal more fun, the James Bond films have always provided a wealth of interesting facts and tidbits that would have otherwise seemed banal, and the first film, ***Dr. No***, set the bar pretty high with its fun facts and fascinating trivia. Ms. Ryder may have learned about the world by reading an encyclopedia, but all film fans had to do was pay attention to James Bond. Ironically, the literary Bond was a "blunt instrument" for Britain, and the only subjects that he was interested in learning were subjects in which he already had a background or were taught by friends. In his transition to the silver screen, 007 (as played by newcomer Sean Connery) showed that he was knowledgeable on a wide variety of topics, and possessed skills his literary predecessor never had, or needed, or would have imagined. The very nature of espionage has changed so dramatically since Fleming's day that the modern secret agent has to have a healthy knowledge of everything. Of course, the fact that Bond is a know-it-all does have its detractors.

German cinema poster © Eon Productions Limited, United Artists Corporation

In *Goldfinger* (1964), when James Bond demonstrates his vast, encyclopedic knowledge by discussing a particular subject, he gets a chilly reception from M (Bernard Lee)—one of the more entertaining running gags in the early films. 007 has made it a point of being the best at everything he does, but not everyone appreciates his expertise. Briefed on gold smuggling over a fine dinner, Bond interrupts his host to critique the shortcomings of his brandy, only to have M bark, "Colonel Smithers is giving the lecture, 007!" Later, in *Diamonds Are Forever* (1971), M derides 007 when he admits to his limited knowledge about diamonds. "Refreshing to know there's one subject you're not an expert on," M says with some satisfaction. Even so, knowledge is power, and the fun facts that emerge from each film have provided us

EVERYTHING I KNOW ABOUT LIFE I LEARNED FROM JAMES BOND

with the kind of information that makes conversation at cocktail parties fun. These facts proved to be as interesting as the film itself. Even the shiest wallflower is the life of the party with a few tidbits of 007's seemingly infinite knowledge.

We'd like to think that nearly every James Bond film is filled with the kind of information that makes interesting dinner conversation, and the following fun facts should make you an expert, no matter who is giving the lecture.

Alpine Skiing.

For only the second time in the film series, the other being *On Her Majesty's Secret Service*, James Bond is shown to be an expert downhill skier in *For Your Eyes Only* (1981). He easily eludes Sergei Barsov and the other Russian assassins, at times turning completely around in his skis. In the novel version of *On Her Majesty's Secret Service*, the literary Bond muses as a teenager, he learned his skiing in the old Hannes Schneider School at St. Anton in Augsburg. He had become pretty good and had won his golden K. Long before it became a popular winter sport, skiing was a means of transportation for Scandinavians needing to cross their snow-covered terrain some four thosuand years ago. In the 1920s, the first organized slalom races took place on mountains all over Europe, including one of the most treacherous runs at Mt. Schilthorn (Piz Gloria) in Switzerland. The first world championship was organized in 1931, and, not long after, the thrill and competition of alpine skiing caught on in the United States. Downhill and slalom skiing made its Olympic debut at the 1936 Garmisch-Partenkirchen Games, with events for both men and women. The Giant slalom first appeared at the 1952 Games in Oslo, Norway, and the super slalom or Super G was introduced at the 1988 Games in Calgary, Canada. Something tells us that Bond isn't quite finished with skiing.

Armageddon.

At the point when Stromberg deploys his stolen nuclear submarines to launch a third world war in *The Spy Who Loved Me* (1977), he makes a Biblical allusion that only 007 would know. He says, "Observe, Mr. Bond, the instruments of Armageddon." Derived from the Hebrew "mountain of Megiddo," Armageddon refers to the geographic location of the final battle between the forces of good and evil mentioned in Revelation 16:16. This climatic struggle between Christ and Antichrist is supposed to culminate with Christ's victory ushering in his thousand-year reign on earth. Over the years, many wars have been deemed Armageddon by contemporary doomsayers, including the English Civil War, the Crimean War, the First World War, and the Gulf War. In fact, the word has become synonymous with any catastrophically destructive battle. But in the context used by Stromberg, Armageddon means the final war between the two superpowers of the United States and Russia. He hopes to profit from the total annihilation of mankind by establishing his new world order under the sea.

Atlantis.

In *The Spy Who Loved Me* (1977), Stromberg names the headquarters of his undersea kingdom after the mythical island of Atlantis. A continent the size of Europe, over twelve thousand years ago, Atlantis boasted great, beautiful cities, advanced technology, and a utopian society. But for some unknown reason, it was subjected to a great cataclysm that reduced its great cities to rubble and plunged its world into the sea, lost forever. The legend of Atlantis has survived for thousands of years, but no one has been able to validate its existence. Around 370 B.C., the Greek philosopher Plato wrote of Atlantis in two of his many dialogues. In "Critias," he described its exact location in the Atlantic Ocean near the Straits of Gibraltar, and told about its destruction ten thousand years earlier. Both "facts" were based upon the two hundred-year-old records of a Greek king named Solon who had heard of Atlantis from an Egyptian priest. In "Timaeus," Plato characterized the island continent as a prosperous nation that sought to enslave other nations that interfered with its plans to expand. He wrote, "Now in this island of Atlantis there was a great and wonderful empire which had rule over the whole island and several others, and over parts of the continent and, furthermore, the men of Atlantis had subjected the parts of Libya within the columns of Heracles as far as Egypt, and of Europe as far as Tyrrhenia." Plato concludes by writing the Atlanteans made a mistake in trying to enslave the Greeks. They were unable to stand up to the military might of Sparta and Athens, and following their defeat in a great naval battle, a natural disaster sealed their fate. Perhaps Stromberg should have taken a closer look at the legend before he named his own kingdom Atlantis.

The Bank of England.

In a late night meeting, Colonel Smithers explains to Bond and M, "The Bank of England is the official depositor of gold bullion, just like Fort Knox, Kentucky, is for the United States." The Bank of England was founded in 1694 to act as the Government's banker and debt-manager. Since then, its role has expanded to include management of the nation's currency and its connection with other country's financial systems. In 1931 the United Kingdom actually left the gold standard, and all of its gold and foreign exchange reserves were transferred to the Treasury. But the Bank of England still handled their management, and continues to manage these reserves to this day.

Baron Samedi.

In *Live and Let Die* (1973), Baron Samedi (Geoffrey Holder) appears first as a performer in a musical extravaganza at the Sans Souci Hotel in San Monique, then later re-appears to Bond and Solitaire at the crossroads, and finally officiates at Solitaire's voodoo sacrifice. 007 easily dispatches him with several punches that send him flying into a coffin filled with deadly snakes. James Bond has never believed in superstitious mumbo-jumbo, and yet he'd be wise to avoid the real Baron Samedi. According to the folkloric traditions of the Caribbean, Baron Samedi is the god of cemeteries and chief of the legion of the dead. In Vodoun beliefs, he is the lord of death and fertility, cemeteries and pestilence, the underworld and the afterlife. He appears as a skeleton, attired in a black or purple top hat and tails, and carries a long walking stick. He demands hot peppers steeped in rum as a sacrificial offering. The first burial in a cemetery or burials performed on Saturday are always dedicated to Baron Samedi. As the personification of death, he cannot be reasoned with or bargained with or destroyed in any way. He has no African counterpart, but is often associated with St. Gerard in Catholicism.

Cliff-top Monasteries of Meteora, Greece.

In *For Your Eyes Only* at the northwest corner of Thessaly, Greece, the cliff-top monasteries of Meteora stand perched atop massive, rocky pinnacles that rise thousands of feet above the ground. These rugged, vertical rocks have become a popular destination for rock climbers today, but more than a thousand years ago, the caves and fissures of the rocks were home to ninth century hermits who sought sanctuary from the ravages of their day. On Sundays, they climbed down from their cells to celebrate mass in Doupiani, and, as more and more people settled in the caves, the Theotokos of Doupiani was established as the first religious order in the rock community. Several centuries later, three monks (Gregory, Moses, and Athanasius) fleeing from Byzantine pirates left the Monastery of Iviron to found the first monastery in the land of the great rock forest (as the region was then known). Called *Stylos* or the Pillar, they built a small wooden hut, and assembled a small community of believers around them. Later, Athanasius constructed a chapel in a cave on the nearby *Platys Lithos* or the Broad Rock, and encouraged others to build more cells and cloisters. At one time, Meteora, which means "suspended in the air," boasted twenty-four separate monasteries, the largest of which being the Monastery of the Holy Trinity, but only six survive today, mostly as museums. Since no ladders or steps were ever built, access to the monasteries was gained by means of a rope-and-pulley system. Monks would descend in nets to the fertile valleys below to grow grapes, corn, and potatoes, and would need to be hoisted back up to winch towers overhanging the chasm. Their monastic homes were like cliff-top fortresses, and withstood many invaders over the centuries. No one could have prepared them, however, for the assault of James Bond and his crew.

The College of Arms.

The College of Arms, located on Queen Victoria Street in

London, is the official repository of the records, the coats of arms, and pedigrees of all of the noble families in the Commonwealth of England. Early in *On Her Majesty's Secret Service* (1969), James Bond pays a visit to the college, and, using his own genealogy as a cover, he consults with Sir Hilary Bray (George Baker) about Blofeld's claim to noble title. Officers of the College are known as heralds; Sir Hilary Bray is the Sable Basilisk (or literary herald). Each officer of arms conducts his own practice in heraldry and genealogy, and charges fees to undertake research. The heralds and pursuivants take each request in turn, a week at a time, and advise on whether they are able to assist in a particular heraldic or genealogical problem, what research they would recommend and what fee would be appropriate. Any person, like James Bond, who approaches the officer in waiting and employs him on some task becomes that herald's client. Coats of arms are still granted by Letters Patent from heralds, and a right to arms can only be established by registration in the official records of the College of Arms of a pedigree showing direct male line descent from an ancestor to the existing requester. Bond discovers that his ancestry dates back to Sir Thomas Bond in 1734, and that his coat of arms features argent on a chevron's sable with three bezants (gold balls). His family motto in Latin is "Orbis Non Suffict," roughly translated as the "world is not enough."

Cruise Missiles.

Blofeld (Max Von Sydow) plots to launch two Tomahawk Cruise missiles on the West in *Never Say Never Again* (1983), and naturally, James Bond is enlisted to stop him. The Tomahawk Cruise missiles are still in use by the U.S. Navy and NATO countries. The Cruise missiles are twenty feet long and twenty-one inches around. At launch, they are assisted by five hundred and fifty-pound solid rocket boosters and weight three thousand two hundred pounds. They can deliver a one thousand-pound bomb and can fly from five hundred to one thousand miles at speeds well over five hundred miles per hour employing their turbofan engines. Cruise missiles can hit a target the size of a single-car garage. And they are only one-tenth the cost of a ballistic "Scud" missile, such as was used by the Iraqis. They are the best bang for the buck, and we are not talking double-entendres here.

Diamonds and Diamond Smuggling.

When James Bond confesses that he does not know much about diamonds, saying they are the "hardest substance found in nature; they cut glass, suggest marriage. I suppose it replaces the dog as the girl's best friend. That's about it," his boss M is delighted, replying that it is "Refreshing to hear that there is one subject you're not an expert on!" The fact of the matter is that 007 learns a great deal about diamonds in ***Diamonds Are Forever***. When Bond takes a look at the diamonds in the funeral parlor, they are all cut and highly polished. In real life, diamonds come as gray pebbles from the mine. They are cut and polished, often, in Holland or in other countries where specialists do the job. The wrong cut on a large stone can cost you six figures. A dentist in his backroom, such as Dr. Tynan, is not going to be cutting millions of dollars in diamonds. Today, diamonds are smuggled more for political reasons than for criminal ones. "Conflict diamonds," such as those James Bond uncovers in ***Die Another Day***, are fuelling rebellions in contemporary Africa. Large diamond companies work with go-betweens who, in turn, work with political groups. In 1999, the UN Security Council sanctioned the UNITA rebels in Angola. Since then, other diamonds have financed violence in the Democratic Republic of Congo, Liberia and Sierra Leone. Diamonds are the cash of the international underworld; very easy to conceal—unlike the stacks of $100 bills seen bulging out of attaché cases in so many lame action films—and to turn into ready money in any large metro area. But of course, one must have a "reliable" fence. Ian Fleming wrote *The Diamond Smugglers* in 1958 as a nonfiction treatise on the world of diamond smuggling.

The Dove.

In *For Your Eyes Only* (1981), James Bond first discovers a dove-shaped pin on the body of Ferrara outside the hockey rink in Cortina, then later sees the same design on the wetsuits of the men who work for Milos Columbo. He suspects Columbo is responsible for his friend's death, but later learns Emile Locque uses the dove as his symbol. Ironically, the dove represents peace, not death. In Judeo-Christian circles, the dove has always symbolized peace and the transcendent power of the Holy Spirit. In Genesis 8:10-11, Noah sends a dove out from the Ark, and the bird returns with a freshly plucked olive leaf in its beak. Noah knew the waters had subsided from the earth, and God was sending him a message of peace and hope. In Matthew 3:16, soon after Jesus is baptized, the Spirit of God is seen descending like a dove and alighting on His shoulder. In ancient times, a dovelike vessel was frequently suspended over the baptismal font, and represented Pentecost. It is indeed a "sick joke" that an assassin would rely on a symbol of peace as his calling card. [Dr. Christmas Jones sports the same graphical design of the dove, seen in *For Your Eyes Only,* as a tattoo on her mid-section in *The World Is not Enough* (1999).]

EVERYTHING I KNOW ABOUT LIFE
I LEARNED FROM JAMES BOND

Electromagnetic Pulse.

In M's office, the discussion began with the threat posed by an electromagnetic pulse to modern computer systems in both *The Man with the Golden Gun* (1975) and *GoldenEye* (1995). When a nuclear device explodes, there is a blast of electromagnetic radiation that may join electrical and electronic systems causing current and voltage surges. In the case of an atomic bomb, there is an electromagnetic pulse through the lower frequencies from 3 Hz to 30 kHz. Therefore, computers, automobiles, cell phones, certainly anything with a microchip may be short-circuited. Scientists suspected this problem since the 1940's, but it became clear in 1962 when the USA was doing high-altitude explosive atmospheric tests detonated in the Pacific Ocean about eight hundred miles from Hawaii. The explosion, Starfish Prime, disrupted radio stations and electrical equipment throughout the fiftieth state. In 1963, therefore, the USA and the Soviet Union signed the Atmospheric Test Ban Treaty to eliminate the threat of EMPs. It is estimated, for example, that a single high-altitude explosion about two hundredmiles above Kansas would create an EMP that would blast the entire USA. Radio frequency links, microcircuits and satellites would be damaged, unless the equipment was turned off at the time of the EMP. How do you protect against EMP damage? Metallic shielding helps as well as surge protectors, filters, etc. plus backup units that are out of range of the EMP burst. There is a possibility that terrorist groups could produce an E-bomb. This E-bomb is a non-atomic explosive device which can be constructed in various ways; one of which is a tube packed with explosives placed inside a copper coil that is set off by a bank of capacitors. We will not go into more details, but this device will create an EMP. For an estimated $400, terrorists could send out an EMP to the United States and devastate any unprotected electrical infrastructure within a certain area. Some experts fear that if an E-bomb is detonated in the right place, it could set the USA back two hundred years for a period of time. We *believe* that Homeland Security is working on this problem.

Enter the Dragon.

In ***The Man with the Golden Gun*** (1975), James Bond walks into the martial arts tournament at Hai Fat's school, and reminds viewers of the plot from Robert Clouse's ***Enter the Dragon*** (1973), starring Bruce Lee. Both Lee's character and Bond are investigating the actions of a reclusive billionaire who owns a martial arts school as well as many other institutions and corporations. ***Enter the Dragon*** was Lee's most popular film in the west, partially because it was produced by Americans and shot in Hong Kong and Los Angeles. Although it cost just under $1,000,000 to produce it, ***Enter the Dragon*** created a market for Hong Kong action films that continues today, despite Lee's death in Hong Kong in 1973. A clear example of the Hong Kong film industry's influence on motion pictures is the "Hong Kong wire work" in which characters seem to float through the air as they attack each other. Wire work is a commonplace in such Western films as the Wachowski Brothers' ***The Matrix*** (1999) and its sequels, horror films and some action films as well as in the more traditional Chinese fantasies such as Ang Lee's ***Crouching Tiger, Hidden Dragon*** (2000). In his performance at the martial arts school, Bond appears a bit sleazy when he kicks his first opponent in the head when he is bowing to him. Bad form, old boy, though the first opponent was decidedly no gentleman, just a bit slow on the uptake. When Chula, his second opponent appears, you may remember how closely he

EVERYTHING I KNOW ABOUT LIFE
I LEARNED FROM JAMES BOND

watches Bond at every moment. Their fight sequence is quite traditional, though Bond's exit in diving through a window is more cinematic than routine. On the other hand, Hai Fat's people were not going to permit him to walk away alive, even if Bond defeated every member of the school *mano a mano*.

Fabergé Eggs.

James Bond tracks a fake Fabergé Egg in ***Octopussy*** (1983) to an island of beautiful women. In the Russian Orthodox Church, Easter is considered the most important and joyous feast day of the year. Following church services, families gather together to celebrate the holy day by exchanging gifts of decorated eggs and three kisses. The eggs represent symbols of renewed life and hope for the coming year. On Easter Sunday in 1884, to mark their twentieth wedding anniversary, Czar Alexander III gave his beloved wife, Czarina Maria Fedorovna, a simple enameled egg that had been crafted by a young jeweler named Peter Carl Fabergé. Inside the egg, much to the delight of the Empress, was a golden yolk which contained a golden hen, which in turn contained a diamond miniature of the royal crown. The egg, which was about five inches tall, reminded Czarina Maria of her homeland, and was so popular among members of the royal court that Alexander commissioned Fabergé to make an Easter egg each year for her. They agreed that the Easter gift would always have the shape of an egg, and would hold a surprise inside. For the next ten years up until Alexander's death in 1894, Fabergé made one intricately designed and individually crafted egg for the Czarina each year. When Nicholas II ascended the throne, he began making two eggs, one for the new Czar to give his wife, Alexandra, and the other for the Dowager Empress. Altogether there were fifty-seven imperial Easter eggs made and presented to the royal family. When the Revolution began, some of the eggs were lost, some were hidden, and some were smuggled out of the country by American physician Armand Hammer. Of the fifty-six originals, forty-four have been located today, and two others have been recently photographed. Today, these eggs are valued at $5,000,000.

Figure Skating.

In *For Your Eyes Only* (1981), James Bond appreciates the beautiful figure skating of Bibi Dahl (Lynn-Holly Johnson) even if he does not reciprocate her sexual advances. People have been ice-skating for thousands of years. In fact, archaeological digs in Bjoko, Sweden, date the first primitive ice skates to 1000 BC. Ice skaters have been racing and otherwise competing against one another for centuries, but it wasn't until 1860, when American-born Jackson Haines combined elements of ballet and dance to ice skating; hence figure skating was born. Figure skating as a competitive sport did not begin until the midto late-19th century in Europe. The first figure skating competitions were held in the 1880's. In 1892, the International Skating Union was formed, and the first World Championship (for men only) was held in St. Petersburg, Russia, in 1896. The first women's championship was held in 1906. Figure skating is the oldest sport in the Winter Olympics. It was contested at the 1908 Olympic Games in London, and then again in 1920 at Antwerp. The events included compulsory figures, in which skaters traced diagrams of the figure eight on the ice, and free skating. Today, free skating counts for two-thirds of the score, together with a short program of required elements. Not surprisingly, some people still don't consider figure skating as a real sport because of its elegance and gracefulness. But it does require hours and hours of practice in order to maintain coordination, balance, fitness, and strength.

Fort Knox Bullion Depository.

The Fort Knox Bullion Depository, as depicted in *Goldfinger* (1964), is the fictional creation of production designer Ken Adam, and not based on any real diagrams or construction plans. While Adam's shiny sets with their stacks of gold bars and recessed lighting look impressive and very realistic, the actual layout and design of the underground vaults remain a top secret. Located approximately thirty miles southwest of Louisville, Kentucky, on a site which was formerly a part of the Fort Knox military reservation, the Depository was built in 1936 at a cost of $560,000. The first gold was moved to the Depository by railroad in January 1937, and the final series of shipments were completed in June 1937. The two-story basement and ground-floor building is constructed of granite, steel and concrete, with its exterior dimensions measuring one hundred and five feet by one hundred and twenty-one feet and forty-two feet high. The vault door weighs more than twenty tons. No one person is entrusted with the combination. Various members of the Depository staff must dial separate combinations known only to them in order to gain access to the vault. The building is equipped with the latest and most modern protective devices, and is virtually impregnable. Had Goldfinger managed to carry out "Operation Grand Slam," he would have been disappointed to learn that Fort Knox is one of several institutions (including the Philadelphia Mint, the Denver Mint, the West Point Bullion Depository, and the San Francisco Assay Office) that maintain the country's gold reserves.

Gold.

In January, 2013, gold was selling at about $1,720.00 per ounce, depending on the rate of exchange and the marketplace. But in 1964, when Auric Goldfinger was planning the crime of the century, James Bond used the then-current rate of exchange, and did some calculations of his own.

> Bond: "Yes, well, I've worked out a few statistics of my own. $15,000,000,000 in gold bullion weighs ten thousand five hundred tons. Sixty men would take twelve days to load it onto two hundred trucks. Now, at the most, you're going to have two hours before the Army, Navy, Air Force, and Marines move in and make you put it back."

Pretty amazing that Bond was able to work those statistics out in his head without the aid of a computer or calculator.

Goya.

After Bond is captured by Dr. No (Joseph Wiseman) and escorted to dinner, Agent 007 stops to notice Goya's "The Duke of Wellington" on an easel next to the stairs in the dining room. This painting was stolen from a museum in 1960 and was never recovered. Francisco Goya is considered by many to be "The Father of Modern Art," and began his painting career in Spain in the 19th century by expressing his thoughts and feelings very frankly. For more than sixty years, Goya pushed the boundaries of traditional art to find a new form of expression, and in turn created some of the finest work of modern art. "The Duke of Wellington" was just one example of his tremendous versatility.

EVERYTHING I KNOW ABOUT LIFE
I LEARNED FROM JAMES BOND

Gun Barrel Rifling.

Each James Bond film begins with its signature scene, in which an assassin's gun barrel follows Bond from right to left, and 007 draws down on him and fires a single shot, killing him. The view from inside the gun barrel, which was accomplished by pointing a pinhole camera through a real gun barrel by Maurice Binder, reveals a series of spiraling grooves. Gunsmiths cut these grooves, known as rifling, into the inner surface of the barrel for a reason. When a bullet or other projectile travels down the length of the barrel, its body cuts into the grooves and forces it to spin. Giving the bullet a spin provides for greater stability and greater accuracy in its trajectory toward a target. Early muskets had a smooth bore, and thus were not very accurate. German gun designers in the seventeenth century developed the technique of rifling, and totally revolutionized the way in which guns were created. By the way, the actor in the famous gun barrel opening is not Sean Connery, but rather his stuntman Bob Simmons. Connery would not film the sequence himself until the movie *Thunderball* (1965), and since then, each actor who has played James Bond has filmed their own sequence at the end of the gunbarrel.

Heraldry.

In the Middle Ages, heraldry was used as a mark of identification to distinguish warriors on a battlefield. Knights were free to choose their own designs, and these designs were marked or "emblazoned" on a warrior's armor and surcoat (or garment worn over a coat of mail). These "coats of arms" identified the knight to his allies and his opponents. However, by the fifteenth century, the duplication of designs forced the King to standardize the markings, and heraldry became a method of standardization. The right to bear a certain coat of arms was linked to heredity and gradually became recognized as evidence of the wearer's noble birth. In 1484, the Herald's College was granted a charter of incorporation by Richard III of England, and it became an executive office to trace ancestry, to approve coats of arms, to confirm titles of honor, and to examine claims to certain rights. All arms, both those established by right of ancient lineage and those recently granted by the crown, were registered with the College of Arms. Even the terms used in heraldry were standardized. Terms such as "engrailed," "nebuly," "inverted," "dancety" and "embattled" were adopted to describe the coats of arms. Charges, which were the figures in the field emblazoned on a coat, were simplified into three specific kinds, including the Ordinaries (chief, pale, bend, fess, chevron, cross, saltire, bar, baton, etc.), the Subordinaries (roundels, fusils, orle, annulets, cinquefoil, etc.), and the Common (hand, fish, lions, bears, birds, mullets, etc.). The colors were also standardized, with two metals (gold and silver (or argent) and five colors, including red (gules), green (vert), blue (azure), black (sable) and purple (purpurs). As the age of chivalry passed, the need for this type of identification also declined, but custom has extended heraldry to this day. In ***On Her Majesty's Secret Service*** (1969), when James Bond goes to Piz Gloria under the guise of Sir Hilary Bray, he carries Charles Boutell's ***Heraldry***, revised by C.W. Scott-Giles and J.P. Brook-Little. (London: Frederick Warne Co., Ltd., 1963.)

RMS Queen Elizabeth.

It certainly is a surprise when we see James Bond jump onto the wreck of the RMS Queen Elizabeth in the Hong Kong

EVERYTHING I KNOW ABOUT LIFE I LEARNED FROM JAMES BOND

harbor and then hear him welcomed aboard by a British voice in *The Man with the Golden Gun* (1975). Like so many others, we tend to forget it is the Queen Mary that we can find at Long Beach, California. The original RMS Queen Elizabeth was decommissioned by the Cunard Line in 1968, due to the increased transatlantic traffic by airplanes and more modern ocean liners. Finally, in 1970, C. Y. Tung, a Taiwanese shipping tycoon, bought the ship at auction to convert it into an ocean-going university. On January 9, 1972, HMS Queen Elizabeth was in Hong Kong harbor being re-conditioned to a more academic environment when fires sprouted throughout the ship. Presumably, it was insured. There were too many fires to put out before the wooden interiors burned down. Never again would Queen Elizabeth walk the decks of this passenger liner. The wreck was in the harbor for many months before it was scrapped for its junk value. Despite the fantasy element of the setting, it certainly is true, as was mentioned in the film, that the price of renting space in Hong Kong is exorbitant. Maybe it really would have been cheaper to run the intelligence office out of the wreck. In any case, building the sets at the acute angle of the wrecked Queen Elizabeth at Pinewood Studios caused quite a challenge to the set designers. There were more than a few problems and injuries for both actors and crews on those sequences shot in the "interior" of the Queen Elizabeth.

Honky.

Like the pejorative term "nigger," which certain racist white groups use to identify African-Americans, the term "honky" is a racist term, dating back to 1946, which certain African-Americans use to identify whites. A dialectical variation on hunky or "bohunk," these derogatory terms identified Hungarian or Polish or Eastern-European factory workers who lived in Midwestern cities, like Chicago. In the late 1920s and early 1930s, the term was corrupted to "honky" as a pejorative to denote people of Slavic ancestry as well as others who worked in factories. By the late fifties, honky came to mean blue-collar whites, and by the sixties, white people in general. The racist term is still socially and legally acceptable for reasons unknown to the authors of this book. For the one and only time in the series, James Bond is referred to as a "honky" (by Mr. Big and his men) in *Live and Let Die* (1973).

Hubris.

Aristotle wrote that hubris was a common theme in Greek tragedy, and often featured prominently in stories in which protagonists felt they were equal to or greater than the gods. To the Greeks, hubris meant that someone who possessed considerable gifts presumed that, because of those gifts, he or she could take advantage of others. Exaggerated pride, arrogance, insolence, aristocratic violence, and unbridled passion were among the worst behavioral traits an individual could have. Central characters in most Greek tragedies were often people of "high estate," like the rich or the famous or the powerful, and they would do inexplicable things simply because they could do them and, in turn, destroy themselves. In other words, a person who was guilty of hubris has gotten too big for his or her britches in a cosmic way, and must be punished by the gods. In *For Your Eyes Only* (1981), Kristatos has misused his great power and wealth in a way that oversteps moral bounds, and faces retribution for his misdeeds.

EVERYTHING I KNOW ABOUT LIFE
I LEARNED FROM JAMES BOND

Jazz.

Jazz represents a typically American style of music, and is considered, with just a handful of other art-forms, one of the few contributions to World culture that the West has made. We hear Dixieland being played by the funeral procession's band in *Live and Let Die*. Jazz is derived from ragtime as well as the blues. The music is characterized by the beat of propulsive syncopation, driving brass bands, deliberate distortions of pitch, and varying degrees of improvisation. Many of jazz's roots are celebrated in the city of New Orleans, particularly in the week before "Mardi Gras". As a seaport city with boats going to and from the spicy islands of the Caribbean and Latin America, the Crescent City thrived with many different musical forms. Ultimately, the city's large black population combined those forms together to create jazz in the early twentieth century.

Junkanoo.

In *Thunderball* (1965), James Bond ducks in and out of the Junkanoo parade, a parade on Boxing Day (December 26) and New Year's Day in Nassau, to evade capture by Fiona Volpe and her men. Thousands of wildly costumed celebrants take to the streets to beat drums, march and dance to an African rhythm with touches of Obeah (West African religion) in the air. The term "Junkanoo" comes from the name John Canoe, an African leader and slave trader on the Gold Coast of Africa. He allegedly seized Fort Brandenbury from the British, thereby becoming a folk hero. Even in pre-emancipation days, the slaves were given three days off to participate in Junkanoo. In the 1950's and 1960's, distinct groups were formed—with such names as the Mexicans, the Valley Boys, the Saxons and the Vikings. Now, prizes are given to the best groups. The parade starts at 2:00 AM and continues until 9:00 AM. Then, the winners are announced. We are considering forming a select group ourselves just for a visit to this rowdy and funfilled event, though Bob's red-haired wife says she will not dance with James Bond, should he appear.

King Midas.

In both the novel and film versions of ***Goldfinger***, the titular character is referred to as the man with the "Midas" touch. King Midas, the oft-maligned figure of Greek and Roman mythology, was an actual, historical figure. By all accounts, he was the most important king of Phrygia because his treaties with other countries gave his people many years of peace and prosperity. But Greek and Roman authors turned him into a character of ridicule that was not very wise. According to the ancient myth, Midas offered Silenus, the wayward companion of Dionysus, food, drink and shelter, and was rewarded for his kindness and hospitality by Dionysus with a wish. King Midas wished that everything he touched would turn to gold, making him the richest man in the world. He returned to his palace, and changed everything, including the palace gates, into gold. After a while, Midas started to get hungry and thirsty, but found that he couldn't eat or drink as all his food and wine turned to gold when he touched it! His servants tried to feed him, but that didn't work either. Eventually, Midas begged Dionysus to remove the spell, and was permitted to wash away his "golden touch" in the river Pactolus. Even to this day, the soil along the riverbank has a golden gleam.

EVERYTHING I KNOW ABOUT LIFE
I LEARNED FROM JAMES BOND

Lawrence of Arabia.

In *The Spy Who Loved Me* (1977), a familiar theme occurs when 007 rides a camel into the desert, one that we have heard before. Many years before *Lawrence of Arabia* (1962) became a box office sensation and Maurice Jarre penned its famous musical theme, Lawrence became famous as a British army officer in the First World War by playing a key role in the Arab Revolt of 1916–18. Thomas Edward Lawrence was born in Wales in 1888 and studied archaeology at Oxford. After graduating with honors in 1910 and serving briefly as a museum curator in Iraq (then Mesopotamia), he joined the army, and was assigned to the Geographical Section of the General Staff in London. Because of his unique knowledge of the Middle East, Lawrence was soon posted to the Department of Military Intelligence in Cairo. In 1916, when the Arabs rebelled against the Turkish Empire, he was dispatched to Mecca on a fact-finding mission, and quickly endeared himself to King Feisal. Feisal, in turn, selected him as his British liaison officer. Under his leadership, Lawrence inspired the Arabs to take the port city of Akaba from the Turks who were allies of the Germans. Their campaign opened a second front that helped turn the tide of war. With decisive victories in Deraa and Damascus, Lawrence helped to raise the Arabs from a collection of feuding rival tribes to a military force of great power. At the end of the war, he tried to help the Arabs form an Arab state in the Middle East, but lost all credibility when Feisal made a separate peace with the British commander, General Allenby. Lawrence returned home to England, and died years later in a tragic motorcycle accident.

Lepidoptery.

In his leisure time at his country home, Quarterdeck, M (Bernard Lee) enjoys lepidoptery, which is a branch of entomology that deals with insects belonging to the large order Lepidoptera, including butterflies and moths; he is right in the middle of mounting a specimen when Bond interrupts him at his home with news of Blofeld. An admiral in the Royal Navy, M follows in the tradition of Sir Joseph Banks, the eighteenth-century English biologist and lepidopterist who accompanied Captain James Cook on his three-year circumnavigation of the globe. M not only collects and studies butterflies but also publishes articles on lepidoptery in scientific journals under a pseudonym; the admiral was an acknowledged expert in a group of small butterflies called Blues and was studying the *Nymphalis Polychorus*. The study of butterflies and moths is an obscure hobby that is enjoyed by a relatively small collection of scientists and enthusiasts. Vladimir Nabokov, the author of **Lolita** and a Russian contemporary of Ian Fleming, was well known for his interest in lepidoptery and shook its world with his very unique discoveries.

Microchips.

Everyone wants microchips, the more complex, the better. High tech industries' desire for microchips motivates Max Zorin, the modern-day Goldfinger, in ***A View to a Kill*** (1985). But what are these microchips? Microchips are a system of integrated circuits, which consist of very large numbers of transistors connected with circuitry and placed within a single silicon microchip. The microchip uses silicon because it is a semiconductor, a material that will conduct electricity somewhat but is not an all-out conductor, such as copper, nor is it an insulator, that prevents conductivity, such as the plastic that covers wires. In turn, the transistor, which does most of the work, is the device that replaced the vacuum tube. We remember old radios that had vacuum tubes. Until they lighted up, you would not even get static on your radio. The transistor contains three layers of semiconductors; each layer can carry a current. A small change in the current or voltage of the inner semiconductor layer produces a great change in the current going through the entire component. The microchip acts as a gate, opening and closing the flow of electricity many, many times a second. Today, modern microchips contain hundreds of thousands of transistors per microchip. You can see why you should not be using them as the center target on your dartboard, no matter what your friends may say after their third beer. Sarcastically suggest they use the zits on their foreheads for targets instead of a microchip. Human skin can grow back; no one will re-create a microchip for you.

Nazi Gold.

In an effort to gain Goldfinger's confidence, Bond entices the eccentric billionaire with a bar of gold that was recovered from a Nazi horde at the bottom of Lake Toplitz, high up in the Austrian Alps, sixty miles from Salzburg. During World War II, Luftwaffe Commander-in-Chief Hermann Goering maintained a villa not far from the lake where he entertained Nazi dignitaries, including Adolf Hitler himself. In the event the fortunes of war turned, the region around Lake Toplitz was intended to be the *Alpenfestung*, the Reich's Alpine Fortress and their last stand. However, by April 1945, Hitler was dead, the Allies were closing in, and time had run out for the Third Reich. Many of the last leaders of the Nazi regime fled there with the hopes of stashing vast quantities of gold and other priceless plunder. To this day, not a single ounce of gold or any other treasure has been recovered from the murky depths of Lake Toplitz, despite persistent rumors to the contrary. Treasure hunters have found crates of counterfeit British pounds, the printing plates, and even the printing press used to make them. Other divers have uncovered propellant charges and controls for rockets, laboratory equipment, weapons, and explosives. But no crates of gold, and certainly not the smelt of six hundred gold bricks "that vanished in 1944 while the Nazis were on the run."

Nerve Gas.

Delta Nine nerve gas is fatal. James Bond warns Goldfinger that he will kill sixty thousand people needlessly with the nerve gas. While hundreds of real nerve gas agents exist and some are fatal, Delta Nine is a fictional creation.

Nuclear Submarines.

As a prelude to World War III, Stromberg high-jacks three nuclear submarines, including one from the United States that just happens to be transporting James Bond, in *The Spy Who Loved Me* (1977). In 1954, one year after the publication of *Casino Royale*, the U.S. Navy launched its first nuclear-powered submarine, the *Nautilus*. The sub had a crew complement of one hundred and five men, was three hundred and twenty-four feet long, and had a maximum speed of twenty-five knots (twenty-nine miles an hour). From 1960 to 1966, forty-one other nuclear-powered submarines, nicknamed "boomers," joined the Nautilus in patrolling the world's seas. Each boat, which was named for an eminent figure in American history, carried sixteen Polaris nuclear missiles that could be launched underwater toward distant targets all around the world. Each missile carried ten times the destructive power of the atomic bombs that were dropped on the cities of Hiroshima and Nagasaki in World War II. Starting in 1972, the Polaris missiles were exchanged for the more accurate Poseidon missiles, and then, in 1979, for the Trident 1 missiles. The "boomers" were eventually replaced by the much larger Ohio-class submarines, the first of which were launched by the U.S. Navy in 1981. In the film, Bond and Anya hitch a ride on the *U.S.S. Wayne*, commanded by Captain Carter. We were both wondering for which eminent figure in American history the *U.S.S. Wayne* was named, "Mad" Anthony Wayne of the American Revolution or John Wayne? The U.S.S. Wayne was also the name of the nuclear submarine commanded by actor Leonard Nimoy in the cold war drama Assault on the Wayne (1971). Enemy agents posing as US Navy crew sabotage the submarine and steal its anti-ballistic missile guidance system

Orchids.

We loved the image of the black orchid in **Moonraker** (1979). Orchids appear in the titles of mystery novels quite often—such as Cynthia Riggs' **The Cranefly Orchid Murders** (Martha's Vineyard Mysteries), Stuart Woods' **Orchid Blues** (Holly Barker Novels), etc. Rex Stout's detective hero, Nero Wolfe, raises orchids. And one of Stout's novels is **Black Orchids**. The idea that a society could become infertile because of close contact with an orchid is not as farfetched as we might imagine. For example, giant pharmaceutical firms—such as Merck, Glaxo, SmithKline, and even the National Cancer Institute of the U.S.—are searching jungles and other areas in the Himalayas and Columbia for various plants to help mankind, including orchids. Along the India/Burma border, the Orchid Society of Malaysia has set up five orchid parks for commercial export of orchids, not all of whom will appear on prom dresses and, perhaps, assist in causing some woman's first child. The pharmaceutical industry has employed orchids both to cause people to procreate (aphrodisiacs) as well as to induce sterility. These beautiful and complex plants have a rich background in modern pharmacology as well as in ancient Greek mythology. As far as any orchid destroying the pyramid builders of the Mayan civilization, however, that was pushing the envelope. Though the Mayans (who were in Central America, not South America) and their civilization did have a quick turnaround after 900 A.D., it was not caused by infertility but rather by the reverse. Their city populations became too large to be fed by their food-delivery systems, and the Mayans retreated into village life, where you can find them today. And they still love orchids.

The Orient Express.

The elegant wooden paneled railway carriages of the Simplon Orient Express that ran from Paris to Istanbul in 1919 were found in many British mystery novels and in such films as John Paddy Carstairs' 1948 *Sleeping Car to Trieste*. Probably the most famous mystery film set on the Orient Express was Sidney Lumet's 1974 ***Murder on the Orient Express*** with Albert Finney as Hercule Poirot. The original Express d'Orient actually left Paris in 1883 and traveled to Vienna. As of June 2001, the Orient Express's route has been shortened to something resembling its original route from Paris to Vienna. But the mystique of the train lives on in ***From Russia with Love*** (1963), and so do two tourist trains that use a slightly more elegant, restored vintage rolling stock version of the 1930's era train. Travelers who enjoy fantasizing about rubbing elbows with mysterious figures and international intrigue still can book tours on the "Venice Simplon Orient Express."

Piranha Fish.

"They can strip a man to the bone in thirty seconds," Blofeld tells his Eastern guests, just moments before he demands an additional hundred million dollars in extortion money from them, in ***You Only Live Twice*** (1967). His words sound a bit ominous, but given the history of these legendary fish, deadly true. Commonly known as the "wolf of the water," the piranhas hunt as a perfect pack, leaving no chance of escape for their prey. The fish are very short in stature, but capable of fast bursts of speed which, when coupled with a mouthful of razor sharp teeth, makes them one of the most deadly of all freshwater predators. The common Piranha fish falls into two main family groups, the *Pygocentrus* and the *Serrasalmus*. The *Pygocentrus* family of piranha features the familiar blunt, bulldog face, while the *Serrasalmus* has a longer more pointed snout. Both varieties are extremely dangerous and deadly. Two of Blofeld's associates, Helga Brandt and Hans, learn first hand how deadly they are.

Poetry.

Moments before the attack on Piz Gloria by Draco's forces, in ***On Her Majesty's Secret Service*** (1969), Tracy distracts Blofeld in the Alpine Room with a poem she quotes. The words that she says to the murderous leader of SPECTRE are actually derived from a play by James Elroy Flecker entitled ***Hassan: A Soldier's Story***:

> Thy dawn, O Master of the World, thy dawn;
> For thee the sunlight creeps across the lawn,
> For thee the ships are drawn down to the waves,
> For thee the markets throng with myriad slaves,
> For thee the hammer on the anvil rings,
> For thee the poet of beguilement sings . . .

While many literary critics might decry Fleming's writing style as pedantic, the use of many literary sources in the novels and films demonstrate just how sophisticated the works really are.

The Pyramids at Giza.

In *The Spy Who Loved Me* (1977), James Bond follows Fekkesh, a middleman negotiating the stolen tracking device for Max Kalba, to the Pyramids at Giza, a necropolis of ancient Memphis, in a suburb of Cairo, Egypt. During an evening show for tourists that tells the history of the three Great Pyramids, Fekkesh is murdered by Jaws, and 007 finds his body with those of the pharaohs. One of the great wonders of the world, the Great Pyramid of Khufu (at Cheops) stands as a monument to the Egyptian pharaoh Khufu of the Fourth Dynasty who died around 2560 B.C. Most contemporary scholars agree this great pyramid was built over a twenty-year period with solid blocks of stone that were cut from quarries hundreds of miles away and transported by slaves using wood to roll them across the plain. No two scholars can agree on how the actual structures were built, but one theory suggests the construction of a spiral ramp that was raised as the pyramidal structure was built. The ramp, which was coated with a kind of silicon substance, eased the displacement of the blocks which were then pushed or pulled into place. For thousands of years, the pyramids of Giza, known alternately as "The Granaries of Joseph" or "The Mountains of Pharaoh," have stimulated the imagination of every person who has seen them. Alexander the Great knelt down and wept when he first saw them, while Napoleon expressed pride to his soldiers, stating, "From the tops of these Pyramids, forty centuries are looking at us." Today, the Great Pyramid is protected, along with the other pyramids and the Sphinx, by a great fence constructed for tourists venturing to the Giza Plateau. Jaws actually has to bite his way through a heavy metal lock and chain in order to reach Fekkesh who has hidden away in one of the ante-chambers of a pyramid. James Bond may not have enjoyed the show, but he hopes that Anya has.

Saint Bernard Dogs.

A Saint Bernard dog comes to James Bond's rescue after he has been thrown free of the bobsled that has presumably taken Blofeld to his death in *On Her Majesty's Secret Service* (1969). The dog wants to comfort him, but Bond sends it off to retrieve a barrel of brandy (Five-Star Hennessy, of course). Legendary for their mountain rescues, Saint Bernard dogs were first bred by the monks of the Saint Bernard Monastic Order in Switzerland in the eleventh century as guard dogs. Because the monastery of Saint Bernard of Montjou was constructed so high in the Swiss Alps, the monks relied on the hardy breed for protection. Later, when the dogs proved how effective they were in rescuing travelers caught in blizzards and avalanches, the legend of the St. Bernard dog grew (helped in large part by a story written by Prior Balalu in 1703). Thanks in part to the shaggy dense coat of the St. Bernard, the dog could weather severe conditions that the average domestic animal could not. The monks soon began using Saint Bernards to save people trapped in the cold Alpine wilderness. Legend added the barrel—filled with all kinds of alcoholic beverages—attached to the dog's collar, and the rest as we say is history.

San Andreas Fault.

When Lex Luther in *Superman* (1978) declares that "we all have our faults, and mine is in California," he is influencing another power-mad megalomaniac in the Bond films. We know that Max Zorin thought he had a good thing going by employing the San Andreas Fault to destroy his competitors in the Silicon Valley. We hear about this fault, this break in the deep underground tectonic plates, every time there is a serious tremor in San Francisco. In 1989, twenty-five miles of this fault broke apart in northern California, from Eureka to San Juan Bautista, during an earthquake called the 1989 Loma Prieta earthquake. Its epicenter was close to San Francisco. The Loma Prieta was the first major earthquake to occur alongside the San Andreas Fault since the 1906 earthquake that resulted in the burning of San Francisco. Sixty-three people died, and there was almost $6 billion in damage to property in the Bay area. This earthquake with its twisting of bridges and highways and demolition of buildings was a reminder that, while *A View from a Kill* was fiction, the San Andreas Fault was a real threat. It became very evident just five years after the filming of the James Bond film. It's not only "not nice to fool Mother Nature," but the old girl might kill you at any time in the Bay area.

SCUBA gear.

SCUBA (Self-Contained Underwater Breathing Apparatus or Aqua-Lung) gear is certainly prevalent in the underwater sequences of *Thunderball*. One of the inventors of the compressed-air SCUBA gear was French engineer and diver Jacques Cousteau in 1943. He later went on to get great publicity for the sport with his film *The Silent World* (1952). The great fight sequence between the SPECTRE frogmen led by Emilio Largo and the American frogmen led by James Bond makes a memorable scene. It is no surprise that SPECTRE would have chosen an Italian to lead this venture, as on December 19, 1941, Italian frogmen entered the harbor in Alexandria, Egypt, and crippled the British battleships Queen Elizabeth and Valiant. It is easy to remember Largo's white hair streaming behind him as he went on the attack. He was a good warrior, but he had to learn how to treat a lady the hard way.

Seven Chakras.

Diversity is the name of the game in international entertainment, and the Bond films have never lacked diversity. With *Tomorrow Never Dies* (1997, a film set in England, Hamburg, Ho Chi Minh City, and the South China Sea, we can still have room for a traditional Indian concept that goes back to the days when Rome was just seven hills with a few sheep grazing on them—the seven chakras. "Chakra" is a Sanskrit term for wheel or disk. It identifies here one of the seven points in the body where energy focuses. True, Dr. Kaufman had mentored Mr. Stamper on how to torture people for days with torture instruments (actually, they were surgical instruments for horses with added fancy handles by the prop department) by prodding into the chakra points of the body. The first chakra is at the base of the spine and has a great deal to do with our physical bodies. The second chakra is based in the womb (or abdomen, sexual organs and lower back for men) and effects emotions and movement. The third chakra is in the solar plexus and is the power chakra. The fourth chakra is the heart chakra; it governs love and unites all the other chakra points. The fifth chakra is at the throat; it affects our ability to communicate with each other and our creativity. The sixth chakra is in the middle of the forehead (the third eye position); it links our thoughts with our emotions. The seventh chakra is at the top of the head; it connects us with a higher power, wisdom and bliss. Now do we really want Stamper to mess with these chakras? Obviously, he was brain dead from his seventh chakra down.

Sharks.

Remember Emilio Largo warning James Bond about how dangerous the Golden Grotto sharks were, the same sharks he kept in his pool, in *Thunderball* (1965)? Well, he certainly gave something away then. Later, when Felix Leiter tells Bond that they are above the Golden Grotto, Bond asks for Leiter to fly his helicopter at a lower altitude, and Bond finds the camouflaged Vulcan bomber. The sharks to be found in the Golden Grotto are Tiger sharks. They have a reputation as man-eaters. Tiger sharks are found throughout the world in warm oceans. They reach about eighteen feet at full growth and are gray in color. It is not hard to provoke an attack by a shark. If you are thrashing about, you'll resemble the irregular vibrations of a wounded fish. If you have a cut or you are a woman who is menstruating, you'll attract them as well. After all, they can sense one drop of blood amid ten million drops of water. Relax; there are only about one hundred shark attacks worldwide in any given year, though a quarter of them do lead to death. Does shark repellant really work? Well, the World War II government-issued stuff pretty much just made the water murky, so that the sharks might not notice your pale

EVERYTHING I KNOW ABOUT LIFE
I LEARNED FROM JAMES BOND

palm in the water. Recently, a New Jersey company called Shark Defense made a shark repellant, called A-2, based on chemical found in dead sharks—pheromones used to communicate. The company claims A-2 repels four species of sharks: Nurse, Lemon, Black Tip and Caribbean Reef. It is testing A-2 on other, larger species. However, we suggest you keep your eyes open and your speargun handy, just like James Bond. No sure-fire repellant is available.

Silicon Valley.

If you know the way to San Jose, you probably know the way to Silicon Valley—the heartland of the US high tech industry, semiconductor land, where the microchip is king. Silicon Valley was Max Zorin's *View to a Kill*(ing) in the 1985 Bond film. Thousands of high-tech companies are headquartered there, including from the Forbes 500: Adobe Systems, Apple Computer, Cisco Systems, Hewlett-Packard, Intel, Oracle Corporation, Sun Systems, Symantec, Yahoo! and many others. It received the name "Silicon Valley" from journalist Don Hoefler in 1971; a reference to the high concentration of semiconductor and computer-related industries in the area. The "Valley" in "Silicon Valley" is a reference to the Santa Clara Valley. San Jose is the largest city in the Silicon Valley. Its population grew from two hundred thousand in 1960 to more than nine hundred thousand people by 2000. The cost of living there is quite high because of the high salaries so many people have gathered from the industries. In 1971, there were approximately one hundred and seventeen thousand high tech jobs; by 1999, there were six hundred and fifteen thousand high tech jobs. The Silicon Valley accounted for about forty percent of California's export trade in 1999. By 2000, the average home cost in the valley was more than twice the national average for major metro areas. If this information is going over your head, we can recommend another aspect of the Silicon Valley, a visit to the wineries around San Jose. Relax and spend some time in the wineries' tasting rooms. Sample their wines slowly, inhale deeply and roll the liquid in your mouth before swallowing. It is what James Bond might do when taking a break from Her Majesty's Secret Service.

Smurfing.

As the U.S. Bank Secrecy Act began to show its teeth on deposits or transfers of $10,000 or more, "smurfing" became the name of the game. Individuals recruited by retailers or the Columbian drug lords would go from bank to bank making deposits just under $10,000 and withdrawing cashier checks to be forwarded out of the country. This proposition was slow and somewhat risky. Therefore, Columbian drug lords starting buying planes to transport loads of cocaine to Mexico, Canada, and elsewhere for ultimate delivery to the USA or Europe. Once the cocaine was out the door, the same planes were loaded with U.S. currency (from $20-30 million) for a trip back to Columbia. There are other methods of laundering drug money that could have been used in ***Licence to Kill*** (1989), but we suggest you focus on finding a superior 401K Plan instead.

Sotheby's.

At the beginning of ***Octopussy*** (1983), 007 meets Jim Fanning at Sotheby's Auction House in order to discover the identity of the seller of "Property of a Lady," and trace the Fabergé egg to Kamal Khan and his associates. For two hundred and sixty years,

EVERYTHING I KNOW ABOUT LIFE
I LEARNED FROM JAMES BOND

Sotheby's has been auctioning off some of the finest books and collectibles and fine art in the world. Samuel Baker, founder of Sotheby's, held the first-ever auction on March 11, 1744, selling a hundred rare books for a few hundred pounds. Modest though his first sale might seem today, he continued to offer many great libraries for auction. Libraries from Prince Talleyrand, John Wilkes, the Marquis of Lansdowne, and even French Emperor Napoleon were all sold through Samuel Baker's auctions. When Baker died in 1778, his estate was divided between his partner George Leigh and his nephew, John Sotheby. For the next hundred years, the Sotheby family dominated the firm, and extended its auctions to include rare prints, medals, and coins. By the end of the First World War, the firm had so successfully expanded its role in the market that Sotheby's moved from its Wellington Street address to its now famous New Bond Street location. Today, more than one hundred Sotheby's offices are spread around the world, and, in 2002, auction sales amounted to approximately $2 billion.

The Space Station.

We always enjoy the sequences in James Bond films where the dozens of minions of the main villain gather together in their laboratory/headquarters to conquer the world. In **Moonraker** (1979), who can forget those dozens of beautiful people walking about in brightly colored outfits preparing to dominate both the Planet Earth and the space around it? The only trouble is, that sequence doesn't remind us of any space stations we ever saw. They remind us of what the luxurious space station in Stanley Kubrick's **2001: A Space Odyssey** (1968) is like. (Do you remember Drax's pheasant hunt starting with a hunting horn blaring the notes from the opening to Richard Stauss' "Thus

Spake Zarathustra"?) Kubrick used Strauss' theme in association with the black monolith in his film ***2001: A Space Odyssey***. The Soviet Mir Space Station, which was launched in 1986 and lasted for over fourteen years, did not have dozens of occupants at any one time. The International Space station, which had its tenth anniversary of continuous human occupation on Nov. 2, 2010, has been visited by over two hundred individuals from many nations. As far as luxurious headquarters, our shots of the space station have always displayed tight quarters and crewmen, not in designer togs, but rather in space suits without their large helmets. Regrettably, after thirty years of missions, the final space shuttle mission ended on July 21, 2011, at the Kennedy Space Center in Florida. The move from government-funded to corporate-funded space exploration paves the way for all sorts of wealthy Drax-like figures to control the final frontier. Let's just hope they don't have plans for world domination, or one day we'll look up at the International Space Station and be forced to pay homage to our new Overlords.

Spiders.

In ***Dr. No,*** James Bond has a very close encounter in his hotel suite with a large tarantula, and then later learns that Honey Ryder dispatched an unwelcome male suitor by placing a black widow spider "underneath his mosquito net." Spiders in the James Bond novels and films are rare, but when they do appear, they are usually deadly. Actor Sean Connery was so morbidly afraid of spiders that the shot of the spider in his bed was originally done with a sheet of glass between him and the spider. When that didn't look realistic enough, the scene was reshot with stuntman Bob Simmons doubling as Agent 007. The fact of the matter is that James Bond really didn't have anything to fear from the tarantula, but should have been keenly aware of black widows. Despite their ferocious appearance and bad reputation, bites from the tarantulas rarely cause any harm. Many people keep these spiders as pets. Their bad reputation can be traced back to an epidemic that broke out in the small town of Taranto in southern Italy in 1370. Occurring every summer for three hundred years, the disease was attributed to the bite of a large, hairy Wolf Spider (known in scientific terms as the *Lycosa Tarantula*). In order to cure the disease, people relied on wild dancing and music. Later in the seventeenth century, science proved that the "tarantula" spider was virtually harmless, and that it was in fact the Black Widow Spider that was the real culprit. Black widow spiders, especially the *female* of the species, are particularly deadly, and inject a poison that can be fatal to some people. Today, the term tarantula is a general one that refers to spiders belonging to the family Theraphosidae, and some of the largest in the world can be found in the state of Arizona. While James Bond reacts to the tarantula by smashing it to pieces with the heel of his shoe, he would be wiser to keep an eye open for Honey so that she doesn't put a black widow in his bed.

Stradivarius.

In ***The Living Daylights*** (1987), Kara Milovy's cello is a famous Stradivarius named Lady Rose, and Bond uses that information to link her and Koskov to an American arms dealer named Whitaker who bought the cello at auction. The six hundred and fifty or so musical instruments, particularly the violins, made by Antonio Stradivari are considered to be among the best and most rare string instruments in the world. Born in 1644, Antonio Stradivari built more than one thousand one hundred instruments in his lifetime at his small shop in Cremona, Italy.

He was renowned for his interpretation of geometry and design, and the violins, harps, guitars, violas and cellos he made were a work of real genius. Many copies of his work, which also bear his name, were made, but they are not necessarily the best instruments. His genuine label uses the Latin inscription *Antonius Stradivarius Cremonensis Faciebat Anno [date]*. This inscription indicates the maker (Antonio Stradivari), the town (Cremona), and "made in the year," followed by a date that is either printed or handwritten. Kara Milovy's cello, Lady Rose, a Stradivarius of Cremona which sold at auction in New York to Brad Whitaker for $150,000, is totally fictitious.

Sumo Wrestling.

In ***You Only Live Twice*** (1967), James Bond first meets Aki at a sumo-wrestling arena in Tokyo, but watches two matches before saying "I love you" to her. Sumo, which is a kind of wrestling for very heavyweight contenders, is the national sport of Japan. It originated in ancient times as part of a religious ceremony to the Shinto gods and has been steeped in ritual and tradition ever since. The basic rules of sumo are simple. The first wrestler, who either touches the floor with something other than his sole or is forced out of the ring by his opponent, loses the match. Sumo-wrestling matches themselves often last only a few seconds, and, in only a few cases, one minute or more.

Taj Mahal.

The Taj Mahal, located in the city of Agra in Northern India as seen in ***Octopussy*** (1983), is one of the Seven Wonders of the Modern World. Renowned for its magnificent architecture and incredible beauty, the familiar image of its gentle pear-shaped dome, square base, and four towering citadels is instantly recognizable all around the globe. The impressive structure is synonymous with India. As a mausoleum of the Mogul Empress Mumtaz Mahal, the Taj is unparalleled on earth, for mortal remains have never been kept in such grandeur. When his beloved wife died in childbirth in 1630, after bearing Shah Jehan fourteen children, the fifth Mogul emperor was so heartbroken with grief over her loss that he decided to build her the finest sepulcher ever—a monument of eternal love. For twenty-two years, over twenty thousand common laborers and master craftsmen worked on the complex on the banks of the river Yamuna in Agra. Material was brought in from all over India and central Asia, and supposedly it took a fleet of one thousand elephants to transport the rare materials to the site. Designed by the Iranian architect Ustad Isa, the structure was finally completed in 1648. Today, tourists from all over the world take the one-and-a-half-hour train from New Delhi to see the magnificent edifice that was built to honor Mumtaz Mahal (Exalted One of the Palace).

TAROT Cards.

One of the recurring visual themes in *Live and Let Die* (1973) is Solitaire's use of Tarot cards to follow Bond's actions from one cliff-hanging adventure to another. It is beautifully imagined as she deals cards that are super-imposed over his flight from London to New York. Designed specifically by Fergus Hall, courtesy of Portal Gallery in London, the Witches Tarot (as it is known) depicts dreamlike fantasies with bold swashes of colors in a style similar to the surrealist movement. (On the back of the cards is a red-and-white design which features the number 007 repeated over and over again.) When she deals the cards, Solitaire is represented by a card featuring the High Priestess, Bond is the Fool, and together they are the Lovers. Later in the film, 007 actually uses the cards against Solitaire to trick her into bed. The Tarot deck contains seventy-eight cards, twenty-two of which are referred to as the Major Arcana. Each card contains an image that represents a specific idea or meaning, and by "reading" the cards in association with other cards the reader is supposed to see the future. Some have traced the Tarot, as an ancient tool of divination, back to the Egyptians and magical wisdom of Thoth, the Egyptian god of inspired written knowledge. Others believe there is a correlation between the Tarot and the Hebrew Kabala. Still others have associated the cards with Gypsies, psychics, spiritualists, magicians, and (of course) witches. The first known deck appeared in Italy in 1440, and three other decks, called the "Visconti Trumps," are considered as the forerunners of decks that are used today. Card makers in Marseilles, France, in the latter half of the fifteenth century standardized the cards, and created a game for nobles. Certain cards, including the ones for Death, the Devil, and the Tower of Destruction, were omitted as offensive. Nearly one hundred years later, these cards were returned to the deck, and were used to tell fortunes. Despite attempts by religious leaders to ban the practice, Tarot reading is very much alive and well today.

Tongs.

Count Lippe in *Thunderball* (1965) has a tong tattoo, indicating his allegiance to the Red Dragon tong of Macau. Earlier in the film series, Dr. No revealed that he had been a member of the tongs. A tong is a Chinese secret society. Many of them exist in Europe and the USA as well as in Asia. They are, by tradition, something that grew up in China in the seventeenth century to protect the peasantry. While the wealthy and powerful could turn to the government, the poor person depended on the tong. In the USA, tongs exist in every large city with a "Chinatown." Most tongs are simply benevolent associations for its hard-working members. Some tongs, however, are still active in controlling gambling, prostitution, and drug sales in the Chinatown area. Mainland Chinese tongs that are bound by kinship and are criminal in nature are called triads. Triads are allegedly responsible for the main flow of opium, which is processed into heroin, from the Golden Triangle of Burma, Thailand and China. We would suggest that tong or triad matters are best left to persons of Chinese ancestry or James Bond to investigate, or not.

The Undertaker's Wind.

In the novel version of *Live and Let Die* (1973), as they approach the Jamaican headquarters of Mr. Big by sea, Quarrel tells James Bond about the "Undertaker's Wind." The Cayman islander says the off-shore breeze blows the bad air out while the night time winds blow the sweet air in from the sea. All year round, Jamaica enjoys temperatures between seventy-five to ninety degrees Fahrenheit, and two delightfully named winds help cool the island: the Doctor's Wind blows gently from inland out to sea, and the Undertakers Wind comes off the sea in the evenings. At tropical twilight, a ten minute-pause brings a quiet melancholy over the island, and then the stars and the moon come out, and the palms begin to whisper and signal the end to the short lull between the two great winds of Jamaica.

JOHN L. FLYNN AND BOB BLACKWOOD

Venetian Glass.

When we first saw *Moonraker* (1979) take us through the expensive glass museum at Venini Glass, we thought, "Surely, there must be a reason for this sequence." Later, as Chang came through with his bokken and his bad attitude, we saw the reason for the sequence. It was barbarian time at the glass museum. The Venetians started producing glass around the eighth century A.D. The Venetians, who traded throughout the Mediterranean, were always on the lookout for new techniques in producing glass. The Fourth Crusades' brutal looting of Constantinople gave the Venetians, who provided the transport for the "crusaders," the chance to add even more glass-making techniques to their business. In 1291, the glassblowers were moved to the island of Murano, outside of central Venice, so that the master glassblower and his apprentices would not be sharing secrets with the hordes of people from all over the world who traveled through the center of Venice. They didn't want them handing out trade secrets in Saint Mark's Square. When Tamerlane and his Mongols conquered Syria in 1402 and kidnapped the Syrian glassblowers, Venice had a lock on the production of quality glass. In the later 1400's, the Venetians produced "Crystallo," the clear transparent product that we think of when we say "glass." The Venetians went on to combine strips of different colored glass with Crystallo to create "Catticino" glass. The Venetians went on to produce "Aventurine," which creates glass with gold, silver, copper or mica flakes throughout the glass. When the Republic of Venice collapsed in the late eighteenth century, the secrets of glassblowing were no more. But by the mid-twentieth century, there was a revival in interest in Venetian glass that continues to this day.

EVERYTHING I KNOW ABOUT LIFE
I LEARNED FROM JAMES BOND

Volcanoes.

Ernst Stavro Blofeld, the head of SPECTRE, wisely chooses an extinct volcano to hide a state-of-the-art rocket base because Japan is known for its nearly two hundred volcanoes in *You Only Live Twice* (1967). How he managed to build it without notice and in such a relatively short period of time is another subject indeed! Japan is home to ten percent of the world's active volcanoes. In fact, the island nation suffers from tremors from these volcanoes or minor earthquakes every day of the year. Japan does suffer severe earthquakes as well. In 1923, the Great Kantō Earthquake shook the country and caused a subsequent fire which killed thirty-eight thousand people in Tokyo alone. Yet, the destruction of Blofeld's hideaway was considered by many to be a geological fluke.

Voodoo.

The derivative of what may be the world's oldest-known religion, Voodoo or Voudoun, dates back some ten thousand years or more to the dawn of human civilization and a West African cult known as "Vodoun," meaning "spirit." Practitioners believed that there were no accidents, and that everything was pre-determined by a snake god that formed the world and everything in it. Music and dance were key elements in the religious rites. When the Europeans began taking Africans to the New World as part of the slave trade, the essential wisdom and beliefs of Vodoun went with them. Voodoo, as we know it today, was born in Haiti. Not only did the slaves invoke their own gods, but they also incorporated rituals of the natives of Hispaniola, the Catholic slavers, and various other ethnic groups from Africa. The result of the different religious groups integrating their beliefs was a new religion known as Voodoo. The serpent figures heavily in the Voodoo faith; in fact, the word Voodoo has been translated as "the snake under whose auspices gather all who share the faith." Bond has little difficulty in dealing with Baron Samedi and his voodoo worshippers in *Live and Let Die* (1973).

World Champion Chess Players.

Boris Spassky, born in 1937 in Leningrad, U.S.S.R., became an international master of chess in 1953 and junior world champion and grandmaster in 1955. In 1960, he defeated David Bronstein for the U.S.S.R. Championship in Leningrad. The ending of this famous match is shown with Kronsteen (Sheybal) playing Spassky's game in *From Russia with Love* (1963). Spassky became a world champion when he defeated another Soviet, Tigran Petrosian, in 1969. A courtly and public figure, Spassky was set to continue the Russian domination of the world of chess. But in 1972, the American Bobby Fischer defeated Spassky in Reykjavik, Iceland, ending thirty-five years of Russian championships. While Spassky returned to Mother Russia, allegedly in disgrace, he still appears occasionally to play in international competitions and make some money. Bobby Fischer, on the other hand, seems to be having problems relating to the world and, after his victory, had not granted a public interview for over thirty years. Just because you won, it doesn't make you a winner, as Kronsteen learned.

CHAPTER THIRTEEN

LIFE LESSONS FROM JAMES BOND

You only live twice or so it seems,
One life for yourself and one for your dreams.
This dream is for you, so pay the price.
Make one dream come true, you only live twice.

—Nancy Springer, ***You Only Live Twice*** (1967)

James Bond's vast range of skills and knowledge is only matched by his clever resourcefulness in dealing with each new challenge that comes his way. In the course of his adventures, 007 has learned many lessons about life, some the hard way (particularly when it has cost him a fellow agent or a loved one). But Bond never makes the same mistake twice. In movie after movie, Agent 007 has demonstrated an encyclopedic knowledge of subjects ranging from deep-sea diving gear and electromagnetic pulses to butterfly collecting and even the history of rare orchids. His vast knowledge continues to increase as he adds new skills and talents with each new assignment. Simply put, James Bond is always learning, and his resourcefulness in handling dangerous situations as they occur reflects a man whose mind is always collecting information. Every important lesson about life, we have learned from 007, and those lessons have helped us handle "dangerous situations" as they have occurred in our own lives. These life lessons not only make the James Bond films very interesting but also provide us with a roadmap to surviving in a world that is not always as black and white.

You Only Live Twice [BR 1967] Photo By: Ronald Grant Archive / Mary Evans / Everett Collection rant Archive 10695652

Alligators and Crocodiles.

"Trespassers will be eaten!" In the first James Bond adventure, ***Dr. No***, 007 fought his first non-human predator, a tarantula, at close range in his hotel room. In the fourth and fifth films, Bond faced predatory sharks and deadly piranhas, respectively. In ***Live and Let Die***, Bond is trapped on an island surrounded by man-eating predators, and must use every ounce of his skill and resourcefulness to survive. Thanks to the incredible stunt work of Ross Kananga, a real-life crocodile hunter, Bond literally

EVERYTHING I KNOW ABOUT LIFE
I LEARNED FROM JAMES BOND

walks to safety across the backs of several crocodiles. During the one hundred-million-year age of reptiles, crocodilians ruled the earth. Today, only twenty-three species remain, many of which are in danger of extinction due to human encroachment on their natural habitat. Of all the species, the crocodile is still regarded as the ultimate predator. Not only is the crocodile a highly intelligent animal, but it also has the largest and most complex set of behaviors of any of its closest relatives. Crocodiles are often distinguished from alligators by their tapered and triangular snouts or the exposed tooth on either side of the lower jaw. Alligators are slightly larger, with a round nose and a darker-colored hide. Some of these lizard-shaped reptiles live to be two hundred years old. They eat anything, even each other, or can go an entire year without eating. From the movie, we learn two valuable life lessons about disabling a crocodile: "One way is to take a pencil and jab it in the pressure point beneath its eye," according to Tee-Hee (Julius Harris), and "the other way is twice as simple. You just reach your hand in its mouth and pull its teeth out." We're hoping that you are never trapped on an island surrounded by alligators and crocodiles, but if you are, don't say we didn't prepare you; always carry a pencil, and be prepared to act swiftly, like a reptile dentist.

The Code Hero.

As it says in the tag line, James Bond is out for revenge in ***Licence to Kill*** (1989). His longtime ally Felix Leiter has been mutilated; Leiter's attractive wife, who grabbed a kiss from Bond at her wedding, was killed and, possibly, raped. His own government and agencies of the American government did not want him to revenge himself upon Franz Sanchez. But Bond ignored their requests. This Bond is a code hero. Like Sam Spade in Dashiell

Hammett's novel ***The Maltese Falcon*** (1929), when a man's partner is killed, he must do something about it, even if the killer is a woman whom he might love (such as the charming Mary Astor in John Huston's 1941 ***The Maltese Falcon***). What means does he use to get revenge on the killer of Della Leiter? As Michael G. Wilson noted, he borrowed the device from Akira Kurosawa's film ***Yojimbo*** (1961) of driving the gang leader into killing other gangsters, just as happened in Hammett's novel ***Red Harvest*** (1929), which was an influence on Kurosawa. In turn, Kurosawa influenced the plot of Sergio Leone's film ***A Fistful of Dollars*** (1964) with Clint Eastwood, which even has some shot-by-shot similarities to Kurosawa's film. In Walter Hill's ***Last Man Standing*** (1996) with Bruce Willis, the influence was from Kurosawa again. Bond's professionalism can go hang. He feels that no one will punish this raving beast, this drug lord, except James Bond. And, he is right. For a number of reasons, taking out Sanchez is on the back burner of everyone's stove, everyone but James Bond's. Government agencies have to do what is best for their government. Individual agents, on the other hand, always see it as a bad thing when another government or a criminal organization starts picking off agents and, especially, the agents' families. It must not be encouraged, for the good of agents everywhere, to paraphrase Sam Spade in ***The Maltese Falcon***. So James Bond did what his government would not do, and we applaud him for it. We suspect, however, that in real life, ***On Her Majesty's Secret Service*** would not be inclined to keep James Bond on the payroll after this event. After all, the terrorist threat could have turned out very bad for both the US and the UK governments. No one wants to be responsible for a terrorist attack that could have been prevented.

EVERYTHING I KNOW ABOUT LIFE
I LEARNED FROM JAMES BOND

Communal Bathing.

In Feudal Japan, the lack of baths or bathing facilities gave rise to the tradition of communal bathing in the "sento," or bathhouse. Typically, males bathe on one side of a large room, which is separated by a tall barrier, and women bathe on the other side. Japanese cleanse themselves first with soap and shampoo in a shower area, then soak with other, newly washed bathers in a single large bath. Since the 1980s, these communal bathhouses have begun decreasing in numbers as more and more Japanese bathe at home. Some more traditional Japanese are concerned that without the kinship of mutual nakedness, their children will not be properly socialized with others. In *You Only Live Twice*, Tiger Tanaka tells Bond that he is going to take his first civilized bath, while 007 quips that he "likes the plumbing." One important life lesson that every Westerner should know is that keeping the water clean is a fundamental part of Japanese bathing. Make sure you are clean, and make sure you have washed off all soap and shampoo before entering a public bath. Getting soap in the bathtub will seriously offend your Japanese hosts as will farting in the water to create the effects of a Jacuzzi.

Death-dealing Double-Entendres.

In *From Russia with Love* (1963), the moviemakers began the use of double-entendres, not double-entendres about sex, which is expected in Bond films, but about dealing death to the opposition. Sometimes the sexuality and the violence are linked. For example, we first hear one when the Bulgarians try to take out Kerim Bey via a bomb in his office. Luckily, Kerim Bey's sexy assistant was insistent that he leave his desk and join her on the settee just before the explosion occurred. We pick up the event as James Bond later enters the bombedout office. Bey explains what happens and says, "The girl left in hysterics." The tongue-in-cheek Bond suggests, "She found your technique too violent." Another death-dealing double-entendre occurs when Bond and Bey are poised outside the hideout of Krilencu (Haggerty) to take out the Bulgarian thug with Bond's AR-7 folding rifle. There is a huge advertising mural painted on an apartment building's wall for ***Call Me Bwana***, a film starring Bob Hope and sex goddess Anita Ekberg that was produced by Bond film producers Broccoli and Saltzman. Krilencu has an emergency exit through the window in the middle of Ekberg's mouth. When Bey's sons dressed as police officers knock on the front door, Krilencu climbs down a rope through the window. When the aggrieved Bey pulls the trigger, Krilencu falls to his death. Bond then quips, "She should have kept her mouth shut." Later, on the water, as Bond shoots up the barrels of high-octane fuel with a Very pistol before the oncoming SPECTRE boats, he says: "Where there's smoke, there's fire." Also, at the end of the film, Rosa Klebb (Lenya) enters Bond and Tania's hotel room in Trieste dressed as a maid. She pulls a gun on Bond, orders everyone around, until finally Tania knocks the gun from her hand. Klebb swings into physical combat mode, tears off her hat and whips out a poisoned knife implanted beneath the toe of her shoe. Bond fends her off with a chair, until Tania shoots Klebb with a pistol. Looking at the body, Tania says, "Horrible woman." Bond notes, "Yes, she's had her kicks." From this point on, death-dealing double entendres are standard in the vocabulary of action heroes, such as Clint Eastwood and Arnold Schwarzenegger. After all, if you can't have fun with your work, why do it? There's always a job available at the local Wal-Mart.

EVERYTHING I KNOW ABOUT LIFE I LEARNED FROM JAMES BOND

Defusing a Nuclear Warhead.

Secret Agent James Bond has spent the time between his assignment in **Goldfinger** (1964) and the events in *The Spy Who Loved Me* (1977) reading up on how to defuse a nuclear warhead. In his earlier mission, 007 was completely clueless as to how to defuse the atomic device that was ticking away in the vault at Fort Knox, but, twelve years later, while trapped aboard the supertanker *Liparus*, Bond demonstrates considerable ease in defusing one of the nuclear warheads in the armory. What happened? From the Ian Fleming novels, we learn that Bond is easily bored, and that, since he only gets one or two big missions a year, 007 maintains his edge by reading dispatches and reports from other agents and instruction manuals on all manner of things. We suspect one of the manuals was one produced by the U.S. Nuclear Regulatory Commission on defusing nuclear warheads. With great skill, he uncouples the primary stage rocket from the warhead itself using tools that do not have an electromagnetic charge of any kind. Bond then unscrews the explosive triggering device from its housing, and carefully removes it from its magnetized hull, paying close attention not to touch off the nuclear material. And finally, he cuts the red wire (instead of the green wire) to disable it completely in order to use the explosive device against Stromberg's forces. At each step of the way, 007 pauses long enough to explain what he is doing to the crew of the nuclear submarine. Now that's what we call leadership! Unfortunately, by the time of his mission in *The World Is not Enough* (1999), Bond has forgotten most of what he learned about defusing a nuclear warhead, and must rely on Dr. Christmas Jones to help him. Or do you think he just wanted her along for company?

Double-Cross.

Kamal Khan plots with General Orlov to double-cross Octopussy, steal her riches, and leave her to die when the nuclear bomb goes off. Thankfully, 007 intervenes and saves the day. The reasons why criminals commit crimes are probably as varied as the crimes themselves. But the one constant that remains the same is that there is no honor among thieves. In the vast majority of James Bond films, the criminal mastermind has proven that he cannot be trusted in dealings with his underlings. Ernst Stavro Blofeld has routinely murdered members of his SPECTRE organization for failing to kill Bond or for committing some other minor offense. Goldfinger gassed members of several Mafia families after they completed assorted deeds for him, while Drax and Stromberg and Kristatos have executed trusted allies and confidants when they no longer served a purpose. The Bond movies teach us that, if we associate with bad people, we are likely to suffer. Thieves tend to run with thieves, and liars with liars, and because of their overall lack of integrity, everyone looks out for himself, and takes advantage of others. Habitual thieves and liars have also been known to be murderers, so death is a very likely possibility for people who fall in with thieves and liars. An important lesson for us all to learn is to let principle, not circumstance, guide our actions in everything that we do. As for habitual thieves and liars, we'd like to remind them "what goes around, comes around."

Dragons.

When they are attempting to penetrate Dr. No's outer defenses on Crab Key Island, Quarrel warns James Bond and Honey about the dragon, but Bond quickly dismisses the Cayman

EVERYTHING I KNOW ABOUT LIFE
I LEARNED FROM JAMES BOND

Islander's warnings as superstition. Honey speaks up, and asks if Bond has ever seen a dragon. He admits that he has not, but still does not believe in them. Later, they encounter an armored tank that has been made up to look like a dragon, and flames from its "mouth" burn Quarrel to a crisp. Much to his dismay, Bond discovers some truth behind the myth. The dragon is a legendary beast in the fairy tales and legends of many European and Asian cultures. Often represented as a monstrous winged and scaly serpent with a crested head and enormous claws, the mythical creature meant something completely different in the two folkloric traditions. In Europe, dragons were portrayed as fire-breathing beasts that represented evil; in Asia, especially China and the Japans, dragons were considered friendly creatures that ensured good luck and wealth. According to medieval legends, dragons horded great treasures in their dens, and the person who killed one supposedly inherited its wealth. In the English epic poem, Beowulf died fighting a dragon guarding its treasure, while Bilbo Baggins in **The Hobbit** steals the treasure of the dragon Smaug. The most famous story found the patron saint of England, Saint George, slaying the dragon of Cappadocia and rescuing the virgin princess from its clutches. Because of this heroic deed, other Christian knights sought out damsels in distress from dragons. We doubt if they found any, unless they were local warlords called the Dragons of Northumberland, etc. James Bond is a latter-day St. George, and the monsters he slays are larger-than-life figures, not unlike the dragon in the story. The dragon is, therefore, a metaphor for the evil that men, like Dr. No, do. Good men, whether they believe in the existence of dragons or not, must always combat evil.

Explosive Decompression.

Early in the film, Bond warns Pussy Galore about firing a Smith and Wesson .45 revolver in the passenger compartment of her jet. He tells her, "If you fire at this close range, the bullet will pass through me and the fuselage like a blowtorch through butter," and will cause them (and anything else that wasn't bolted down) to be sucked out into space. Not surprisingly, during the climatic struggle, Goldfinger's golden gun goes off and blasts a whole in the window, depressurizing the cabin. Bond is able to brace himself, but Goldfinger is sucked out of the cabin to his death. The reality of the situation is that, if a small caliber bullet were to penetrate a pressurized airplane, the passengers would not be sucked out the windows from "explosive decompression." Explosive decompression only occurs with huge holes. For instance, a terrorist bomb blew out a large section of the fuselage of TWA Flight 727 over Athens in 1986, and only four people were killed due to explosive decompression. Since a 9mm or .38 caliber bullet makes a hole less than an eighth of an inch, the effect of a bullet hole on cabin pressure is not enough to be measurable. The notion of explosive decompression from a bullet hole is actually an urban myth originated by *Goldfinger*. Explosive decompression or not, we still think it's not a good idea to wave a gun around on board an aircraft at thirty-five thousand feet, particularly in today's climate.

Golden Girls and gold paint.

Not long after bedding Goldfinger's girlfriend Jill Masterson, Bond is knocked unconscious by Odd-Job. When Bond finally awakens, he discovers that Jill is dead, her body covered in

EVERYTHING I KNOW ABOUT LIFE I LEARNED FROM JAMES BOND

gold paint. The official coroner's report says that Jill Masterson (Shirley Eaton) died of "skin suffocation" by being coated in gold, a complication often associated with cabaret dancers. While skin occlusion does not affect oxygen respiration, it does affect blood pressure. A body completely covered in paint (gold or otherwise) will cause a spontaneous and potentially dangerous rise in blood pressure. At any rate, since human skin plays little or no role in respiration, don't assume that your girlfriend who is covered from head to toe in gold paint died of skin suffocation. You might ask around to find out who is painting up your girlfriend from head to toe, however.

Haiku.

Ian Fleming's novel begins with a haiku from the famous Japanese poet Basho (1634–1694): "You only live twice: / Once when you are born, / And once when you look death in the face." The haiku, a seventeen-syllable verse consisting of three metrical units of five, seven, and five syllables, is one of the most important forms of traditional Japanese poetry. Most critics date the haiku to the famous verses of the Edo-period (1600–1868) when masters like Basho, Yosa Buson and Kobayashi Issa were writing "hokku," a term which literally means "starting verse." But this is actually a misconception. Hokku was not meant to be read alone as an independent poem, but rather as the first starting link of a much longer chain of verses known as "haika." While it was not uncommon for a poet to compose a hokku by itself without composing the rest of the chain, hokku verse merely set the tone for the rest of the poetic chain. In the 1890's, Masaoka Shiki formalized this verse form as haiku, so that it could be written, read, and understood as a complete poem unto itself, rather than part of a longer chain. Fleming's allusion suggests that everyone, including James Bond, faces life twice, once when we are born and once when we die. For those dear readers who are more literal-minded, we point out that Bond "dies" in the pre-titles sequence and lives a second time, following the credits.

Honorable Alternatives.

When James Bond first meets Octopussy, she commends him for having given her father Major Dexter Smythe an "honorable alternative" to facing trial for treason and ultimately a firing squad. 007 had once been charged with bringing him to justice. We can learn something about honor and dignity from Bond's actions. In our society, when someone commits a crime or some offense against society, we demand retributive justice . . . proverbially, an eye for an eye. Our laws, which are based upon Judeo-Christian beliefs, assure us that everyone receives equal treatment according to the principles of righteousness and rectitude in all things. In our courts, justice is depicted as a blind woman holding two scales, each of which must be balanced. But that is not always the case. Regrettably, some criminals do go free, while some innocents are convicted of crimes they did not commit. But that is really not the dilemma that Bond wrestles with . . . 007 is supposed to be the "blunt instrument" of law, bringing criminals who have broken society's rules to face justice, but instead he practices a rare form of justice that has little place in our Judeo-Christian society. In the back-story, which is actually taken from Ian Fleming's short novel ***Octopussy***, Major Dexter Smythe was a British army officer who was seconded to MI6, and assigned to find a horde of Chinese gold (in the novel, Nazi gold). While tracking the gold, he murdered his guide,

EVERYTHING I KNOW ABOUT LIFE
I LEARNED FROM JAMES BOND

Jannes Oberhauser, and then disappeared with the treasure. Twenty years later, Bond tracked him to his hideaway in Sri Lanka (Jamaica, in the story), and gave him twenty-four hours to clear up his affairs. Smythe committed suicide rather than face the disgrace of a public court martial and execution. For the Carthaginian general Hannibal who tried to invade Rome with his famous elephants, suicide seemed an honorable alternative to being a captive or even possibly a slave of the Roman people. Among the warrior elite, who followed the teachings of Buddha, suicide was considered an honorable alternative to being killed by others or continuing a life in shame or misery. Eastern religious beliefs have always advocated suicide to avoid an inevitable death at the hands of others, or to escape a longer period of unbearable pain or psychological misery. 007 offers Smythe that "honorable alternative." Justice is still served, but instead of costing his government millions of dollars on a public trial, of which the outcome is still uncertain and putting a fellow agent through the embarrassment, Bond gives the Major a dignified out. We think that everyone would like a twenty-four-hour period at the end of our lives to settle our affairs and would most likely welcome an honorable alternative.

Industrial Lasers.

Auric Goldfinger's new toy is an industrial laser, and he boasts that "it can project a spot on the moon or, at closer range, cut through solid metal." He then offers to demonstrate its capability of cutting through solid metal (and flesh) while Bond is strapped precariously to his workbench. Later in the film, Goldfinger uses his laser to cut through the steel doors of Fort Knox. As depicted on screen, the device is large and cylindrical in shape, with a coil of electrically charged wire and a thin nozzle for the beam of light. In ***Die Another Day*** (2002), Mr. Kil threatens both Jinx and 007 with an automated laser system that, eventually, causes his own death. Today, industrial lasers are used in our world for a variety of routine tasks from correcting vision and maintaining global communication to drawing maps and printing documents. They can indeed "project a spot on the moon" and are presently being tested as a defensive weapon. But please don't hold your breath for one like Buck Rogers' pistol, unless this is ***Moonraker***.

Leadership Skills.

In the epic battle aboard the *Liparus* in ***The Spy Who Loved Me*** (1977), James Bond demonstrates the kinds of leadership skills that are necessary to command large forces of men. As a commander in the Royal Navy, 007 knows that the first thing a good leader must possess is a clear understanding of his or her own needs and goals. Next he must know the resources and skills of the men under his command. Knowledge helps a leader deal with each person as an individual who has a unique contribution to make towards achieving a goal. Then the leader must have excellent oral and/or written communications skills, and those skills must include intelligence gathering as well as giving commands. Next, the leader influences the performance of the group and individual members through his or her actions. Setting the example is probably the most important leadership skill of all because it effectively shows others the proper way to conduct themselves. And finally, a good leader knows how to share leadership by delegating authority to other members of the group and teaching them the skills necessary to succeed. Effective teaching means increasing the knowledge, skills and attitudes of the group and its members. Bond knows that good leadership is the result of many years of experience in the careful application of these fundamental leadership skills.

Mountaineering.

Even though his parents were killed in a mountain climbing accident years before, James Bond has frequently shown us that he has the skills to climb tall edifices in a single bound. In ***Diamonds Are Forever*** (1971), he scales the exterior of Willard White's Las Vegas casino with little more than a piton-gun and a couple of strong ropes. Scaling a mountain, such as the rugged rock face that supports the monastery of St. Cyril in ***For Your Eyes Only*** (1981), is a bit more detailed and takes a great deal more time and effort. Mountaineering requires a big commitment, and is not meant to be taken lightly. Usually, climbers will start building their skills by scaling a small rock or hacking up a frozen waterfall, and then work their way into mountaineering. They must also conquer their fear of falling, which is what keeps most of us with our feet firmly planted on the ground. Once vertical, they know there is no room for doubt, or stupid mistakes. Typical gear that is needed for this sport includes a good pair of rock climbing shoes, comfortable clothing that is wind and waterproof, a harness, backpack, carabineers, chalk and chalk bag, ropes, a helmet, a crash pad, a belay device, cams, nuts, quickdraws, and lots of patience. Most mountain climbers dream of ascending one or all of the Seven Summits, including Kilimanjaro, Denali, Everest, Elbrus, Aconcagua, Vinson Masif, and Carstensz. While we're certain the view from the top is spectacular, send us a postcard, and we'll take your word for it. Clearly, mountaineering is not for the faint of heart.

JOHN L. FLYNN AND BOB BLACKWOOD

Poppies and Drug Smuggling.

From his poppy fields on San Monique, Kananga is producing heroin which he plans to smuggle into the United States and distribute through a chain of Fillet of Soul restaurants—two tons of heroin, to be exact, with a street value well over a billion dollars. As the by-product of poppies, heroin is the focal point of several Bond adventures and an Ian Fleming story titled "The Poppy Is Also a Flower." Made as a British film in 1966 by Terence Young, the director of three James Bond movies, *Poppies Are Also Flowers* followed a group of narcotics agents from the UN working to stem the heroin trade from Iran. Eventually, they decide to inject a radioactive compound into a seized shipment of opium, and follow it through the distribution chain. With the help of CIA operatives, Bond destroys Kananga's poppy fields, and literally blows up the source of the heroin.

Possession Is Nine-Tenths of the Law.

When James Bond recites the old adage about "possession being nine-tenths of the law" to Kananga, he is actually recalling a contentious debate from the 1700's on copyright law. In the late seventeenth and early eighteenth century, intellectual property was considered the same as landed property. Authors argued that they were the sole owners of their literary works, but certain publishers also felt that they had the right of the public to reproduce certain works for public consumption. A 1709 statute gave writers ownership for a term of twenty-one years for books already in print and fourteen years for new books, with the possibility of a second fourteen-year term. But even after the passage of the statute, many London-based booksellers still laid claim to certain literary properties. In a landmark case, a majority of judges (nine) ruled in favor of granting authors due rights to their literary property, but only for a specified period of time. Accordingly, Samuel Johnson wrote, "Possession is nine-tenths of the law—or, as I would like to understand it, the law is mostly about property . . . common lawyers had an easier time thinking about copyright in terms of property rights." Rightly or wrongly, the person who possesses something usually has a greater legal right to it than anyone else.

Radiation Decontamination.

According to the ***Radiation Safety Manual***, people must follow several specific methods of decontamination in order to reduce radiation exposure and minimize the absorption of radionuclides through the skin; but then we already learned that life lesson in ***Dr. No***. After James Bond and Honey are brought into Dr. No's headquarters, they are forced to undergo a very harsh decontamination procedure. They are forced to remove their clothing because it is contaminated, and then specific hot spots on their skin are located using a spectrometer. Soap and lukewarm water (or detergent) is used to remove most of the contamination and to prevent its spread to the clean areas of their bodies. When the spectrometer reveals that the contamination still exists, they must wash again using plenty of soap and a soft brush. Both Bond and Honey also thoroughly wash their hair with liquid soap and water rinse. Afterwards, Honey wraps her hair in a towel to keep the contaminated water from running onto the face and shoulders. Thankfully, the soap and water reduce the contamination on their bodies to an acceptable level, and they are allowed to get dressed in new clothes. Since their old clothes are saturated with radiation, the garments are placed in a radioactive waste disposal unit. It's always a good idea to keep one of those around. So, the life lesson is: the next time you are exposed to a dose of radiation, get rid of your clothes immediately and take a lukewarm shower with soap, preferably with a beautiful woman.

Resignation.

When M removes James Bond from Operation Bedlam in *On Her Majesty's Secret Service* (1969), 007 dictates his letter of resignation to Miss Moneypenny, and asks that she kindly present it to his boss. Naturally, Bond has no desire to resign from Her Majesty's Secret Service, and Miss Moneypenny cleverly changes the wording to read a "leave of absence." But James Bond's threat to resign does have the power to shock his boss, and possibly force him to reconsider 007's assignment to Operation Bedlam. Resignation or the formal notification of resigning is a huge gamble, and should not be considered lightly. As a life lesson, we feel that it is one of the most invaluable ones that we have learned in the James Bond films. If you feel you have exhausted all your options, then you have but one option left, and that is to threaten to resign. But simply threatening to resign will not work. You must be prepared to resign, if your bluff is called by your boss. Write a formal letter, identifying problems as you see them, and provide your boss with reasonable solutions to the problems. Submit it, anticipate the best, and prepare for the worst.

Revenge.

In *For Your Eyes Only* (1981), when Sir Timothy Havelock and his wife are murdered by a Cuban hit man in front of their daughter, Melina Havelock decides to avenge their deaths

EVERYTHING I KNOW ABOUT LIFE
I LEARNED FROM JAMES BOND

by killing all those responsible. James Bond reminds her that vengeance is never a good thing, "The Chinese have a saying: Before setting off on revenge, you first dig two graves," but she refuses to listen to him. In our culture, the notion of revenge is actively promoted by the words and phrases that we use in our daily, colloquial speech. Words like payback, punish, and reprisal and phrases like "Don't get mad, get even," "Let the punishment fit the crime," and "Revenge is a dish best served cold" are part of our popular culture. Even the Bible advocates "an eye for an eye." For those who can simply walk away from a bad situation, without any reprisals, we say, "More power to you!" But the rest of us mere mortals get caught up in the moment and find it difficult to shrug off blatant wrongdoings. No one wants to appear weak; no one wants to end up like those sad sacks who spend the rest of their lives complaining about what someone did to them years before. Revenge is a potent, expedient way to get even for any injuries or offenses, perceived or otherwise. Like Karma, revenge seems like the perfect means to bring the scales of justice back into balance and restore order to the universe. Unfortunately, revenge also causes people to act blindly with anger, rather than with reason. We excuse our blind rage by sighting the principle of an eye for an eye, and completely miss the rest of Romans 12:19, which says that "Vengeance is mine; I will repay, saith the Lord," James Bond is trying to remind us that revenge is never healthy, and that it affects everyone involved. The act of harming someone in retaliation for something harmful that they have done to you never resolves the initial harm.

"Shoes Off" Custom.

When Bond sits down at the Sumo Wrestling arena in *You Only*

Live Twice (1967), and then later enters Dikko Henderson's home, he removes his black moccasin shoes without hesitation 007 is aware that Japanese custom dictates that visitors remove their shoes before entering a house or other residence. Originally, the floors in all Japanese homes were covered with straw mats, known as "tatamis." In order to keep the tatamis clean for sitting upon, all outdoor footwear was left at the door. The custom is deeply-rooted in Japanese traditions, and, while modern homes have replaced the tatami-mat floors with more Western-style interiors furnished with tables and chairs, this "shoes off" custom has not changed. Foreign visitors can easily startle or even anger their Japanese hosts by walking into a home without first removing their shoes. In the mid-nineteenth century, for instance, the first American consul to Japan, Townsend Harris, shocked Japanese by walking straight in to see the shogun in Edo Castle without taking off his shoes. To save face, we recommend that you remove all outdoor footwear at the entrance to a Japanese house or dwelling, and place them right in the "geta-bako," or shoe cupboard.

Triscadecaphobia.

When James Bond breaks free of his captors at Draco's secret headquarters in ***On Her Majesty's Secret Service*** (1969), he bursts through a closed door into an elegant den, throws a knife and hits a calendar on a bookshelf. Draco says, "But today is the thirteenth, Commander Bond," and he replies, "I'm superstitious." Going as far back as ***From Russia with Love*** (1963), James Bond has remained mockingly superstitious, particularly about the number thirteen. Triscadecaphobia is the irrational fear of the number 13. Many believe Friday the 13th is an especially unlucky day, but not everyone holds with

EVERYTHING I KNOW ABOUT LIFE I LEARNED FROM JAMES BOND

that particular belief. In Ancient Rome, the citizens considered the sixth day of the week to be lucky, and dedicated it to their beautiful Venus. Muslims claimed Friday as the day in which Allah created Adam, and also saw it as the day when Adam and Eve ate the forbidden fruit. Christians call the day on which the Romans crucified Christ Holy Friday, and say there were thirteen present during the Last Supper when Jesus said goodbye to his apostles before being crucified. The first recorded instance of an unlucky Friday the 13th, happened in October 1307 when the Pope, in league with the King of France, signed the death sentence of "the Knights Templar." All of them were burned as heretics, including their Grand Master, Jacques DeMolay. The early Scandinavians believed the number 13 meant bad luck because of the evil cruel Loki, the thirteenth demigod among a pantheon of twelve other gods. So, while there are a number of reasons why many would fear the number 13, there is no explicit evidence that the number (or the day) spells bad luck. Simply for James Bond and our life lesson, it represents a day to take notice and caution.

Witticisms.

With James Bond strapped onto a metal table in the laboratory (and the industrial laser pointing directly at him from above), Goldfinger warns, "Choose your next witticism carefully, Mister Bond. It may be your last." A witticism is a cleverly witty and often biting remark, and Bond is well known for his pithy remarks, however ironic and dangerous they might be. We think it's a very good idea that you should always choose your witticisms carefully, because you never know when what you say may be the last thing you say. James Bond: "I think you made your point. Thank you for the demonstration."

SAMPLE FACTOIDS SPREAD THROUGHOUT THE BOOK

THE TEN BEST JAMES BOND FILMS

1. *Goldfinger* (1964)
2. *On Her Majesty's Secret Service* (1969)
3. *The Spy Who Loved Me* (1977)
4. *From Russia with Love* (1963)
5. *GoldenEye* (1995)
6. *Live and Let Die* (1973)
7. *Thunderball* (1965)
8. *Dr. No* (1962)
9. *Tomorrow Never Dies* (1997)
10. *Skyfall* (2012)

SAMPLE FACTOIDS SPREAD THROUGHOUT THE BOOK

THE FIVE WORST JAMES BOND FILMS

1. *The Man with the Golden Gun* (1975)
2. *A View to a Kill* (1985)
3. *Moonraker* (1979)
4. *Quantum of Solace* (2008)
5. *Never Say Never Again* (1983)

THE TOP TEN JAMES BOND GIRLS

1. Honey Ryder (Ursula Andress)
2. Pussy Galore (Honor Blackman)
3. Jinx (Halle Berry)
4. Solitaire (Jane Seymour)
5. Tracy (Diana Rigg)
6. Domino Petachi (Kim Basinger)
7. Tiffany Case (Jill St. John)
8. Octopussy (Maud Adams)
9. Tatiana Romanov (Daniela Bianchi)
10. Sévérine (Bérénice Marlohe)

SAMPLE FACTOIDS SPREAD THROUGHOUT THE BOOK

FAVORITE JAMES BOND SPOOFS

1. *Austin Powers: International Man of Mystery* (1997)
2. *Our Man Flint* (1965)
3. *In Like Flint* (1967)
4. *Austin Powers: The Spy Who Shagged Me* (1999)
5. *The Silencers* (1966)
6. *Austin Powers in Goldmember* (2001)
7. *The Return of the Man from U.N.C.L.E.* (1983)
8. *Casino Royale* (1967)
9. *The Nude Bomb* (1980)
10. *Spy Hard* (1996)

TELEVISION SHOWS INSPIRED BY THE JAMES BOND FILMS

- *The Man from U.N.C.L.E.* (1964)
- *The Girl from U.N.C.L.E.* (1966)
- *Amos Burke—Secret Agent* (1965)
- *The Wild, Wild West* (1965)
- *Get Smart* (1965)
- *I, Spy* (1965)
- *The Prisoner* (1967)
- *Alias* (2001)

SAMPLE FACTOIDS SPREAD THROUGHOUT THE BOOK

FAVORITE JAMES BONDS

1. Sean Connery
2. Pierce Brosnan
3. Roger Moore
4. Timothy Dalton
5. Daniel Craig
6. David Niven
7. Barry Nelson
8. George Lazenby
9. Peter Sellers
10. Woody Allen

THE RIVALS OF JAMES BOND

- Napoleon Solo (Robert Vaughn)
- Illya Kuryakin (David McCallum)
- Maxwell Smart (Don Adams)
- Matt Helm (Dean Martin)
- John Drake (Patrick McGoohan)
- Simon Templar (Roger Moore)
- Derek Flint (James Coburn)
- Austin Powers (Michael Meyers)
- Indiana Jones (Harrison Ford)
- James T. West (Robert Conrad)

SAMPLE FACTOIDS SPREAD THROUGHOUT THE BOOK

TOP TEN REASONS WHY *GOLDFINGER* IS THE BEST BOND FILM

1. Sean Connery as the Best James Bond
2. The Aston Martin DB-5 (with modifications) as the Best Bond Car
3. Pussy Galore and pussy galore (including Jill, Tilly Masterson, Dink, Mei-Lei)!
4. Auric Goldfinger as the Best Bond Villain
5. Odd-Job as the Best Bond Henchman The Megalomaniac's Plan "Operation Grand Slam"
6. Guy Hamilton's Direction
7. The Raid on Fort Knox
8. The Clever One-Liners
9. Ken Adam's Sets

TEN TRIED AND TRUE INGREDIENTS FOR SUCCESS IN A JAMES BOND FILM

1. An Attractive, Well-Dressed Secret Agent
2. Beautiful, Buxom Bond Girls
3. A Larger-than-Life Megalomaniac Bent on World Domination

SAMPLE FACTOIDS SPREAD THROUGHOUT THE BOOK

4. His Loyal, Incredibly Strong Manservant (preferably mute)
5. Cool Gadgets with an Introduction by Q
6. An Equally Cool Car with Special Modifications
7. Thrilling Locations (which include magnificent sets)
8. Edge of Your Seat Stunts
9. Pithy One-Liners
10. An Action-Packed Climax Featuring a Cast of Thousands

FAVORITE JAMES BOND CARS, VEHICLES AND OTHER MODES OF TRANSPORT

1. Aston Martin DB-5 (from *Goldfinger* [1964] to *No Time to Die* [2021])
2. *Lotus Esprit* (from *The Spy Who Loved Me* [1977])
3. Little Nellie (from *You Only Live Twice* [1967])
4. BMW Z-3 Roadster (from *GoldenEye* [1995])
5. Aston Martin Vanquish (from *Die Another Day* [2002])
6. *Moonraker-6* Space Shuttle (from *Moonraker* [1979])
7. BMW Z-8 Roadster (from *The World Is not Enough* [1999])
8. Aston Martin DB-7 (from *On Her Majesty's Secret Service* [1969])
9. Acrostar Jet (from *Octopussy* [1983])
10. Rocket-Jet Pack (from *Thunderball* [1965])

SAMPLE FACTOIDS SPREAD THROUGHOUT THE BOOK

LIST OF JAMES BOND'S CARS AND VEHICLES

1. *Dr. No* (1962)
    - 1961 Sunbeam Alpine Series II
    - Chevrolet Bel-Air Taxi
2. *From Russia with Love* (1963)
    - Rolls Royce
    - Bentley 4 ½ Liter convertible
    - Citroën Traction Avant
    - Chevrolet delivery vehicle
3. *Goldfinger* (1964)
    - Aston Martin DB5
    - Ford Mustang convertible
    - Ford Ranchero
    - 1964 Lincoln Continental
    - Rolls Royce Phantom III
4. *Thunderball* (1965)
    - Aston Martin DB5
    - Ford Mustang convertible
    - BSA 650cc Lightning motorcycle
5. *You Only Live Twice* (1967)
    - Toyota 2000 GT convertible with Japanese SS modifications
6. *Toyota Crown Casino Royale* (1967)
    - 1933 4 ½ Liter Supercharged Bentley convertible
    - Lotus Formula 3 race car
    - Jaguar E Roadster

SAMPLE FACTOIDS SPREAD THROUGHOUT THE BOOK

7. *On Her Majesty's Secret Service* (1969)
    - Aston Martin DBS
    - 1969 Ford Cougar convertible
    - Mercedes Benz sedan
8. *Diamonds Are Forever* (1971)
    - 1971 Ford Mustang Mach 1
    - Moon Buggy
    - 1971 Ford sedan
    - Honda All Terrain Vehicle
    - Aston Martin DBS
9. *Live and Let Die* (1973)
    - New York taxis
    - U.S. sedans from Ford
    - London double-decker bus
    - Morris/Austin Mini Moke
    - 1963 Chevrolet Impala
10. *Man with the Golden Gun* (1975)
    - AMC Hornet hatchback
    - AMC Matador car-plane
    - RC3 Seabee Seaplane
11. *The Spy Who Loved Me* (1977)
    - Lotus Esprit submersible
    - Kawasaki 900 with sidecar Ford Taurus
    - Small bus
12. *Moonraker* (1979)
    - MP Roadster
    - Venetian gondola/hovercraft
    - Glastron speedboat/hang glider
13. *For Your Eyes Only* (1981)
    - Lotus Esprit Turbo 2.2
    - Citroën 2CV
    - Yamaha XJ 500 winterized motorcycles

SAMPLE FACTOIDS SPREAD THROUGHOUT THE BOOK

14. *Octopussy* (1983)
    - BMW 5 Series sedans with police paint
    - BMW motorcycle
    - Mercedes 250 SE
    - Mercedes
    - Alfa Romeo GTV
    - VW bug
    - Rolls Royce
15. *Never Say Never Again* (1983)
    - Yamaha XJ 650 Turbo motorcycle with rocket-assist
    - Chevrolet Camaro
    - 4 ¼ Liter Bentley convertible
    - Renault Turbo
    - Mercedes SL convertible
16. *A View to a Kill* (1985)
    - Renault 11 taxi
    - 1985 Ford LTD
17. *The Living Daylights* (1987)
    - Aston Martin DBS V8 Vantage
    - Audi 200 Quattro
    - Land Rover
18. *License to Kill* (1989)
    - Kenworth W900B trucks
    - Lincoln Mark VII LSC
19. *GoldenEye* (1995)
    - BMW Z3 roadster
    - Aston Martin DB5
    - Ferrari 355 GTS
    - Cagiva motorcycle
    - Russian T22 tank
20. *Tomorrow Never Dies* (1997)
    - BMW 750iL sedan

SAMPLE FACTOIDS SPREAD THROUGHOUT THE BOOK

- BMW Cruiser R1200C
- Aston Martin DB5

21. *The World Is not Enough* (1999)
    - BMW Z8
    - Aston Martin DB5
    - Bentz boat with Q modifications

22. *Die Another Day* (2002)
    - Aston Martin V12 Vanquish with Q modifications
    - Jaguar XKR convertible with Graves' modifications

23. 1957 Ford Fairlane convertible *Casino Royale* (2006)
    - Aston Martin DB-5
    - Christensen 163' Yacht
    - 2006 Aston Martin DBS

24. *Quantum of Solace* (2008)
    - Aston Martin DBS V12
    - 52m Benetti Luxury Motor Yacht

25. *Skyfall* (2012)
    - Aston Martin DB-5

26. *Spectre* (2015)
    - Aston Martin DB-10

27. *No Time to Die* (2021)
    - Aston Martin DB-5

APPENDIX 1:

WHO WILL BE THE NEXT JAMES BOND?

As this book goes to press in April 2022, less than six months after the release of *No Time to Die*, Daniel Craig's replacement as the next James Bond has yet to be announced. EON's Producers Barbara Broccoli and Michael Wilson have a huge task ahead of them in selecting the next person to be 007. While speculation abounds with oddsmakers in Las Vegas and around the world, no single actor has emerged as the odds-on favorite for the next film. But there's really no rush, We've still got plenty of time to get the Aston Martin shined up and 007's tuxedo pressed before work begins on Bond 26. And yes, even though James Bond was mortally wounded at the end of the last movie, James Bond will return . . .

At press time, here are the top ten leading contenders for the role of James Bond 007:

1. **Henry Cavill**. Cavill was considered too young (at age twenty-two) when Craig was selected fifteen years ago. Now, after

APPENDIX 1

roles as Superman and Napoleon Solo, the ruggedly handsome Cavill may be a bit too mature to commit fifteen years (or more) to play James Bond in the next four to five films. He also may not be done playing the Man of Steel, if Christopher Nolan has anything to say about it.

2. **Tom Hardy** has played similar roles, in particular *Inception* (2010), looks good in a tuxedo, and is one of the few actors on the list who could guarantee box-office following the phenomenal success of the Daniel Craig Bond films. However, with Mad Max and Venom roles open to him, he may be too committed to other franchises to play 007.

3. **Richard Madden**, the thirty-six-year-old Scottish actor, has been scoring points as BBC's *Bodyguard* and Robb Stark in *Game of Thrones*, and continues to move up the list with few (if any) negatives on his side. He is a strong contender, especially to those who loved listening to Sean Connery's Scottish brogue as the agent with the license to kill. The only question would be whether Madden could juggle appearing as Ikaris from *The Eternals* (2021) in the MCU sequels as well as playing Bond.

4. **Dominic Cooper** played Ian Fleming in the BBC-produced miniseries, *Fleming: The Man Who Would be Bond* (2014), and he still remains as our favorite pick to be the next James Bond. He is known for his portrayal of comic book characters Jesse Custer on AMC's *Preacher* (2016–2019) and young Howard Stark in the Marvel Cinematic Universe. He looks great in the fight scenes and is charming to women. His only real drawback is that he is forty-four years-old, perhaps too old for a fifteen-plus year contract with EON.

5. **Cillian Murphy** has the acting chops and star-power to take over the role of James Bond, but at forty-five, he may be a bit too old, like Dominic Cooper, to play 007 long term. EON is definitely looking for an actor to carry the role for four to five

APPENDIX 1

films. His boyish features may also work against him when Bond is called upon to exercise his license to kill. And more often than not, Murphy takes on secondary roles because of their complexity to play. We see him as a long-shot at this point.

6. **Jamie Dornan** demonstrated he could make women hot and bothered in his sex scenes in the *Fifty Shades* trilogy, and proved that he also had a darker edge in *The Fall*. But does he have the charisma or the star power to play Bond, James Bond? We're really not sure, but then neither of us picked Daniel Craig as Bond. We both wanted Clive Owen, and still maintain that Owen would have been an outstanding 007. As for Dornan, at least he has first-hand experience working with whips and chains.

7. **Régé-Jean Page.** Like Dornan, women swooned over Page's handsome, eligible bachelor from Netflix's *Bridgerton* (2020) when he first stepped out on the scene. Even former 007 Pierce Brosnan told *Entertainment Tonight* that Page would make a "wonderful" choice to replace Craig, but let's face facts. He has no track record when it comes to fighting had guys or gunning down an enemy agent in cold blood. We're openminded enough to welcome an actor of color to the role, like Idris Elba or Colin Salmon who played Charles Robinson during the Brosnan years. But we just don't think Page is the right one for the job. Ironically, Page will be breathing new life into Simon Templer (aka the Saint) in a new big screen adaptation of the spy Roger Moore played before becoming 007.

8. **Idris Elba.** Speaking of Idris Elba, we both like him a great deal! He is cool, calm and collected, and has already proven to us he would make an outstanding James Bond, considering his work as Luther, a British detective. Unfortunately, like several others on the list, he may be too old. Elba is entering his fifties, and would not be available to commit to many more films as 007.

APPENDIX 1

"I know the rumors about Bond have always chased me," he said, in a recent interview. "Listen, my poor mum is like 'One day you're going to get it!' I was like 'Mum, I'm good, I've got Luther!' I'm definitely doing that." We love him as Luther, and will continue to follow his career.

9. **James Norton** has a proven track record with the number and variety of the roles he has played, from the disillusioned soldier in *War & Peace* (2016) to the ethically-challenged figure in *McMafia*. He earned a nomination for the British Academy Television Award for Best Supporting Actor in 2015 for his performance as ex-convict Tommy Lee Royce in *Happy Valley*. At six-foot-one, he is also the tallest actor on the list. Norton seems very nice and young, perhaps too bland to be Bond? Or maybe that's exactly what Barbara Broccoli and Michael Wilson are looking for . . . a blank slate upon which to write their next 007.

10. **Tom Hiddleston.** The first time we saw Hiddleston on screen was in Woody Allen's fever dream *Midnight in Paris* (2011) as F. Scott Fitzgerald. Clearly, he looked just like the author of *The Great Gatsby* (1925), and it was a winning performance opposite Owen Wilson. Then Hiddleston morphed into Loki in the Marvel Cinematic Universe, turning a bad guy into a three-dimensional cartoon character. He is quite good as Loki, even in his own television series. Could he play Bond? Absolutely, Hiddleston has the acting chops to play any character. Would he want to play James Bond when he's having so much fun as Loki? We're really not sure . . .

As this book goes to press, the actual odds are . . .

Tom Hardy—10/3
Regé-Jean Page—6/1

APPENDIX 1

James Norton—8/1
Henry Cavill—10/1
Idris Elba—10/1
Tom Hiddleston—22/1
Cillian Murphy—28/1
Richard Madden 33/1
Jamie Dornan—100/1

APPENDIX 2:

OTHER 00-AGENTS

Seven must be a lucky number, for James Bond 007 has survived while many of his fellow 00-agents have died in the line of duty. We're really not quite certain how many 00-agents work for MI6; that number has varied over the years, from a little as three in the novel *Moonraker* to what appears to be nine in the film version of *Thunderball*. We have also read mentions of a 0013, so perhaps that number goes higher than we had anticipated. Based on what we know, here's a list of other 00-agents:

- **Agent 002:**
    1. Bill Fairbanks Assassinated by Francisco Scaramanga (a.k.a. *The Man with the Golden Gun*) in Beirut 1969.
    2. In *The Living Daylights*, another 002 participated in a training exercise in Gibraltar with 004 and Bond, but was eliminated early from the exercise.
    3. Another 002 was rescued from Portuguese police headquarters in Macao in 1954 (according to Pearson's *James Bond: The Authorized Biography*).

APPENDIX 2

- **Agent 003:**
    1. Name Unknown—He was found dead in Siberia in *A View To A Kill* with the computer chip by 007.
    2. "Jack" was killed by Diavolo, the main villain, in the *Everything or Nothing* Bond video game (2004).
    3. A third 003 was badly injured in 1951 according to *James Bond: The Authorized Biography*.
- **Agent 004:**
    1. Frederick Warder participated with 002 and 007 in the training exercise in Gibraltar in *The Living Daylights*, but was murdered by a KGB agent.
    2. Another 004 was based in Britain in *The Facts of Death*.
- **Agent 005:**
    1. Stuart Thomas was missing, presumed dead, in *Colonel Sun*.
- **Agent 006:**
    1. Alec Trevelyan faked his death in 1986, and re-emerged as the head of the Janus crime syndicate.
- **Agent 007:**
    1. Nomi (Lashana Lynch) appears as 007's replacement in *No Time to Die* (2021).
- **Agent 008:**
    1. While his name is unknown, Agent 008 has been mentioned twice (in *Goldfinger* and *The Living Daylights*) as Bond's replacement.
- **Agent 009:**
    1. Name Unknown, he was assassinated by Mischka and Grischka in the film, *Octopussy*.

APPENDIX 2

  2. Another was sent by M in *The World Is not Enough* to assassinate Renard.
  3. Another died in Hungary in 1955, according to Pearson's *James Bond: The Authorized Biography*.
  4. Another 009 is mentioned as the next in seniority after Bond in *Thunderball*.
- **Agent 0011.**
  1. Name Unknown, he was lost in Singapore, according to *Moonraker*.
  2. **Agent 0012.** Although not mentioned on screen, the novelization of *The World Is not Enough* suggests the agent whose death Bond is investigating at the start of the film is 0012.
- **Agent 00?.**
  1. Named Captain Norman Nash, this un-numbered 00-agent was killed by "Red" Grant in *From Russia with Love*.
  2. Agent 00? Silva (Javier Bardem) was trained by M and placed as an agent in Hong Kong in *Skyfall* (2012). During the course of the movie, he never reveals his 00-number, but we are both convinced he earned his license to kill.
  3. Additional 00-agents are glimpsed during briefing scenes in *Thunderball* and *The World Is not Enough* but no information is provided. The latter film establishes that at least one 00-agent is female.

APPENDIX 2

APPENDIX 3:

SPECTRE AGENTS

SPECTRE has a system where all of its operatives are numbered. In the novels each member's number rotates each month (during *Thunderball* Largo is No 1 and Blofeld is No 2). However, in the films, the numbering seems more constant, perhaps acting as a hierarchy. This is what we know about SPECTRE's Agents:

No 1: Ernst Stavro Blofeld. Head of SPECTRE.

No 2: Emilio Largo (Adolfo Celi). He was in charge of the plot to steal British nuclear weapons and blackmail NATO, and was killed by his lover Domino (*Thunderball*).

No 3: Rosa Klebb (Lotte Lenya). Formerly head of operations for SMERSH, she defected to SPECTRE and worked on the scheme to steal the Lektor decoding machine. She was killed by Tatiana Romanova. (*From Russia with Love*). A later unnamed No 3 (Burt Kwouk) acted as a control room technician in SPECTRE's Japanese headquarters (*You Only Live Twice*).

APPENDIX 3

No 4: An unnamed control room technician (Michael Chow) in SPECTRE's Japanese headquarters (*You Only Live Twice*).

No 5: Kronsteen (Vladek Sheybal). As SPECTRE's Director of Planning and a master chess player, Kronsteen was executed by Blofeld when he failed to defeat James Bond with his fool-proof plot. (*From Russia with Love*). A later unnamed No 5 (Philip Stone) was a member of SPECTRE who provided consultation for the Great Train Robbery (*Thunderball*).

No 6: Colonel Jacques Boitier (Rose Alba/Bob Simmons). Jacques Boitier was an assassin who killed two members of the British Secret Service before he was killed by Bond (*Thunderball*).

No 7: An unnamed member of SPECTRE who was blackmailing a double agent (*Thunderball*).

No 9: An unnamed member of SPECTRE who assisted in No 11's drug-dealing scheme. However, he was embezzling funds and was executed by Blofeld (*Thunderball*).

No 10: An unnamed member of SPECTRE (André Maranne) who organized the assassination of a French anti-matter specialist who had defected to the Russians (*Thunderball*).

No 11: Helga Brandt (Karin Dor). Helga Brandt was a SPECTRE operative working in Japan as Osato's secretary. She was executed by Blofeld for her failure to kill Bond. (*You Only Live Twice*) An unnamed member of SPECTRE who was embezzling funds, and had to be executed by Blofeld (*Thunderball*).

APPENDIX 4:

PRODUCTION NOTES

DR. NO

- Producer Cubby Broccoli's wife, Dana, recommended Sean Connery for the James Bond role in *Dr. No* after she saw Connery in Walt Disney's ***Darby O'Gill and the Little People*** (1959).
- Richard Burton, Cary Grant, Rex Harrison, Trevor Howard, Roger Moore and David Niven were actors considered for the James Bond role in *Dr. No.*
- Despite being an early critic of Sean Connery as James Bond, Ian Fleming was so impressed by his performance in *Dr. No* that he created a Scottish background for James Bond.
- Directors John Frankenheimer and Alfred Hitchcock both turned down directing *Dr. No.* Terence Young agreed to helm the film in their place. Among the directors also considered for helming *Dr. No* were

APPENDIX 4

Bryan Forbes, Guy Green and Guy Hamilton. Hamilton eventually directed Goldfinger in 1964.
- When *Dr. No* opened in Italy, the Vatican condemned the film for its moral perspective. Stunt man Bob Simmons is the man in the opening gun barrel sequence in *Dr. No*, *From Russia with Love* and *Goldfinger*. Sean Connery replaced him in *Thunderball* (1965).

FROM RUSSIA WITH LOVE

- At an estimated cost of $2 million, roughly double the expense of *Dr. No, From Russia with Love* grossed over $78 million worldwide vs. over $59 million gross for *Dr. No*.
- In the pre-titles adventure, the faux Bond who is killed resembles Sean Connery quite closely. A re-shoot added a moustache on the actor.
- The "McGuffin"—the Lektor encryption machine whose possession drove the plot of From Russia with Love—was based on Ian Fleming's real World War II work with the group that broke the German Enigma machine's secret code.
- Rumor has it that there was no love lost between the women who played the fighting Gypsy girls in *From Russia with Love*. Martine Beswicke was allegedly a favorite of Director Terence Young, and Aliza Gur was not. We do see Beswicke again in Terence Young's *Thunderball* (1965) as Bond's assistant Paula Caplan.

APPENDIX 4

GOLDFINGER

- Margaret Nolan, who appears briefly as Bond's masseuse, Dink, also appears during the credits painted in gold. An aircraft hanger bears the sign "Welcome General Russhon," a reference to the film's technical advisor Lieutenant-Colonel Charles Russhon.
- *Goldfinger* was the first Bond film to be shown on commercial television in the United States, on September 17, 1972. It won the highest Neilson ratings for a motion picture on television to that date. Forty-nine percent of American viewers saw it.
- Both Orson Welles and Theodore Bikel were both in the running for the part of Auric Goldfinger. Gert Fröbe won it.
- Goldfinger's first name, Auric—not Eric—is from the Latin term for gold, "aurum".

THUNDERBALL

- *Thunderball* with an estimated budget of $9 million grossed over $140 million worldwide and led the field in both the USA and the United Kingdom for 1965.
- Underwater sets were built in the open sea for *Thunderball,* probably the first in film history, which permitted long underwater fight sequences. Special

APPENDIX 4

Effects Coordinator John Stears won an Oscar for his efforts on this film.
- Perhaps due to the effect of Shrublands, we do not see 007 smoking in this film.
- *Thunderball* is the first film in which 007 makes love to a woman, Domino, beneath the sea. The SCUBA gear and seawater were apparently no hindrance.
- Patricia Fearing (Molly Peters) was nude behind the opaque glass of her shower screen giving her a first for a "Bond girl"; the women who danced in the titles were nude as well, but the lighting and artwork were more than fig leaves.

CASINO ROYALE (1967)

- *Casino Royale* was the first 007 novel by Ian Fleming. Its production rights were sold for a song for a 1954 dramatization with Barry Nelson as an American "Jimmy Bond" on the *Climax* series on CBS TV in the USA. Producer Charles K. Feldman obtained the rights to make this film outside of the "official" James Bond film series produced by Cubby Broccoli and his relatives. Feldman decided to make it a parody of the most successful film series in existence.
- With an estimated $12 million budget, *Casino Royale* was seen as an extremely high budget, about twice what its first budget had been. Ultimately, the film took in about $39 million, ultimately a good return on the investment, and it grossed in the top three films in the U.S. for 1967, behind *You Only Live Twice*.

APPENDIX 4

- Someone saw the value in the name ***Casino Royale***. In 1999, MGM paid Sony $10 million for all rights to the name and the Bond character. That same year, Sony had agreed to the sale because of a suit brought by MGM that caused Sony to pay MGM $5 million and to promise to deliver the rights to them.
- Part of the problem with the wandering storyline of ***Casino Royale*** was caused by the fact that five directors worked on the film: Val Guest, Ken Hughes, John Huston, Joseph McGrath and Robert Parrish. Val Guest had the challenge of tying all of the loose ends together.
- In addition to script problems, ***Casino Royale*** had problems with the actors. Peter Sellers allegedly would disappear for days at a time. Producer Charles K. Feldman finally cut off Sellers, and Guest had to finish the film without him. In addition, Orson Welles loathed Peter Sellers, called him an "amateur," and the two actors refused to be on the set together at the same time.

YOU ONLY LIVE TWICE

- For the first time in the series (but certainly not the last), the plotline of ***You Only Live Twice*** bears little resemblance to Ian Fleming's novel.
- Ernst Stavro Blofeld's face appears in ***You Only Live Twice*** for the first time in the series. In the next film, ***On Her Majesty's Secret Service***, he is played by Telly Savalas. In the following film, ***Diamonds***

Are Forever, Charles Gray plays the criminal mastermind.
- In *You Only Live Twice*, 007 is not seen behind the wheel of a car.
- Burt Kwouk, who played the Red Chinese Agent in *Goldfinger*, returns as a SPECTRE contractor in Blofeld's control room.
- Neither Kissy Suzuki's name nor Aki's last name is given in *You Only Live Twice*, unlike main characters in other Bond films in the series.
- Charles Gray, who appears as Dikko Henderson in *You Only Live Twice*, returns as Ernst Stavro Blofeld in *Diamonds Are Forever* (1971).

ON HER MAJESTY'S SECRET SERVICE

- George Lazenby, thirty, in *On Her Majesty's Secret Service* was the youngest 007 at age thirty. The other actors made their first film at the following ages: Pierce Brosnan, forty-three; Sean Connery, thirty-two; Timothy Dalton, forty-one; and Roger Moore, forty-six.
- The only actor to play 007 who was not born and reared in the UK was George Lazenby, an Australian.
- Robert Campbell, John Richardson, Anthony Rogers, Roy Thinnes and Adam West were in the running for the role of James Bond. Timothy Dalton felt he was too young for 007. Roger Moore was

APPENDIX 4

starring in the long-running *The Saint* TV series (1962–69) and was not available.
- Though Sean Connery was offered a relatively high $1 million salary to play 007 again, he refused.
- *On Her Majesty's Secret Service* has the only opening gun barrel sequence of the series in which 007 drops to one knee before firing into the camera.

DIAMONDS ARE FOREVER

- Lana Wood, the sister of star Natalie Wood who played Natalie's younger sister in John Ford's *The Searchers* (1956), played Plenty O'Toole in *Diamonds Are Forever*. For some reason, all of her lines were dubbed by another actress. Ms. Wood went on to appear for another ten years in show business.
- Ernst Stavro Blofeld made his last appearance in an "official" James Bond film in *Diamonds Are Forever* as writer and executive producer Kevin McClory retained the rights to the character, who appeared in McClory's *Never Say Never Again* (1983).
- There is no question the model for Willard Whyte (Jimmy Dean), the politically powerful, billionaire recluse who was keeping himself in a penthouse remote from the rest of Las Vegas, is based on Howard Hughes. Hughes kept himself in utter privacy in penthouses in Las Vegas in the late 1960's and early 1970's. By chance, James Bond film producer Cubby Broccoli was a longtime friend of Hughes, from Hughes filmmaking days in Tinseltown. Broccoli

received complete freedom to use Hughes' Las Vegas properties for this film in return for a 16mm advance print of all James Bond films.

LIVE AND LET DIE

- United Artists requested an American as 007 in ***Live and Let Die*** and suggested Paul Newman, Robert Redford or Burt Reynolds to replace Sean Connery. Producer Cubby Broccoli insisted on a British actor and suggested Roger Moore. Other 007 candidates were Michael Billington, John Gavin, Michael McStay, Simon Oates, and John Ronane.
- Roger Moore was Ian Fleming's first pick to play James Bond, but he was not available.
- Roger Moore shot the opening gun-barrel sequence hatless in ***Live and Let Die***, a first for a James Bond series film.
- For ***Live and Let Die***, Sean Connery allegedly said "no" to $5.5 million to play 007 one more time.
- ***Live and Let Die*** was the only film in the 007 film series to date without an appearance by Q (Desmond Llewelyn). Fan pressure brought Q back for ***The Man with the Golden Gun*** (1975) and many other films until his death after the filming of ***The World Is not Enough*** (1999).

APPENDIX 4

THE MAN WITH THE GOLDEN GUN

- In an interview with *The Hollywood Reporter*, Producer Cubby Broccoli said he would not completely redo any Bond film, but there were parts of ***The Man with the Golden Gun*** that he would do differently.
- Rumor has it that ***The Man with the Golden Gun*** broke through the Iron Curtain and was screened within Moscow's Kremlin. We don't know if any royalties were paid.
- The site for Scaramanga's island in ***The Man with the Golden Gun*** is Khow-Ping-Khan, near Phuket off the coast of Malaya. Almost immediately it was known as James Bond Island and became a getaway vacation location. Later, it is seen briefly in ***Tomorrow Never Dies*** (1997).
- Christopher Lee (Scaramanga) is a cousin of Ian Fleming; both Lee and Fleming worked in military intelligence during World War II. They often golfed together at a club near London. Though Lee was considered for the role of 007 in ***Dr. No***, Fleming still liked Roger Moore for the role.
- Allegedly at the Khow-Ping-Khan location, Roger Moore found a cave filled with bats. Knowing Christopher Lee's history for playing Count Dracula in the 1950s and 1960s, Moore told him that his subjects were awaiting his commands.

APPENDIX 4

THE SPY WHO LOVED ME

- Richard Kiel, who played the henchman Jaws in *The Spy Who Loved Me*, had played a similar part as the henchman of a criminal mastermind played by Patrick McGoohan in the previous year's thriller *Silver Streak* (1976).
- Director Stanley Kramer oversaw the lighting for production designer Ken Adams in *The Spy Who Loved Me*, as Claude Renoir's vision starting going in shooting the film.
- Victor Tourjansky, an assistant director in several films, played the "man with the bottle" who questions his sobriety when he sees 007 drive his Lotus Esprit submersible out of the water and onto the beach in *The Spy Who Loved Me*. He reprises again in *Moonraker*, where he gasps at 007 piloting his gondola on St. Mark's Square. In *For Your Eyes Only*, he is a customer of the lodge when 007 skis off his table.
- The story of *The Spy Who Loved Me* is very loosely based on Fleming's novel. Since 007 did not figure prominently in Fleming's work, he insisted that Eon had to come up with a brand-new plotline.
- At the end of *The Spy Who Loved Me*, a sign says: "James Bond will return in *For Your Eyes Only*. That was before *Star Wars* (1977) and *Close Encounters of the Third Kind* (1977) did huge box office; the next film to be produced was *Moonraker* (1979) with its outer space plot and futuristic concepts. *Moonraker*

APPENDIX 4

took in over $200 million worldwide, and *The Spy Who Loved Me* was put off until 1981.

MOONRAKER

- While there are many French locations in the joint British-French production of *Moonraker*, some of the facilities used in the U.S. would actually have been used by anyone seeking entrée to outer space: the Rockwell International facility in Palmdale, California, and the Kennedy Space Center in Titusville, Florida.
- Lois Chiles (Dr. Holly Goodhead)—a top fashion model and 1970s film actress (*The Way We Were*, *The Great Gatsby* and *Death on the Nile*)—was considering retiring from show business until *Moonraker* Director Lewis Gilbert accidentally was sitting next to her on an airliner and pitched the film to her.
- James Bond's pilot and lover in *Moonraker*, played by Corinne Clery, had starred in the sexually explicit *The Story of O* (1975), the French film based on an erotic novel. Clery's career in French and Italian films plus European TV continues to date.
- Jaws (Richard Kiel) features prominently in two Bond films—*The Spy Who Loved Me* and *Moonraker*—yet, following the line of strong silent henchmen, he has only one short line in one film, *Moonraker*. When he opens a bottle of champagne with his steel teeth in the ruins of the space station, he toasts Dolly by saying: "Well, here's to us."

APPENDIX 4

- Allegedly, Jaws was recycled for *Moonraker* because of many letters from children asking Cubby Broccoli to bring him back. Jaws is a crowd pleaser.
- In the pre-titles adventure, Jaws throws 007 out of an airplane without a parachute. Bond skydives and rips off (literally) the pilot's parachute. The sequence was done without any special effects; taking over a month and dozens of jumps to make this sequence look good on the editor's bench.

FOR YOUR EYES ONLY

- When Roger Moore balked at appearing in *For Your Eyes Only*, the producers examined Michael Billington, Nicholas Clay, Lewis Collins, Michael Jayston, Ian Ogilvy, David Robb and David Warbeck as potential 007 actors. Financial persuasion moved Moore to reprise the role.
- Allegedly, the bald man who attempts to eliminate 007 at the film's sequence, before the titles, was supposed to be a parody of Blofeld, a regular 007 opponent. It was an in-joke at the expense of producer Kevin McClory, who had gained the legal rights to both SPECTRE and Blofeld's character. McClory went on to co-write the story and be an executive producer of *Never Say Never Again* (1983) with Sean Connery as 007 and Max von Sydow as Blofeld.
- In *For Your Eyes Only*, John Glen permitted singer Sheena Easton to be on-camera during the opening

credits of the film, the first such appearance in a 007 series film.
- Cassandra Harris, who was then married to future 007 Pierce Brosnan, played Countess Lisl von Schlaf in *For Your Eyes Only*. She died of cancer in 1991 after having a child with the Irish actor.
- Tula, the stage name of Caroline Cossey who played the tall girl at the pool in the white outfit in *For Your Eyes Only*, was later revealed to once have been a man named Barry Cossey. She has had a career as a fashion model and appeared in rock videos.

OCTOPUSSY

- James Brolin, star of *Westworld* (1973) and *Gable and Lombard* (1976), was given a screen-test when Roger Moore allegedly dragged his heels about playing 007 again in *Octopussy*.
- In casting the title role of *Octopussy*, the producers looked at Sybil Danning, Faye Dunaway and Persis Khambata before turning to Maud Adams. Adams had played Scaramanga's lover in *The Man with the Golden Gun* (1975).
- Bernard Lee, who had originated the role of M in *Dr. No* and had played the role in the first ten films of the series, died of cancer in 1981. In *Octopussy*, Robert Brown, the Admiral Hargraves of *The Spy Who Loved Me* (1977), replaced Lee as M.
- In *Octopussy*, Q (Desmond Llewelyn), instead of skulking in his laboratory or just dropping off

equipment at an exotic location, becomes a real field operator.
- In *Octopussy*, Roger Moore favors the 9x19mm Walther P5 rather than his usual Walther PPK for most of the motion picture.

NEVER SAY NEVER AGAIN

- Kevin McClory, the producer of *Thunderball* through Eon Productions, won the right to do a remake of *Thunderball* in a lawsuit against Eon Productions (Cubby Broccoli's company). Broccoli was hanging onto every detail of *Never Say Never Again* to prevent it intruding on his *Octopussy* (1983) film in the "official" James Bond series that premiered first in 1983. Johnny Carson on the NBC *Tonight Show* TV show asked Connery who was the best villain he faced. Connery, fresh from show biz legal battles, said, "Cubby Broccoli."
- *Never Say Never Again* got its title from Mrs. Connery, Micheline Roquebrune. When Connery reminded her he had vowed never to do another Bond film, she said, "Never say 'never' again." Since Connery had a large measure of control over the film, he picked the title.
- *Never Say Never Again* grossed $54 million in the North American market vs. $68 million for *Octopussy*. Both films did well in other markets, though Connery sued Producer Jack Schwartzman for non-payment of part of his $5 million salary. In

turn, Schwartzman sued Director Irvin Kershner for expenses above the budget.
- Bernie Casey, an African American actor, played Felix Leiter in *Never Say Never Again*, the only African American to play that role until Jeffrey Wright in Casino Royale.
- Steven Seagal advised on martial arts in *Never Say Never Again*, and, allegedly, broke Sean Connery's wrist while demonstrating a slick move on the set.
- Kim Bassinger, who played Domino in *Never Say Never Again*, went on to win an Oscar for Best Supporting Actress for ***L.A. Confidential*** (1997).
- Barbara Carrera (Fatima Blush) refused to have a "body double" for her erotic sequence with Sean Connery. Hmmm...

A VIEW TO A KILL

- Roger Moore and Patrick Macnee were old friends. Throughout the 1960s, Macnee starred at Elstree Studios in ***The Avengers*** TV series opposite Honor Blackman (Pussy Galore in ***Goldfinger***) and later opposite Diana Rigg (Mrs. James Bond in ***On Her Majesty's Secret Service***) from 1961 to 1969. Roger Moore was also at Elstree shooting ***The Saint*** TV series from 1962 to 1969.
- Roger Moore (James Bond) and Lois Maxwell (Miss Moneypenny), who as the faithful secretary of M had been in every Bond film, ended their affiliation with the Bond films with *A View to a Kill*.

APPENDIX 4

- The opening sequence of *A View to a Kill* was the first time James Bond is engaged in espionage on Russian soil.
- Christopher Walken was the only Bond villain in the "official series" to have received an Oscar for acting, Best Supporting Actor in *The Deer Hunter* (1978), before his appearance in a Bond film, *A View to a Kill*.
- The then little-known actor Dolph Lundgren, a companion of Grace Jones (May Day), played a walk-on KBG agent in the racetrack sequence with Christopher Walken.

THE LIVING DAYLIGHTS

- ***The Living Daylights*** was the first Bond series film with Timothy Dalton—a star of the London stage, TV shows and other films—as 007. Though many fans liked Pierce Brosnan, he was signed up to continue the long running ***Remington Steele*** (1982–87) TV series. Sean Bean, Sam Neill and many other actors were in the running for the part.
- The major role of General Pushkin in *The Living Daylights* had originally been created for Walter Gotell as General Gogol, the charming and clever role Gotell had played in *The Spy Who Loved Me*, *Moonraker*, *Octopussy* and *A View to a Kill*. When Gotell fell ill, John Rhys-Davies carried the plot forward as General Pushkin, while Gotell was able to do a cameo as Gogol. Though Gotell continued

APPENDIX 4

his film career for another ten years, the producers did not develop General Gogol's role after *The Living Daylights*.
- Brad Whitaker (Joe Don Baker) is such an egocentric villain that all of the statues of the military geniuses in his office bear a resemblance to himself. Baker would go on as good guy CIA Agent Jack Wade in **GoldenEye** (1985) and **Tomorrow Never Dies** (1997).
- The orchestra conductor in Kara's last musical sequence is John Barry, the composer who scored most of the earlier films in the 007 series. *The Living Daylights* was his last Bond film to date; Barry has won five Oscars and is a prolific composer.

LICENCE TO KILL

- Producer Cubby Broccoli was determined to keep costs down on his estimated $40 million budget for *Licence to Kill*, so he moved most of the filming to Mexico, which provided the *Isthmus* (read General Manuel Noriega's *Panama*) backgrounds for the film. Ernest Hemingway's house in the Key's was picked for Bond's meeting with M. The Keys' Seven Mile Bridge was used for the armored car sequence and would be used again in James Cameron's *True Lies* (1999) with Arnold Schwarzenegger. *Licence to Kill* grossed $156 million worldwide.
- *Licence to Kill* is the first film in the "official series" not to be named after an Ian Fleming novel or short story, though the plot borrows from Fleming's novel *Live*

and Let Die as well as his short story "The Hildebrand Rarity." The first working title for the film was *License Revoked* before it was changed to *Licence to Kill*, with the British spelling of the word "licence."
- Robert Brown (M), Timothy Dalton (James Bond), and Caroline Bliss (Miss Moneypenny) said farewell to the James Bond series with *Licence to Kill*.
- Desmond Llewelyn (Q) reveled in portraying an agent in the field in *Licence to Kill*; he had more onscreen time than in any other James Bond film.
- David Hedison returned from *Live and Let Die* (1973) to play Felix Leiter again; he was the only actor who has played Leiter twice, until Jeffrey Wright in the Craig films.

GOLDENEYE

- *GoldenEye* (1995) was Pierce Brosnan's first appearance as James Bond. Pierce had been offered the role of James Bond in *The Living Daylights*, but lost out due to his contractual obligations to the television series *Remington Steele*. Before Pierce Brosnan was cast as James Bond, Liam Neeson, Mel Gibson, Sam Neill, Hugh Grant and Lambert Wilson were all rumored to be in the running for the role.
- The movie *GoldenEye* (1995) shares its title with the name of Ian Fleming's estate in Jamaica and a 1989 television movie about the secret life of Ian Fleming.
- Because the series was caught up in litigation, the six-and-a-half-year hiatus between the release of

APPENDIX 4

Licence to Kill and *GoldenEye* represents the longest gap between Bond films since the series first started in 1962.
- During production on the film, several changes had to be made to the script because the plot was close to James Cameron's *True Lies* which was released at the time.
- *GoldenEye* marks the first time that the role of M was played by a woman (Judi Dench).

TOMORROW NEVER DIES

- *Tomorrow Never Dies* had an estimated budget of $110 million. Approximately $100 million came into the production company from product placements: Aston Martin, BMW, Heineken, L'Oréal, Omega, etc. Its worldwide gross was $346 million.
- The working title for the film was *Tomorrow Never Lies*, as *Tomorrow* was the name of Carver's newspaper which manufactured its news for the public. Allegedly, a mistake was made in typing or faxing the title, and the producers preferred the current title.
- Instead of Ho Chi Minh City (Saigon) in Vietnam, where Elliot Carver's Asian office was situated, the film was actually shot in Bangkok, Thailand, when political problems arose with the Vietnamese government.
- Michelle Yeoh, who made a living in Hong Kong martial arts films before *Licence to Kill*, did most of her action sequences herself.

- The original U.S. Navy "stealth ship" was the USS Sea Shadow, approximately one hundred and sixty feet long. Its shape from a ship model, obtained by the producers, guided the production designer.
- Terri Hatcher found out she was pregnant after she got the role of Carver's wife. The director shot her sequences as soon as possible.

THE WORLD IS NOT ENOUGH

- In *On Her Majesty's Secret Service*, we learn for the first time that James Bond's family motto is "The World Is not Enough." That seemed like an appropriate title for a Bond movie, considering that the producers had run out of Ian Fleming titles. The film's rumored titles included ***Death Waits for No Man***, ***Fire and Ice***, ***Pressure Point*** and ***Dangerously Yours***.
- Sharon Stone was M-G-M's first choice for the role of Elektra King, but the producers went with Sophie Marceau after her turn in Mel Gibson's ***Braveheart*** (1995).
- The Scottish castle used as MI6's secret headquarters is the same castle used in ***Highlander***. It's called the "Eilean Donan Castle" and is located near the Isle of Skye, West Scotland.
- A portrait of the first M (as played by Bernard Lee) hangs in the castle.
- Desmond Llewelyn makes his final appearance as Q; regrettably, the actor died in a freak automobile

accident shortly after the movie was released. The video release is dedicated to Llewelyn.

- Peter Jackson, the successful director of the *Lord of the Rings* trilogy, was first considered to direct, but producer Barbara Broccoli didn't like *The Frighteners*, and reconsidered.

DIE ANOTHER DAY

- *Die Another Day* was released on the fortieth anniversary of the first "official" James Bond film, *Dr. No* (1962). References to all of the previous "official" films are made both overtly—the Bell Textron Jet Pack from *Thunderball* (1965) and Colonel Klebb's shoe/dagger from *From Russia with Love* (1963) in Q's office—and covertly—the surfing sequence filmed at Hawaii's "Jaws" beach in honor of Richard Kiel's villainous Jaws from *The Spy Who Loved Me* (1977) and *Moonraker* (1979).
- *Die Another Day* has more than a passing resemblance in its plot to Ian Fleming's novel *Moonraker*, though its title is not from Fleming's work. Ian Fleming, who borrowed James Bond's name from the writer of *A Field Guide to the Birds of the West Indies* that Fleming found in his Caribbean office, would have applauded to see James Bond borrow the same book in Cuba and pretend to be an ornithologist when meeting Jinx in *Die Another Day*.
- Madonna, who sang the title song and was responsible for the lyrics, had an uncredited role as Verity,

APPENDIX 4

the fencing master with a propensity to be laced up in leather and with a friendship with Miranda Frost.
- While shooting the early Korean sequence, Pierce Brosnan injured his knee badly while running to a hovercraft on *License to Kill*. He was out of action for a period of weeks.
- While the U.S. Air Force had developed a new "stealth" aircraft that has a certain invisibility at distances over two miles, it has not transferred this technique to any ground vehicles.

CASINO ROYALE

- The "Vesper" that James Bond orders at Casino Royale is taken from the novel. It consists of three parts gin (Gordon's was Bond's choice), one part vodka (Bond preferred a grain vodka be used; e.g. Absolut) and half part of Kina Lillet. The ingredients are shaken over ice until cold, served in a cocktail glass with a slice of lemon peel for garnish.
- This was the third adaptation of the Ian Fleming novel of the same name. The first adaptation was a televised episode of *Climax!* (1954), and the second was a comic adaptation in 1967. Barry Nelson played Agent Jimmy Bond, and David Niven played Sir James Bond, respectively.
- James Bond's letter of resignation via the Mi6 intelligence intranet read: "M—I hereby tender my resignation with immediate effect. Sincerely, James Bond". This is the third James Bond movie where James

Bond has resigned. The first was *On Her Majesty's Secret Service* and the second was *Licence to Kill*.
- Most of the cars seen in the movie are made by Ford Motor Company. In the scene where Bond acts as a valet the cars in the parking lot are Land Rovers, Volvos, Jaguars and other Ford Motor Company's cars.
- Part of the location filming included the world-famous Atlantis resort in Nassau, the Bahamas.
- The Black-and-White sequence that occurs early in the film was taken right from Ian Fleming's history of James Bond, in which 007 earns his eponymous title by assassinating several men.

QUANTUM OF SOLACE

- *Quantum of Solace* is the first direct sequel in the series. The storyline starts roughly thirty minutes after the events in *Casino Royale* (2006).
- This is the first James Bond movie to utilize the now rebuilt (for a second time) Albert R. Broccoli 007 Stage which burnt down (for a second time) one week after *Casino Royale* finished filming there in 2006.
- Though the title is borrowed from an Ian Fleming short story, the story was conceived by Michael G. Wilson, one of the series producers.
- The Aston Martin DBS car makes a return in this movie due to a three-picture $100-million deal that car company Ford has for exclusive vehicle product-placement rights.
- Plans to film near the Incan ruins at Machu Picchu,

APPENDIX 4

Peru were scratched due to uncertain weather conditions in the area.
- Dennis Gassner's production design is meant as a homage to the pioneering work of Bond production designer Ken Adam.

SKYFALL

- *Skyfall* was the twnty-third film in the EON series, and marked the fiftieth anniversary of the James Bond films.
- The Aston Martin DB5 makes a welcome return to action in *Skyfall* when it is called out of mothballs to save 007's life one more time. The Ford Motor Company had a three-picture $100-million deal that began with the remake of **Casino Royale** and continued through **Quantum of Solace**.
- As a publicity stunt to promote the release of the film, Daniel Craig as James Bond 007 escorts Queen Elizabeth II's double to the London Summer Olympics in 2012 by "leaping" from a helicopter and "parachuting" into the royal seats at the game.
- The mug Q drinks from in his lab has the letter "Q" from the game Scrabble printed on it, complete with the number "10", the point value of the letter Q in the board game.
- The opening credits feature Bond periodically shooting at targets, Shanghai dragons, Silva's skull logo, and the Skyfall mansion from which Bond's eyes stare out.

APPENDIX 4

SPECTRE

- SPECTRE was the twenty-fourth film in the EON series, and came out in 2015.
- The Ford Motor Company produced a specially-designed Aston Martin DB10 for the movie **SPECTRE**.
- At age fifty, Monica Bellucci played the oldest Bond girl in the series. Her character's name was Lucia Sciarra.
- Dr. Madeliene Swann (Léa Seydoux) is a psychologist running a secret medical clinic in the Alps, which calls to mind Ernst Stavro Blofeld's secret medical clinic in the Alps in *On Her Majesty's Secret Service* (1969).
- The secret terrorist organization Quantum from **Casino Royale** (2006) and **Quantum of Solace** (2008) was referred to as SPECTRE in non-English prints of QOS.

NO TIME TO DIE

- *No Time to Die* was the twenty-fifth film in the EON series, and came out in 2021.
- **James Bond's** code number 007 is assigned to a female agent named Nomi.
- James Bond dies during the course of the mission.
- *No Time to Die* was Daniel Craig's last outing at James Bond.

APPENDIX 4

JAMES BOND'S PERSONAL BEST SCORECARD

FILM TITLE	SEXUAL ENCOUNTERS	MISSION KILLS	MATINIS/ OTHER DRINKS	"BOND, JAMES BOND"
Dr. No	3	5	2/6	1
FRWL	4	12	1/3	0
GOLDFINGER	3	10	1/8	1.5
THUNDERBALL	3	25*	0/4	0
YOLT	4	25*	1/5	0
CR	1	7	1/5	0
OHMSS	4	8	1/7	2
DAF	1	7	1/4	1
LALD	3	7	0/3	1
TMWTGG	2	1	0/4	2
TSWLM	3	25*	1/4	1
MOONRAKER	3	14	1/3	1
FYEO	2	11	0/5	2
NSNA	4	25*	2/5	0

APPENDIX 4

OCTOPUSSY	2	14	1/4	1
AVTAK	4	5	0/6	2
TLD	2	7	3/5	1
LTK	2	14	0/5	1
GoldenEye	3	14	1/3	1
TND	3	25*	1/6	1
TWINE	3	19	1/5	2
DAD	3	25*	2/7	1
CR	1	10	1	1
QOS	1	17**	6	0
SKYFALL	2	25*	Plenty	1
SPECTRE	1	235	Plenty	1
NO TIME TO DIE	1	988***		

*The number 25 is an estimate. During epic battle scenes in which James Bond is using machine guns and grenades, maintaining an accurate body is nearly impossible.

**After killing 17 guys in far too many stunt scenes, we lost track . . .

***The number 988 is an estimate, becuase we don't know how how many people were still left on the island when the nukes arrive, and kill Bond. Less than a thousand?

APPENDIX 4

JAMES BOND'S SEXUAL CONQUESTS (FILM BY FILM)*

FILM TITLE	GIRL #1	GIRL #2	GIRL #3	GIRL #4
Dr. No	Sylvia Trench	Miss Taro	Honey Ryder	
FRWL	Sylvia Trench	Vida	Zora	Tatiana Romanova
GOLDFINGER	Dink	Jill Masterson	Pussy Galore	
THUNDERBALL	Patricia Fearing	Fiona Volpe	Domino	
YOLT	Lady Fiona			
CR	Ling	Aki	Helga Brandt	Kissy Suzuki
OHMSS	Tracy	Ruby Bartlett	Nancy	Chinese Girl
DAF	Tiffany Case			
LALD	Miss Caruso	Rosie Carver	Solitaire	
TMWTGG	Andrea Anders	Mary Goodnight		
TSWLM	Log Cabin Girl	Arab Beauty	Major Anya Amasova	
MOONRAKER	Corinne Dufour	Dr. Holly Goodhead	Manuela	
FYEO	Countess Lisl von Schlaf	Melina Havelock		
NSNA	Patricia Fearing	Lady in Bahamas	Fatima Blush	Domino Petachi
OCTOPUSSY	Magda	Octopussy		
AVTAK	Submarine Girl	May Day	Pola Ivanova	Stacy Sutton
TLD	Girl on Boat	Kara Milovy		
LTK	Lupe Lamora	Pam Bouvier		
GoldenEye	Natalya Simonova	Xenia Onatopp	Caroline	

APPENDIX 4

TND	Professor Inga Bergstrom	Paris Carver	Wai Lin	
TWINE	Dr. Molly Warmfish	Elektra King	Dr. Christmas Jones	
DAD	Jinx Johnson	Miranda Frost		
CR	Vesper Lynd			
QOS	Strawberry Fields			
SKYFALL	Sévérine	Eve Moneypenny*	unknown woman	
SPECTRE	Lucia Sciarra	Dr. Swann	Estrella	
NTTD	Dr. Swann			

APPENDIX 4

Note: James Bond may not remember all their names, but we do! 007 had a number of near misses, including Bonita in *Goldfinger*, Buttercup and Vesper Lynd in *Casino Royale*, nine of the allergy girls in *On Her Majesty's Secret Service*, the girl with something on her chest and Plenty O'Toole in *Diamonds Are Forever*, Saida and Chew Me in *The Man with the Golden Gun*, Bibi Dahl in *For Your Eyes Only*, Jenny Flex in *A View to a Kill*, Peaceful Fountains of Desire in *Die Another Day*, Solange Dimitros in *Casino Royale* and Camille in *Quantum of Solace*. And alas, Miss Moneypenny has come close so many times with 007, including *Skyfall*, but never consummated their obvious flirtation. Always the bridesmaid, never the bride.

APPENDIX 4

JAMES BOND'S ENEMIES (FILM BY FILM)

FILM TITLE	EVIL ORGANIZATION	VILLIAN	HENCHMAN	FEMME FATALES/ OTHER
Dr. No	SPECTRE	Dr. No	Prof. Dent	Miss Taro
FRWL	SPECTRE	Kronsteen	Grant	Rosa Klebb
GOLDFINGER	Presumably SPECTRE	Goldfinger	Odd Job	
THUNDERBALL	SPECTRE	Largo	Mr. Vargas	Fiona Volpe
YOLT	SPECTRE	Blofeld	Hans	Helga Brandt
CR	SMERSH	Le Chiffre	Dr. Noah	Vesper Lynd
OHMSS	SPECTRE	Blofeld	Gunther	Irma Bunt
DAF	SPECTRE	Blofeld	Mr. Wint	Mr. Kidd
LALD	Black Mafia	Kanaga/Mr. Big	Tee-Hee	Rosie Carver
TMWTGG	Red China	Francisco Scaramanga		
TSWLM	Stromberg Industries	Carl Stromberg	Jaws	
MOONRAKER	Drax Enterprise Corporation	Sir Hugo Drax	Jaws	
FYEO	Soviet Union	Aristotle Kristatos	Emile Locque	Blofeld
NSNA	SPECTRE	Maxim Largo	Lippe	Fatima Blush
OCTOPUSSY	Kamal Khan and Orlov	Kamal Khan	Gobinda	General Orlov
AVTAK	Zorin Industriesl	Max Zorin	Scarpine	May Day
TLD	Soviet Union	Gen. Georgi Koskov	Necros	Brad Whitaker
LTK	Drug Cartels	Franz Sanchez	Dario	May Day

APPENDIX 4

GoldenEye	Janus Syndicate	Alec Trevalyan		Xenia Onatopp
TND	Carver Media Group	Elliot Carver	Stamper	
TWINE	King Industry	Renard	Cigar Girl	Elektra King
DAD	North Korea	Gustav Graves	Zao	Miranda Frostl
CR	Quantum	Le Chiffre	Mr. White	Steven Obanno
QOS	Quantum	Dominic Green	General Medrano	Steven Obanno
SKYFALL	Silva	Patrice		Séverine
SPECTRE	Spectre	Blofeld	Hinx	Estrella
NTTD	Spectre	Blofeld Safin		

APPENDIX 4

007'S BOX OFFICE NUMBERS AND RANKINGS

FILM TITLE	WORLDWIDE BOX OFFICE	BUDGET	RANKING	"BOND... JAMES BOND"
Dr. No	$59,500,000	$1,100,000	24	Sean Connery
FRWL	$78,900,000	$2,000,000	22	Sean Connery
GOLDFINGER	$124,900,000	$3,000,000	17	Sean Connery
THUNDERBALL	$141,200,000	$9,000,000	15	Sean Connery
YOLT	$111,600,000	$9,500,000	20	Sean Connery
CR	$35,000,000	$12,000,000	25	David Niven
OHMSS	$64,600,000	$7,000,000	23	George Lazenby
DAF	$116,000,000	$7,200,000	19	Sean Connery
LALD	$126,400,000	$7,000,000	18	Roger Moore
TMWTGG	$97,600,000	$13,000,000	21	Roger Moore
TSWLM	$185,400,000	$14,000,000	11	Roger Moore
MOONRAKER	$202,700,000	$34,000,000	8	Roger Moore
FYEO	$194,900,000	$28,000,000	9	Roger Moore
NSNA	$138,000,000	$36,000,000	16	Sean Connery
OCTOPUSSY	$183,700,000	$27,500,000	11	Roger Moore
AVTAK	$152,400,000	$30,000,000	14	Roger Moore
TLD	$191,200,000	$30,000,000	10	Timothy Dalton
LTK	$156,200,000	$40,000,000	13	Timothy Dalton
GoldenEye	$350,700,000	$80,000,000	8	Pierce Brosnan
TND	$335,300,000	$110,000,000	9	Pierce Brosnan
TWINE	$352,030,660	$135,000,000	7	Pierce Brosnan

APPENDIX 4

DAD	$424,700,000	$142,000,000	6	Pierce Brosnan
CR	$594,239,066	$150,000,000	4	Daniel Craig
QOS	$586,090,727	$200,000,000	5	Daniel Craig
SKYFALL	$1 billion*	$200,000,000	1	Daniel Craig
SPECTRE	$889.7 million	$245 million	2	Daniel Craig
NTTD	$774.2 million	$250 million	3	Daniel Craig

Note: Daniel Craig and Pierce Brosnan appeared in the top money-makers, while the next closest was Roger Moore for *Moonraker*. Sean Connery's best effort was *Thunderball*. The final total of *Skyfall* of over $1 billion makes it the most successful Bond film of all time.

APPENDIX 4

007 REMAKES AND RETREADS: HAVEN'T I HEARD THAT ONE BEFORE

FILM	PLOT
Dr. No	When a fellow agent is killed, Bond is sent to the Caribbean, and uncovers a megalomaniac ruling an island nation with plans to topple U.S. rockets. A naïve young woman assists him with his mission.
FRWL	With James Bond in pursuit of a rare decoding machine, the world's deadliest assassin sets his sights on 007.
GOLDFINGER	James Bond must prevent a megalomaniac from irradiating the gold supply of the U.S. in order to increase the wealth of his own stock. A female confederate switches sides, and helps 007 avert the catastrophe in the end.
THUNDERBALL	When Ernst Stavro Blofeld threatens to destroy a major U.S. city with two nuclear warheads seized by his SPECTRE organization, 007 dives to the rescue. His love interest is a woman named Domino (Derval).
YOLT	Blofeld arranges for his SPECTRE organization to kidnap both an American and a Russia spacecraft, and it's up to James Bond to stop World War III. A female Japanese agent assists 007.

APPENDIX 4

DAF	If his demands are not met, Blofeld plots to destroy the world with a space-based laser weapon, which is powered by sunlight focused through diamonds, and 007 is the only one who can stop him.
LALD	When three agents are killed, Bond is sent to the Caribbean, and uncovers a megalomaniac ruling an island nation with plans to topple a drug market. A naïve young woman assists him with his mission. Isn't this just a remake of *Dr. No*?
TMWGG	With James Bond in pursuit of a rare solar-powered device, the world's deadliest assassin sets his sights on 007. Isn't this just a remake of *From Russia With Love*?
AVTAK	James Bond must prevent a megalomaniac from destroying Silicon Valley in order to increase the madman's wealth of his own stock in microchips. A female confederate switches sides, and helps 007 avert the catastrophe in the end. Isn't this just a remake of *Goldfinger*?
NSNA	When Ernst Stavro Blofeld threatens to destroy a major city with two nuclear warheads seized by his SPECTRE organization, 007 dives to the rescue. His love interest is a woman named Domino (Petachi). Isn't this just a remake of *Thunderball*?

TSW LM	Carl Stromberg arranges for his organization to kidnap both an American and a Russia submarine, and it's up to James Bond to prevent World War 3. A female Russian agent assists 007. Isn't this just a remake of *You Only Live Twice*?
DAD	If the Western powers refuse his demands to withdraw from Korea, Gustav Graves plots to destroy the world with a space-based laser weapon, powered by sunlight through diamonds, and 007 is the only one who can stop him. Isn't this just a remake of *Diamonds Are Forever*?

FILMOGRAPHY OF THE JAMES BOND FILMS

Dr. No (1962). Great Britain: EON Productions, one hundred and nine minutes. Director: Terence Young. Producers: Albert R. Broccoli and Harry Saltzman. Screenwriters: Richard Maibaum, Johanna Harwood, and Berkely Mather. Based on the novel by Ian Fleming. Cinematographer: Ted Moore. Special Effects Supervisor: Frank George. Cast: Sean Connery, Ursula Andress, Joseph Wiseman, Jack Lord, Bernard Lee, Lois Maxwell, Anthony Dawson, Zena Marshall, Eunice Gayson, and Peter Burton. *World Premiere:* Odeon Leicester Square, London, on October 5, 1962.

APPENDIX 4

From Russia with Love (1963). Great Britain: Eon Productions, one hundred and fifteen minutes. Director: Terence Young. Producers: Albert R. Broccoli and Harry Saltzman. Screenwriters: Richard Maibaum and Johanna Harwood. Based on the novel by Ian Fleming. Cinematographer: Ted Moore. Special Effects Supervisor: John Stears. Cast: Sean Connery, Daniela Bianchi, Pedro Armendariz, Lotte Lenya, Robert Shaw, Bernard Lee, Eunice Gayson, Walter Gotell, Lois Maxwell, Desmond LLewelyn, Vladek Sheybal, Aliza Gur and Martine Beswicke. *World Premiere:* Odeon Leicester Square, London, on October 8, 1963.

Goldfinger (1964). Great Britain: EON Productions, one hundred and nine minutes. Director: Guy Hamilton. Producers: Albert R. Broccoli and Harry Saltzman. Screenwriters: Richard Maibaum and Paul Dehn. Based on the novel by Ian Fleming. Cinematographer: Ted Moore. Special Effects Supervisors: John Stears and Frank George. Cast: Sean Connery, Gert Frobe, Honor Blackman, Shirley Eaton, Tania Mallet, Harold Sakata, Bernard Lee, Lois Maxwell, Richard Vernon, Nadja Regin, Margaret Nolan, and Desmond LLewelyn. *World Premiere:* Odeon Leicester Square, London, on September 17, 1964.

Thunderball (1965). Great Britain: EON Productions, one hundred and thirty minutes. Director: Terence Young. Producers: Kevin McClory, Albert R. Broccoli and Harry Saltzman. Screenwriters: Jack Wittingham, Richard Maibaum and John Hopkins. Based on the novel by Ian Fleming. Cinematographer: Ted Moore. Special Effects: John Stears. Cast: Sean Connery, Claudine Auger, Adolfo Celi, Luciana Paluzzi, Rik Van Nutter, Guy Doleman, Molly Peters, Martine Beswicke, Bernard Lee, Desmond Llewelyn, Lois Maxwell, Roland Culver, Earl Cameron, Paul Stassino, Rose Alba, Philip Locke, George

APPENDIX 4

Pravda, Michael Brennan, Leonard Sachs, Edward Underdown, Bob Simmons, Reginald Beckwith and Maryse Guy Mitsouko (uncredited). *World Premiere:* Hibiya Cinema, Tokyo, Japan, December 9, 1965.

Casino Royale (1967). USA and Great Britain: Columbia Pictures Corporation and Famous Artists Productions, one hundred and thirty-one minutes. Directors: Val Guest, Kenneth Hughes, John Huston, Joseph McGrath, and Robert Parrish. Producers: Charles K. Feldman and Jerry Bresler. Screenwriters: Wolf Mankowitz, John Law and Michael Sayers. Uncredited Screenwriters: Woody Allen, Val Guest, Ben Hecht, Joseph Heller, Terry Southern, Billy Wilder and Peter Sellers. Based on the novel by Ian Fleming. Cinematographer: Jack Hildyard. Special Effects Supervisors: Cliff Richardson and Roy Whybrow. Cast: Peter Sellers, Ursula Andress, David Niven, Orson Welles, Joanna Pettet, Daliah Lavi, Woody Allen and Deborah Kerry. *World Premiere:* Odeon Leicester Square, London, April 13, 1967.

You Only Live Twice (1967). Great Britain: EON Productions, one hundred and seventeen minutes. Director: Lewis Gilbert. Producers: Albert R. Broccoli and Harry Saltzman. Screenwriters: Roald Dahl and Harold Jack Bloom. Based on the novel by Ian Fleming. Cinematographer: Freddie Young. Special Effects Supervisors: John Stears. Cast: Sean Connery, Akiko Wakabayashi, Mie Hama, Tetsuro Tamba, Teru Shimada, Karin Dor, Donald Pleasence, Bernard Lee, Lois Maxwell, Desmond Llewelyn, Tsai Chin, Burt Kwouk, Ronald Rich, and Charles Gray. *World Premiere:* Odeon Leicester Square, London, on June 12, 1967.

APPENDIX 4

On Her Majesty's Secret Service (1969). Great Britain: EON Productions, one hundred and forty minutes. Director: Peter Hunt. Producers: Albert R. Broccoli and Harry Saltzman. Screenwriters: Richard Maibaum. Additional Dialogue by Simon Raven. Based on the novel by Ian Fleming. Cinematographer: Michael Reed. Special Effects Supervisor: John Stears. Cast: George Lazenby, Diana Rigg, Telly Savalas, Gabriele Ferzetti, Ilse Steppat, Bernard Lee, Lois Maxwell, Desmond Llewelyn, George Baker, Angela Scoular, Catherine Schell, Julie Ege, Joanna Lumley, Anouska Hempel, Jenny Hanley, Bernard Horsfall, and Yuri Borionko. *World Premiere:* Odeon Leicester Square, London, on December 18, 1969.

Diamonds Are Forever (1971). Great Britain: EON Productions, one hundred and twenty minutes. Director: Guy Hamilton. Producers: Albert R. Broccoli and Harry Saltzman. Screenwriters: Richard Maibaum and Tom Mankiewicz. Based on the novel by Ian Fleming. Cinematographer: Ted Moore. Special Effects Supervisors: Leslie Hillman and Whitney McMahon. Cast: Sean Connery, Jill St. John, Charles Gray, Lana Wood, Jimmy Dean, Bruce Cabot, Putter Smith, Bruce Glover, Norman Burton, Joseph Furst, Bernard Lee, Desmond Llewelyn, Leonard Barr, and Lois Maxwell. *World Premiere:* Las Vegas, Nevada, December 17, 1971.

Live and Let Die (1973). Great Britain: EON Productions, one hundred and twenty-one minutes. Director: Guy Hamilton. Producers: Albert R. Broccoli and Harry Saltzman. Screenwriter: Tom Mankiewicz. Based on the novel by Ian Fleming. Cinematographer: Ted Moore. Special Effects Supervisors: Derek Meddings and Rick Baker. Cast: Roger Moore, Jane Seymour, Yaphet Kotto, Bernard Lee, Lois Maxwell, David

Hedison, Gloria Hendry, Geoffrey Holder, Julius Harris, Clifton James, Madeline Smith, and Tommy Lane *World Premiere:* Odeon Leicester Square, London, on July 5, 1973.

The Man with the Golden Gun (1975). Great Britain: EON Productions, one hundred and twenty-five minutes. Director: Guy Hamilton. Producers: Albert R. Broccoli and Harry Saltzman. Screenwriters: Richard Maibaum and Tom Mankiewicz. Based on the novel by Ian Fleming. Cinematographer: Ted Moore and Oswald Morris. Special Effects Supervisors: John Stears. Cast: Roger Moore, Christopher Lee, Britt Ekland, Maud Adams, Hervé Villechaize, Clifton James, Richard Loo, Soon-Tek Oh, Marc Lawrence, Bernard Lee, Lois Maxwell, Marne Maitland, Desmond Llewelyn and Chan Yiu Lam. *World Premiere:* Location and Date: Odeon Leicester Square, London, December 18, 1974; released in 1975 to general cinemas.

The Spy Who Loved Me (1977). Great Britain: EON Productions, one hundred and twenty-five minutes.Director: Lewis Gilbert. Producer: Albert R. Broccoli. Screenwriters: Christopher Wood and Richard Maibaum. Based on the novel by Ian Fleming. Cinematographer: Claude Renoir. Special Effects Supervisor: John Evans. Cast: Roger Moore, Barbara Bach, Curt Jurgens, Richard Kiel, Caroline Munro, Walter Gotell, Geoffrey Keen, Bernard Lee, Desmond Llewelyn, Lois Maxwell, Michael Billington, Edward de Souza, Valerie Leon, and George Baker. *World Premiere:* Odeon Leicester Square, London, on July 7, 1977.

Moonraker (1979). Great Britain: EON Productions, one hundred and twenty-six minutes. Director: Lewis Gilbert. Producers: Albert R. Broccoli. Screenwriters: Christopher

APPENDIX 4

Wood. Based on the novel by Ian Fleming. Cinematographer: Jean Tournier. Special Effects Supervisors: René Albouze, Charles Assola, John Evans, Serge Ponvianne and John Richardson. Cast: Roger Moore, Lois Chiles, Michael Lonsdale, Richard Kiel, Corinne Clery, Bernard Lee, Geoffrey Keen, Desmond Llewelyn, Lois Maxwell, Toshirô Suga, Emily Bolton, Blanche Ravalec and Walter Gotell. *World Premiere:* Odeon Leicester Square, London, on June 26, 1979.

For Your Eyes Only (1981). Great Britain: EON Productions, one hundred and twenty-seven minutes. Director: John Glen. Producer: Albert R. Broccoli. Screenwriters: Richard Maibaum and Michael G. Wilson. Based on the novel by Ian Fleming. Cinematographer: Alan Hume. Special Effects Supervisor: John Evans. Cast: Roger Moore, Carole Bouquet, Topol, Lynn-Holly Johnson, Julian Glover, Cassandra Harris, Jill Bennett, Michael Gothard, John Wyman, Geoffrey Keen, Lois Maxwell, Desmond Llewelyn, and Walter Gotell. *World Premiere:* Odeon Leicester Square, London, on June 24, 1981.

Octopussy (1983). Great Britain: EON Productions, one hundred and thirty-one minutes. Director: John Glen. Producer: Albert R. Broccoli. Screenwriters: George MacDonald Fraser, Richard Maibaum, and Michael G. Wilson. Based on the short story by Ian Fleming. Cinematographer: Alan Hume. Special Effects Supervisors: John Evans and John Richardson. Cast: Roger Moore, Maud Adams, Louis Jourdan, Kristina Wayborn, Kabir Bedi, Steven Berkoff, David Meyer, Tony Meyer, Desmond Llewelyn, Robert Brown, Lois Maxwell, Michaela Clavell, Vijay Amritraj, and Walter Gotell. *World Premiere:* Odeon Leicester Square, London, on June 6, 1983.

APPENDIX 4

Never Say Never Again (1983). UK/USA/W. Germany: Talia Films, one hundred and thirty-four minutes. Director: Irvin Kershner. Producer: Jack Schwartzman. Screenwriters: Kevin McClory, Jack Whittingham, and Lorenzo Semple, Jr. Based on the novel **Thunderball** by Ian Fleming. Cinematographer: Douglas Slocombe. Special Effects Supervisor: Ian Wingrove. Cast: Sean Connery, Klaus Maria Brandauer, Max Von Sydow, Barbara Carrera, Kim Basinger, Bernie Casey, Alec McCowen, Edward Fox, Pamela Salem, Rowan Atkinson and Valerie Leon. *World Premiere:* Los Angeles, CA, on October 7, 1983.

A View to a Kill (1985). Great Britain: EON Productions, one hundred and thirty-one minutes. Director: John Glen. Producers: Albert Broccoli and Michael Wilson. Screenwriters: Richard Maibaum and Michael Wilson. Based on a story by Ian Fleming. Cinematographer: Alan Hume. Special Effects Supervisors: John Richardson. Cast: Roger Moore, Christopher Walken, Tanya Roberts, Grace Jones, Patrick Macnee, Patrick Bauchau, David Yip, Fiona Fullerton, Manning Redwood, Alison Doody, Willoughby Gray, Desmond Llewelyn, Robert Brown, Lois Maxwell, and Walter Gotell. *World Premiere: San Francisco, California, May 22, 1985.*

The Living Daylights (1987). Great Britain: EON Productions, one hundred and thirty minutes. Director: John Glen. Producers: Albert R. Broccoli and Michael G. Wilson. Screenwriters: Richard Maibaum and Michael G. Wilson. Based on the short story by Ian Fleming. Cinematographer: Alec Mills. Special Effects Supervisors: John Richardson and Chris Corbould. Cast: Timothy Dalton, Maryam d'Abo, Joe Don Baker, Art Malik, Jeroen Krabbé, John Rhys-Davies, Andreas Wisniewski, Thomas Wheatley, John Terry, Geoffrey Keen, Robert Brown,

APPENDIX 4

Walter Gotell, Caroline Bliss, and Desmond Llewelyn. *World Premiere:* Odeon Leicester Square, London, on June 29, 1987.

Licence to Kill (1989). Great Britain/USA: EON Productions, one hundred and thirty-three minutes. Director: John Glen. Producers: Albert R. Broccoli and Michael G. Wilson. Screenwriters: Michael G. Wilson and Richard Maibaum. Based on characters by Ian Fleming. Cinematographer: Alec Mills. Special Effects Supervisors: Chris Corbould, Laurencio Cordero and Sergio Jara. Cast: Timothy Dalton, Carey Lowell, Robert Davi, Talisa Soto, Anthony Zerbe, Frank McRae, David Hedison, Wayne Newton, Benicio Del Toro, Anthony Starke, Everett McGill, Desmond Llewelyn, Pedro Armendariz, Jr., Robert Brown, and Priscilla Barnes. *World Premiere:* Odeon Leicester Square, London, June 13, 1989.

GoldenEye (1995). Great Britain: EON Productions, one hundred and thirty minutes. Director: Martin Campbell. Producers: Barbara Broccoli and Michael G. Wilson. Screenwriters: Michael France, Jeffrey Caine and Bruce Feirstein. Based on characters by Ian Fleming. Cinematographer: Phil Meheux. Special Effects Supervisor: Derek Meddings. Cast: Pierce Brosnan, Sean Bean, Izabella Scorupco, Famke Janssen, Joe Don Baker, Judi Dench, Robbie Coltrane, Gottfried John, Desmond Llewelyn, Samantha Bond, Alan Cumming, and Michael Kitchen. *World Premiere:* Dorothy Chandler Pavilion, Los Angeles, California, on November 13, 1995.

Tomorrow Never Dies (1997). Great Britain/USA: EON Productions, one hundred and nineteen minutes. Director: Roger Spottiswoode. Producers: Barbara Broccoli and Michael G. Wilson. Screenwriters: Bruce Feirstein. Characters by Ian

APPENDIX 4

Fleming. Cinematographer: Robert Elswit. Special Effects Supervisor: Chris Corbould. Cast: Pierce Brosnan, Jonathan Pryce, Michelle Yeoh, Teri Hatcher, Ricky Jay, Götz Otto, Joe Don Baker, Vincent Schiavelli, Judi Dench, Desmond Llewelyn, Samantha Bond, Colin Salmon, Geoffrey Palmer, Julian Fellowes, Terence Rigby and Cecile Thomsen. *World Premiere:* Odeon Leicester Square, London, on December 9, 1997.

The World Is not Enough (1999). Great Britain/USA: EON Productions, one hundred and twenty-nine minutes. Director: Michael Apted. Producers: Barbara Broccoli and Michael G. Wilson. Screenwriters: Neal Purvis and Robert Wade. Characters by Ian Fleming. Cast: Pierce Brosnan, Sophie Marceau, Robert Carlyle, Denise Richards, Judi Dench, Desmond Llewelyn, John Cleese, Robbie Coltrane, Samantha Bond, Colin Salmon, and Maria Grazia Cucinotta. *World Premiere:* Senator Theater, Baltimore, Maryland, on November 8, 1999.

Die Another Day (2002). Great Britain/USA: EON Productions, one hundred and twenty-nine minutes. Director: Lee Tamahori. Producers: Barbara Broccoli and Michael G. Wilson. Screenwriters: Neal Purvis. Characters by Ian Fleming. Cast: Pierce Brosnan, Halle Berry, Toby Stephens, Rosamund Pike, Rick Yune, Judi Dench, John Cleese, Michael Madsen, Will Yun Lee, and Emilio Echevarria. *World Premiere:* Odeon Leicester Square, London, on November 18, 2002.

Casino Royale (2006). Great Britain/USA: EON Productions, one hundred and six minutes. Director: Martin Campbell. Producers: Barbara Broccoli and Michael G. Wilson. Screenwriters: Paul Haggis, Neal Purvis, and Robert Wade. Characters by Ian Fleming. Cast: Daniel Craig, Eva Green, Mads Mikkelsen,

Caterina Murino, Judi Dench, Giancarlo Gianini, Jeffrey Wright, and Jesper Christensen. *World Premiere:* Odeon Leicester Square, London, on November 14, 2006.

Quantum of Solace (2008). Great Britain/USA: EON Productions, one hundred and six minutes. Director: Marc Forster. Producers: Barbara Broccoli and Michael G. Wilson. Screenwriters: Paul Haggis, Neal Purvis, and Robert Wade. Characters by Ian Fleming. Cast: Daniel Craig, Olga Kurylenko, Mathier Amalric, Judi Dench, Giancarlo Gianini, Gemma Arterton, Jeffrey Wright, David Harbour, and Jesper Christensen. *World Premiere:* Odeon Leicester Square, London, on October 29, 2008.

Skyfall (2012). Great Britain/USA: EON Productions, one hundred and six minutes. Director: Sam Mendes. Producers: Barbara Broccoli and Michael G. Wilson. Screenwriters: John Logan, Neal Purvis, and Robert Wade. Characters by Ian Fleming. Cast: Daniel Craig, Javier Bardem, Judi Dench, Ralph Fiennes, Naomie Harris, Berenice Marlohe, Albert Finney, Ben Whishaw, Rory Kinnear, Ola Rapace, Helen McCory, and Nicholas Woodeson. *World Premiere:* Odeon Leicester Square, London, on November 9, 2012.

Spectre (2015). Great Britain/USA: EON Productions, one hundred and twenty minutes. Director: Sam Mendes. Producers: Barbara Broccoli and Michael G. Wilson. Screenwriters: John Logan, Neal Purvis, and Robert Wade. Characters by Ian Fleming. Cast: Daniel Craig, Christoph Waltz, Ralph Fiennes, Naomie Harris, Ben Whishaw, Rory Kinnear, Léa Seydoux, Monica Bellucci, David Bautista, and Andrew Scott. *World Premiere:* Odeon Leicester Square, London, on November 6, 2015.

APPENDIX 4

No Time to Die (2021). Great Britain/USA: EON Productions, one hundred and sixty-three minutes. Director: Cary Joji Fukunaga. Producers: Barbara Broccoli and Michael G. Wilson. Screenwriters: Robert Wade, Phoebe Waller-Bridge, and Cary Joji Fukunaga. Characters by Ian Fleming. Cast: Daniel Craig, Christoph Waltz, Ralph Fiennes, Naomie Harris, Ben Whishaw, Rory Kinnear, Léa Seydoux, Rami Malek, Jeffrey Wright, Lashana Lynch. *World Premiere*: Royal Albert Hall, London, on September 28, 2021.

BIBLIOGRAPHY

PRIMARY SOURCES

(ORIGINAL JAMES BOND NOVELS BY FLEMING)
FLEMING, IAN

Casino Royale. London: Jonathan Cape, 1953.
Diamonds Are Forever. London: Jonathan Cape, 1956.
Dr. No. London: Jonathan Cape, 1958.
For Your Eyes Only. London: Jonathan Cape, 1960.
From Russia with Love. London: Jonathan Cape, 1957.
Goldfinger. London: Jonathan Cape, 1959.
Live and Let Die. London: Jonathan Cape, 1954.
Moonraker. London: Jonathan Cape, 1955.
Octopussy. New York: Signet, 1966.
On Her Majesty's Secret Service. London: Jonathan Cape, 1963
The Man with the Golden Gun. New York: Signet, 1965.
The Spy Who Loved Me. London: Jonathan Cape, 1962
Thunderball. London: Jonathan Cape, 1961.
You Only Live Twice. New York: Viking, 1964.

BIBLIOGRAPHY

(Original James Bond Short Stories by Fleming)

"Agent 007 in New York." *New York Herald Tribune* (newspaper). October 1963.
Broken Claw. New York: Putnam, 1990.
Cold Fall. New York: Putnam, 1995.
Death Is Forever. New York: Putnam, 1992.
For Special Services. New York: Coward, 1982.
"For Your Eyes Only." *For Your Eyes Only* (story collection). London: Jonathan Cape, 1960.
"From a View to a Kill." *For Your Eyes Only* (story collection). London: Jonathan Cape, 1960.
Golden Eye (novelization). London: Hodder & Stoughton, 1995.
Icebreaker. New York: Putnam, 1983.
Licence Renewed. New York: Marex, 1981.
Licence to Kill (novelization). New York: Putnam, 1989.
Man from Barbarosa. New York: Putnam, 1991.
Never Send Flowers. New York: Putnam, 1993.
Nobody Lives Forever. New York: Putnam, 1986.
No Deals, Mr. Bond. New York: Putnam, 1987
"Octopussy." *Playboy*. March and April 1966 (Original James Bond Novels by Gardner) Gardner, John.
"Quantum of Solace." *Cosmopolitan*. May 1959.
"Risico." *For Your Eyes Only* (story collection). London: Jonathan Cape, 1960.
Role of Honor. New York: Putnam, 1984.
Scorpius. New York: Putnam, 1987.
Seafire. New York: Putnam, 1994.
"The Hildebrand Rarity." *Playboy*. March 1960.
"The Living Daylights." *The Sunday Times* (newspaper). 4 February 1962.

BIBLIOGRAPHY

"The Property of a Lady." *The Ivory Hammer* (Sotheby's Annual). 1963.
Win, Lose or Die. New York: Putnam, 1989.

(Original James Bond Novels by Benson) Benson, Raymond

"Blast from the Past," *Playboy.* January 1997.
Die Another Day (novelization). New York: Boulevard Books, 2002.
Doubleshot. New York: Putnam, 2000.
High Time to Kill. New York: Putnam, 1999.
Man with the Rose Tattoo. New York: Putnam, 2002.
"Midsummer Night's Doom," *Playboy.* January 1999.
Never Dream of Dying. New York: Putnam, 2001.
The Facts of Death. New York: Putnam, 1998.
The World Is not Enough. (novelization). New York: Boulevard Books, 2002.
Tomorrow Never Dies (novelization). London: Hodden & Stoughton, 1997.
Zero Minus Ten. New York: Putnam, 1997.

(Other Original James Bond Novels)

Deaver, Jeffrey, *Carte Blanche.* Simon and Schuster, 2011.
Faulks, Sebastian, *Devil May Care.* Penguin Books, 2008.
James Bond and Moonraker. New York: Jove Books, 1979.
Markham, Robert, *Colonel Sun.* New York: Signet, 1968.
Mascott, R.D., *003 ½: The Adventures of James Bond Junior.* Random House, 1967.
Wood, Christopher, *The Spy Who Loved Me.* New York: Warner Books, 1977.

BIBLIOGRAPHY

(The James Bond Junior Books) Higson, Charlie

Blood Fever. Ian Fleming Productions, 2006.
By Royal Command. Ian Fleming Productions, 2008.
Double or Die. Ian Fleming Productions, 2007.
Hurricane Gold. Ian Fleming Productions, 2007.
Silver Fin. Ian Fleming Productions, 2005.

(The Moneypenny Diaries) Westbrook, Kate (Samantha Weinberg)

Guardian Angel. Thomas Dunne Books, 2008.
Final Fling. Thomas Dunne Books, 2010.
Secret Servant. Thomas Dunne Books, 2009.

(Unofficial Works and Self-Published Titles)

Batsford, B.T., *Your Deal, Mr. Bond.* 1997
Fleming, Ian, *Alligator.* 1962.
Hatfield, Jim, *The Killing Zone.* A Charter Book, 1985.

SECONDARY SOURCES, BOOKS

Amis, Kingsley, *The James Bond Dossier.* New York: New American Library, 1965.
Barnes, Alan and Marcus Hearn, **Kiss Kiss Bang Bang!.** London: Batsford, 1997.
Bennett, John and Janet Wollacott, **Bond and Beyond.** New York: Macmillan, 1987.
Benson, Raymond, **James Bond Bedside Companion.** New York: Dodd-Mead, 1986.

BIBLIOGRAPHY

Brosnan, John, *James Bond in the Cinema*. New York: A.S. Barnes, 1977; 2nd, 1981.

Cork, John and Bruce Scivally, *Bond: The Legacy*. New York: Abrams, 2002.

Dougall, Alastair, *James Bond: The Secret World of 007*. London: Dorling Kindersley, 2000.

Hibbin, Sally, *The Official James Bond Movie Book*. New York: Hamlyn, 1987.

James Bond: The Authorized Biography. London: Jonathan Cape, 1973.

Lane, Andy and Paul Simpson, *The Bond Files: The Unofficial Guide to the World's Greatest Secret Agent*. London: Virgin, 1998.

McInerney, Jay et. Al, *Dressed to Kill: James Bond—The Suited Hero*. London: Flammarion, 1996.

McReynolds, B.S., *The 007 Dossier*, New York: B.S. Book Publishing, 1999.

Pearson, John, *The Life of Ian Fleming*. London: Jonathan Cape, 1965.

Pfeiffer, Lee and Philip Lisa, *The Incredible World of James Bond*. New York: Citadel, 1995.

Rye, Graham, *The James Bond Girls*. New York: Citadel, 1998.

Rubin, Steven Jay, *The Complete James Bond Movie Encyclopedia*. New York: Chicago: McGraw Hill, 2003.

Snelling, O.F., *James Bond: A Report*. New York: Spearman, 1964.

Tanner, William, *The Book of Bond, or Every Man His Own 007*. New York: Viking, 1965.

The James Bond Films. New York: Talisman, 1981.

Turner, Adrian, *Goldfinger: From A to Z*. London: Bloomsbury, 1998.

Yenne, William, *Secret Weapons of World War II: The

BIBLIOGRAPHY

Techno-Military Breakthroughs that Changed History. New York, NY: Berkeley Books, 2003.

SECONDARY SOURCES, DVD

A View to a Kill, 1985, Special 007 Edition DVD. MGM Home Entertainment, 2000, **Inside 'A View to a Kill'**. Documentary.
Cubby Broccoli—The Man Behind Bond. Documentary. Audio Commentary Featuring Director Guy Hamilton, the Cast and Crew.
Double-O-Stuntmen. Documentary. Audio Commentary Featuring Director Guy Hamilton, the Cast and Crew.
Gilbert, Lewis, dir. ***Moonraker***. 1979. Special 007 Edition. MGM Home Entertainment, 2000.
Glen, John, dir. ***Licence to Kill***, 1989. MGM Home Entertainment, 1999, **Inside 'Licence to Kill'**. Documentary. Audio commentary featuring director John Glen and cast members. Audio commentary 2 featuring producer Michael Wilson and others.
Guest, Val, John Huston and others, dirs. ***Casino Royale***. 1967. DVD.
Hamilton, Guy, dir. ***Diamonds Are Forever***. 1971, Special 007 Edition. DVD.
Home Entertainment, 2000, **Inside 'The Man with the Golden Gun'**. Documentary.
Inside 'Moonraker'. Documentary.
Kershner, Irvin, dir. ***Never Say Never Again***. 1983. DVD, NSNA Company, 2000.
MGM Home Entertainment, 2000, **Inside 'Diamonds Are Forever'**. Documentary.
MGM HomeEntertainment, 2003, **Inside 'Die Another**

BIBLIOGRAPHY

Day'. Documentary. Audio Commentary with Director Lee Tamahori and Producer Michael G. Wilson. Audio Commentary with Pierce Brosnan and Rosamund Pike.

MGM Home Entertainment, 2000, *Inside 'From Russia with Love'*. Documentary. Audio Commentary Featuring Director Terrence Young and Members of the Cast and Crew.

MGM Home Entertainment, 2002. *Psychedelic Cinema*. With Val Guest, documentary.

MGM Home Entertainment, 1999, *The Secrets of 007*. Documentary. Audio Commentary featuring Director Roger Spottiswoode. Second Audio Commentary by Second Unit Director Vic Armstrong and Producer Michael G. Wilson.

Spottiswoode, Roger, dir. *Tomorrow Never Dies*. 1997, Special 007 Edition. DVD.

Tamahori, Lee, dir. *Die Another Day*. 2002, DVD, Special Edition.

The Man with the Golden Gun. 1975, Special 007 Edition DVD. MGM.

The Men Behind the Mayhem: The Special Effects of James Bond. Documentary. Audio Commentary Featuring Director Lewis Gilbert, the Cast and Crew.

The Music of James Bond. Documentary. Audio Commentary featuring Director John Glen and Members of the Cast and Crew.

Thunderball. 1965, Special 007 Edition DVD.

MGM Home Entertainment, 1999, *The Making of 'Thunderball'*. Documentary.

The 'Thunderball' Phenomenon. Documentary. Audio Commentary Featuring Director Terrence Young and Audio Commentary by the Cast and Crew.

Young, Terence, dir. *From Russia with Love*, 1963, DVD, Special 007 Edition.

BIBLIOGRAPHY

SECONDARY SOURCES, CD-ROM

Encyclopedia Britannica. 2003, Deluxe Edition. CD-ROM.

SECONDARY SOURCES, INTERNET

"Absolutely James Bond 007", www.ajb007.co.uk//.
"Airship FAQ", myairship.com/faq/index.html.
"Annual Report 2004: The State of the Drugs Problem in the European Union and Norway", www.emcdda.europa.eu/publications/annual-report/2004_en.
ATV Connection Magazine, atvconnection.com/articles/honda-atv-history-in-the-beginning-3/.
Berardinelli, James. "Review of *Moonraker*", 1996, www.reelviews.net/reelviews/moonraker.
Berkeley Seismological Laboratory, seismo.berkeley.edu/outreach/faq.html.
"Bond & the Navy", www.mjnewton.demon.co.uk/bond/navy/html.
BMW 750 iL (1997), Internet Auto Guide. autoguide.com.
Brain, Marshall and Tom Harris, "How GPS Receivers Work" electronics.howstuffworks.com/gadgets/travel/gps.
"Chakras", www.sacredcenters.com/chakras.
Cross, Robin, "The Nazi Expedition" www.channel4.com/.
DEA Congressional Testimony, "Money Laundering by Drug Trafficking Organizations" Feb. 28, 1996, irp.fas.org/congress/1996.

BIBLIOGRAPHY

DEA Congressional Testimony, Panama, June 13, 2000, www.govinfo.gov.

Dobry, Gary, "The Body Politic", www.onthecanvas.com.

DragTimes. www.dragtimes com.Lincoln-Mark-VII-Timeslip-5531.

Ebert, Roger, Review of *Moonraker*, *Chicago Sun-Times*. Jan. 1, 1979, http://rogerebert.suntimes.com/.

"Electromagnetic Pulse" www.physics.northwestern.edu.

"Fleet Ballistic Missile Submarines-SSBN", www.navy.mil/Resources.

Freudrich, Ph.D., Craig, "How Space Stations Work", http://science.howstuffworks.com/space-station.html.

"How Space Shuttles Work", science.howstuffworks.com/space-shuttle.

"Fujifilm", global.fujifilm.com.

Geer, Carri, "Suspect Has Slot-cheating Conviction" *Las Vegas Review-Journal*, June 11, 1998, lasvegassun.com.

HH-65A Dolphin, www.geocities.com/CapeCanaveral.

"History of Horse Racing, The", www.mrmike.com/explore.

"History of Star Wars, The", www.supershadow.com/starwars.

Internet Movie Database, www.imdb.com.

Internet Movie Database Pro., www.imdbpro.com.

James Bond Film Dossiers, www.jamesbondmm.co.uk.

James Bond Lifestyle, www.jamesbondlifestyle.com.

Kwan, Matthew, Cali Drug Cartel Marketing Analysis, http://www.darkside.com.au/mba/cali.html.

M16: The Home of James Bond, www.mi6.co.uk/sections/movies.

Marks' Site, James Bond-007 Cars, jaguar.4t.com/bondcars.

"Media Moguls Have Second Thoughts", www.usatoday.com/money/.

BIBLIOGRAPHY

"Media Moguls on Board: Murdoch, Malone and the Cato Institute", www.alternet.org.
Newton, Matthew, www.mjnewton.demon.co.uk.
Phil Hawksley's BM Bikes, www.bmbikes.co.uk.
Pletka, Danielle, "End Nuclear Extortion", American Enterprise Institute for Public Policy Research. www.aei.org/.
"Robert Maxwell", www.answers.com.
"Robert Maxwell: A Profile", news.bbc.co.uk.
"Rupert Murdoch", www.answers.com.
Sekeres, Andrew, "Institutionalization of the Chinese Tongs in Chicago's Chinatown", gangresearch.net/ChicagoGangs/tongs.
Stott, David, "Identification Parade", www.channelweb.co.uk/feature.
Tam, Kevin R, "Queen Elizabeth", www.uncommonjourney.com.
"Tango Stories", www.elportaldeltango.com.
Tanner, Bill, "The Spy Who Came Out of the Closet, Part 2", jamesbondlifestyle.com.
"Ted Turner", www.answers.com/Ted%20Turner.
"Tomorrow Never Dies", http://www.jamesbond-shop.com.
UN Security Council, "Global Policy Forum", www.globalpolicy.org.
Vakin, Ph.D., Sam, "The Industrious Spies", samvak.tripod.com.
Von Dassanowsky, Robert, "Casino Royale at 33", www.brightlightsfilm.com/28/casinoroyale1.html.
"Why GPS?", www.trimble.com/gps/why.html.
Williams, JD, John, "The Demonization of Anabolic Steroids I: What Makes these Hormones so Evil?", www.worldclasssbodybuilding.com.

ABOUT THE AUTHORS

Born in Chicago, Illinois, in the 1950s, **Dr. John L. Flynn** is a three-time Hugo Award–nominated author, psychologist, teacher, and college dean. In 1977, he received the M. Carolyn Parker Award from the University of South Florida for excellence in creative writing. He received his Bachelor's and Master's degrees in English from the University of South Florida and worked as an English teacher in Baltimore, Maryland. He published his first book *Future Threads* in 1985. In 1998, he earned his PhD as a clinical psychologist from the University of Southern California. He has published nearly twenty books and dozens of articles. He currently resides in Lake Worth, Florida.

Bob Blackwood taught English, literature, film study, and photography at Wilbur Wright College in Chicago until 2000. For more than forty years, he has reviewed books on film criticism and film history for *Choice* magazine.

His book *From the Silent Era to "The Sopranos": Italian American Gangsters in Trend-Setting Films and Television Shows* contains critical commentary on the major Italian American gangster films and TV shows from *The Black Hand* (1906) to *The Sopranos* (1999–2005).

ABOUT THE AUTHORS

Blackwood began reading the James Bond novels in the 1950s and is a life-long devotee to Ian Fleming. He has co-authored two books with John L. Flynn: *Everything I Know About Life I Learned From James Bond* and *Future Prime: Top Ten Science Fiction Films*.

JOHN L. FLYNN

FROM OPEN ROAD MEDIA

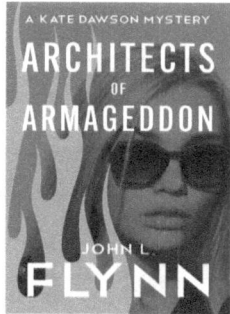

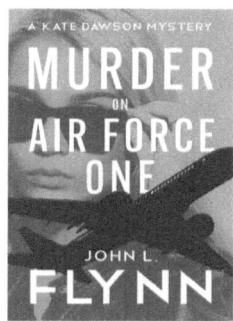
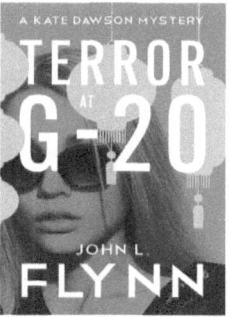

Find a full list of our authors and titles at www.openroadmedia.com

FOLLOW US
@OpenRoadMedia

www.ingramcontent.com/pod-product-compliance
Lightning Source LLC
Chambersburg PA
CBHW030330240426
43661CB00052B/1586